Game-Based Education Approaches to Inclusive Business Management

Giuseppe Modarelli
University of Turin, Italy

Christian Rainero
University of Turin, Italy

Stefano Amelio
University of Insubria, Italy

IGI Global
Publishing Tomorrow's Research Today

Published in the United States of America by
IGI Global
701 E. Chocolate Avenue
Hershey PA, USA 17033
Tel: 717-533-8845
Fax: 717-533-8661
E-mail: cust@igi-global.com
Web site: https://www.igi-global.com

Library of Congress Cataloging-in-Publication Data

Names: Modarelli, Giuseppe, 1991- editor. | Rainero, Christian, 1977- editor. | Amelio, Stefano, editor.
Title: Game-based education approaches to inclusive business management / edited by Giuseppe Modarelli, Christian Rainero, Stefano Amelio.
Description: Hershey, PA : Business Science Reference, [2025] | Includes bibliographical references and index. | Summary: "The book advocates for a transformative approach that integrates game-based learning and working methodologies to instigate a shift towards inclusivity, social responsibility, and overall well-being"-- Provided by publisher.
Identifiers: LCCN 2024002237 (print) | LCCN 2024002238 (ebook) | ISBN 9798369311721 (h/c) | ISBN 9798369311738 (ebook)
Subjects: LCSH: Educational games. | Organizational behavior--Social aspects. | Social responsibility of business. | Well-being.
Classification: LCC LB1029.G3 G27 2024 (print) | LCC LB1029.G3 (ebook) | DDC 371.33/7--dc23/eng/20240212
LC record available at https://lccn.loc.gov/2024002237
LC ebook record available at https://lccn.loc.gov/2024002238

Vice President of Editorial: Melissa Wagner
Managing Editor of Acquisitions: Mikaela Felty
Managing Editor of Book Development: Jocelynn Hessler
Production Manager: Mike Brehm
Cover Design: Phillip Shickler

British Cataloguing in Publication Data
A Cataloguing in Publication record for this book is available from the British Library.

Table of Contents

Detailed Table of Contents

Corporate social responsibility (CSR) initiatives have expanded to encompass a wide array of endeavors aimed at fostering inclusivity across society. This chapter delves into the role of CSR in promoting inclusivity within the realms of game-based learning and professional employment. Through an examination of existing literature and case studies, this chapter underscores the significance of CSR endeavors in fostering a more inclusive environment for diverse populations, including individuals with disabilities, minorities, and marginalized groups. Game-based learning and professional employment stand out as domains with profound implications for social and economic impact. This thematic analysis explores the intersection of these two areas and their contributions to broader social and economic outcomes. By integrating methods of game-based learning with inclusive employment practices, businesses can play a pivotal role in advancing social equity while simultaneously enhancing organizational performance and fostering innovation.

This conceptual chapter proposes an innovative way for organisations to engage new stakeholders through video games. This concept requires an explanation of the psychological mechanisms that permit an effective learning process through games and video games. In the educational field, simulation-based video games are effective learning tools because they motivate gamers-learners through an immersive virtual experience to improve themselves in competitive challenges. Shifting to the organisational dimension, video games can be used to upgrade primary stakeholders. An organisation is interested in establishing new relationships with new stakeholders and enhancing the relationships with existing stakeholders. Nowadays, stakeholders want to feel closer to organisations and prefer to establish relationships with those organisations which reflect their values and ethical principles. Thus, organisations must intercept these values and principles to engage existing and new stakeholders, and video games can contribute to helping the organisation achieve this goal.

Higher education is undergoing a transformation towards student-centered approaches, moving away from traditional methods to embrace innovative methodologies that encourage active student participation in learning. This chapter explores the benefits of adopting non-conventional teaching methodologies to enhance student engagement and socialization across various subjects, as well as their acquisition of relevant knowledge and skills. A specific activity within the "Games of Marketing" project is detailed, which has been implemented over five academic years with high student approval. In summary, this chapter highlights the shift towards student-centered learning in higher education and the exploration of innovative teaching methodologies through the "Games of Marketing" project. It emphasizes the project's adaptability, its impact on student engagement, and its potential to enhance learning outcomes across diverse educational settings.

Pre-vetting inspection is a critical process to enhance safety and environmental protection onboard tanker ships. The current study firstly proposes a serious game design model, namely GAMESIRE 2.0, for crew upskilling in tanker vetting requirements. This study considers recently updated requirements of Ship Inspection Report (SIRE 2.0) Programme of Oil Companies International Marine Forum (OCIMF). Using GAMESIRE 2.0 model, preliminary design of a serious game-based training is conducted in preparation for SIRE 2.0 Clause # 4.2.1, which focuses on navigational procedures on passage planning and execution. Further maritime studies might utilize GAMESIRE 2.0 model to design additional serious games in SIRE 2.0 context. In fact, scope of GAMESIRE 2.0 model can be extended through other maritime inspection regimes such as Chemical Distribution Institute (CDI), Tanker Management Self-Assessment (TMSA), Dry Bulk Management Standard (DRYBMS), etc. Consequently, this study contributes to third-party standards on enhanced safety and environmental protection in tanker shipping industry.

Preface

Trends, Perspectives and Criticalities in Game-Based Approaches for Diversity and Inclusion

It seems necessary to consider as the incipit of this book a reference to the etymology of the word on which the scientific contribution is structured and takes its steps. DIVERTIRE (from Italian) TO FUN (ant. divèrtere) v. tr. [from latin. have fun, proper. «to turn elsewhere», comp. of di(s)- and vertĕre «to turn»] (I amuse, etc., ant. I amuse, you amuse, etc.). –Turn elsewhere, push away, divert (https://www.treccani.it/vocabolario/divertire/). Therefore, the meaning can be traced back to that of making people take another direction (https://www.etimo.it/?term=divertire). Precisely from this term it is necessary to reconsider the human dimension in the places where social functions are carried out, with ever deeper attention to the dynamic perspective of inclusion, because TO FUN (DIVERTIRE – in Italian) and DIVERSE (DIVERSO in Italian) (divèrso, adj. and s. m. [latin. divĕrsus, propr. passive part of divertĕre «to deviate», comp. of di(s)- and vertĕre «to turn»]. – turned in another direction) have the same root and describe univocal dimensions of "direction towards" something or someone. Hence the need to use the game seems to be crucial, in a society that functionalizes and subserves to itself its dynamics, underlying the system architectures of social networks, new technologies, the broad spheres of ideal and ideic attribution in construction of structurally engineered fabrics on the basis of reproducting the real in the virtual; synthetic projections of an apparatus that transposes and moves elsewhere, therefore entertains in an unusual, alternative and functional way, the social dimension that is expressed in the daily perspective, tangible and otherwise, of work. Here the game-based dynamic takes on and finds value in a constructivist reference framework, guaranteeing the achievement of what is prescribed in the current SDGs as grand socio-economic-environmental challenges, especially in parallel with what a socially constituted responsibility should be able to define in the the scope of inclusiveness in the business & management area.

People are increasingly immersed in the digital world, the gateway to which passes through any technological device equipped with an Internet network. The time spent scrolling through feeds on social networks or watching one episode after another on the main streaming platforms flows like a flow that catalyzes attention towards the digital world. One or more alter egos of a virtual transposition of reality, the conceptual reproduction of the evident in a more subtle and feeble portion of infinite dimensions. Today's society is therefore conceptually regulated by the logic of gaming which encourages people to continuously connect to avoid the fomo effect (fear of missing out) thus being rewarded by likes and the arrival of new followers the more active one is in the communities online.

Since the 1980s there has been a tendency to consider society as a whole as a global network, also thanks to the advent of the Internet, one of the key innovations of the twentieth century. The possibility therefore of communicating, interacting and interfacing with other spatial dimensions distant from each other in real time has allowed the emergence, or rather the re-emergence, of a social construct such as that of the network. To date, thanks to the COVID-19 pandemic, the concept of network organization has begun to be reconsidered within the corporate paradigm. Therefore, in the cooperative perspective that companies can also implement to overcome and deal with crises, the network has become a re-emerging social construct. From here the cooperative dynamic can be understood as inherent to the articulations of the interactive game system. Similarly, disruptive innovations of the twenty-first century, such as blockchain, are characterized by a system architecture based on the dynamics of gaming, thus further identifying respective underlying social constructs of networking and systems of incentives and rewards, cooperation and competition at within a larger "gaming society".

One of the most revolutionary technologies of the last decades is certainly the blockchain, a digital register, decentralized and distributed in a peer to peer network in which the archived data can be viewed by all participants in a safe, secure and transparent way. The system architecture underlying the blockchain has the characteristics of game dynamics in which the network participants are the nodes, whose task is to mine, i.e. verify the operations and then validate them and add another block to the chain. Thus was born the competition to be the first to share the solution to the mathematical problem deriving from the hash algorithm and obtain the reward. Therefore, mining is nothing else, which is the digital transposition of real work based on objective goals and real wages.

The game dynamics incorporated into the blockchain system architecture allows operations to be certified temporally, giving value to the digital resources recorded in the blocks connected to each other through an alphanumeric code called hash.

Like a modern "cluedo", the blockchain would make the process of entering data on the network transparent as well as the agents identifiable. Thanks to the structure for levels of increasing decryption difficulty used in the mining process for the certification of the data on the digital and widespread register, the parallelism with the game dynamics is made more evident than ever. In fact, on the one hand, just as the rules of a game cannot be changed or tampered with except through cheating, any tampering with the register and fraudulent behavior would be identified and isolated from the system.

In the same way, to participate in any game you need to have the necessary tools to start a game, so to participate in the mining process you need to have computational hardware, cooling systems and a large amount of electricity without forgetting the continuous maintenance of the devices. Currently, the complexity of the mathematical problems underlying the decryption process, such as the bitcoin mining process, is requiring increasingly greater resources that are difficult to find in the activity of a single individual. In this way the logic of encouraging collaboration becomes a common factor such as the aim of winning a game during the gaming session, so each miner makes their resources available to guarantee the greatest contribution to the solution of the problem and obtain a greater reward, which is distributed proportionally to the use of the resources contributed.

The objective of the contribution is not to explain how the blockchain works; in fact, this is given as already known and reference is made to the scientific literature of reference for further clarifications. Rather, the contribution aims to explain a conceptual parallel in reference to blockchain as an emerging technology based on a pre-existing social construct, such as the network organization thus taken into consideration in its predominant features in light of the dynamics of a society ideally centered on gaming.

The importance and relevance of the topic is specified through the Trend Analysis on NgramViewer Google Analytics Tool (Figure 1, accessed on 11th Feb. 2024). The tendency is quite redundant and non-linear. And since the Eighties and Nineties the theme of gaming started again to have relevance and boost interest. Today it is possible to draw attention to a topic that has been developed under different profiles for hundreds of years.

Figure 1. Ngram Viewer Analysis

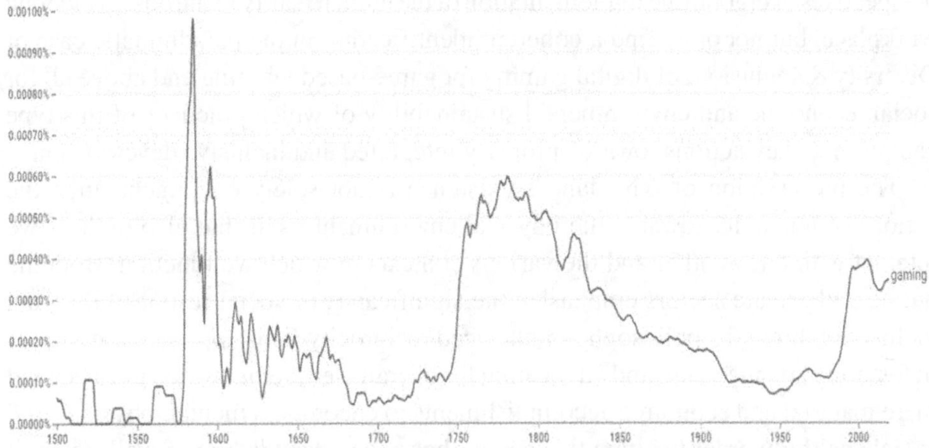

In line with what has been said, blockchain technological innovation presents itself as a new revelation on a par with the Internet with the third industrial revolution. Today we are witnessing a multitude of scientific publications on blockchain but almost none of these are linked to another emerging or, as previously stated, re-emerging dimension of the network organization. During the COVID-19 pandemic, the latter was considered as the anti-crisis panacea as well as organizational innovation although it is a social construct coeval with man. As far as gaming is concerned, literature in this sense is found in sectors as diverse as education, psychology, pedagogy, sociology, personal growth, sport, marketing and only for a few years within the dynamics corporate.

The intent of this collective contribution and above all of the preface to it, is not so much to identify a gaming dynamic in the emerging blockchain technology, but to ideally and conceptually exploit its basic assumptions to redefine the concept of "gaming society" in which we are now immersed in. In this regard, concepts re-emerging from pedagogical practice and theory can be taken up in conjunction with the emergence of digital technologies, artificial intelligence, augmented and virtual reality. All these dimensions do nothing but create perspectives, which if well integrated together can and must be exploited at the service of man in the context in which he carries out his social functions. The contribution moves in this direction and therefore consists on the one hand in increasing the literature inherent to the topic, on the other, in providing a transversally alternative perspective and in integrating the evolutionary perspective of the network society within the corporate sphere and technological applications such as blockchain which by their very nature relate to the dynamics of gaming activities. In this sense, the crucial themes of the great challenges, of the objectives of the 2030 Agenda and of the dynamic perspectives of ergonomic implementation of the human reality in the post-pandemic workplace, but not only, find a coherent identification in the paradigmatic case of Diversity & Inclusion, of digital gaming for game-based learning and above all for social, economic and environmental sustainability of which practices of this type can promote key actions towards properly integrated and inclusive development.

The preservation of our planet's existence is not solely contingent upon the actions of humanity towards the physical environment itself, but also on how we interact with one another and the various contexts in which we function. Both the public and private sectors emphasize the significance of social responsibility and inclusivity through a philosophy of balanced reciprocity. This approach is essential in fostering advancement and advocating for overall well-being, which goes beyond mere material and economic accomplishments to encompass mental, physical, and social health. In order to attain this comprehensive understanding of well-being, it is imperative to maintain a harmonious equilibrium between our professional and personal lives while simultaneously managing our relationships with colleagues in a respectful and all-encompassing manner that appreciates and values diversity. As part of our obligations, we are entrusted with the task of discovering solutions that facilitate the comprehension, acceptance, and dissemination of these underlying principles. We are entrusted with the task of discovering solutions and pursuing these aforementioned fundamental objectives within the domains where we dedicate the majority of our time: organizations and work environments.

Frequently, the workplace environment itself can become a hindrance to overall well-being. However, in relation to the Sustainable Development Goals (SDGs) outlined by the 2030 Agenda, a multitude of scholars, academics, and practitioners are proposing alternative solutions on a global scale within each area specified by the Agenda itself, in order to achieve sustainability in a socially-driven and all-encompassing manner. In accordance with the objectives set forth by this publication, it would be of utmost importance to initiate investigations from the perspectives of organizations, economics, work-life balance, and life itself, conducting extensive research and inquiries into methods of reducing inequalities and fostering inclusivity, all the while examining the deep-rooted human paradigms associated with learning approaches. By doing so, both Game-Based-Learning and Game-Based-Working can generate numerous advantages in promoting organizational well-being.

Currently, scientific production relating to play as a learning dynamic, in parallel with the Diversity & Inclusion perspective, appears to be limited. In fact, 61 results emerged from a literary gap analysis of this type on the SCOPUS database, and only 5 results narrowing the field to the business, management & accounting area alone. For this reason, the contribution proposes a key orientation of dissemination and scientific discussion on the topic, acting as an exploratory, orientation and directive anchor towards avant-garde and potentially operational development horizons.

Governments, both collectively and individually, have dedicated a significant amount of time and effort over the course of several decades to the development and implementation of various actions, reforms, and policies. However, it has been widely recognized that the most successful actions often originate from the grassroots level, serving as exemplary practices that others can emulate and adopt.

The proposed stimulus outlined in this book aims to identify specific areas of interest that have the potential to foster advancements in public governance, private enterprises, organizational structures, and the creation of value. This endeavor is not limited to these areas alone but encompasses a broader scope of possibilities.

The impetus behind the creation of this book stems from the urgent need to address the existing imbalance in the current state of affairs in relation to various forms of inequality. Additionally, it aims to ensure the optimal well-being of individuals in the workplace, both through idealistic and practical perspectives. The research findings presented in this book offer valuable insights that will be beneficial to a diverse range of stakeholders. These include policymakers, managers from both the public and private sectors, educators at all levels, occupational psychologists, and researchers who can explore new and uncharted avenues of investigation. The collective knowledge derived from this endeavor will contribute to the continuous cycle of development within society and extend well beyond its immediate impact.

Durkheim, a prominent sociologist and educator from the 19th and early 20th centuries, was a proponent of positivist culture. He advocated for the notion that individuals must be educated in accordance with the society in which they reside. The ultimate goal of education, in Durkheim's perspective, is to transform the "individual self" into a "social self". This implies that individuals should possess the ability to comprehend and abide by the laws and norms that govern collective life. Society, through its influential role as a model, does not seek to repress individuals but rather facilitate their complete realization. In this context, companies serve as microcosms of socially organized life and provide a reference point for individuals to express their true selves. Furthermore, they exert a transformative force on both individuals and society as a whole. By imitation, as Bandura expressed in the social learning view, integrating Durkheim's perspective of understanding collective norms and uniforming to these ones, if we live in a "pseudo-gaming society", we will adopt its norms into reality, in our workplaces etc. So, it is necessary to reconduct these issues to our uses and our needs for well-being. Therefore, it is crucial to adopt a perspective of inclusion based on Bio-Psycho-Social principles, which recognize individuals in their entirety and account for all aspects of their functioning. In light of these considerations, the well-being of both individuals and groups can be fostered through inclusive actions and mechanisms that embrace diversity as a core value.

Disability, race, religion, language, and other factors become pivotal determinants of success or failure in creating an environment conducive to work. It is imperative to cultivate a culture of social responsibility within companies that extends beyond mere superficial gestures. In Western societies, significant legislation has been enacted to protect individuals with disabilities from discrimination in the workplace and during the employment process. Against the backdrop of a melting pot society, emerging values appear to offer a paradigmatic approach to addressing the complex issue of unity and diversity in the context of cultural and subcultural relationships.

Cultural, social, economic, linguistic, and various other diversities, when taken as a whole, can be deemed as constituting a disability for all intents and purposes. This notion aligns with the general definition put forth by the International Classification of Functioning (ICF) - World Health Organization, which defines disability as the challenges faced by individuals in their physical, personal, or social functioning in one or more key domains of life. These challenges arise from the interaction between a person's health condition and contextual factors. In essence, this definition encompasses a wide range of variables, including contextual, personal, and social influences. When it comes to the realm of literature, there has been a noticeable trend of overlooking disability and its development, resulting in a constant flattening effect. However, the game, as a pedagogical approach to inclusion, offers a potential solution to this issue.

Numerous scholars and researchers, such as Gorbanev et al. (2018), Light and Robert (2010), Arnab et al. (2015), Speelman et al. (2019), Kafai (2017), Paeßens and Winther (2021), Wang et al. (2016), Briot et al. (2017), Carrión et al. (2020), have highlighted the game's role in fostering inclusivity. By analyzing the contributions of book chapters that delve into the dynamics between public-private organizations and organizations of different sizes (large, small, and medium-sized), we can gain insights into how the game can serve as a key tool for promoting inclusion. The works of Flyvbjerg (2011), Heale and Twycross (2018), Crowe et al. (2011), Gomm, Foster & Hammersley (2000), Aberdeen (2013), and Yin (2012) provide valuable perspectives on this matter.

The core idea is to draw attention to the potential synergy between internal social responsibility actions and their external repercussions and positive effects. This involves aligning private company policies with public initiatives such as the Sustainable Development Goals (SDGs) and Governmental Agendas. By addressing the complex challenges of inclusivity and striving for integral well-being, through reciprocal actions, we can create a conducive environment for all individuals. The works of Low (2014), Duthler and Dhanesh (2018), Mory, Wirtz & Göttel (2016), Falk and Fischbacher (2006), and Adu-Gyamfi et al. (2021) shed light on these interconnected relationships.

Within the theoretical framework of the book, the theme of diversity and the dialogue of cultures can be explored through the lens of the French philosopher Jullien (2010). Jullien's perspective encompasses three dimensions: universal, uniform, and common. The universal dimension refers to universally prescribed norms, which stand in contrast to the individual or the singular. The uniform dimension acknowledges the existence of differences and presents them as alternatives. Lastly, the common dimension represents the space where relationships are formed, shared, and founded.

The editors of the book aim to address two fundamental research questions that serve as the foundation for their research actions and potential managerial implications. They aim to highlight the current reality in Western society, and beyond, which emphasizes the all-encompassing inclusion of diversity, specifically with regards to inclusion. The understanding of disability in this context aligns with the holistic profiles presented by the ICF and how it can be subverted by the game-driven approach.

Considering the research questions and providing comprehensive answers to them, the editors of the book offer a detailed overview of its main focus, which centers around the examination of diversity and disability in relation to government guidance. Additionally, they emphasize the utilization of a "game" perspective as a crucial element in ensuring internal social responsibility, which in turn leads to positive external consequences.

The study delves into the vast academic managerial literature on corporate social responsibility, while also drawing insights from various fields such as sociology, psychology, and pedagogy. By incorporating these multidisciplinary perspectives, the researchers aim to align their work with the goals outlined in Agenda 2030, which sets forth a comprehensive framework for sustainable development.

In the context of Western society, the prevailing modes of thought have undergone a transformative process throughout history, gradually evolving into what can be described as a "global system" that has become increasingly globalized. Contrary to initial expectations, this process of cultural globalization has not resulted in a homogenized culture, but rather has stimulated critical thinking and intellectual elaboration. Consequently, as thoughts are critically examined in light of the changing society, existing paradigms are subject to questioning, leading to a sense of frustration and dissatisfaction within established knowledge. This, in turn, motivates individuals to dismantle cognitive monoliths and restructure the present civilization towards a future that aligns with their aspirations.

In this ongoing transformation, societies undergo both positive and negative changes, but nevertheless continue to evolve and adapt. As societies become more institutionalized and systemic in nature, they inadvertently marginalize minority groups, who nonetheless strive for social change and actively engage in efforts to address inequality. These individuals recognize the urgent need to work towards a more inclusive society, wherein disparities are eliminated and equal opportunities are provided for all.

Socio-political and cultural shifts and transformations often serve as catalysts for significant turning points, wherein long-held beliefs, practices, norms, and values are challenged. These breaking points create opportunities for the emergence of new cultural forms and perspectives, thereby paving the way for societal progress and the advancement of collective consciousness.

In this particular context, it is crucial to comprehend culture as an amalgamation of values, norms, and conceptions that society imposes upon itself. However, subsequent to undergoing a process of modification, individuals who no longer feel a sense of belonging to a particular culture, or who were not originally part of a culture, tend to embark on a journey of socially redesigning their existence. The individual who no longer perceives themselves as an integral part of a given community, which encompasses a set of rules, values, visions, and beliefs, finds themselves expelled from their natural environment and subsequently struggles to regain their rightful place within the social fabric. Conversely, when examining welcoming societies, we discover that their strength lies in embracing diversity and embracing the creation of new and co-constructed shared values. These societies do not view the "other" as an adversary, but rather as a source of inspiration for evolutionary rebirth. Nevertheless, it is imperative to acknowledge that sporadic initiatives centered around welcome and integration are insufficient in achieving a comprehensive coexistence of diversity. Instead, a collective commitment is required, one that is grounded in the logic of assimilation and directed towards dialogue and constructive confrontation. Within this framework, the term "diversity" should not be understood as mere difference, but rather as a means of enrichment. In today's interconnected world, characterized by globalized networks and instantaneous communication, the notion of diversity manifests primarily as cultural plurality. Consequently, diversity should be perceived as an inherent mental representation, which the process of globalization has sought to diminish but has not succeeded in eliminating. On the contrary, globalization has often served to exacerbate diversity. In light of this, a society built upon cultural diversity, and by extension, diversity in general, necessitates the existence of organizations capable of implementing inclusive and intercultural strategies. Once again, in situations where the state and governments are frequently absent or have limited influence, responsible citizens who have organized themselves to live and work together propose alternative strategies that incorporate and formalize the ideologies that governments and development agendas strive to achieve. At this critical juncture, case studies have been examined and regarded as a bastion of a society characterized by contrasting and paradoxical elements, which persist to this day.

The main dimensions through which an individual encounters diversity encompass family, school, society, and the work environment. It is essential to pay heed to the concept of diversity, which is often expressed in its plural form, signifying the existence of diversity in various forms and manifestations. This diversity is not solely confined to ethnic-cultural social structures linked to immigration and genetic factors. Rather, it encompasses the multiplicity of affective experiences, cognitive styles, and environmental and familial stimuli that are expressed within socially organized contexts such as companies. An inclusive society, organization, or company cannot evade the challenges posed by diversity and inequality. These challenges are highlighted in the 10th Sustainable Development Goal (SDG) outlined by the United Nations for the year 2030. This SDG advocates for and directs efforts towards the recognition, preservation, interaction, and integration of all forms of diversity. From an early stage in life, diversity permeates every sphere of society, beginning with the educational institution. It is through this exposure that individuals learn to differentiate between themselves and others within the realm of their own individuality. (Garcia-Prieto, Bellard & Schneider, 2003; Spradlin & Parsons, 2008).

The protection of diversity in all its forms, dimensions, expressions, and place/environment is of utmost importance. It is crucial to recognize the significance of heterogeneity in a fragmented society, as it emphasizes individuality and sharing in the face of an epistemological cultural challenge posed by diversity as a value (Homan, 2019). Keeping in line with simulative Game Based Learning (GBL) (Plass, Homer & Kinzer, 2015; Qian & Clark, 2016; Ifenthaler, Eseryel & Ge, 2012; Pivec, Dziabenko & Schinnerl, 2003), the concept of Game Based Working (GBW), an acronym coined by the editors, holds the potential to create inclusive and emotionally charged experiences that can greatly impact occupational well-being, particularly for individuals integrated into routine mechanisms. A key aspect of both GBL and GBW is the participative element, which involves the exchange of ideas and solutions, a willingness to listen and present, and an active structuring of one's own learning and life experiences, all of which can be shared as tacit personal baggage within the entire group. By acting as a mediator, games can effectively break down barriers and reduce cultural and social distances between individuals within a heterogeneous group that shares a common purpose. This common purpose fosters aggregation, defines roles and perspectives, and ultimately leads to a sense of unity. GBW can take various forms, all grounded in the belief that everything becomes more effective and productive in terms of group performance when it is made enjoyable. Consequently, rules, goals and objectives, results and feedback, and the overall structure of operations serve to motivate commitment, involve and generate adrenaline, enhance cognitive skills, and improve attention. Similarly, co-operative learning (Doolittle, 1997; Li & Lam, 2013; Dansereau, 1988; Pratt, 2003; Johnson & Johnson, 1986; Balkcom, 1992) diminishes the competitive component and opens the door for inclusiveness and commitment (Marr, 1997). In this regard, there is also a strong emphasis on rewards and recognition (Hansen, Smith & Hansen, 2002; Ruffini & Modarelli, 2015; Ali & Ahmed, 2009), group dynamics, and the reduction of potential conflicts (Song, 2013; Baral, 2017; Braem et al., 2012; Padmala & Pessoa, 2011). The direct involvement, along with the challenging yet achievable goals (Marchington & Wilkinson, 2005), further contribute to the effectiveness of GBW. In addition to the studies conducted by Piaget (1977), Vygotskij (1981), Freud (1986), Wood, Bruner, and Ross (1976) that identify play as a learning and inclusion practice, new avenues of research have emerged in the first decades of the new millennium (Bourgonjon & Soetaert, 2013; Gee, 2008; Prensky, 2003; Davis & Ferdig, 2009; Barzilai & Blau, 2014; de Freitas & Maharg, 2011), leading to the development of "serious games" used for work purposes and holding significant interest within the research community.

In view of the consistent and steady perspectives in counteracting the prevailing trend of interest, which is the exponential growth in the production of literary works centered around the theme of the pedagogical game, as well as the continuous attention given to companies and their attitudes towards disability issues, the aim of this editorial project is to stimulate both the academic world and practitioners to adopt an inclusive perspective when analyzing the business environment, whether it be in the public or private sector. The main objective is to examine how the pedagogical use of games can contribute to the overall value of an organization, not simply as a form of superficial corporate social responsibility, but as a means of generating intrinsic value for the organization itself and for society as a whole. Additionally, this approach aims to promote well-being and reduce inequalities, as outlined in the Sustainable Development Goals (SDGs). By starting with organizations as social entities, both in the public and private sectors, and recognizing their role as agents of social aggregation, we can foster an inclusive society, thereby embracing sustainable modernity and shaping the future.

The proposed outline seeks to provide a stimulus that enables the identification of specific areas of interest capable of promoting organizational value within the framework of public-private governance, particularly in relation to the aforementioned issues. By focusing on these niche areas, we can uncover untapped potential and create opportunities for the development of innovative approaches and solutions. Ultimately, this approach will contribute to the enhancement of organizational value and the realization of a more inclusive and sustainable society, under its ideological consideration of "game" architecture.

The collective contribution is made up of the following research studies, considering introductory chapters and specific application of GBL-GBW approaches for Diversity & Inclusion (D&I) in Business and Management area:

1) Perceptions, Criticalities, and Potential of game-Based Trainings for Inclusion: A Literary Review and Evidence From the Field

This study, involving perception, criticalities and potentials of game-based trainings, provides a literary review and an historical background alo examining the field in terms of educational games evolutionary aspects to promote diversity and inclusion (D&I) in work environments. The main points of departure are the following ones: (i) To create an equitable and sustainable society, diversity and inclusion are essential; (ii) playing games may be a valuable tool for promoting D&I values, learning, teamwork, and personal growth; (iii) the management of diversity in the workplace aims to provide safe and supportive environments for people with diverse backgrounds. In this sense, th research aims to understand the evolution of the concept of games and diversity as well as the potential advantages and risks of educational games for D&I in work environments.

2) Managing With the "Diverse": A Gaming Perspective for the Promotion of a More Inclusive and Sustainability-Oriented Culture

This research highlights the need for new tools in training programs to facilitate the acquisition of domain-specific knowledge and the cultivation of mindsets conducive to engaging with complex system dynamics, promoting innovative and transdisciplinary thinking. This discussion contribution presents and evaluates gaming strategies that foster diversity and a holistic approach to sustainability. While not exhaustive, this contribution aims to stimulate discussions on nurturing a culture aligned with sustainable development principles in educational and corporate settings, focusing on three key themes: gaming to advance the Sustainable Development Goals (SDGs), enhance communication skills through education, and raise awareness about inequalities and disabilities in the workplace. Emphasizing the importance of interdisciplinary approaches in addressing complex challenges, the study underlines the role of gamification in advocating for the SDGs, improving communication effectiveness, and addressing inequalities. Despite limitations in exploring gaming debates systematically, the study sheds light on the potential of gamification to promote sustainability-oriented behaviors in diverse work environments, suggesting avenues for further research and exploration.

3) Gamification Against Inequalities at Work: A Systematic Literature Review

This research study, thanks to a rigourous literature review, demonstrates that the attainment of well-being and inclusion remains a formidable challenge, highlighted by persistent issues such as work-life balance and discrimination. The research highlights a significant gap in the literature on the limited exploration of gaming as a means to enhance the inclusion of individuals with disabilities in professional environments, despite its recognized potential. The study contributes shaping an overview of gamification's role in promoting worker well-being and equality, emphasizing the need for continued interdisciplinary research to inform best practices and advance sustainable workplace inclusivity, according to the Agenda 2030 SDGs.

4) Promoting Inclusivity: Corporate Social Responsibility in Game-Based Learning and Professional Employment

Corporate social responsibility (CSR) efforts have expanded to include a wide range of initiatives aimed at promoting inclusion across society. This study explores the role of his CSR in promoting inclusivity in the fields of game-based learning (GBL) and professional employment. Through a review of existing literature and case studies, the authors highlights the importance of CSR efforts in promoting a more inclusive environment for people, including people with disabilities, minorities, and marginalized groups. The purpose of this research is to consider how CSR efforts intersect with promoting inclusion by GBL approaches. The authors conceptually discover the paradigms, cases and applicative evidences supporting the effectiveness of CSR-driven inclusion efforts.

5) Digital Game-Based Learning as a Tool for Intercepting Stakeholders' Tendencies

This research introduces a novel approach for organizations to connect with new stakeholders using video games, exploring the psychological mechanisms that facilitate effective learning in this process. The study considers simulation-based video games in education as useful and powerful tools in order to engage learners in immersive virtual experiences that enhance their skills through competitive challenges. The research also explores the organizational context correlating video games approaches that can also be utilized to engage primary stakeholders, establishing and strengthening relationships with stakeholders by aligning their values and principles to tendecnies in their preferences. Video games are considerd an alternative way for improving Game-Based-Learning in the business and management area.

6) Game-Learning in Action: A Serious Board Game on Human Capital Reporting: How Games Improve Human Capital Management and Reporting

The study proposed highlights potentials about games implementations related to educational area. Although the game proposed has been tested so far within universities, it is actually designed as a full-fledged game that serves different types of learners (students, professionals, managers, other employees, etc.). It focuses on key aspects related to human resources, such as D&I, employment and remuneration, health and safety, labor practices, human rights, skills and knowledge, training and education. Another contribution of the game proposed is methodological in nature and enriches the existing sparse literature on the impact of game-based learning on sustainability and reporting aspects. The aforementioned game is designed as a serious game and is increasingly recognized as an effective means of improving learning outcomes and helping learners focus on the target topic. The authors recognize that this research does not objectively measure student learning outcomes, and we believe that the results remain important and of practical interest. This is consistent with the idea that careful planning of game design elements is essential when developing educational materials at any level. These results confirm that serious games have significant potential as educational tools.

7) Transformative Learning in Higher Education: Unveiling the Impact of Innovative Teaching Strategies Through the Games of Marketing

The search for GBL activities led the authors to structure a proposal where the knowledge in the subjects is evaluated in group activities within a gymkhana called Games of Marketing set in series referred to the students. To analyze the effect of this activity, a behavioral model is proposed comparing students who enjoyed the activity with those who did not, confirming the existence of significant differences in the elements that build satisfaction and indirectly the recommendation byparticipants. By this work the authors seek to describe the GBL activities and arouse curiosity among teachers to be able to adapt and implement them in their classes. The study elucidates and clarifies the expedients related to a practical application of GBL approache in ambit of Business and management area, in the specific: marketing.

8) Investigating the Potential of Maritime Serious Game Design in SIRE 2.0 Context: GAMESIRE 2.0

This research aims to introduce a model for designing serious games specific to SIRE 2.0 inspections in the maritime sector. The study also includes the initial design of a serious game for maritime use, known as GAMESIRE 2.0. The primary goal is to offer valuable insights into incorporating gamification into SIRE 2.0 inspection training. It is emphasized that the research objectives are deeply rooted in the serious games literature and an industrial survey of serious gaming in the maritime field. Consequently, this study is seen as making both a theoretical contribution to the literature and a practical one to the maritime industry.

9) The Role of Relationships as Protagonists in Role-Playing Games

The advent of various digital learning modalities, including e-learning, m-learning, and AI-based education, has fundamentally transformed individual, social, and professional interactions. This global phenomenon transcends demographic boundaries, prompting interdisciplinary inquiry from fields such as sociology, cognitive sciences, and emerging specializations like cyberpsychology. However, it also raises critical concerns, including misinformation, privacy invasions, and social isolation. Noteworthy innovations such as AI and collaborative platforms, exemplified by tools like Microsoft Teams and Asana, are redefining professional engagement and productivity. This study prioritizes an exploration of the interplay between technology and user relationships while offering recommendations for enhancing communication and relational dynamics in digital environments. The critical research references to Eric Berne (1910-1970), the pioneer of Transactional Analysis, whose seminal 1964 work, "Games People Play", remains a foundational text in psychology, reflecting a transformative approach to psychotherapy developed in the late 1950s that continues to serve as a framework for analyzing interpersonal dynamics through the concept of "games" representing individuals' roles within their contexts.

Giuseppe Modarelli
University of Turin, Italy

REFERENCES

Aberdeen, T. (2013). Yin, RK (2009). Case study research: Design and methods. Thousand Oaks, CA: Sage. *The Canadian Journal of Action Research, 14*(1), 69-71.

Adu-Gyamfi, M., He, Z., Nyame, G., Boahen, S., & Frempong, M. F. (2021). Effects of internal CSR activities on social performance: The employee perspective. *Sustainability (Basel)*, 13(11), 6235. DOI: 10.3390/su13116235

Ali, R., & Ahmed, M. S. (2009). The impact of reward and recognition programs on employee's motivation and satisfaction: an empirical study. *International Review of Business Research Papers, 5*(4), 270-279.

Arnab, S., Lim, T., Carvalho, M. B., Bellotti, F., De Freitas, S., Louchart, S., Suttie, N., Berta, R., & De Gloria, A. (2015). Mapping learning and game mechanics for serious games analysis. *British Journal of Educational Technology*, 46(2), 391–411. DOI: 10.1111/bjet.12113

Balkcom, S. (1992). Cooperative Learning. Education research consumer guide. Academic Press.

Baral, S. K. (2017). Role of emotional intelligence to handle conflicts and team building: An analytical study. *Splint International Journal of Professionals*, 4(2), 85.

Barzilai, S., & Blau, I. (2014). Scaffolding game-based learning: Impact on learning achievements, perceived learning, and game experiences. *Computers & Education*, 70, 65–79. DOI: 10.1016/j.compedu.2013.08.003

Bourgonjon, J., & Soetaert, R. (2013). Video games and citizenship. CLCWeb. *Comparative Literature and Culture*, 15(3), 8.

Braem, S., Verguts, T., Roggeman, C., & Notebaert, W. (2012). Reward modulates adaptations to conflict. *Cognition*, 125(2), 324–332. DOI: 10.1016/j.cognition.2012.07.015 PMID: 22892279

Briot, J. P., de Azevedo Irving, M., Vasconcelos Filho, J. E., de Melo, G. M., Alvarez, I., Sordoni, A., & de Lucena, C. J. P. (2017). Participatory management of protected areas for biodiversity conservation and social inclusion: Experience of the SimParc multi-agent-based serious game. *Multi-Agent-Based Simulations Applied to Biological and Environmental.*

Carrión, M., Santórum, M., Sampredro, C., Paredes, A., Ortiz, Y., Samaniego-Santillán, P., & Maldonado-Garcés, V. (2020, July). Designing a serious game for labor inclusion of people with intellectual disabilities using iPlus methodology. In *International Conference on Applied Human Factors and Ergonomics* (pp. 603-610). Springer. DOI: 10.1007/978-3-030-51828-8_79

Crowe, S., Cresswell, K., Robertson, A., Huby, G., Avery, A., & Sheikh, A. (2011). The case study approach. *BMC Medical Research Methodology*, 11(1), 1–9. DOI: 10.1186/1471-2288-11-100 PMID: 21707982

Dansereau, D. F. (1988). Cooperative learning strategies. In *Learning and study strategies* (pp. 103–120). Academic Press. DOI: 10.1016/B978-0-12-742460-6.50013-X

Davis, N., & Ferdig, R. E. (2009). What is special about teacher education for virtual schooling? *Journal of Technology and Teacher Education*, 17(4), 425–435.

de Freitas, S., & Maharg, P. (2011). Digital games and learning: Modelling learning experiences in the digital age. In *Digital games and learning*. Continuum International.

Doolittle, P. E. (1997). Vygotsky's Zone of Proximal Development as a Theoretical Foundation for Cooperative Learning. *Journal on Excellence in College Teaching*, 8(1), 83–103.

Duthler, G., & Dhanesh, G. S. (2018). The role of corporate social responsibility (CSR) and internal CSR communication in predicting employee engagement: Perspectives from the United Arab Emirates (UAE). *Public Relations Review*, 44(4), 453–462. DOI: 10.1016/j.pubrev.2018.04.001

Falk, A., & Fischbacher, U. (2006). A theory of reciprocity. *Games and Economic Behavior*, 54(2), 293–315. DOI: 10.1016/j.geb.2005.03.001

Flyvbjerg, B. (2011). *Case study. The Sage handbook of qualitative research, 4*, 301-316.

Freud, S. (1986). Al di là del principio di piacere (1920). In Opere di Sigmund Freud (OSF) vol. 9. L'Io e l'Es e altri scritti 1917-1923, Bollati Boringhieri, Torino.

Garcia-Prieto, P., Bellard, E., & Schneider, S. C. (2003). Experiencing diversity, conflict, and emotions in teams. *Applied Psychology*, 52(3), 413–440. DOI: 10.1111/1464-0597.00142

Gee, J. P. (2008). *Learning and games*. MacArthur Foundation Digital Media and Learning Initiative.

Gomm, R., Foster, P., & Hammersley, M. (2000). Case study method: Key issues, key texts. Case study method, 1-288.

Gorbanev, I., Agudelo-Londoño, S., González, R. A., Cortes, A., Pomares, A., Delgadillo, V., Yepes, F. J., & Muñoz, Ó. (2018). A systematic review of serious games in medical education: Quality of evidence and pedagogical strategy. *Medical Education Online*, 23(1), 1438718. DOI: 10.1080/10872981.2018.1438718 PMID: 29457760

Hansen, F., Smith, M., & Hansen, R. B. (2002). Rewards and recognition in employee motivation. *Compensation and Benefits Review*, 34(5), 64–72. DOI: 10.1177/0886368702034005010

Heale, R., & Twycross, A. (2018). What is a case study? *Evidence-Based Nursing*, 21(1), 7–8. DOI: 10.1136/eb-2017-102845 PMID: 29146764

Ifenthaler, D., Eseryel, D., & Ge, X. (2012). Assessment for game-based learning. In *Assessment in game-based learning* (pp. 1–8). Springer. DOI: 10.1007/978-1-4614-3546-4_1

Johnson, D. W., & Johnson, R. T. (1986). Mainstreaming and cooperative learning strategies. *Exceptional Children*, 52(6), 530–561. DOI: 10.1177/001440298605200608 PMID: 2938962

Jullien, F. (2010). *L'universale e il comune. Il dialogo tra culture*. Laterza.

Kafai, Y. B. (2017). Connected gaming: An inclusive perspective for serious gaming. *International Journal of Serious Games*, 4(3). Advance online publication. DOI: 10.17083/ijsg.v4i3.174

Li, M. P., & Lam, B. H. (2013). *Cooperative learning*. The Hong Kong Institute of Education.

Light, R. L., & Robert, J. E. (2010). The impact of Game Sense pedagogy on Australian rugby coaches' practice: A question of pedagogy. *Physical Education and Sport Pedagogy*, 15(2), 103–115. DOI: 10.1080/17408980902729388

Low, M. P. (2014). Internal corporate social responsibility: An overview. *Australian Journal of Basic and Applied Sciences*.

Marr, M. B. (1997). Cooperative learning: A brief review. *Reading & Writing Quarterly*, 13(1), 7–20. DOI: 10.1080/1057356970130102

Mory, L., Wirtz, B. W., & Göttel, V. (2016). Factors of internal corporate social responsibility and the effect on organizational commitment. *International Journal of Human Resource Management*, 27(13), 1393–1425. DOI: 10.1080/09585192.2015.1072103

Padmala, S., & Pessoa, L. (2011). Reward reduces conflict by enhancing attentional control and biasing visual cortical processing. *Journal of Cognitive Neuroscience*, 23(11), 3419–3432. DOI: 10.1162/jocn_a_00011 PMID: 21452938

Paeßens, J., & Winther, E. (2021). Game design in financial literacy: exploring design patterns for a collaborative and inclusive serious game from different perspectives. In *Game-based learning across the disciplines* (pp. 43–59). Springer. DOI: 10.1007/978-3-030-75142-5_3

Piaget, J. (1977). The role of action in the development of thinking. In *Knowledge and development* (pp. 17–42). Springer US. DOI: 10.1007/978-1-4684-2547-5_2

Pivec, M., Dziabenko, O., & Schinnerl, I. (2003, July). Aspects of game-based learning. In *3rd International Conference on Knowledge Management* (Vol. 304).

Plass, J. L., Homer, B. D., & Kinzer, C. K. (2015). Foundations of game-based learning. *Educational Psychologist*, 50(4), 258–283. DOI: 10.1080/00461520.2015.1122533

Pratt, S. (2003). Cooperative learning strategies. *Science Teacher (Normal, Ill.)*, 70(4), 25.

Prensky, M. (2003). Digital game-based learning. *Computers in Entertainment*, 1(1), 21. DOI: 10.1145/950566.950596

Qian, M., & Clark, K. R. (2016). Game-based Learning and 21st century skills: A review of recent research. *Computers in Human Behavior*, 63, 50–58. DOI: 10.1016/j.chb.2016.05.023

Ruffini, R., & Modarelli, G. (2015). Retribuzione e motivazione nella pubblica amministrazione oggi. RU Risorse umane nella pubblica amministrazione, 29(6).

Song, D. (2013). Research on diversity, conflicts and performance in creative team management. *African Journal of Business Management*, 7(39), 4139–4148.

Speelman, E. N., Rodela, R., Doddema, M., & Ligtenberg, A. (2019). Serious gaming as a tool to facilitate inclusive business; a review of untapped potential. *Current Opinion in Environmental Sustainability*, 41, 31–37. DOI: 10.1016/j.cosust.2019.09.010

Spradlin, L. K., & Parsons, R. D. (2008). *Diversity matters: Understanding diversity in schools*. Cengage Learning.

Vygotsky, L. S. (1981). The Genesis of Higher Mental Functions. In Wertsch, J. V. (Ed.), *The Concept of Activity in Soviet Psychology*.

Wang, R., DeMaria, S.Jr, Goldberg, A., & Katz, D. (2016). A systematic review of serious games in training health care professionals. *Simulation in Healthcare*, 11(1), 41–51. DOI: 10.1097/SIH.0000000000000118 PMID: 26536340

Wood, D., Bruner, J. S., & Ross, G. (1976). The role of tutoring in problem solving. Journal of Child Psychology and Psychiatry, 17, 89-100.

Yin, R. K. (2012). *Case study methods*. Academic Press.

Section 1
"Framing the Topic": An Introduction

Chapter 1
Perceptions, Criticalities, and Potentials of Game-Based Trainings for Inclusion:
A Literary Review and Evidence From the Field

Giuseppe Modarelli
University of Turin, Italy

Christian Rainero
https://orcid.org/0000-0003-3112-8886
University of Turin, Italy

ABSTRACT

Diversity and inclusion (D&I) are pivotal in cultivating a favorable society, profoundly influencing both individual and collective welfare within educational and occupational contexts. Contemporary studies underscore the role of gaming as a potent medium for advancing D&I principles, thereby bolstering collaboration and personal growth. Furthermore, proficient management of diversity within work environments not only adheres to legal standards but also yields economic advantages, such as heightened job satisfaction. To explore significant dimensions of the D&I research domain related to the lens of pedagogical gaming, the authors propose (a) a comprehensive review of the literature, also considering a historical developmental overview of the concepts of diversity and gaming; (b) an empirical field study aimed at assessing the primary potentials, along with positive and negative perceptions, as well as critical challenges associated with pedagogical gaming methodologies.

DOI: 10.4018/979-8-3693-1172-1.ch001

1. INTRODUCTION

Diversity and inclusion (D&I) represent fundamental values for building an equitable and sustainable society (Winters, 2013). These principles are inextricably intertwined with the world of education, training, and work, influencing individual and collective well-being at personal and working level (Roberson, 2006; Farndale et al., 2015; Garg & Sangwan, 2021; Kirton, 2020). In this scenario, gaming emerges as a valuable tool for promoting the values of diversity and inclusion, encouraging learning, collaboration, and personal growth (Shliakhovchuk, 2018; Lehan, Hussey & Babcock, 2020; Modarelli, Rainero, & Amelio, 2024; Cole & Zammit, 2020). Workplace diversity management has recently garnered attention, with organizations striving to establish an equitable environment that is considerate, respectful, and supportive of individuals from diverse backgrounds Patrick & Kumar, 2012; Davis, Frolova & Callahan, 2016). The goal of diversity management is to develop policies, practices, and strategies that ensure the inclusion of individuals with varied identities in the workplace. Apart from meeting legal obligations, diversity management also offers economic advantages, such as enhanced job satisfaction and organizational appeal (Chakraborty & Chatterjee, 2020). Research has shown that workplace diversity policies are most effective when endorsed by both top management and employees themselves (Scarborough et al., 2019).

Gender diversity, sexual orientation, ethnicity, religion, disability etc., represent only a few dimensions of diversity. In today's global economy, companies must prioritize creating inclusive workplaces for innovation, problem-solving and employee happiness. Game-based pedagogies offer a potential solution to address diversity and inclusion in the workplace. Employers can design dynamic learning experiences that promote empathy, teamwork, and interechanging solutions for communication and team building (Wolfe, Bowen & Roberts, 1989). Organizations are promoting inclusive spaces for individuals with disabilities, emphasizing support and adjustments for equal opportunities. Leadership plays a crucial role in fostering change and implementing best practices (Vito & Sethi, 2020). Ethnicity, gender, disability, religion etc., diversity management is essential for fostering inclusive workplaces, addressing disparities, and balancing diversity initiatives. Research on employee relations in diverse environments can reveal obstacles and facilitators for enhancing positive interactions.

Gamification is a popular tool, approach, and method for enhancing motivation, fostering competition, and improving learning outcomes in various settings. It has been used in education, customer engagement, and business applications. Gamification strategies focus on understanding user preferences and promoting economic and performance-oriented approaches. It has been shown to improve learning activities, enhance assessment feedback, and enhance computational thinking among young learners. In supply chain management, gamification has been used to bridge the gap between gaming experiences and real-world problem-solving. Despite potential drawbacks, gamification remains a versatile tool for reshaping learning experiences and driving behavioral changes (Hamari, Koivisto & Sarsa, 2014; Caponetto, Earp & Ott, 2014; Marczewski, 2013). Serious games are designed to produce specific outcomes, such as learning, skill enhancement, behavior modification, or cognitive evaluation. They combine game design with instructional design principles to create immersive experiences. Personalization is crucial, as it optimizes learning processes and performance. Serious games have been used in healthcare, urban planning, and cognitive assessment. They use adaptive approaches, dynamic difficulty levels, and sensors to improve individual functions and cognitive aspects. Participatory game prototyping balances domain content and playability (Susi, Johannesson & Backlund, 2007; Laamarti, Eid & El Saddik, 2014; Wouters, P., Van der Spek, E. D., & Van Oostendorp, H. (2009).

With the aim of considering predominant aspects of the D&I research field connected to the perspective of pedagogical gaming, the authors propose: (a) a review of the literature also from the point of view of a historical evolutionary excursus of the concept of diversity and gaming; (b) a field investigation at an empirical level aimed at validating the main potential, positive and negative perceptions, as well as critical issues of pedagogical gaming approaches. To this end, the authors proposed a survey on a sample of 50 teachers from secondary schools in Italy, who had the opportunity to participate and/or implement pedagogical gaming dynamics.

This chapter explores the pedagogical underpinnings, potentials, risks, criticalities and positive or negative perceptions related to game-based pedagogies and training for promoting inclusive environments.

The research therefore aims to answer a clear research question dictated, on the one hand, by the need to make coherent and homogeneous a framework of reference inherent to the evolution of the D&I area in relation to the more poorly investigated dimension of gaming instrumental to vision pedagogical and the implementation of inclusive dynamics in the framework of business and management, focused on the potential to produce positive effects on workplace well-being, on work-life balance (WLB) (Guest, 2002) and above all towards the broader horizon of great challenges oriented to the prerogatives expressed by SDGs (Farouk, 2021). Therefore, the research attempts to answer the following questions:

RQ1: what is the evolutionary dimension that has allowed the establishment of gaming practices as a relevant factor for inclusiveness and diversity management?

RQ2: What are the main developments that gaming-based approaches can bring to working environments in terms of D&I practices?

2. BACKGROUND: CONTEMPORARY TRENDS IN D&I

2.1. Gender Diversity

Gender diversity management is a crucial component of organizational policies aimed at fostering inclusive and fair workplaces. Research underscores the significance of gender diversity management in addressing disparities and promoting equity across gender dimensions (Mazure & Jones, 2015) (Mousa, Massoud & Ayoubi, 2020). Organizational use of inclusive language and strategies ensures appropriate representation and analysis based on sex and gender (Sczesny, Moser & Wood, 2015). Military projects focused on regendering aim to redefine participation within a military framework outside the scope of gender mainstreaming projects, potentially minimizing the likelihood of institutional change (Duncanson & Woodward, 2015; Samuels et al., 2023). Nursing students' perceptions of gender-defined roles in nursing emphasize strategies for addressing stereotypes, using gender-inclusive language, ensuring gender diversity in teams, and revising curricula to overcome gender-based differences in promoting inclusivity (Prosen, 2022; Carter, 2020) . Strategies for fostering inclusive medical imaging environments must account for attributes that facilitate the inclusion of diverse forms of gender diversity, including ethnicity, culture, age, physical ability, among others (Venter & Hodgson, 2020). Particularly, efforts to establish a gender identity-inclusive learning environment within medical education stress the importance of addressing gender identity diversity to ensure inclusion in an educational context (Baecher-Lind et al., 2023). Educators trained in gender-inclusive teaching strategies have shown success in managing classrooms, with education playing a pivotal role in the effectiveness of implementation. The findings underscore the need for holistic approaches to address management challenges and cultivate a supportive environment for the enactment of gender-inclusive policies. Initiatives like safe spaces in organizational settings strive to involve transgender and gender-diverse employees in gender diversification efforts, fostering greater inclusion and career development opportunities for marginalized groups in society. Organizations can foster an environment that values individuality and promotes diversity and inclusion by integrating gender-inclusive practices with resilience-building programs (Feldman et al., 2006; Shore, Cleveland & Sanchez, 2018). Gender diversity and inclusion represent areas where learning institutions are intensifying efforts to dismantle gendered roles and stereotypes, thereby fostering inclusive environments. Various sexual orientations and gender identities are starting to acknowledge the significance of creating a more supportive environment for LGBTQ+ members. Research strongly indicates that organizational policies in the workplace should endorse and offer expanded opportunities for LGBTQ+ employees, as well as their partners and family members (Quinn et al., 2015).

In STEM workplaces, diversity and inclusion efforts advocate for acknowledging and supporting LGBTQ individuals within organizational settings to cultivate a more inclusive sense of belonging. There is a critical need for work in LGBTQ+ diversity management, as emphasized in a case study focusing on the visibility of LGBTQ+ staff in universities. The study emphasized the necessity of incorporating more explicit symbols of LGBTQ+ visibility into institutional cultures and policies to ensure that all individuals are included in a university setting (C. Lee, 2022). Research has also examined the financial implications of managing LGBTQ+ diversity, indicating that organizations prioritizing the inclusion of LGBTQ+ employees are more successful in attracting and retaining top talent (Corral, 2024). Additionally, the inclusion of LGBTQ+ individuals in the workplace has been shown to positively impact gender diversity, illustrating how diversity and inclusion initiatives intersect across various diversity levels (Maji et al., 2023). Systemic disparities have been identified as significant for LGBTQ+ professionals in STEM fields, highlighting the need for workplaces to become more inclusive and protective of LGBTQ identities (Sona et al., 2022). Policies should be inclusive and protective of LGBTQ+ individuals in workplace and departmental practices, ensuring that all individuals can benefit from a supportive and affirming work environment. Workplace diversity and inclusion policies positively incentivize the health and well-being of LGBTQ+ employees (Mara, Ginieis & Brunet-Icart, 2021). Therefore, an inclusive and safe environment must be established for each individual (Fielding, 2004).

2.2. Disability Diversity

Organizations have also embraced a model that promotes the creation of inclusive spaces for individuals with disabilities. Workplace policies should be as attentive and responsive as possible to employees with disabilities, emphasizing the importance of extending support and accommodations for equal opportunities (Nafukho et al., 2010; Westen, 1985). Such organizations are likely to establish more inclusive and supportive work environments by taking a comprehensive view of the social and environmental impacts on individuals with disabilities. The role of leadership in fostering actual change and an inclusive environment is crucial (Gould et al., 2020; Hurtado, Alvarado & Guillermo-Wann, 2015), as leaders enable organizations to implement best practices into practical strategies and approaches for successful diversity and inclusion initiatives involving disabled employees. Managing disability as a diversity factor necessitates an understanding of how disability can impact core HR practices such as job retention, accommodation, and termination (Sang et al., 2021). Exploring employers' perspectives on challenges and strategies for better recruiting, retaining, and advancing employees with physical disabilities is essential to comprehend the obstacles and opportunities (Kuppers, 2026; Thomas, 2014) in managing disability diversity (Munsell et al., 2022; Zulmi et al., 2021).

2.3. Ethnic Diversity

Ethnic diversity management is a critical component of fostering inclusive workplaces that appreciate a variety of cultural backgrounds (Collier, 2001; Aigner, 2014; Janssens & Zanoni, 2014) . Kapilashrami et al. (2021) emphasize the importance of addressing ethnic disparities in various aspects such as exposure, protection, and clinical management to ensure fair treatment of healthcare personnel. Achieving ethnic inclusion through balancing diversity initiatives is essential for effective diversity management strategies (Janssens & Zanoni, 2014). The significance of strategic management and leadership has grown in organizations with diverse ethnic workforces, underscoring the need to comprehend workplace dynamics in ethnically diverse settings. Research on employee relations in such environments can reveal obstacles and facilitators to enhancing positive interactions among employees from diverse ethnic backgrounds. The ethnic and gender makeup of the workplace is closely linked to charitable giving within organizations, with attention drawn to the increasing representation of female and ethnic minority workers in recent years (Leslie et al., 2013). Employees' perceptions of favoritism towards members of their own ethnic group within the workplace can impact organizational dynamics. Managing perceptions of ethnic homophily is crucial to prevent detrimental workplace relationships and outcomes (Lee & Reade, 2014). Ethnic homophily, a sociological descriptive paradigm, denotes individuals' propensity to interact preferentially with those of similar ethnic backgrounds, fostering social support and belonging, particularly among minorities. While Granovetter emphasizes the significance of weak ties for employment (1973; 2018), Putnam (2000) acknowledges that strong ethnic networks can enhance social capital, with their impact being context-dependent, potentially facilitating or obstructing inclusivity and equity. Birnir and Waguespack (2011) and Shore et al. (2011), confirm that addressing ethnic homophily perceptions is a step towards fostering a truly inclusive environment, where diversity is highly valued, and collaboration between employees from diverse ethnic backgrounds is encouraged.

2.4. Gamification and Serious Games

Gamification and serious gaming are innovative methodologies that effectively enhance inclusion and diversity. By fostering motivation, personalizing experiences, offering immediate feedback, and promoting collaboration, gamification, alongside serious gaming, can raise awareness and facilitate experiential learning in diverse contexts. Gamification has garnered significant interest across various domains by integrating elements of game design into non-game contexts. The ability of gamification to enhance motivation and foster friendly competition through collaboration in diverse settings, such as education, customer engagement, or employee performance, has made it a popular tool for driving behavioral change (Hamari, Koivisto & Sarsa, 2014; Caponetto, Earp & Ott, 2014; Marczewski, 2013). Organizations are increasingly utilizing gamification techniques to enhance customer engagement by incorporating gaming-style incentives and mechanisms that promote desired behaviors (Yang et al., 2017). Even in business applications, the integration of elements like competition, teamwork, curiosity, and problem-solving effectively engages users and enhances performance in mobile banking services (Baptista & Oliveira, 2017). Therefore, the concept of adaptive gamification in educational research explores how tailored gamification approaches can better meet the learning needs of users (Bennani et al., 2021). In the realm of statistics education, approaches such as challenge-based gamification design, featuring elements like points, levels, leaderboards, and clear objectives, are believed to support effective learning practices and study designs to improve learning outcomes (Legaki et al., 2020). By incorporating features like scores, challenges, and rewards, gamification in education creates interactive learning environments that boost student motivation and render the exploration of complex concepts enjoyable. Tools like GamiTool have been developed for Massive Open Online Courses to assist instructors in effectively integrating gamification strategies, sharing workloads, and maximizing usability within gamified learning environments (Ortega-Arranz, 2022). Additionally, methods such as gamification have been implemented in fields such as science, demonstrating enhanced impacts on student performance by incorporating game elements to boost engagement and motivation for learning (Ismail et al., 2021; Alsawaier, 2018). A fundamental aspect in most gamification strategies is the understanding of user preferences, typically favoring an economical and performance-oriented approach within a gamified setting. These gamification techniques have significantly improved learning activities, elevating assessment feedback and interaction in educational settings. Moreover, gamification has been explored for its potential in enhancing computational thinking among young learners and adding value to various educational tasks (Olmo-Muñoz, 2023; Thielsch & Niesenhaus, 2017; Ortiz Rojas, Chiluiza & Valcke, 2017). Within supply chain management, gamification has been utilized to solicit responses from participants to address issues or make decisions, effectively bridging the gap between gaming experiences and real-world problem-solving (Sainath & Sai, 2023; Poonsawad, Srisomphan & Sanrach, 2022; Hung, 2018; Schöbel et al., 2019).A comparison of case-based learning methods with gamification strategies indicates that challenge- and immersion-based approaches lead to efficacy in educational contexts (Zafar et al., 2022). Particularly intriguing are the integrations where gamification strategies are leveraged to enhance the utilization and impact of blockchain technology within student-centered learning environments, thereby fostering creativity, innovation, and interactivity in educational spheres (Aini et al., 2022; Parizi & Dehghantanha, 2018; Aini, Lutfiani, & Zahran, 2021). Nevertheless, it is crucial to recognize the potential drawbacks of gamification, as research has suggested that gamified assessments can negatively impact students' perceptions and content knowledge (Hammedi et al., 2017). Limiting gamification to assessment mechanisms alone may impede student engagement and performance outcomes (Aini, 2019). Despite these concerns, gamification in e-learning presents a powerful driver for active learning, offering an enjoyable approach to acquiring knowledge (Kapp, 2012). Consequently, gamification stands as a versatile and potent tool for reshaping learning experiences, enhancing user engagement, and prompting behavioral changes across various life domains. Incorporating game design elements holds promise for creating highly interactive and engaging learning environments that inspire participants to collaborate effectively and engage in innovative learning practices (Meske et al., 2017; Patricio et al., 2020). Understanding users' interests remains paramount in most gamification strategies, with an emphasis on an economic and performance-driven approach in gamified experiences.

Serious games are typically created with a primary objective beyond mere entertainment and are intended to produce specific outcomes, such as learning, skill enhancement, behavior modification, or cognitive evaluation. The development of serious games involves a meticulous process that merges elements of game design with instructional design principles to craft immersive and compelling learning experiences. Personalization is a crucial feature in serious games as tailoring game elements to individual player characteristics can optimize learning processes and performance results. Notably, the incorporation of personalization in participatory design of serious games strives to comprehend game mechanics that intertwine with domain content, fostering meaningful and engaging experiences for players. These games aim not only to enhance learning but also to influence users' perceptions and behaviors towards achieving particular objectives. By incorporating elements like points, leaderboards, levels, and rewards, serious games heighten motivation and engagement in non-game contexts through gamification strategies. The utilization of serious games has been shown to enhance treatment adherence in healthcare settings and facilitate training for healthcare professionals. These specialized serious games serve the purpose of promoting treatment adherence in health-related contexts Susi, Johannesson & Backlund, 2007; Laamarti, Eid & El Saddik, 2014; Wouters, Van der Spek & Van Oostendorp, 2009). Furthermore, serious games play a supportive role in enhancing education across various domains, including dementia care, through immersive learning experiences (Carlier et al., 2023). The development of serious games for health interventions holds promise for enhancing adherence and user engagement through effective design and development processes (Libe et al., 2020). These games often employ adaptive and personalized approaches to cater to individual needs and preferences, thereby enriching the overall user experience significantly (Gurbuz & Celik, 2022). Due to their ability to dynamically adjust difficulty levels while considering educational constraints, serious games encourage learners to stay motivated, engaged, and ultimately achieve their learning objectives successfully (Streicher & Smeddinck, 2016). Severe games have a history in urban planning, with examples like Minecraft being used for participatory design in urban development projects (Delaney, 2022). For instance, serious games have been designed to support children experiencing school refusal, aiming to enhance learning experiences and engagement through innovative methods (Høiseth et al., 2021). Furthermore, the expansion of learning content, refinement of gameplay, and adjustment of difficulty levels in serious games have been improved through the use of prototypes and collaboration with various stakeholders in the design process. These games blend entertainment elements with educational content purposefully to achieve specific learning outcomes. Serious games have also been instrumental in the cognitive assessment of elderly individuals, with games like whack-a-mole demonstrating promising usability and validity testing among this demographic (Ampatzidou & Gugerell, 2018). The design of such serious games necessitates a solid foundation in game mechanics and instructional design principles to create intuitive and engaging learning experiences (Westera, 2022).

Games that integrate brain-computer interface (BCI) sensors provide a new platform to improve the brain's functions and cognitive aspects of an individual (Sung et al., 2012). The learning outcome of an individual player can be assessed, and afterward, the inference can be combined to evaluate the overall effectiveness of serious games (Carlier et al., 2022). However, participatory game prototyping has emerged as a productive way to generate engaging and relevant serious games, seeking a balance between domain content and playability.

Games incorporating BCI sensors offer a novel avenue for enhancing cognitive functions and aspects of individuals (Sung et al., 2012). The assessment of an individual player's learning outcomes can be conducted, followed by the integration of inferences to assess the overall efficacy of serious games (Carlier et al., 2022). Nonetheless, participatory game prototyping has emerged as an effective method for creating immersive and pertinent serious games, aiming to strike a balance between subject matter expertise and usability.

2.5. Putnam's Influencing View

In Robert D. Putnam's influential publication "Bowling Alone" from 2000 (Putnam, 2000), he examines the decay of civic traditions in contemporary society, attributing it to a decrease in community involvement and social capital (Andrews, 2011). Putnam underscores the waning sense of community and the breakdown of social frameworks that have resulted in heightened disconnection among individuals (Andrews, 2011; Bauman, 2013; Mack & Khare, 2016). He stresses the significance of reestablishing connections both symbolically and practically, using communal bowling as a metaphor for rebuilding social bonds (Spalding, 2006). Putnam's evaluation of the repercussions of diminishing social capital in the United States identifies five core components of social capital: communal organizational vitality, participation in civic matters, community service, informal socializing, and social confidence (Andrews, 2011). The notion of social capital, as popularized by Putnam in "Bowling Alone," has incited substantial scholarly discussion due to its linkage with voluntary groups and its influence on economic progress (Foster et al., 2021). Putnam's work has been pivotal in drawing attention to the decline in civic engagement and the role of social capital in nurturing communal cohesion (Wouters et al., 2009). He is recognized for highlighting personal isolation as a noteworthy social issue, shedding light on the consequences of reduced social interactions within communities (Greenwald & Beery, 2001). Through his research, Putnam stresses the necessity for individuals to actively engage in communal endeavors to combat the erosion of social capital (Borlido & Coromina, 2018). Putnam's analysis of social capital and civic engagement has influenced various domains, including public policy, sociology, and community health services (Andrews & Wankhade, 2014). His exploration of the correlation between social capital and public service effectiveness has spurred further investigation into the impact of social connections on the efficiency of public services (Andrews & Wankhade, 2014). Putnam's work has also played a key role in shaping dialogues on democratic community development and the role of face-to-face communication in fostering civic participation (Flavin-McDonald & Barrett, 1999). By emphasizing the significance of social frameworks and community bonds, Putnam underscores the importance of social capital in advancing democratic governance and citizenship (Silva et al., 2013). Additionally, Putnam's examination of the decline in social capital in America has raised apprehensions regarding the influence of contemporary phenomena such as television on social interactions (Olken, 2009). He has emphasized the need for individuals to actively participate in communal activities to prevent the erosion of social capital and cultivate a sense of belonging (Borlido & Coromina, 2018). Putnam's metaphor of "bowling alone" has become synonymous with the trend of decreasing social interactions and serves as a poignant symbol of the challenges facing modern communities (Robison et al., 2002). Despite this declination, authors like Modarelli, Rainero & Amelio (2024) find the American context as a wide range plethora for game-based solutions toward inclusive approaches in the work environment. However, Putnam's job continues to inspire researchers to explore the dynamics of social capital, community engagement, and their implications for societal well-being and cohesion, and the game-based solution would be a derivation appendix fruitful for investigations.

3. CONTEXTUALIZATION: AN HISTORICAL ANCHORAGE OF PEDAGOGICAL GAME

In the current global economy, companies aiming for innovation and competitiveness must prioritize fostering inclusive workplaces to reap benefits beyond legal compliance, including enhanced innovation, problem-solving, and employee satisfaction (Mor Barak & Daya, 2013; Royall, McCarthy & Miller, 2022; Stevens, Plaut & Sanchez-Burks, 2008). Despite increased recognition of the importance of diversity and inclusion, many organizations effectively promote them (Modarelli, Rainero & Amelio, 2024; Mazur, 2014; Kuknor & Bhattacharya, 2022; Shore, Cleveland & Sanchez, 2018), by contrast the majority struggle for applicating game-based approaches of training programs and working procedures, often reinforcing biases, and proving ineffective in the long term (Möhlen et al., 2018; Schmölz et al., 2017). Game-based pedagogies offer a promising approach to addressing diversity and inclusion challenges by creating engaging learning experiences that encourage empathy, teamwork, and understanding among employees (Apostolakis et al., 2016). Despite their potential benefits, it is currently uncertain if game-based strategies can effectively promote diversity and well-being in the workplace (Greipl, Moeller & Ninaus, 2020) and properly on this arrangement, the authors try to build a road-map for navigating the plethora of existing information and misinformation on the theme. Based on the premise that work is "a process involving hands, head, and heart" (Rich, Lepine & Crawford, 2010; Ashforth & Humphrey, 1993), as stated by Bekker (2011), the job well-being and/or negative influence variables can be traced back to two sources, per the first reference model (general) (Bakker & Demerouti, 2007). These sources are (a) job demands and (b) job resources. In addition, not merely these forms of harrashments in the area of working well-being should be considered, but with the same importance, discrepancies due to the diversities in working environments create dangers on the WLB (Sang & Powell, 2013). Inclusive workplaces are essential for fostering a sense of acceptance and belonging among all employees, regardless of their differences, according to Shore et al. (2011). In these environments, fairness and equality are highly valued, ensuring that every individual has an equal opportunity for growth, advancement, and recognition (Mikkelson, 2013). However, corporate leaders must continue to be committed to addressing biases, eliminating barriers to inclusion, and promoting serence climate on the job.

The first traces of inclusive play date back to Egypt and Ancient Greece and Roman Empire, where physical education was considered fundamental to the development of all citizens, regardless of their physical or social abilities (Liboriussen & Martin, 2016; Sebbane, 2001; Andreu-Cabrera et al., 2010; Kurke, 1999; Goldhill, 2017; Coleman, 2000; Alföldi-Rosenbaum, 1971During the Middle Ages, education became more elitist and play lost its inclusive role (Elliott, 2004) However, with the advent of the Enlightenment and the industrial revolutions, the importance of play for learning and social development was rediscovered (Ewers, 2019; Schreiber, 2021; Cambi & Staccioli, 2007; Dasen & Vespa, 2021; Swaddling, 1999; Plummer, 1898). The evolutionary timeline of games as a social pedagogical practice can be divided into several eras: (a) Ancient, (b) Classical, (c) Medieval, (d) Renaissance, (e) Enlightment and Industrial Revolution and (e) 20th century, with the rise of digital gaming.

Table 1. Game as pedagogical tool – evolutionary timeline

Game as pedagogical tool - evolutionary timeline		References
(a) Ancient era	Games have been a significant part of human culture since ancient times, serving as amusement, instruction, and religious rites in various aspects of society. The remnants of ancient civilizations, such as Mesopotamia, Egypt, and China, provide insights into their social structures and cultural customs through various games.	Finkel (2007); Dasen & Vespa (2021); Liboriussen & Martin (2016); Bell (1979);
(b) Classical era	During the Classical Era, Greco-Roman civilization valued games as a means to showcase cultural identity, athletic skills, and intellectual abilities. The Olympic Games and Panhellenic athletic tournaments attracted athletes from Greece. Philosophers like Plato and Aristotle praised games for their educational value in fostering bravery, temperance, and justice.	Becker (1967); Miller (2004); Swaddling (1999); Plato (1992) Serra (2018); Plummer (1898); Piazza (2006); Zanardi (1985);
(c) Medieval era (d) Reinassance era	During the Middle Ages and Renaissance, games evolved into complex representations of moral education, courtly culture, and creative inventiveness. Nobility used games like backgammon and chess as symbols of social standing and intelligence, with sophisticated game sets. Allegorical games like the "Game of the Goose" blended moral education with religious and ethical lessons, addressing societal issues. During the Renaissance, games like Tarot cards and mathematical riddles and puzzles emerged as means of intellectual inquiry and creative expression. Games served as tools for socializing, education, and enjoyment for all social classes.	Murray (1978); Bell (1979); Elliott (2004);

continued on following page

Table 1. Continued

Game as pedagogical tool - evolutionary timeline		References
(e) Enlightment and Industrial Revolution	During the Enlightenment and Industrial Revolutions, games underwent significant changes reflecting the evolving social, technological, and economic landscape. Games became more rationalized and standardized, leading to their widespread popularity across various socioeconomic classes. Industrial capitalism also made games more commercialized, allowing the public to purchase mass-produced toys and board games. As the middle class grew, leisure activities increased, leading to advancements in entertainment and game design. New pastimes emerged, including mechanical puzzles, parlor games, amusement parks, and carnival attractions	Huizinga (1955); Boulton (1974); Schreiber (2021); Bell (1979); Ewers (2019); Landow (2009); Sutton-Smith (1997);
(f) 20th century era	The 20th century saw a significant transformation in the gaming industry, with the rise of digital technology and the creation of classic video games like Pac-Man, Space Invaders, and Pong. The popularity of home gaming consoles like the Atari 2600 and Nintendo Entertainment System democratized gaming, encouraging a new wave of game creators and gamers. The development of immersive virtual and augmented reality (AR) experiences has made gaming more feasible, and professional players, teams, and tournaments have turned gaming into a competitive sport. The evolution of digital gaming is shaping the way we play, learn, and interact in the digital age, offering new possibilities and problems for developers, players, and society. Sociocultural viewpoints emphasize the value of group learning and social contact in game-based situations, and games offer cooperative problem-solving and peer-to-peer mentorship. Games are increasingly recognized as effective tools for training, education, and behavior modification, with applications in various sectors and situations. The 20th century saw a significant evolution in the concept of inclusive education. In 1948, the Universal Declaration of Human Rights established the right to education for all, regardless of race, sex, religion, nationality or ability. In the 1950s and 1960s, the first special education programs dedicated to students with disabilities were developed. In the 70s and 80s, the school integration model established itself, which involved the inclusion of students with disabilities in regular classes. In the 1990s, we moved to the school inclusion model, which considers diversity as a resource for the learning of all students.	Newman (2004); Kent (2001); Wolf (2001); Galarneau & Zibit, 2007; Vygotsky (1978); Steinkuehler & Squire (201); Gee (2007); United Nations. General Assembly. (1949). Universal declaration of human rights (Vol. 3381). Department of State, United States of America; Skinner (1963); Piaget (1954); Csikszentmihalyi (1990; 2013);

Source: authors' elaboration

3.1. Gaming as a Tool for Inclusive Education in the 21st Century

The concept of diversity and inclusion (D&I) has deep roots in human history (Özbilgin, 2009). Since the earliest societies, people have recognized and appreciated the variety of cultures, traditions and perspectives (Diller, 2014). However, it is only in recent decades that D&I has become a central theme of public discourse and social policies (Hunt, Layton & Prince, 2015; Roberson, 2006). In the 21st century, play has taken on an increasingly important role in inclusive education (Bettelheim, 1972). Several studies have shown that the game can be used to: (a) promote the learning of new skills and knowledge, (b) develop social and emotional skills, (c) encourage collaboration and teamwork and (e) increase self-esteem and self-confidence (Alsawaier, 2018; Poonsawad, Srisomphan & Sanrach, 2022; Hung, 2018; Schöbel et al., 2019; Parizi & Dehghantanha, 2018; Kapp, 2012; Meske et al., 2017). The gaming approach can be used in both formal and informal training contexts, for example: at school, in professional training centers, in companies, in non-profit organizations (Beltadze, 2016; Camerer & Knez, 1997). There are numerous examples of inclusive play that are used around the world (Modarelli, Rainero & Amelio, 2024). Among these, it is possible to mention: (a) role-playing games that simulate real-life situations, (b) board games that promote cooperation and collaboration, (c) simulation games that allow you to experiment with new professions and (d) playful activities that use new technologies (Graham & Gray, 1969). The use of games in educational and training contexts entails some ethical implications that are important to consider. Among these, we can mention: (a) the need to ensure the accessibility of the game to all students, (b) the importance of promoting values of respect and inclusion, (c) the protection of students' personal data and (d) responsible use of new technologies (Kim & Werbach, 2016). An important factor in the evolution of D&I was the rise of the civil rights movements in the 20th century. These movements, such as the African American civil rights movement and the feminist movement, fought against discrimination and inequality based on race, gender, and other factors. They have helped raise awareness of the need to create more inclusive and just societies for all (Morris, 1984) The increasing globalization and interconnectedness of the world have led to a greater awareness of human diversity (Berger & Huntington, 2002). People are increasingly exposed to different cultures and ideas, which has led to a greater understanding and appreciation of difference (Kavesh, 2024). Despite the progress made, D&I remains a major challenge in many companies (Vaz Torres, Vasques-Menezes & Presotti, 2017). Discrimination and inequality persist in many forms, and many people continue to feel excluded and marginalised (Roithmayr, 2003). However, D&I also represents an opportunity to create more cohesive, innovative, and prosperous societies. Some key points in the history of D&I can be found in the following timeline (Tab.2).

Table 2. Key points in the history of D&I with specific details on the Italian educational and working context

YEAR	DESCRIPTION
GENTILE REFORM (1923):	Before the Gentile reform, the Italian school system was characterized by strong social selection and little attention to individual differences. Education was often reserved for a small elite. The Gentile reform, while representing a step forward for Italian education, consolidated an elitist and homogeneous school model, with little attention to the needs of students with difficulties
1948:	Universal Declaration of Human Rights adopted by the United Nations General Assembly.
1964:	Civil Rights Act passed in the United States, prohibiting discrimination based on race, color, religion, sex, and national origin.
1970-1980:	Beginning of a debate on the need for a more inclusive school that is attentive to diversity. First regulations that recognize the right to education for all, but school integration still remains an exception.
1975:	World Conference of Women in Mexico City, which adopts the Mexico City Declaration on the Equality of Women.
1992:	Law n. 104/1992 - Introduces the concept of "handicap" and defines the rights of people with disabilities, including the right to education. Provides for the inclusion of students with disabilities in mainstream schools, with the necessary support. The Minister of Education at the time, Antonio Falcucci, was a strong supporter of this law and actively committed to promoting school integration.
1995:	World Conference on Women in Beijing, adopting the Beijing Platform for Action for the Empowerment of Women.
1999:	Law n. 68/1999 containing provisions for the right to work of disabled people, promotes the inclusion and integration of disabled people into the workplace. It introduces the obligation to hire for companies with more than 15 employees, defines the reserve quotas for public administrations and establishes targeted placement services.
2000:	Millennium Development Goals adopted by the United Nations, which include a goal to promote gender equality and the empowerment of women.
2000:	Moratti Reform: Introduces the concept of "diversity" and emphasizes the importance of inclusion for all students. Introduces the Individualized Educational Plan (PEI).
2008:	Legislative Decree n.81/2008 (Consolidated Law on Workplace Safety), guarantees the health and safety of workers, including people with disabilities. It provides for adaptations of workplaces and equipment to promote work inclusion.
2015:	Sustainable Development Goals adopted by the United Nations, which include a goal to reduce inequality and promote peaceful and inclusive societies.
2015:	Law n. 107/2015 "Buona Scuola" – with the introduction of this law a process of school reform takes place in a radical way with particular attention to the inclusion policy.
2015:	Legislative Decree n.151/2015, reforms Law 68/99, simplifying procedures and strengthening targeted placement services. It introduces new tools to promote job placement, such as inclusive internships and job placement paths.

continued on following page

Table 2. Continued

YEAR	DESCRIPTION
2017:	Legislative Decree 66/2017: Defines the concept of "special educational needs" (SEN) and broadens the range of students to whom support measures are addressed.
...:	Subsequent ministerial notes provided clarifications and updates on the methods of implementing the rules, defining roles, tasks and operational tools.

Source: authors' elaboration

In Italy, D&I is a relatively recent topic. The adoption of specific laws and policies to promote D&I is relatively recent. However, in recent years there has been a growing awareness of the importance of D&I, both in the public and private sectors.

Important considerations on the Italian development timeline are to be considered as follows (Tab.3).

Table 3. Key points in the history of D&I in Italy

YEAR	DESCRIPTION
2006:	*Law against discrimination based on sexual orientation and gender identity.*
2012:	*National plan for equity and social inclusion.*
2016:	*Charter of principles for promoting diversity and inclusion in public administrations.*
2020:	*National plan for gender equality*

Source: authors' elaboration

D&I is an ongoing process that requires ongoing commitment from all sectors of society. It is important to continue working to create more inclusive and just societies for all.

The use of games as an educational and training tool has ancient roots, dating back to the first civilisations. Throughout history, its value has been recognized in various fields, including children's education, professional training, and military training.

In recent times, attention has focused on the potential of gaming to promote diversity and inclusion, both in educational and workplace contexts. This interest was born from the awareness that diversity represents a richness and a precious resource for society, and that inclusion is fundamental to guarantee everyone equal opportunities for success.

In conclusion, the use of games as an approach to education, training and work can represent a valid tool for promoting diversity, inclusion, and well-being. Through play, it is possible to create more welcoming, stimulating, and sustainable environments, where everyone can express their potential and contribute to collective success.

3.2. Inclusive and Diversified Education: Evolutionary Scenario Inherent to the SDGs

The use of games as an educational and training tool, with deep roots in history, has taken on an increasingly central role in promoting diversity, inclusion, and well-being in line with the Sustainable Development Goals (SDGs) of the 2030 Agenda.

The Sustainable Development Goals (SDGs) of the United Nations 2030 Agenda represent a fundamental framework for promoting diversity, inclusion, and well-being in all areas of life, including education, training, and work.

Goal 4 aims to ensure equitable and inclusive quality education for all. Gaming can be used to achieve this by promoting active and participatory learning for all students.

Therefore, play promotes inclusive and welcoming learning environments, enhancing individual and cultural differences (UNESCO, 2015). Through play, the following are promoted: (a) social and emotional skills (Boghian & Cojocariu, 2023) and the fight against stereotypes and prejudices (UNICEF, 2019).

The game would thus make training more engaging and effective, facilitating experiential learning (Tan, 2018). The game encourages: (a) teamwork and collaboration (UNESCO, 2019), development of transversal skills (European Commission, 2017).

As regards the issues of Workplace Wellbeing and Sustainable Environments, the following objectives are found in the 2030 Agenda: (i) objective 3: Health and well-being, such that gaming would be able to reduce stress and anxiety, improving mood and motivation (Kopp, 2018), promoting Creativity and productivity (Tremblay, 2019), as well as increasing the sense of belonging (Van Leeuwen & Westwood, 2008); (ii) objective 8: Inclusive economic growth, full employment and decent work. Gaming, in relation to working environments, would contribute to creating healthy and safe (OSHA, 2020), ergonomic and comfortable (NIOSH, 2016) working environments, promoting important awareness of respect for the environment and the human sphere of workers (ISO, 2015).

As an evolutionary scenario, play, understood as an atavistic social practice continually in progress, under the aegis of the 2030 Agenda and the D&I policies inherent to management, by 2030, an increase in inclusive learning environments in schools and in universities (UNESCO, 2021); a development of educational gaming platforms accessible to all (European Commission, 2020) and a diffusion of gaming practices in companies to promote workplace well-being (World Health Organization, 2019).

Therefore, the use of games represents a powerful tool to achieve the SDGs, promoting diversity, inclusion and well-being in educational, work and social contexts.

The literature indicates that unbalanced work-life balance (WLB) can lead to depression, stress, lower productivity, higher exhaustion, and absenteeism. Additionally, it can cause negative emotional impacts like loneliness, irritability, worry, and guilt, with more mental health symptoms compared to those who perform work-related activities in hostile working environments (Issahaku, Anthony & Bakari, 2020; Mann & Holdsworth, 2003; Sanin, J2020; Yamada, 1999; Cantone & Wiener, 2017; Schindeler, 2021).

4. THEORETICAL DIMENSION: GAME-BASED LEARNING THEORY

A referring framework for comprehending the complexity of human behavior, culture, and learning is offered by game-based theory. Games have been crucial in forming societies, promoting social interaction, and preserving cultural values for next generations. From its initial iterations to current versions, this theory has changed, incorporating ideas from game studies, psychology, anthropology, and archeology (Squire, 2005). This chapter attempts to clarify the cultural relevance, cognitive advantages, and useful applications of game-based approaches in promoting inclusive learning environments, improving decision-making abilities, and tackling difficult issues in modern society through an interdisciplinary approach.

The relevance of play in human society is underscored by game-based theory (Plass, Homer & Kinzer, 2015), since gaming transcends both time and culture, from early board games to contemporary electronic games. Human experience has been replicated and stimulated by games. Game-Based Learning Theory, also known as game-based learning (GBL) (Tobias, Fletcher & Wind, 2014), is the utilization of games or game components in educational environments to enhance learners' engagement, motivation, and results. GBL has become increasingly popular as a novel educational approach, supported by a growing body of research illustrating its efficacy.

Various theories underpin game-based learning, with some of the most crucial being: according to Behaviorism theory, GBL leverages positive reinforcement principles, such as points, badges, and rewards, to stimulate desired behaviors and learning outcomes (Skinner, 1963); following Cognitive theory, games can facilitate active learning, experimentation, and problem-solving, contributing to the acquisition of knowledge and the enhancement of cognitive skills (Piaget, 1954); constructivist theory confirms that GBL empowers students to construct their knowledge through immersive and interactive experiences, fostering independent and meaningful learning (Vygotsky, 1978). The flow Theory considers GBL as able to induce a state of 'flow' in learners, marked by total absorption and intrinsic motivation, thereby optimizing the learning process (Csikszentmihalyi, 1990).

In this way, it is possible to shape the borders of active learning (Dewey, 2022) and GBL (Ifenthaler, Eseryel & Ge, 2012) opening horizons of application towards game-based working experiences (GBW) (Romero, 2015). GBL and the application of this approach within the business and management environment (e.g. GBW), presents numerous advantages compared to conventional learning methodologies: i.e. enhanced engagement and motivation, offering challenges, feedback opportunities, and a sense of progression; enhanced retention of knowledge, thanks to the immersive and interactive nature of GBL experiences; development of soft skills due to the fact that games can aid in the cultivation of skills like problem-solving, critical thinking, collaboration, and communication; fostering a positive learning environment because games can establish a fun and relaxing atmosphere, reducing anxiety levels and promoting learning (Hartt, Hosseini & Mostafapour, 2020).

GBL can find application across a broad spectrum of educational contexts, including, school education, business training and lifelong learning.

5. METHODOLOGICAL ISSUES: DESIGN, GAP, AND FIELD ANALYSIS

The authors carried out a multilevel gap analysis specifically focused on finding literary references on the topic of D&I, game-based approaches, SDGs and well-being, in scientific journals in the sector, as per Modell reference (2022).

Therefore, the subsequent literature review, aimed at identifying and validating the previously identified gap, is expressly based on a systematic search referring to 25 journals of international relevance in the field of education which will specifically consider research on the topic and who have published or are expected to publish related research studies.

The list of journals's databases questioned is reported in tab.4, also considering the number of referring articles on the total amount of published studies.

Table 4. Journals' databases questioned and articles retrieved on the topic

Journal Title	Retrieved Articles on the Theme
Education Sciences	12
Frontiers in Education	6
International Review of Education	2
Computers & Education	2

continued on following page

Table 4. Continued

Journal Title	Retrieved Articles on the Theme
Higher Education Quarterly	1
Journal of Education	1
The Journal of Higher Education	0
Childhood Education	0
Journal of Educational Psychology	0
The Journal of Educational Research	0
The Educational Forum	0
Early Years Educator	0
Education + Training	0
Journal of Teacher Education	0
Innovait Education and Inspiration for General Practice	0
Educational Researcher	0
The Journal of Experimental Education	0
Educational Theory	0
Studies in Higher Education	0
British Journal of Educational Psychology	0
History of Education Quarterly	0
Review of Educational Research	0
Educational Philosophy and Theory	0
British Journal of Special Education	0
Advances in Physiology Education	0

Source: Authors' elaboration on journals' databases.

The questionnaire design follows the research methodological prerogatives provided by Krosnick (2018) and Acharya, (2010). The questionnaire, as reported in table 5 is structured on five areas of investigation interest considered under 26 descriptors: (i) sesations on game-based training; (ii) positive considerations; (iii) perplexities; (iv) potentials for D&I; (v) perceived influence on working well being.

The five areas and the 26 descriptors, finalized to a systematic mapping of sensations, positive considerations, perplexities, potentials for D&I and perceived influence on eorking well being have been structured asking to "Gemini" Ai, Google Tool:

"Imagine you are a participant in a game-based training in a company. Express your considerations in this regard, your doubts and potential, especially for the D&I area at working level. How much does the practice of game-based training influence well-being at work? Please, take into account the main literary production on the theme D&I".

On the basis of the response provided by "Gemini" Ai Google Tool, reference dimensions and descriptors were structured to ensure a broad mapping of the frame subjected to the human response of the fifty participants selected as a sample for the study.

On the one hand, this provides an innovative form of integration between human-technology interactions to support research. On the other hand, the approach is methodologically structured as it is based on prevailing literature.

Table 5. Questionnaire design

Questionnaire game based training The data processed will be collected anonymously and will not be attributable to individual persons.					
Fill in where indicated by the spaces and place a cross in the boxes designated for the answer: **Gender:** □M □F **Age:** □20-29 □30-44 □45-65					
Answer by placing a cross based on the agreement/ disagreement scale shown below on the right.	**Answers**				
Graduated scale	**1**	**2**	**3**	**4**	**5**
Descriptor	**Scarce**	**Not very much**	**On average**	**Enough**	**Highly**
1. Sensations:					
Satisfaction and fun					
Motivation and commitment					
Self-confidence					
Understanding and awareness					
Connection and collaboration					
Relationality					
Reciprocity					
2. Positive considerations:					
Development of active and engaging learning					
Development of transversal skills					
Development of Problem solving approach					
Development of critical thinking					
Improved teamwork					
Promotion of inclusive environments					
Promotion and respect for differences					
Mutual understanding					
Communication improvement					
3. Perplexities					
Lack of inclusiveness (involuntary exclusion)					

continued on following page

Table 5. Continued

Overemphasis on competition					
Difficulty in evaluating learning					
4. Potentials for D&I					
Raising awareness on diversity and inclusion issues					
Promotion of reflection and dialogue					
I develop inclusive behaviors					
Creating a welcoming working environment					
5. Perceived influence on well-being at work					
Increased motivation and involvement					
Stress reduction					
Serene working climate and valorization of differences					

Source: authors' elaboration on "Gemini Ai Google Tool (accessed 20th June 2024)

The research design that the authors propose is based on the one hand on a gap analysis relating to the review of the main literary references; on the other hand, the authors provide a survey-based field study, formalized through an analysis of the positive and critical sensations, perceptions and perceptions relating to the game-based training application/participation.

Using the keywords "diversity" AND "inclusion" AND "game" AND "SDG" AND "well being" as search terms, the authors dentify a specific gap in literature, verifying that only six specialized journals, on twentifive analyzed, published research integrating D&I with the dimension of SDGs and well being in relation to the gaming approach.

The following query correlated research terms with each other reproducing a literary context characterized by a gap, potentially defining a research area possible of further developmental investigation. In this way, the query (Title AND Abstracts) "diversity" AND "inclusion" AND "game" AND "SDG" AND "well being", highlited twentifour papers in concerning the ambit. The originality and the relevance of the research has been verified.

Given this starting dimension, the research architecture is extended thanks to the ad hoc structured research questions (RQ1 and RQ2), relating to the object of study.

6. RESULTING EVIDENCE

In addition to the starting gap analysis, structured functionally and instrumentally to the literary review, the authors designed a field analysis focused on a survey-based investigation.

A sample of n. 50 (one eliminated – total. n. 49) teachers of the high school in Italy, involved on a randomized criteria of samplig, elicited by the participation and/ or implementation experience in game based learning/training processes.

The sample details concern: gender (25 males and 24 females, respectively 51% and 49%); average age (20-29 years old – 39%; 30-44 years old – 47%; 45-65 years old – 14%).

Figure 1. Sensations on Game based training (Authors' elaboration)

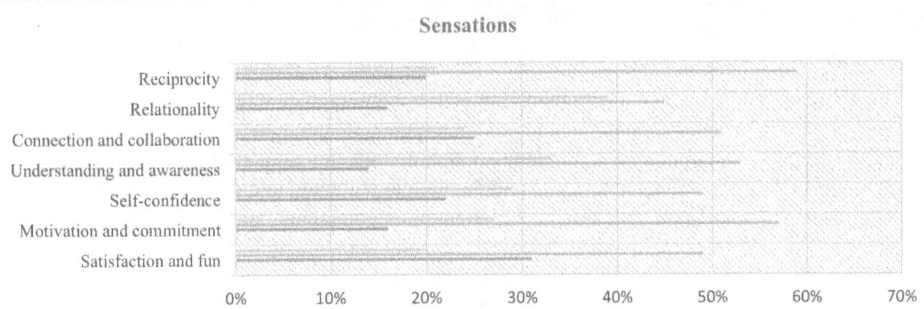

	Satisfaction and fun	Motivation and commitment	Self-confidence	Understanding and awareness	Connection and collaboration	Relationality	Reciprocity
5	20%	27%	29%	33%	24%	39%	21%
4	49%	57%	49%	53%	51%	45%	59%
3	31%	16%	22%	14%	25%	16%	20%
2	0%	0%	0%	0%	0%	0%	0%
1	0%	0%	0%	0%	0%	0%	0%

5 4 3 2 1

Figure 2. Positive considerations on game based training (Authors' elaboration)

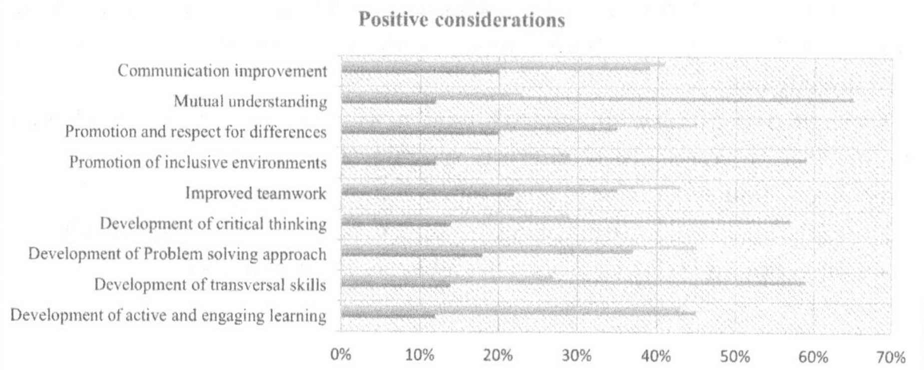

	Development of active and engaging learning	Development of transversal skills	Development of Problem solving approach	Development of critical thinking	Improved teamwork	Promotion of inclusive environments	Promotion and respect for differences	Mutual understanding	Communicatio n improvement
5	43%	27%	45%	29%	43%	29%	45%	23%	41%
4	45%	59%	37%	57%	35%	59%	35%	65%	39%
3	12%	14%	18%	14%	22%	12%	20%	12%	20%
2	0%	0%	0%	0%	0%	0%	0%	0%	0%
1	0%	0%	0%	0%	0%	0%	0%	0%	0%

5 4 3 2 1

Figure 3. Perplexities on game based training (Authors' elaboration)

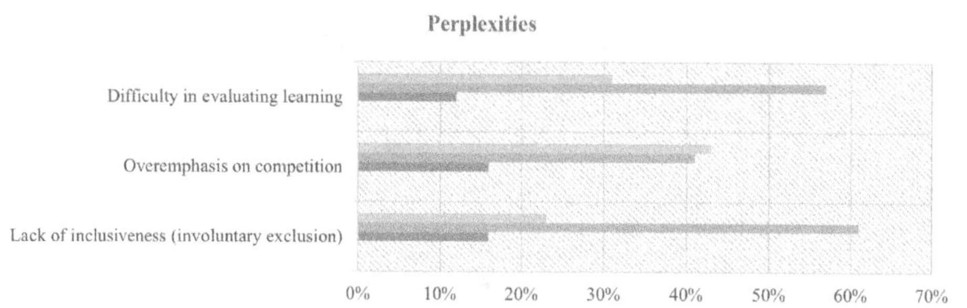

	Lack of inclusiveness (involuntary exclusion)	Overemphasis on competition	Difficulty in evaluating learning
5	23%	43%	31%
4	61%	41%	57%
3	16%	16%	12%
2	0%	0%	0%
1	0%	0%	0%

5 4 3 2 1

Figure 4. Potentials for D&I on game based training (Authors' elaboration)

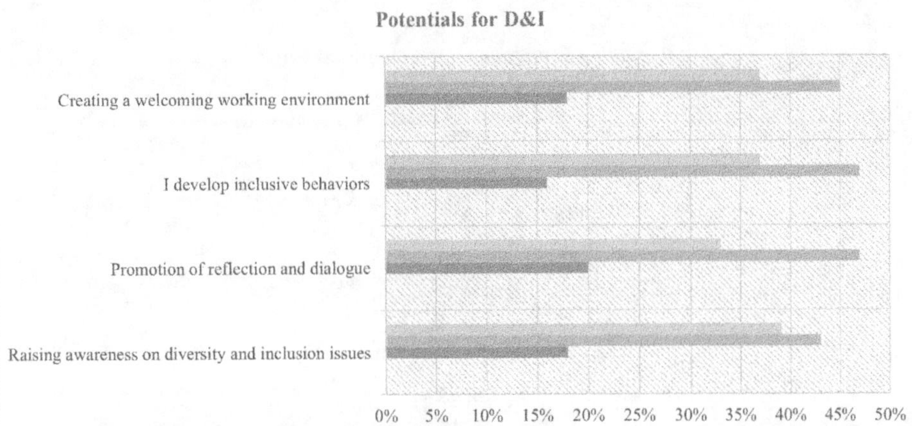

	Raising awareness on diversity and inclusion issues	Promotion of reflection and dialogue	I develop inclusive behaviors	Creating a welcoming working environment
5	39%	33%	37%	37%
4	43%	47%	47%	45%
3	18%	20%	16%	18%
2	0%	0%	0%	0%
1	0%	0%	0%	0%

5 4 3 2 1

Figure 5. Perceived influence on well-being at work on Game based training (Authors' elaboration)

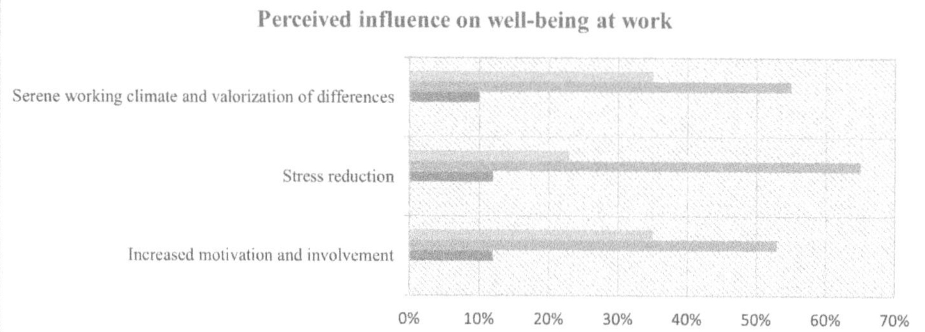

	Increased motivation and involvement	Stress reduction	Serene working climate and valorization of differences
5	35%	23%	35%
4	53%	65%	55%
3	12%	12%	10%
2	0%	0%	0%
1	0%	0%	0%

5 4 3 2 1

As regards the first dimension of the sensations expressed and perceived by the selected sample, in reference to the game based training sessions experienced (Figure.1), the evidence would demonstrate that the majority of the descriptors used pertain to Satisfaction and fun, Motivation and commitment, Self-confidence, Understanding and awareness, Connection and collaboration, Relationality and Reciprocity. The highest percentage levels show more than good agreement (4 Likert scales).

As regards the second dimension of the positive considerations expressed by the selected sample, in reference to the game based training sessions experienced (Figure 2), the evidence would demonstrate that the majority of the descriptors relate with a high degree of agreement (5 Likert scale) a: Development of Problem solving approach, Improved teamwork, Promotion and respect for differences and Communication improvement. In addition, with a good level of accordance (4 Likert scale): Development of active and engaging learning, Development of transversal skills, Development of critical thinking, Promotion of inclusive environments, Mutual understanding.

As regards the third dimension of the perplexities expressed and perceived by the selected sample, in reference to the game based training sessions experienced (Figure 3), the evidence would demonstrate that the majority of the descriptors used relate with a good degree of accord (4 Likert scale) to Lack of inclusiveness (involuntary exclusion) and Difficulty in evaluating learning and with a high degree of agreement to Overemphasis on competition.

As regards the fourth dimension inherent to the potential for D&I expressed and perceived by the selected sample, in reference to the game based training sessions experienced (Figure 4), the evidence would demonstrate that the majority of the descriptors used pertain to the most cases with a good degree of agreement (4 Likert scale) on Raising awareness on diversity and inclusion issues, Promotion of reflection and dialogue, development of inclusive behaviors, Creation of a welcoming working environment.

As regards the fifth and final dimension inherent to the influences on well-being at work perceived and expressed by the selected sample, in reference to the game based training sessions experienced (Figure 5), the evidence would demonstrate that the majority of the descriptors used refer in most cases with a good degree of agreement (4 Likert scale) to Increased motivation and involvement, Stress reduction, Serene working climate and valorization of differences.

6. CRITICAL DISCUSSION AND CONCLUSION

Diversity management plays a pivotal role in contemporary organizations, with the primary goal of establishing an inclusive setting where individuals from various backgrounds are not only acknowledged but also esteemed (Köllen, 2021). An innovative method that has garnered attention in fostering inclusion is the integration of gamification or serious gaming (AlSaad & Durugbo, 2021). . Gamification entails infusing game elements into non-game scenarios to amplify engagement, motivation, and learning outcomes, as noted by Trinidad et al. (2021). Through the utilization of gamification principles, organizations can develop interactive and immersive experiences that stimulate participation and collaboration among employees from diverse backgrounds, as highlighted by Zhang (2021). Studies indicate that gamification can offer substantial advantages (Hung, A. C. Y. (2018); Schöbel et al. 2019; Kapp, 2012; Meske et al., 2017; Patricio et al., 2020; Thielsch & Niesenhaus, 2017; Ortiz Rojas, Chiluiza & Valcke, 2017) in educational settings, such as advancing school inclusion for students with disabilities, as emphasized by Caldas (2024) and Filho (2024). By reshaping the learning environment into a dynamic and motivating domain, gamification can address individual learning requirements and preferences, fostering an inclusive and student-centric educational approach, according to Caldas (2024). Nonetheless, despite its potential, for further research is imperative to investigate the implementation of gamification in inclusive special education to ensure its efficacy in promoting transformative and inclusive educational practices, as indicated by Filho (2024).

In the domain of human resources management, gamification has been identified as a sustainable tool that can bolster endeavors towards inclusivity within organizations, according to Kumar et al. (2021). By embracing an inclusive outlook towards the local community, society, and resources, gamification strategies can enhance not only employee engagement and performance but also contribute to a more inclusive organizational culture, according to Kumar et al. (2021). Furthermore, gamification has been acknowledged as a valuable strategy for enhancing recruitment processes by rendering them more appealing, collaborative, and efficient, as explored by Singh (2022). The utilization of gamification has also been examined in the context of knowledge management processes, where it has been found to positively influence employees' motivation and involvement with knowledge management systems, as highlighted by Sampaio et al. (2019). Through the integration of gamification elements into knowledge exchange and learning processes, organizations can foster a more captivating and inclusive setting that encourages the generation, transfer, and dissemination of knowledge among employees, as posited by Sampaio et al. (2019). This approach can be particularly advantageous in nurturing a culture of inclusivity and collaboration within organizations.

Moreover, the incorporation of gamification in health interventions, such as stress management and diabetes self-care, has exhibited promising outcomes in engaging and motivating individuals to adopt healthy habits, according to Hoffmann et al. (2017) and Theng et al. (2015). By infusing gamified components into web-based health interventions, organizations can heighten user interest and enjoyment, ultimately enhancing user experience and adherence to health programs, as suggested by Brown et al. (2016). Additionally, gamification has proven effective in enhancing glycaemic control among patients with type 2 diabetes mellitus, underscoring its potential in promoting healthy behaviors and self-care practices, as demonstrated by Kaihara et al. (2021). In the educational realm, gamification has been increasingly employed to elevate student learning motivation, engagement, and performance, according to Limantara et al. (2023). Through the design of gamified learning management systems, educators can fashion interactive and immersive learning encounters that cater to diverse student needs and preferences, ultimately fostering a more inclusive educational milieu, as highlighted by Limantara et al. (2023). Furthermore, it has been demonstrated in research by Biçen & Kocakoyun (2018) that the incorporation of gamification techniques has the capability to enhance student engagement in classroom activities and elevate student aspirations for achievement. The overall incorporation of gamification across a range of sectors, such as education, human resources management, and health interventions, offers a promising avenue to advance inclusivity and diversity within both organizational and educational settings.

Through capitalizing on the captivating and stimulating elements of gamification, organizations have the potential to establish inclusive atmospheres that address the varied needs and preferences of individuals hailing from diverse backgrounds. Nevertheless, there is a pressing need for further investigation and examination to gain a comprehensive understanding of the capacity of gamification in fostering inclusivity and diversity in diverse contexts. This underscores the necessity for continued scholarly inquiry and exploration to unlock the full potential of gamification in promoting inclusivity and diversity across a spectrum of environments.

The document provided by Shan et al (2021) delves into a case study involving a collaboration with an immigrant services organization, shedding light on the crucial practices that contribute to the efficacy of diversity work. These practices encompass the establishment of a diverse and inclusive organizational culture, the provision of continuous learning opportunities, and the implementation of diversity training initiatives. Furthermore, the study underscores the pivotal role of reflection and lifelong learning in the context of diversity work.

The study was carried out by Gast, Schildkamp & van der Veen in 2017, shedding light on the complexities and nuances associated with team-based professional development interventions. In this comprehensive literature review, an analysis is conducted on the impacts of team-based professional development interventions in the realm of higher education. The review meticulously identifies various factors that can either impede or facilitate such interventions at different levels, including the individual, team, and organizational spheres. The author, Woolfson (2024), with an extremely recent article, underscores the critical need for transformative strategies to enhance the inclusivity and effectiveness of educational programs catering to children with SEND (special educational needs and disabilities).

On another hand, the Brazilian Physiological Society several years ago organized a conference and symposium dedicated to promoting the active involvement of women in the field of science during their Annual Congress. These initiatives were specifically designed to address the glaring underrepresentation of women in scientific research and aimed to inspire and encourage physiologists to prioritize gender balance within the discipline. This event, as documented by Mello-Carpes et al. in 2019, highlighted a significant step towards fostering gender diversity and inclusivity within the scientific community.

Despite several studies on the theme of D&I, angles remain unexplored or underestimated. Fortunately, in the last years scholars and companies (Modarelli, Rainero & Amelio, 2024) are fostering efforts in implementing action of D&I as policies based on game-training solutions. This atavistic, and even contemporary approach, tool and method, could better match the goals of sustainable development expressed by the UN Agenda 2030. With this prerogative scholarly pieces delve into the myriad challenges and unresolved issues surrounding the implementation of inclusive work.

This academic chapter delves into the concept of diversity work and its significance in fostering inclusive and equitable engagement within organizational settings, providing a critical evidence-based mapping of criteria and dimensions related to the evolution of D&I paradigms, game-based approaches, potential perspectives and perceptions on game-based solutions for the organizational area.

Through an innovative and theoretically anchored methodological dynamic, the authors provide an exemplary and clear roadmap, useful to policy makers, public and private managers, managers and directors of schools and universities, as well as non-profit organizations to encourage the meeting of job supply and demand on a more inclusive basis, promoting dignity of work itself and enjoyable productivity, in a framework of balance between WLB and achievement of SDGs.

Diversity and inclusion represent fundamental pillars for building an equitable and sustainable society. These principles are inextricably intertwined with the world of education, training and work, influencing individual and collective well-being. In this scenario, gaming emerges as a valuable tool for promoting the values of diversity and inclusion, encouraging learning, collaboration and personal growth.

The concept of inclusive education has undergone a profound evolution over time. From the first experiences of special education dedicated to students with disabilities, it has been possible to arrive to a broader approach that values the individual differences of all students.

Diversity, inclusion and play are key elements to building a more sustainable and inclusive future. The integration of these principles into education, training and work is fundamental to promoting individual and collective well-being, contributing to the achievement of the SDGs.

In conclusion, the use of games as an approach to education, training and work can represent a valid tool for promoting diversity, inclusion and well-being. Through play, it is possible to create more welcoming, stimulating and sustainable environments, where everyone can express their potential and contribute to collective success.

In this sense, the evolutionary dimension that has allowed the affirmation of gaming practices as a relevant factor for inclusiveness and the management of diversity is the pedagogical value inherent in the dynamics of gaming itself, as in its infancy today (RQ1). On the other hand, the developments that game-based approaches can bring to work environments in terms of D&I practices are intrinsically connected to the sustainable development policies currently in force (RQ2). Therefore, the use of games as an educational and training tool, with deep roots in history, has taken on an increasingly central role in promoting diversity, inclusion and well-being in line with the Sustainable Development Goals (SDGs) of the 2030 Agenda.

Potential limitations of the study are inherent in the sample size, which is currently still small. Developments in the field can be proposed not only on the sample of teachers, but also on other types of professionals who operate by applying game-based approaches. Comparative perspectives can guarantee interesting answers to the investigation dimension.

REFERENCES

Aini, Q. (2019). Understanding How Gamification Influences Behaviour in Education. *International Journal of Advanced Trends in Computer Science and Engineering, 8*(1.5), 269–274. DOI: 10.30534/ijatcse/2019/4781.52019

Aini, Q., Azizah, N., Salam, R., Santoso, N. P. L., & Millah, S. (2022). iLearning Education Based on Gamification Blockchain. *Indonesian Journal of Electrical Engineering and Computer Science*, 26(1), 531. DOI: 10.11591/ijeecs.v26.i1.pp531-538

Aini, Q., Lutfiani, N., & Zahran, M. S. (2021). Gamification based on blockchain technology to enhance student centered learning. *CCIT Journal*, 14(1), 100–110. DOI: 10.33050/ccit.v14i1.1268

Alföldi-Rosenbaum, E. (1971). *The finger calculus in antiquity and in the Middle Ages: Studies on Roman game counters I.* Walter de Gruyter.

AlSaad, F. M., & Durugbo, C. M. (2021). Gamification-as-innovation: A review. *International Journal on Management of Innovation & Technology*, 18(05), 2130002. DOI: 10.1142/S0219877021300020

Alsawaier, R. S. (2018). The effect of gamification on motivation and engagement. The International Journal of Information and Learning Technology, 35(1), 56-79.

Ampatzidou, C., & Gugerell, K. (2018). Participatory Game Prototyping – Balancing Domain Content and Playability in a Serious Game Design for the Energy Transition. *CoDesign*, 15(4), 345–360. DOI: 10.1080/15710882.2018.1504084

Andreu-Cabrera, E., & González, M. C. (2010). Play and childhood in ancient Greece. *Journal of Human Sport and Exercise*, 5(3), 339–347. DOI: 10.4100/jhse.2010.53.04

Andrews, R. (2011). Social Capital and Public Service Performance: A Review of the Evidence. *Public Policy and Administration*, 27(1), 49–67. DOI: 10.1177/0952076710394399

Andrews, R., & Wankhade, P. (2014). Regional Variations in Emergency Service Performance: Does Social Capital Matter? *Regional Studies*, 49(12), 2037–2052. DOI: 10.1080/00343404.2014.891009

Apostolakis, K. C., Kaza, K., Psaltis, A., Stefanidis, K., Thermos, S., Dimitropoulos, K., . . . Daras, P. (2016). Path of Trust: A prosocial co-op game for building up trustworthiness and teamwork. In Games and Learning Alliance: 4th International Conference, GALA 2015, Rome, Italy, December 9-11, 2015, Revised Selected Papers 4 (pp. 80-89). Springer International Publishing. DOI: 10.1007/978-3-319-40216-1_9

Ashforth, B. E., & Humphrey, R. H. (1993). Emotional Labor in Service Roles: The Influence of Identity. *Academy of Management Review*, 18(1), 88–115. https://www.jstor.org/stable/258824. DOI: 10.2307/258824

Baecher-Lind, L., Sutton, J. M., Bhargava, R., Chen, K. T., Fleming, A., Morgan, H., Morosky, C. M., Schaffir, J., Sonn, T., Royce, C., Stephenson-Famy, A., & Sims, S. M. (2023). Strategies to Create a More Gender Identity Inclusive Learning Environment in Preclinical and Clinical Medical Education. *Academic Medicine*, 98(12), 1351–1355. DOI: 10.1097/ACM.0000000000005334 PMID: 37478137

Bakker, A. B. (2011). An evidence-based model of work engagement. *Current Directions in Psychological Science*, 20(4), 265–269. DOI: 10.1177/0963721411414534

Bakker, A. B., & Demerouti, E. (2007). The job demands-resources model: State of the art. *Journal of Managerial Psychology*, 22(3), 309–328. DOI: 10.1108/02683940710733115

Baptista, G., & Oliveira, T. (2017). Why So Serious? Gamification Impact in the Acceptance of Mobile Banking Services. *Internet Research*, 27(1), 118–139. DOI: 10.1108/IntR-10-2015-0295

Bauman, Z. (2013). Liquid modernity. John Wiley & Sons.

Becker, M. (1967). *The ancient Roman world.* Holt, Rinehart and Winston.

Bell, R. (1979). *Board and table games from many civilizations.* Oxford University Press.

Beltadze, G. N. (2016). Game theory-basis of higher education and teaching organization. *International Journal of Modern Education and Computer Science*, 8(6), 41. DOI: 10.5815/ijmecs.2016.06.06

Bennani, S., Maalel, A., & Ghezala, H. B. (2021). Adaptive Gamification in E-learning: A Literature Review and Future Challenges. *Computer Applications in Engineering Education*, 30(2), 628–642. DOI: 10.1002/cae.22477

Berger, P. L., & Huntington, S. P. (Eds.). (2002). *Many globalizations: Cultural diversity in the contemporary world*. Oxford University Press. DOI: 10.1093/0195151461.001.0001

Bettelheim, B. (1972). Play and education. *The School Review*, 81(1), 1–13. DOI: 10.1086/443059

Birnir, J. K., & Waguespack, D. M. (2011). Ethnic inclusion and economic growth. *Party Politics*, 17(2), 243–260. DOI: 10.1177/1354068810391149

Boghian, I., & Cojocariu, V. M. (2023). Using games to build social emotional learning skills. Revista Romaneasca pentru Educatie Multidimensionala, 15(1), 622-656.

Borlido, T., & Coromina, L. (2018). Social Capital as Cause and Consequence of Rural Touristic Development: The Case of Lindoso (Portugal). *European Journal of Tourism Research*, 19, 71–85. DOI: 10.54055/ejtr.v19i.326

Boulton, W. B. (1974). *The language of games: An aesthetic criticism*. Springer.

Cambi, F., & Staccioli, G. (2007). *Il gioco in Occidente. Storia, teorie, pratiche*. Armando Editore.

Camerer, C., & Knez, M. (1997). Coordination in organizations: A game-theoretic perspective. Organizational decision making, 158-188

Cantone, J. A., & Wiener, R. L. (2017). Religion at work: Evaluating hostile work environment religious discrimination claims. *Psychology, Public Policy, and Law*, 23(3), 351–366. DOI: 10.1037/law0000132

Caponetto, I., Earp, J., & Ott, M. (2014, October). Gamification and education: A literature review. In European conference on games based learning (Vol. 1, p. 50). Academic Conferences International Limited

Carlier, S., Naessens, V., Backere, F. D., & Turck, F. D. (2023). A Software Engineering Framework for Reusable Design of Personalized Serious Games for Health: Development Study *(Preprint)*. DOI: 10.2196/preprints.40054

Carter, B. (2020). Achieving diversity, inclusion and equity in the nursing workforce. *Revista Latino-Americana de Enfermagem*, 28, e3254. DOI: 10.1590/1518-8345.0000-3254 PMID: 32074212

Chakraborty, S. K., & Chatterjee, L. (2020). Rationales of Gender Diversity Management Policies and Practices in India: An Exploratory Empirical Study in the Indian IT/ITeS Industry. *Equality, Diversity and Inclusion*, 39(6), 667–688. DOI: 10.1108/EDI-04-2019-0124

Cole, A., & Zammit, J. (2020). *Cooperative gaming: Diversity in the games industry and how to cultivate inclusion*. CrC Press. DOI: 10.1201/9780429324826

Coleman, K. (2000). Entertaining Rome. *OXFORD UNIVERSITY SCHOOL OF ARCHAEOLOGY MONOGRAPH*, 54, 210–258.

Collier, P. (2001). Implications of ethnic diversity. Economic policy, 16(32), 128-166; Aigner, P. (2014). Ethnic diversity management in theory and practice. *Journal of Diversity Management (Online)*, 9(2), 111.

Corral, R. J. P. (2024). Impact of Hybrid and on-Site Work Arrangements on Employee Motivation and Job Satisfaction in the BPO Industry: A Cross-Sectional Study. *Open Journal of Social Sciences*, 12(02), 205–230. DOI: 10.4236/jss.2024.122013

Csikszentmihalyi, M. (1990). The domain of creativity.

Csikszentmihalyi, M. (2013). *Flow: The psychology of happiness*. Random House.

Dasen, V., & Vespa, M. (2021). Ancient play and games: In search of a definition. Play and Games in Classical Antiquity: Definition, Transmission, Reception, 5-16;

Davis, P. J., Frolova, Y., & Callahan, W. (2016). Workplace diversity management in Australia: What do managers think and what are organisations doing? *Equality, Diversity and Inclusion*, 35(2), 81–98. DOI: 10.1108/EDI-03-2015-0020

Delaney, J. (2022). Minecraft and Playful Public Participation in Urban Design. *Urban Planning*, 7(2). Advance online publication. DOI: 10.17645/up.v7i2.5229

Dewey, J. (2022). *How we think*. DigiCat.

Diller, J. V. (2014). *Cultural Diversity*. Cengage Learning.

Duncanson, C., & Woodward, R. (2015). Regendering the Military: Theorizing Women's Military Participation. *Security Dialogue*, 47(1), 3–21. DOI: 10.1177/0967010615614137

Elliott, L. (2004). *Children and Games in the Middle Ages*. Crabtree Publishing Company.

European Commission. (2017). Key Skills for a Societal Change. https://op.europa.eu/en/publication-detail/-/publication/297a33c8-a1f3-11e9-9d01-01aa75ed71a1/language-en

Ewers, H. H. (2019). Children's Games and Children's Literature between the Enlightenment and Romanticism. *Filoteknos*, (9), 86–97.

Farndale, E., Biron, M., Briscoe, D. R., & Raghuram, S. (2015). A global perspective on diversity and inclusion in work organisations. *International Journal of Human Resource Management*, 26(6), 677–687. DOI: 10.1080/09585192.2014.991511

Farouk, A. D. (2021). The role of sustainable development goals (SDGs) in social inclusion. Available at *SSRN* 3984863. DOI: 10.2139/ssrn.3984863

Feldman, M. S., Khademian, A. M., Ingram, H., & Schneider, A. S. (2006). Ways of knowing and inclusive management practices. *Public Administration Review*, 66(s1), 89–99. DOI: 10.1111/j.1540-6210.2006.00669.x

Fielding, N. (2004). Working in hostile environments. Qualitative research practice, 248-260.

Finkel, I. (2007). Ancient board games in perspective: *Papers from the 1990 British Museum colloquium, with additional contributions*. British Museum Press.

Flavin-McDonald, C., & Barrett, M. H. (1999). The Topsfield Foundation: Fostering Democratic Community Building Through Face-to-Face Dialogue. *New Directions for Adult and Continuing Education*, 1999(81), 25–36. DOI: 10.1002/ace.8103

Foster, M. K., Meinhard, A., & Berger, I. E. (2021). *The Role of Social Capital: Bridging*. Bonding or Both., DOI: 10.32920/ryerson.14638890

Garg, S., & Sangwan, S. (2021). Literature review on diversity and inclusion at workplace, 2010–2017. *Vision (Basel)*, 25(1), 12–22. DOI: 10.1177/0972262920959523 PMID: 33806403

Gast, I., Schildkamp, K., & van der Veen, J. T. (2017). Team-based professional development interventions in higher education: A systematic review. *Review of Educational Research*, 87(4), 736–767. DOI: 10.3102/0034654317704306 PMID: 28989192

Gee, J. P. (2007). *Good video games and good learning: Collected essays on video games, learning, and literacy*. Peter Lang. DOI: 10.3726/978-1-4539-1162-4

Goldhill, S. (2017). Play in Ancient Greece: An interview with Simon Goldhill. *American Journal of Play*, 9(3), 287–299.

Gould, R., Harris, S. P., Mullin, C., & Jones, R. (2020). Disability, Diversity, and Corporate Social Responsibility: Learning From Recognized Leaders in Inclusion. *Journal of Vocational Rehabilitation*, 52(1), 29–42. DOI: 10.3233/JVR-191058

Graham, R. G., & Gray, C. F. (1969). Business games handbook.

Granovetter, M. S. (1973). The strength of weak ties. *American Journal of Sociology*, 78(6), 1360–1380. DOI: 10.1086/225469

Greenwald, H. P., & Beery, W. L. (2001). Reducing Isolation Among Inner-City Elders: An Outcome Evaluation. *Health Promotion Practice*, 2(3), 233–241. DOI: 10.1177/152483990100200307

Greipl, S., Moeller, K., & Ninaus, M. (2020). Potential and limits of game-based learning. *International Journal of Technology Enhanced Learning*, 12(4), 363–389. DOI: 10.1504/IJTEL.2020.110047

Guest, D. E. (2002). Perspectives on the study of work-life balance. *Social Sciences Information. Information Sur les Sciences Sociales*, 41(2), 255–279. DOI: 10.1177/0539018402041002005

Gurbuz, S. C., & Celik, M. (2022). Serious Games in Future Skills Development: A Systematic Review of the Design Approaches. *Computer Applications in Engineering Education*, 30(5), 1591–1612. DOI: 10.1002/cae.22557

Hamari, J., Koivisto, J., & Sarsa, H. (2014, January). Does gamification work? a literature review of empirical studies on gamification. In 2014 47th Hawaii international conference on system sciences (pp. 3025-3034). IEEE.

Hammedi, W., Leclerq, T., & Riel, A. C. R. (2017). The Use of Gamification Mechanics to Increase Employee and User Engagement in Participative Healthcare Services. *Journal of Service Management*, 28(4), 640–661. DOI: 10.1108/JOSM-04-2016-0116

Hartt, M., Hosseini, H., & Mostafapour, M. (2020). Game on: Exploring the effectiveness of game-based learning. *Planning Practice and Research*, 35(5), 589–604. DOI: 10.1080/02697459.2020.1778859

Høiseth, M., Alsos, O. A., Holme, S., Ek, S., & Gabrielsen, C. T. (2021). Serious Game Design to Support Children Struggling With School Refusal. *International Journal of Serious Games*, 8(2), 109–128. DOI: 10.17083/ijsg.v8i2.416

Huizinga, J. (1955). *Homo ludens: A study of the play-element in culture*. Beacon Press.

Hung, A. C. Y. (2018). Gamification as Design Thinking. *International Journal on Teaching and Learning in Higher Education*, 30(3), 549–559.

Hunt, V., Layton, D., & Prince, S. (2015). Diversity matters. McKinsey & Company.

Hurtado, S., Alvarado, A. R., & Guillermo-Wann, C. (2015). Creating inclusive environments. *Journal Committed to Social Change on Race and Ethnicity*, 1(1), 60–81.

Ifenthaler, D., Eseryel, D., & Ge, X. (2012). Assessment for game-based learning. In *Assessment in game-based learning: Foundations, innovations, and perspectives* (pp. 1–8). Springer New York. DOI: 10.1007/978-1-4614-3546-4_1

Ismail, M. F., Iksan, Z. H., & Ariffin, R. (2021). Effects of Using Gamification Techniques on Achievement in Science Subject. *International Journal of Academic Research in Business & Social Sciences*, 11(12). Advance online publication. DOI: 10.6007/IJARBSS/v11-i12/11769

Janssens, M., & Zanoni, P. (2014). Alternative diversity management: Organizational practices fostering ethnic equality at work. *Scandinavian Journal of Management*, 30(3), 317–331. DOI: 10.1016/j.scaman.2013.12.006

Kapilashrami, A., Otis, M., Omodara, D., Nandi, A., Vats, A., Adeniyi, O. V., Speed, E., Potter, J., Eder, B., Pareek, M., & Bhui, K. (2021). Ethnic Disparities in Health &Amp; Social Care Workers' Exposure, Protection, and Clinical Management of the COVID-19 Pandemic in the UK. *Critical Public Health*, 32(1), 68–81. DOI: 10.1080/09581596.2021.1959020

Kapp, K. M. (2012). *The gamification of learning and instruction: game-based methods and strategies for training and education*. John Wiley & Sons.

Kavesh, M. A. (2024). Welcoming the foreigner: Notes on the possibility of multispecies hospitality. *American Anthropologist*, 126(1), 109–119. DOI: 10.1111/aman.13938

Kent, S. (2001). *The ultimate history of video games: From Pong to Pokémon and beyond...the story behind the craze that touched our lives and changed the world*. Crown.

Kim, T. W., & Werbach, K. (2016). More than just a game: Ethical issues in gamification. *Ethics and Information Technology*, 18(2), 157–173. DOI: 10.1007/s10676-016-9401-5

Kirton, G. (2020). Diversity and inclusion in a changing world of work. In *The future of work and employment* (pp. 49–64). Edward Elgar Publishing. DOI: 10.4337/9781786438256.00011

Köllen, T. (2021). Diversity management: A critical review and agenda for the future. *Journal of Management Inquiry*, 30(3), 259–272. DOI: 10.1177/1056492619868025

Kopp, S. (2018). The Power of Play: How to Spark Adult Learning and Innovation. https://www.mckinsey.com/featured-insights/themes/how-to-unlock-the-power-of-learning

Krosnick, J. A. (2018). Questionnaire design. The Palgrave handbook of survey research, 439-455. DOI: 10.1007/978-3-319-54395-6_53

Kuknor, S. C., & Bhattacharya, S. (2022). Inclusive leadership: New age leadership to foster organizational inclusion. *European Journal of Training and Development*, 46(9), 771–797. DOI: 10.1108/EJTD-07-2019-0132

Kuppers, P. (2016). Diversity: Disability. *Art Journal*, 75(1), 93–97. DOI: 10.1080/00043249.2016.1171549

Kurke, L. (1999). Ancient Greek board games and how to play them. *Classical Philology*, 94(3), 247–267. DOI: 10.1086/449440

Laamarti, F., Eid, M., & El Saddik, A. (2014). An overview of serious games. *International Journal of Computer Games Technology*, 2014(1), 358152.

Landow, G. P. (2009). *Victorian types, Victorian shadows: Biblical typology in Victorian literature, art, and thought*. Routledge.

Lee, C. (2022). Coming Out in the University Workplace: A Case Study of LGBTQ+staff Visibility. *Higher Education*, 85(5), 1181–1199. DOI: 10.1007/s10734-022-00884-y PMID: 35730026

Lee, H., & Reade, C. (2014). Ethnic Homophily Perceptions as an Emergent IHRM Challenge: Evidence From Firms Operating in Sri Lanka During the Ethnic Conflict. *International Journal of Human Resource Management*, 26(13), 1645–1664. DOI: 10.1080/09585192.2014.958514

Legaki, N. Z., Xi, N., Hamari, J., Karpouzis, K., & Assimakopoulos, V. (2020). The Effect of Challenge-Based Gamification on Learning: An Experiment in the Context of Statistics Education. *International Journal of Human-Computer Studies*, 144, 102496. DOI: 10.1016/j.ijhcs.2020.102496 PMID: 32565668

Lehan, T., Hussey, H., & Babcock, A. (2020). Mission unaccomplished: Beyond "talk [ing] a good game" to promote diversity and inclusion. *Journal of Educational Research and Practice*, 10(1), 12. DOI: 10.5590/JERAP.2020.10.1.12

Leslie, L. M., Snyder, M., & Glomb, T. M. (2013). Who Gives? Multilevel Effects of Gender and Ethnicity on Workplace Charitable Giving. *The Journal of Applied Psychology*, 98(1), 49–62. DOI: 10.1037/a0029943 PMID: 22985116

Libe, C., Grenouillat, A., Lagoutte, J., Jean, C., & Maranzana, N. (2020). *Creativity and Innovation for Children: Presentation and First Experiment of New (Serious).* Game., DOI: 10.35199/EPDE.2020.40

Liboriussen, B., & Martin, P. (2016). Games and gaming in China. *Games and Culture*, 11(3), 227–232. DOI: 10.1177/1555412015615296

Maji, S., Yadav, N., & Gupta, P. (2023). LGBTQ+ in Workplace: A systematic Review and Reconsideration. *Equality, Diversity and Inclusion*, 43(2), 313–360. DOI: 10.1108/EDI-02-2022-0049

Mara, L. C., Ginieis, M., & Brunet-Icart, I. (2021). Strategies for coping with LGBT discrimination at work: A systematic literature review. *Sexuality Research & Social Policy*, 18(2), 339–354. DOI: 10.1007/s13178-020-00462-w

Marczewski, A. (2013). Gamification: a simple introduction.

Mazur, B. (2014). Building diverse and inclusive organizational culture-best practices: A case study of Cisco Co. Journal of Intercultural Management, 6(4.1), 169-179;

Mazure, C. M., & Jones, D. P. (2015). Twenty Years and Still Counting: Including Women as Participants and Studying Sex and Gender in Biomedical Research. *BMC Women's Health*, 15(1), 94. Advance online publication. DOI: 10.1186/s12905-015-0251-9 PMID: 26503700

Mello-Carpes, de Paiva Abreu, Staniscuaski, Souza, Campagnole-Santos, & Irigoyen. (2019). Actions developed by the Brazilian Physiological Society to promote women's participation in science. Academic Press.

Meske, C., Brockmann, T., Wilms, K., & Stieglitz, S. (2017). Social collaboration and gamification. Gamification: Using game elements in serious contexts, 93-109;

Mikkelson, G. M. (2013). Growth is the problem; equality is the solution. *Sustainability (Basel)*, 5(2), 432–439. DOI: 10.3390/su5020432

Miller, S. G. (2004). *Ancient Greek athletics*. Yale University Press.

Modarelli, G., Rainero, C., & Amelio, S. (2024). Games, diversity and occupation: A bidimensional CSR perspective for adaptive organisations. *Social Responsibility Journal*, 20(9), 1787–1808. DOI: 10.1108/SRJ-07-2023-0390

Modell, S. (2022). Accounting for institutional work: A critical review. *European Accounting Review*, 31(1), 33–58. DOI: 10.1080/09638180.2020.1820354

Möhlen, L. K., Handle-Pfeiffer, D., Proyer, M., Schmölz, A., & Kremsner, G. (2018, November). Playful Social Inclusion: Approaching Inclusive Thinking and Acting Through Game Based Learning. In *Proceedings of the 17th European Conference on e-Learning* (pp. 383-93)

Mor Barak, M. E., & Daya, P. (2013). Fostering inclusion from the inside out to create an inclusive workplace. Diversity at work: The practice of inclusion, 391-412.

Morris, A. D. (1984). *The origins of the civil rights movement*. Simon and Schuster.

Mousa, M., Massoud, H. K., & Ayoubi, R. M. (2020). Gender, diversity management perceptions, workplace happiness and organisational citizenship behaviour. *Employee Relations*, 42(6), 1249–1269. DOI: 10.1108/ER-10-2019-0385

Munsell, E. G. S., Kudla, A., Su, H., Wong, J., Crown, D., Capraro, P., Trierweiler, R., Park, M., & Heinemann, A. W. (2022). Employers' Perceptions of Challenges and Strategies in Hiring, Retaining, and Promoting Employees With Physical Disabilities. *Rehabilitation Counseling Bulletin*, 67(3), 177–189. DOI: 10.1177/00343552221130304

Murray, H. J. R. (1997). *Hamlet on the Holodeck: The future of narrative in cyberspace*. MIT press.

Nafukho, F. M., Roessler, R. T., & Kacirek, K. (2010). Disability as a Diversity Factor: Implications for Human Resource Practices. *Advances in Developing Human Resources*, 12(4), 395–406. DOI: 10.1177/1523422310379209

Newman, J. (2004). *Videogames*. Routledge. DOI: 10.4324/9780203642900

Olken, B. A. (2009). Do Television and Radio Destroy Social Capital? Evidence From Indonesian Villages. *American Economic Journal. Applied Economics*, 1(4), 1–33. DOI: 10.1257/app.1.4.1

Olmo-Muñoz, J. (2023). Exploring Gamification Approaches for Enhancing Computational Thinking in Young Learners. *Education Sciences*, 13(5), 487. DOI: 10.3390/educsci13050487

Ortega-Arranz, A., Asensio-Pérez, J. I., Martínez-Monés, A., Bote-Lorenzo, M. L., Ortega-Arranz, H., & Kalz, M. (2022). GamiTool: Supporting instructors in the gamification of MOOCs. *IEEE Access : Practical Innovations, Open Solutions*, 10, 131965–131979. DOI: 10.1109/ACCESS.2022.3228762

Özbilgin, M. (2009). Equality, diversity and inclusion at work: yesterday, today and tomorrow. Equality, diversity and inclusion at work: a research companion, 1-16.

Parizi, R. M., & Dehghantanha, A. (2018, August). On the understanding of gamification in blockchain systems. In 2018 6th international conference on Future Internet of Things and Cloud Workshops (FiCloudW) (pp. 214-219). IEEE DOI: 10.1109/W-FiCloud.2018.00041

Patricio, R., Moreira, A., Zurlo, F., & Melazzini, M. (2020). Co-creation of new solutions through gamification: A collaborative innovation practice. *Creativity and Innovation Management*, 29(1), 146–160. DOI: 10.1111/caim.12356

Patrick, H. A., & Kumar, V. R. (2012). Managing workplace diversity: Issues and challenges. *SAGE Open*, 2(2). DOI: 10.1177/2158244012444615

Piaget, J., & Cook, M. T. (1954). The development of object concept.

Piazza, F. (2006). L'argomentazione come gioco linguistico. Il punto di vista aristotelico. *Giornale di Metafisica*, 389–396.

Plass, J. L., Homer, B. D., & Kinzer, C. K. (2015). Foundations of game-based learning. *Educational Psychologist*, 50(4), 258–283. DOI: 10.1080/00461520.2015.1122533

Plato, . (1992). *Laws*. Cambridge University Press.

Plummer, E. M.The Olympic Games in Ancient Times. (1898). II. The Olympic Games in Ancient Times. *American Physical Education Review*, 3(1), 1–18. DOI: 10.1080/23267224.1898.10649670

Poonsawad, A., Srisomphan, J., & Sanrach, C. (2022). Synthesis of problem-based interactive digital storytelling learning model under gamification environment promotes students' problem-solving skills. *International Journal of Emerging Technologies in Learning*, 17(5), 103–119. DOI: 10.3991/ijet.v17i05.28181

Prosen, M. (2022). Nursing Students' Perception of Gender-Defined Roles in Nursing: A Qualitative Descriptive Study. *BMC Nursing*, 21(1), 104. Advance online publication. DOI: 10.1186/s12912-022-00876-4 PMID: 35509039

Putnam, R. D. (2000). Bowling alone: America's declining social capital. In *Culture and politics: A reader* (pp. 223–234). Palgrave Macmillan US.

Quinn, G. P., Sánchez, J., Sutton, S. K., Vadaparampil, S. T., Nguyêñ, G. T., Green, B. L., Kanetsky, P. A., & Schabath, M. B. (2015). Cancer and Lesbian, Gay, Bisexual, Transgender/Transsexual, and Queer/Questioning (LGBTQ) Populations. *CA: a Cancer Journal for Clinicians*, 65(5), 384–400. DOI: 10.3322/caac.21288 PMID: 26186412

Rich, B. L., Lepine, J. A., & Crawford, E. R. (2010). Job engagement: Antecedents and effects on job performance. *Academy of Management Journal*, 53(3), 617–635. DOI: 10.5465/amj.2010.51468988

Roberson, Q. M. (2006). Disentangling the meanings of diversity and inclusion in organizations. *Group & Organization Management*, 31(2), 212–236. DOI: 10.1177/1059601104273064

Robison, L. J., Schmid, A. A., & Barry, P. J. (2002). The Role of Social Capital in the Industrialization of the Food System. *Agricultural and Resource Economics Review*, 31(1), 15–24. DOI: 10.1017/S1068280500003439

Roithmayr, D. (2003). Locked in inequality: The persistence of discrimination. *Michigan Journal of Race & Law*, 9, 31.

Romero, M. (2015). Work, games and lifelong learning in the 21st century. *Procedia: Social and Behavioral Sciences*, 174, 115–121. DOI: 10.1016/j.sbspro.2015.01.634

Royall, S., McCarthy, V., & Miller, G. J. (2022). Creating an inclusive workplace: The effectiveness of diversity training. *J. Glob. Econ. Trade Int. Bus*, 3, 39–55.

Sainath, K. L., & Sai, K. T. (2023). Supply Chains Are Playing Games: A Review Literature on Gamification in Supply Chain. *Journal of Future Sustainability*, 3(1), 59–66. DOI: 10.5267/j.jfs.2022.11.005

Samuels, M. A. B., De Angelis, K., Gibson, H., Han, J., Laurence, J., Matthew, K. E., & Yu, J. (2023). *Inclusion in the American military: A force for diversity.* Rowman & Littlefield.

Sang, K., Calvard, T., & Remnant, J. (2021). Disability and Academic Careers: Using the Social Relational Model to Reveal the Role of Human Resource Management Practices in Creating Disability. *Work, Employment and Society*, 36(4), 722–740. DOI: 10.1177/0950017021993737

Sang, K., & Powell, A. (2013). Equality, diversity, inclusion and work–life balance in construction. In *Human resource management in construction* (pp. 163–196). Routledge.

Sanin, J. R. (2020). "I Don't Belong Here": Understanding Hostile Spaces. In Me Too Political Science (pp. 112-121). Routledge.

Scarborough, W. J., Lambouths, D.III, & Holbrook, A. (2019). Support of Workplace Diversity Policies: The Role of Race, Gender, and Beliefs About Inequality. *Social Science Research*, 79, 194–210. DOI: 10.1016/j.ssresearch.2019.01.002 PMID: 30857662

Schindeler, E. (2021). Workplace: Hostile Environment. In *Encyclopedia of Security and Emergency Management* (pp. 947–953). Springer International Publishing. DOI: 10.1007/978-3-319-70488-3_256

Schmölz, A., Karpouzis, K., Pfeiffer, D., & Koulouris, P. (2017). Doing Social Inclusion: Aiming to Conquer Crisis through Game-Based Dialogues and Games.

Schöbel, S., Janson, A., Hopp, J. C., & Leimeister, J. M. (2019, July). Gamification of online training and its relation to engagement and problem-solving outcomes. In Academy of Management Proceedings (Vol. 2019, No. 1, p. 11949). Briarcliff Manor, NY 10510: Academy of Management. DOI: 10.5465/AMBPP.2019.11949abstract

Schreiber, E. (2021). The Virtue of Play: Games and Stories for Children in Three Pedagogical Texts of the Enlightenment. *Eighteenth-Century Studies*, 54(3), 613–632. DOI: 10.1353/ecs.2021.0041

Sczesny, S., Moser, F., & Wood, W. (2015). Beyond sexist beliefs: How do people decide to use gender-inclusive language? *Personality and Social Psychology Bulletin*, 41(7), 943–954. DOI: 10.1177/0146167215585727 PMID: 26015331

Sebbane, M. (2001). Board games from Canaan in the Early and Intermediate Bronze Ages and the origin of the Egyptian Senet game. *Tel Aviv : Journal of the Institute of Archaeology of Tel Aviv University*, 28(2), 213–230. DOI: 10.1179/tav.2001.2001.2.213

Serra, M. (2018). *Il gioco del disaccordo: persuasione, comunità, linguaggio in Wittgenstein e Platone (con un terzo incomodo)/The game of disagreement: persuasion, community, language in Wittgenstein and Plato (with a third wheel)*. Rivista Italiana di Filosofia del Linguaggio.

Shan, H., Cheng, A., Peikazadi, N., & Kim, Y. (2021). Fostering diversity work as a process of lifelong learning: A partnership case study with an immigrant services organisation. *International Review of Education*, 67(6), 771–790. DOI: 10.1007/s11159-021-09929-3 PMID: 34840346

Shliakhovchuk, E. (2018). Using video games in intercultural, diversity and inclusion education. In *ICERI2018 Proceedings* (pp. 10326-10336). IATED DOI: 10.21125/iceri.2018.0946

Shore, L. M., Cleveland, J. N., & Sanchez, D. (2018). Inclusive workplaces: A review and model. *Human Resource Management Review*, 28(2), 176–189. DOI: 10.1016/j.hrmr.2017.07.003

Shore, L. M., Randel, A. E., Chung, B. G., Dean, M. A., Holcombe Ehrhart, K., & Singh, G. (2011). Inclusion and diversity in work groups: A review and model for future research. *Journal of Management*, 37(4), 1262–1289. DOI: 10.1177/0149206310385943

Silva, F. C., Clark, T. N., & Cabaço, S. (2013). Culture on the Rise: How and Why Cultural Membership Promotes Democratic Politics. *International Journal of Politics Culture and Society*, 27(3), 343–366. DOI: 10.1007/s10767-013-9170-7

Skinner, B. F. (1963). Operant behavior. *The American Psychologist*, 18(8), 503–515. DOI: 10.1037/h0045185

Sona, A. J., Santana, J. L., & Saitta, E. K. H. (2022). Looking Through a Prism: A Systematic Review of LGBTQ+ STEM Literature. *Journal of Chemical Education*, 100(1), 125–133. DOI: 10.1021/acs.jchemed.2c00391

Spalding, E., & Wilson, A. H. (2006). Bowling Together. *English Education*, 38(2), 102–122. DOI: 10.58680/ee20065073

Squire, K. (2005). Game-based learning: Present and future state of the field. New York, NY: Masie Center E-Learning Consortium.

Steinkuehler, C., & Squire, K. D. (2012). Games, learning, and society: Learning and meaning in Stevens, F. G., Plaut, V. C., & Sanchez-Burks, J. (2008). Unlocking the benefits of diversity: All-inclusive multiculturalism and positive organizational change. *The Journal of Applied Behavioral Science*, 44(1), 116–133.

Streicher, A., & Smeddinck, J. D. (2016). *Personalized and Adaptive Serious Games*. DOI: 10.1007/978-3-319-46152-6_14

Sung, Y., Cho, K., & Um, K. (2012). A Development Architecture for Serious Games Using BCI (Brain Computer Interface) Sensors. *Sensors (Basel)*, 12(11), 15671–15688. DOI: 10.3390/s121115671 PMID: 23202227

Susi, T., Johannesson, M., & Backlund, P. (2007). Serious games: An overview.

Sutton-Smith, B. (1997). *The ambiguity of play*. Harvard University Press.

Swaddling, J. (1999). *The ancient Olympic games*. University of Texas Press.

Tan, G. (2018). Gamification in Education: What is it and How Does it Work? https://edtechmagazine.com/higher/software/gamification

Thielsch, M. T., & Niesenhaus, J. (2017). User experience, gamification, and performance. The Wiley Blackwell handbook of the psychology of the internet at work, 79-101.

Thomas, C. (2014). Disability and diversity. In *Routledge international handbook of diversity studies* (pp. 43–51). Routledge.

Tobias, S., Fletcher, J. D., & Wind, A. P. (2014). Game-based learning. Handbook of research on educational communications and technology, 485-503. DOI: 10.1007/978-1-4614-3185-5_38

Tremblay, M. S. (2019). The Importance of Play in Promoting Healthy Development in Children. https://publications.aap.org/pediatrics/article/119/1/182/70699/The-Importance-of-Play-in-Promoting-Healthy-Child

UNESCO. (2015). Education 2030: Incheon Declaration and Framework for Action. https://uis.unesco.org/sites/default/files/documents/education-2030-incheon-framework-for-action-implementation-of-sdg4-2016-en_2.pdf

UNICEF. (2019). State of the World's Children 2019: Children in a Changing World. https://www.unicef.org/reports/annual-report-2019

Van Leeuwen, L., & Westwood, D. (2008). Adult play, psychology and design. *Digital Creativity (Exeter)*, 19(3), 153–161. DOI: 10.1080/14626260802312665

Vaz Torres, C., Vasques-Menezes, I., & Presotti, L. (2017). Cultural diversity and inclusion in organizations: State of the art and challenges. Organizational Psychology and Evidence-Based Management: What Science Says About Practice, 227-242.

Venter, R., & Hodgson, H. K. G. (2020). Strategies for Inclusive Medical Imaging Environments for Sexual and Gender Minority Patients and Radiographers: An Integrative Literature Review. *Journal of Medical Imaging and Radiation Sciences*, 51(4), S99–S106. DOI: 10.1016/j.jmir.2020.05.009 PMID: 32622654

Vito, R., & Sethi, B. (2020). Managing change: Role of leadership and diversity management. *Journal of Organizational Change Management*, 33(7), 1471–1483. DOI: 10.1108/JOCM-04-2019-0116

Vygotsky, L. S. (1978). *Mind in society: The development of higher psychological processes*. Harvard University Press.

Westen, P. (1985). The concept of equal opportunity. *Ethics*, 95(4), 837–850. DOI: 10.1086/292687

Westera, W. (2022). The Devil's Advocate: Identifying Persistent Problems in Serious Game Design. *International Journal of Serious Games*, 9(3), 115–124. DOI: 10.17083/ijsg.v9i3.547

Winters, M. F. (2013). From diversity to inclusion: An inclusion equation. Diversity at work: The practice of inclusion, 205-228.

Wolf, M. J. P. (2001). *The medium of the video game*. University of Texas Press.

Wolfe, J., Bowen, D. D., & Roberts, C. R. (1989). Team-building effects on company performance: A business game-based study. *Simulation & Games*, 20(4), 388–408. DOI: 10.1177/104687818902000401

Woolfson, L. M. (2024). Is inclusive education for children with special educational needs and disabilities an impossible dream? *The British Journal of Educational Psychology*, bjep.12701. DOI: 10.1111/bjep.12701 PMID: 38890011

Wouters, E., Meulemans, H., & Rensburg, H. C. J. (2009). Slow to Share: Social Capital and Its Role in Public HIV Disclosure Among Public Sector ART Patients in the Free State Province of South Africa. *AIDS Care*, 21(4), 411–421. DOI: 10.1080/09540120802242077 PMID: 19266407

Wouters, P., Van der Spek, E. D., & Van Oostendorp, H. (2009). Current practices in serious game research: A review from a learning outcomes perspective. Games-based learning advancements for multi-sensory human computer interfaces: techniques and effective practices, 232-250.

Yamada, D. C. (1999). The phenomenon of workplace bullying and the need for status-blind hostile work environment protection. *Geological Journal*, 88, 475.

Yang, Y., Asaad, Y., & Dwivedi, Y. (2017). Examining the impact of gamification on intention of engagement and brand attitude in the marketing context. *Computers in Human Behavior*, 73, 459–469. DOI: 10.1016/j.chb.2017.03.066

Zafar, U., Khattak, M., Zafar, H., & Rehman, H. (2022). Let's Play Games: A Comparison of Case-Based Learning Approach With Gamification Technique. *Cureus*. Advance online publication. DOI: 10.7759/cureus.27612 PMID: 36059319

Zanardi, M. (1985). Metafora e gioco nel "Cannocchiale aristotelico" di Emanuele Tesauro. Studi secenteschi, 26, 25.

Zulmi, M. M., Prabandari, S. P., & Sudiro, A. (2021). Inclusive Human Resource Management (HRM) Practices for Employees With Disabilities as an Effort to Manage Diversity. *Estudios de Economía Aplicada*, 39(12). Advance online publication. DOI: 10.25115/eea.v39i12.6002

Section 2

Grand Challenges and Game-Based Learning for Sustainable Development

Chapter 2
Managing With the "Diverse": A Gaming Perspective for the Promotion of a More Inclusive and Sustainability-Oriented Culture

Andrea Caccialanza
https://orcid.org/0000-0002-0861-6796
University of Bologna, Italy

Barbara Barabaschi
https://orcid.org/0000-0003-4254-8421
Università Cattolica del Sacro Cuore, Italy

ABSTRACT

This study explores the mechanisms involved in integrating and balancing individual and organizational interests, focusing on how to manage diversity, particularly the 'diverse'. This chapter traces the elements that define and characterize the "diverse" and the organizational diversity. In particular, this chapter aims to analyze the potential of gaming as an innovative approach not only for greater integration of the diverse in organizations, but also to assess its perspective of integrating this goal in a context of promoting sustainability in the corporate environment. This discussion will then be articulated to the examination of the relationships between gaming and the promotion of the SDG agenda, gaming and the education for an effective communication, gaming to sensitize toward inequalities and disability on the job. Finally, conclusions and research agenda are proposed.

DOI: 10.4018/979-8-3693-1172-1.ch002

1. THE "DIVERSE" IN ORGANIZATIONS

The diffusion of multicultural and multinational organizations implied new challenges for the management of and development of working groups that are required to cooperate for reaching a competitive business model and successful market positioning (Cox & Blake, 1991; Kraus et al., 2019). However, the co-existence of several backgrounds, personal goals and expectations could lead to resistance from the endorsement of a transversal and cross-country working environment (Marquart-Pyatt, 2016). Consequently, understanding the mechanisms underlying the integration and balancing of individual and organizational interests involves developing mechanisms to manage diversity, and, more specifically, the "diverse". Moreover, this distinction and the consequent need to categorize into logical categories the variety of individuals involved in the functioning of an organization first requires the definition of "cultural diversity". As stated by Cox (1994, p. 5) cultural diversity can be described as "the representation in one social system of people with distinctly different group and a number of minority groups". Distinction therefore between groups and the need to operate in complex, multicultural organizational systems make it clear early on how this need is not diminishing over time. There is an unprecedented and pressing need for people to be able to deal with the complex dynamics of the world in which we live, to constantly assess our surroundings, and to adapt to and operate in them by continuously reviewing our frames of reference (Fabricatore & Lopez, 2012). Diversity could be embraced as a concept that encompasses the traditional categories of race, ethnicity, gender, sexual orientation, socioeconomic status, age, physical abilities, religious beliefs, political beliefs, or other ideologies (Patrick & Kumar, 2012). The spread of this new research area on "diversity" can be identified accordingly with Roberson (2019, p. 70) through the combination of organizational psychology and organizational behavior perspectives; so, we suppose that "we have really only just begun to understand diversity and diversity management as a science".

Additionally, Waldman and Sparr (2023) noted that the constant pressure for attention to "different," results in penalizing and detrimental to another concept of equal magnitude, namely "unity". The interdependence between the two concepts is not easy to operationalize or implement, especially at a time when they may appear to be in apparent contradiction. In fact, valuing "diversity" may lead to neglect of "unity", while the winning solution seems to be the proposal of integrated strategies that enhance the advantages of both diversity and unity while neutralizing their downside. Clearly strategies with such a high purpose cannot disregard continuous observation and assessment of the organization and adopt a contingent approach to the continuous and dynamic change of scenario (Griffin et al., 2020).

While the difficulties of implementing such an integrated and complex approach may argue in favour of non-action in this regard, in the belief that the cost of these operations is excessive, the potential impacts of non-action also need to be assessed. The avenues of intervention can be analyzed both through the definition of centers of responsibility delegated to control and monitor the issue, as well as to the definition of specific approaches. In this regard, several scholars (e.g., Williams & Wade-Golden, 2023; Ponomareva et al., 2022) emphasize how the role of the "chief diversity officer" is characterized by a multifaced leadership style and strong interaction with top management levels in order to propose an integration of these principles at every level of the company and trigger "genuine" organizational change. In addition, with reference to the definition of different approaches, Georgeac and Rattan (2023) focused on organizational diversity cases and investigated their content, prevalence, and consequences for underrepresented groups. The authors identified two different approaches for organizations: the business case, as example of instrumental rhetoric claim that refers to the positive impact on business performance, and the fairness case, a non-instrumental rhetoric that opt for diversity as the best one.

Since these strategies do not emerge naturally and in integrated way in the vast majority of organizations, the need to promote ongoing education and awareness of the issue therefore emerges (Bernstein et al., 2020). Thus, training activities and programs require new tools for the assimilation of domain-specific knowledge and the development of mindsets that enable people to engage in complex system dynamics, in other words, "playful, innovative, trans-disciplinary thinking in which systems can be analyzed, redesigned, and transformed into something new" (Zimmerman & Chaplin, 2013).

Gaming approaches for promoting not only diversity but also a necessary and integrated approach to sustainability will be introduced and reviewed in the next section.

2. THE GAMING APPROACH FOR SUSTAINABILITY-ORIENTED CULTURE

Gamification, serious games, and game-based learning exhibit distinctions, yet concurrently pursue analogous objectives. Indeed, all three approaches aim to enhance participant motivation, foster learning, and address problems through the integration of gaming elements. This chapter distinguishes among gamification, serious games, and game-based learning, pointing out why conflating them is improper. Starting with gamification, the term emerged in 2008 and gained recognition predominantly in the 2010s. The most known definition of gamification is provided by Seaborn & Fels (2015, p.17) that formulated shared definition, defined as "the intentional use of game elements for a gameful experience of non-game tasks and contexts". Consequently, the action of including game's elements, such as, points, levels, badges, leader boards, quests, and so on, in tasks and contexts that are typically considered non-game related (Deterding, 2011). This definition is probably the most comprehensive, despite other scholars priorly provided similar definitions, such as the one proposed by Zichemann & Cunningham (2011, p. IX), referred to gamification as "the process of game-thinking and game mechanics to engage and solve problems". Gamification is closely related to tow other concepts: serious games and game-based learning. Literature, often use the term "serious game" interchangeably with the term "game-based learning". However, it's incorrect due to the fact that one could refer to game-based learning as an approach implemented in educational context and that relies on fully-fledged games, better known as serious games, therefore, representing serious games only as a tool in the educational process (Schrader, 2023). One of the main differences between serious games and gamification is the orientation toward learning, that for serious games represents their main goal, whereas for gamification, most of the times, it doesn't depict as the main goal. In fact, gamification is not necessary about learning but it can be applied to several contexts, such as the working environment one. Since serious games are fully developed games, another difference relies on the diverse levels of gaming mechanisms and elements contained in both concepts (Pappas, 2023). On one hand, serious games are designed with a narrative purpose to involve the player in a story with a rich sensory experience, characterized by texts, sounds, graphics, animations and characters which the player can relate him selves with (Schrader, 2023). On the other hand, gamification doesn't follow an actual game structure, even if it might make tasks feel game-like, it only employs games element, that are selected based on the tasks needs. Despite both gamification and serious games share the aim to engage players, they proposed different ways of interaction. Gamification, due to its rewarding-based nature, use game elements to reward players for participating and motivate them, for example by giving point, while serious games tend to use more subtle rewarding systems, which due to the teaching purpose, considers the completion of the game as maximum reward, since it means that the participant has conquered the necessary skills required to beat the game. To conclude gamification can be consider as a broader concept compared to serious games and game-based learning, since it only includes game elements and applies them to the real world, but all three concepts share the same interest in using positive gaming experiences for the sake of a serious purpose. This is also source of misunderstandings about the use of these terms and the relationship within them. As stated by Amory & Seagram (2003, p.1), "the relationship between educational theories, game design and game development are used to develop models for the creation of complex learning environments". This broad perspective on the expanded use of this concept thus opens up different purposes and perspectives of this technique. In particular, the authors underline more specifically that the "game object model", is capable to combine theory and game design, while also define the basis for the development of the "persona outlining model" and the "game achievement model". Game achievement model is an efficient, well conceptualized, and supportive model that can be particularly adapted for complex learning environments.

Accordingly with Modarelli (2023, p. 2) the game "would become a key mediator for establishing inclusive perspectives in work environments, but not only, in organizations of all kinds and in learning dynamics, properly useful for considering the person as a whole and in all operating conditions". This cross-sectional perspective and aimed at analyzing the different perspectives involved had already been emphasized earlier by World Health Organization (2007), however, it does not cease to be a valid orientation and a stage of maturity and development still not always reached. With reference to this contribution to the literature we stress the importance of anchoring this discussion according to clear guidelines of theoretical development based on previous studies, to propose its further development in research agenda (see point 3.1.). To this end, Figure 1 summarizes the dimensions under analysis and the areas and modes of interaction development.

Figure 1. Research conceptual framework

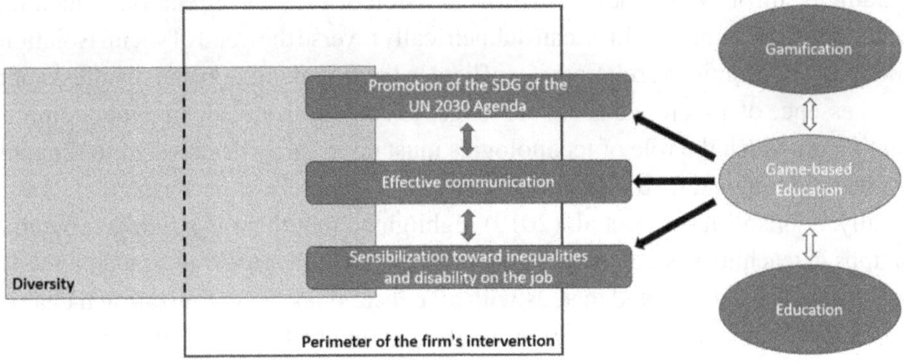

Source: own elaboration

According to our perspective, gamification can be understood as a complementary and integrative element or tool of the processes of education and training, but also providing for a two-way interaction that enriches the respective relevant literatures, such as the education's related one (see white arrows in the right part of Figure 1). This section aims also to provide examples of gamification and the theoretical foundation for the implementation of gamification perspectives in the promotion of more sustainable oriented culture that prior studies adopted to propose a definition, measure the efficiency and identify boundary conditions of applications (e.g., Davies, 2016; Dicheva et al., 2015; Nguyen, 2017; Nah et al., 2014; Noemí & Máximo, 2014), such as in this case the perimeter of the firm's intervention (See the white bow in Figure 1). In particular, Douglas & Brauer (2021) in their review highlighted that gamification has been adopted for different sustainability education context, such as namely: energy reduction, transportation, air quality, waste management, and water conservation. Despite they didn't reveal any hierarchy in the effectiveness of these games - as we also support in our non-hierarchical interaction -, what clearly emerge is that gamification appears to be a promising avenue for preventing climate change. Similarly, Meya and Eisenack (2018) found that gaming fosters the sense of personal responsibility, the confidence in politics for climate change mitigation, and improve the optimism about international cooperation in climate politics. Consequently, it is confirmed also with this specific perspective that gaming can be an integrative instrument of conventional educational and communication methods (see dark grey boxes in Figure 1). This dynamic interaction prompted us to make the concept of "Game-based education" central both in the (self-explanatory) interplay between gamification and education, and in its central role in introducing sensitivities within the company toward more specific issues related to corporate sustainability per-se (see the black arrows in Figure 1). Consistently, Modarelli (2023, p.2) proposed a "paradigm shift towards the self-realizing vision of the self in relation, which the dynamics of the game provides, can diametrically reverse the trend of social isolation, emerging opportunisms, relational conflicts in the fragmentation and disintegration of the essence of a society that can no longer to communicate, albeit hyper communicating, in which the role of technologies must necessarily be elevated to the rank of a healing tool and facilitator, not of offense, nor merely of performance". Additionally, Alonso-Martínez et al. (2019) highlighted that there is a hidden potential for apps in teaching sustainability at in combination with more traditional methods. However, it should be noted that, as with all educational and organizational change elements within organizations, there are also potential educational effects, which if not evaluated can lead to failure of the educational intervention. In particular, Tonda et al. (2018) identified and mapped four negative effects, and they found that the "loss of performance" was the most occurring "dark side" effect.

As a result, it emerges how an innovative and dynamic technique such as gamification is also associated with goals and objectives that use technology and to promote a vision of integral and integrated development with sustainable development principles. Consequently, since we cannot systematically assume or map any kind of corporate interaction with the external environment or the countless variables of internal and external interaction for the examination of the topic of "diverse" in organizations we have selected three key topics in analogy with current future research trends (Bernstein et al., 2020).

As anticipated priorly in Fig. 1, therefore, to propose an effective explanation of several applications of the gaming approach, we propose three specific focuses: (2.1.) gaming and the promotion of the SDG agenda, (2.2.) gaming and the education for an effective communication, (2.3.) gaming to sensitize toward inequalities and disability on the job.

2.1. Gaming and the Promotion of the SDG Agenda

This section provides perspective and critical consideration throughout the implementation of Gaming and the promotion of UN 17 SDGs, with specific focus on: SDG 1 – No poverty; SDG 4 – Quality education; SDG 5 Gender equality; and SDG 10 - Reduced inequalities. Several studies on these issues will be the bases for this discussion (e.g., Ebron, 2023; Sinicropi & Cortese, 2021; Heras-Saizarbitoria et al., 2022; Rosati & Faria, 2019). We resume these goals under the concept of social inclusion defined as "a process ensuring that those at risk of poverty and social exclusion gain the opportunities and resources to actively participate in economic, social, political, and cultural life (Council of The European Union, 2004). In contemporary societies, social inclusion also depends on access to and the use of technologies, which have become pervasive in all areas of everyday life. That's why the term e-inclusion defined by the European Commission as "all efforts by the public and private sector; civil society and the technology community to ensure the full participation of individuals and communities in today's knowledge-based society by (1) addressing the various inequalities that occur at the level of access, motivation, skills and usage related to ICT; and by (2) establishing policies and programs that build upon the use of ICT to achieve wider inclusion objectives" (European Commission, 2010, p.18).

E-inclusion entails socio-economic processes promoting access to technologies and related services, awareness of its opportunities and the willingness and confidence to use digital devices in everyday life. Moreover, e-inclusion can refer both to inclusive digital tools as well as use of digital tools to achieve broader inclusion and empowerment goals.

Empowerment is put forward as one of the main goals of e-inclusion. Selwyn & Facer (2007, p.6) for example affirm that the focus of e-inclusion is to "enable all individuals to make informed and empowered choices about the use of ICT whilst ensuring these individuals have ready access to the resources required to enable them to act on these choices."

The double nature of play (that is instrumental and fun) has encouraged various actors to consider the use of digital games as an engaging, entertaining means to induce some form of change (knowledge and skill acquisition, attitudinal, behavioral or social change). In literature, different terms have been proposed to refer to games dealing with complex issues such as migration, poverty, war, discrimination, sustainability, etc., one of them is serious games[1], to differentiate them from those aiming to mere entertainment Zyda (2005).

In our work we will focus on serious games fostering changes in attitudes and behaviors about diversity and social inclusion as recommended by UN in its Agenda 2030.

In economic organizations, for example, they have been increasingly used as learning tools to provide employees especially with soft but also hard skills. Beneficial results from their use are proven in the literature, also if limits have been observed in less structured learning contexts, for example, with scares use of technologies, when potential users have no access or are not able to use digital devices, or finally when educators are unfamiliar with video games (Lavoué et al. 2019). Considering the promotion of SDG Agenda, serious games are also used to raise awareness of and change players' perspectives on the specific topic addressed (Shliakhovchuk, 2018). When the games represent social and political issue, usually the games are used with the aim to persuade.

On the specific social issue of inclusion, other two principles are crucial, that of representation and that of identification. In this case a relevant factor to consider is to what extent those we seek to empower or include are already playing games if they feel represented in the game and are able to identify with game features. These factors seem to widely influence the success of game-based initiatives.

During the last decades, a growing number of higher education institutes and universities have created educational tools for sustainable development (Annan-Diab & Molinari, 2017) aiming to foster policies and practices. Nevertheless, as Berzosa et al. (2017) indicate, researchers have avoided to use such tools mainly due to the lack of clear and specific objectives. This requires innovative educational approaches that promote authentic educational content and thinking about sustainable development (Blanco-Portela et al., 2017). Serious games are part of the desired innovation process. If we consider the topic of environmental governance, games are used as participatory tools to promote change processes in learning and in social habits (Rodela, 2013).

As such, games function as tools in which the participants learn by doing serious gaming points of strength are in the mix of impacts derived from experience: i) cognitive, consists in the acquisition of new or restructuring of existing knowledge, ii) normative that is, a shift in perceptions, viewpoints, and values and iii) relational that is, a better understanding of others way to think and other expectations (Jean et al., 2013). Researchers have also showed that serious gaming can change individual perceptions and increases understanding of viewpoints of others by offering actors a place to debate, negotiate, exchange perspectives used in decision-making and learn about the trade-offs between decisions. From the learning perspective, literature highlights that all the three types of learning are present; cognitive learning is the most identified learning outcome, but there is also evidence for normative and relational learning outcomes (Stanitsas et al., 2019).

Therefore, serious gaming has already been used in relation to the so-called inclusive business (very attentive to diversity management and inclusion issues) towards meeting the SDGs. In fact, serious games primarily focused on stimulating inclusive decision-making and empowering actors as well as creating space to collectively discuss.

Scholars demonstrated that although the vast majority of serious games are designed to educate users to sustainable development as a whole, their focus is often on a single dimension of it. In particular, environmental management games are the most popular. The economic dimension is the least popular, while the social dimension is gaining in popularity (Stanitsas et al., 2019). The evolution in the (academic and political) debate on how to build sustainable societies has highlighted a lack of social dimension in this debate. Since globalization and the recurrent economic crisis emphasized the growing diversity in social structures and the related risk of social inequalities affecting sustainable development processes, games need to be designed to take into consideration the system complexity in which every action can affect other part of the same system.

In addition, according to Fabricatore and López (2012) digital games reproducing complex systems need to be conceived to stimulate a 'spirit of inquiry' to explore different scenarios and give learners the ability to face uncertainty, accept failure and think about different strategies, that are crucial skills in organizations inspired by sustainable values. This happens, for example, in games designed to develop problem-solving attitude in the management of urban waste elementary school students and undergraduate students. In this type of game, users are required to guide the development of a city adopting management strategies, matching economic growth, environmental protection, as well as considering social implications potentially caused by their actions. These games allow learners to test their behaviors in complex systems involving a great number of stakeholders related each other in order to conserve the nature and to maintain clean the city (Janakiraman et al., 2018).

Another interesting experience has been proposed by the United Nations in 2017, with the launch of 'The World's Future' digital game having the aim to promote a systems perspective on global challenges and increase the general awareness of their interconnected nature. In this game educators, teachers and researchers are required to sensibilize their audience about the challenges and opportunities related to the pursuit of the SDGs in complex systems. The game is integrated by user-tests and feedback sessions. Players are engaged in role-playing, where they need to solve conflicts and negotiate or empathize with each other. Thanks to the use of cards and tokens, players are called to manage the complex interrelations among different SDGs, create in-game partnerships and finally defining possible scenarios to implement the 2030 Agenda. Skills that the game aims to develop are active problem-solving and emotional engagement, persuasion, engaging in social simulations, participants, reflexivity, and independent critical thinking in the pursuit of SDGs (United Nations, 2018).

In this context, it is necessary to better train future professionals who are going to work in companies, as well as in other types of entities (public entities and educational centers, among others) where they are ought to o report economic, social, and environmental information committed to the 2030 Agenda.

On this regard the education system may play an important role in fostering equity and respect, supporting individuals to understand perspectives and needs of people who is "diverse", for example, living in other parts of the world or belonging to another generation or gender. In particular, teaching about sustainable development requires to confront students with ethical issues, indicators of social well-being while preserving the natural environment. (Prado et al, 2020).

It has been demonstrated that the use of serious games affected the degree of knowledge of SDGs. However, serious games in education system seems do not affect the level of priority students recognize them. Nevertheless, the most important skills they allow to develop are creativity, critical attitudes and systemic thinking play the role of a social entrepreneur able to manage resources, not only reducing waste but also creating employment, transport, housing, and telecommunications in an economically and socially sustainable way.

2.2. Gaming and the Education for an Effective Communication

This section provides perspective and critical consideration throughout the implementation of gaming and the promotion of effective communication, with specific focus on how to promote gaming strategies to improve the internal and external sustainability communication (e.g., Peterková et al., 2022; Hunt et al., 2015).

According to Shliakhovchuk (2018), videogames are an expressive medium that may increase individual familiarity with complex situations in a relatively simple way. In this sense, as already pointed out, they promote critical thinking and reflexivity, improve the understanding about the topics they deal with, consequently stimulates decision and action-taking processes, and, at the same time, reinforces social-activist messages (Lavander, 2011). Serious video games have been conceived to support ethics, human-rights education and to overcome issues in intercultural communication, e.g. for learning about different cultures and facilitating relations among people coming from diverse countries of origin. That's why assessment analysis revealed that students after playing *Darfur Is Dying*, were more willing to help Darfurian people than those who had read on mass media about the situation in Darfur those who played *Homeless: It Is No Game* were sensibilized to the problems of homeless people, and this having played *Spent*, revealed higher levels of awareness about poor people conditions in the society (Peng, 2010).

The global market proposes a wide range of video games of different quality and effectiveness levels. They are available online. Many of them are free while others may be purchased at accessible prices.

Serious videogames may be grouped according to the values they aim to express and attitudes they want to incentivize, like empathy for migrant people, generating positive attitudes towards diversity and people from other societies and cultures; respect and understanding towards people in different life circumstances; respect of human-rights overcoming stereotypes and prejudice that teach tolerance, diversity, and inclusion.

Combining video-game play with other forms of formal instructions (teacher-led discussions, textbook readings, written homework assignments, etc.) could rise the effectiveness of communication and results, making formal learning settings more affordable. Instruction combined with video games allow an increase of up to 40% in student learning comparing with traditional lecture instruction (Shliakhovchuk, 2018). Traditional educational methodology focusses on the learning aspects while video games on the active engagement factor to increase users' motivation. Usually, video games, are not added to, but integrated into the existing curriculum. Starting from the teaching aims, educators must carefully consider users profile and the complexity of the topic. For games organized in various modules, it's also possible to opt for a whole game or a part of it.

From a methodological point of view, other suggestions emerged from the literature on how to improve videogame effectiveness in educational context, such as using pre-videogame activities, in-class videogame activities and post-videogame activities.

The use of *pre-video gameplay activities* allowing to collect and systematize what students already know about a topic. For example, if the video concerns refugee issues, students can share what they know about this phenomenon, about why and how people leave their countries of origin, and debate on migrants' integration in the host societies. Videogame trailers and players' reviews can be used to exchange views about the video game's protagonists, events, storyline, setting. The educator may explain the most relevant theories and models before the video game is played. After playing the video game, students can share considerations and argument if their ideas coincide with the ones in the video game.

In-class video gameplay activities allow a deeper understanding of the topic. The educator may choose to play the whole game or selected parts or levels of it, in order to focus on specific issues. Alternatively, the instructor can ask students to play the game before the class session, and selected parts that can be repeated in the classroom. The role of the educator is to define the difficulty levels based on students' previous performance, provide timely hints and think-aloud approaches, and help students through the problem-solving process of critical scenarios. The educator should continually monitor students and provide and receive feedback to optimally scaffold students' game-play experience. Interactive learning is encouraged through timely observation and discussions. It is important to stimulate the students to apply what they have learned. The time devoted to teaching and to students' hands-on playing should be properly balanced.

Post-video game activities are performed to assess and consolidate comprehension and learning outcomes. Debriefing may help to link game-playing experiences and real life. Personal reactions to the playing experience; main events and problems analysis; learning outcomes after playing experience connected to the real world can represent the basis of collective discussion in the post-playing experience. (Fritzsche, 2014).

All the activities described below, answer to the need for videogames to adapt to the specific context the game is used in. While there is currently very little research on adaptation of gamification, more studies have been devoted to adaptation in serious games. Many methods involve adjusting the level of difficulty and adapt the help given to players, the training intensity, or the educational scenario (Pedersen, et al., 2010; Göbel et al., 2010), the quests presented to the player so to define different gameplay scenarios.

2.3. Gaming to Sensitize Toward Inequalities and Disability on the Job

This section provides perspective and critical consideration throughout the implementation of gaming and the sensibilization toward disability on the job (e.g., Ainscow, 2020; Bešić et al., 2023; Corbett, 2001).

Most serious games aim at facilitating gamers' thinking or problem-solving skills trying to realize a gameplay experience that does not solely use masked activities. The level of players' involvement and the quality of the game's content contribute to players' ability to socialize with these contents and transfer learning outcomes into his everyday life, to develop sensitivity, to better understand other people's actions and to empathize with members of minority groups. An extension of serious games is represented by serious moral games, implemented to promote moral sensitivity in business, a precondition of ethical decision-making and behavior in all types of organizations. Their approach is comprehensive of corporate social responsibility practices and diversity and inclusion policies. Nevertheless Tanner et al. (2022) study on these videogames, contrary to previous ones, highlighted that self-reflection and the exposure to pro-social issues do not foster moral sensitivity. Although the development of serious moral games is relevant to demonstrate the interest around the topic of gaming and social sustainability and inclusion, the lack of convergent findings in literature convinced us to maintain the focus of our analysis on serious game in a broad sense.

According to Michael and Chen (2006) serious games extend far beyond traditional teaching facts and memorization, but include all aspects of education such as teaching, training, and informing and can be addressed to all gender and generations at work, or to people with disabilities.

The recent work of Hardteveld et al. (2020) focuses on issues of equity, inclusivity, and diversity, underlying that these crucial challenges in contemporary societies are not sufficiently represented in technical education (see for example that addressed to engineers who realize video games). Authors believe that it would instead be useful to enrich the training paths of those who design videogames for educational purposes with the contribution of the rich literature developed in the field of educational science starting from experiences of social inclusion through the use of videogames. On one hand, they found evidence that game-based learning supports positive outcomes and provides an equitable learning environment; on the other, they also note several challenges that are further discussed.

Indeed, videogames may be useful to foster diversity and inclusion culture in people behaviors in the society as a whole, but also to improve working experience of people suffering from disabilities.

Training through game playing can be appropriate for persons with disabilities, who often have difficulty in applying the acquired knowledge to the physical world or in generalizing to different situations in a cost-effective and safe way (Michael & Chen, 2006).

Digital gaming can be a key site of exclusion for people with disability through inaccessible interfaces and lack of representation. Gaming can also be a key site of inclusion and disabled gamers have become active agents of change against inaccessibility and lack of representation. Some have even created employment opportunities for themselves and other people with disability. In serious games, feedback on the player's success or failure is given visually and/or audibly. This feedback serves to convey a sense of accomplishment and to motivate individuals to change their behaviors and try again (Oblinger, 2004).

In literature, we can find several examples of serious games realized to improve people with disabilities (working and everyday) life quality using serious games.

In the following we cite few examples considered interesting for our work. One is the Stanford Pocketschool project that focusses on mobile empowerment of underserved, poor communities around the world. Skills and knowledge are not simply delivered to the community, but people are enabled and encouraged to become more active and give back to their community in a sustainable manner. Mobile technology is considered a suitable option to achieve this goal, given that it is becoming ever more widely adopted in developing countries. Examples of work done within the Stanford project include the development of storytelling and educational gaming applications to empower children and adults living in poor rural communities in Asia, Africa, and Latin America (Kim et al., 2011). In the case of the children, a non-profit institution called 'Innovations for Learning' took care of manufacturing and distributing a mobile device that the children could use to create stories and share them with others around the world. In the case of the adults, a mobile farming simulation game was created to promote understanding of micro-credits and stimulate entrepreneurship propensity in farming. The authors believe that the key to success of these programs in underserved communities lies in the combination of education, infrastructural support with the aim of empowerment in everyday life.

Some games that are available for public use are the result of participatory design in which people from the target community participated in the design of the game. Soul Control, for instance, emerged from a design concept developed by NEET (Not [engaged] in Education, Employment or Training) youth who took part in games design course. It addresses gang culture and crime. Nintendo has also used cocreation to create game concepts for certain target groups such as children with learning attention deficit disorder (Walsh, 2009) and sighted children (Willems et al., 2011). Working with the target groups by enabling them to act as experts has resulted in game concepts for Wii. The Wii game that aims at blind children is designed to allow blind children do not only have to play games with other blind children but giving them the possibility to interact in game play with their sighted peers. The game *The discoverer* has become accessible to the wide public.

Another group of digital game among those with social purposes, is the one requiring a higher level of user interaction (so the user need having a medium-high level of digital skills). Examples are *Causeworld*, where users check into a certain location and have the opportunity to support a good cause such as the Red Cross *or* other social movements/associations. *Recyclebank* encourages recycling and other 'green' activities by offering rewards, shop discounts and the opportunity to share one's accomplishments with others. *Free Rice* is an online quiz in which correct answers result in rice donations to the United Nations World Food Program.

Finally, Ellis, Leaver & Kant in their recent volume devoted to "Gaming Disability. Disability Perspective on Contemporary Videogames" (2023), collected many examples of innovation and inclusion, from fan communities recognizing

Overwatch character *Symmetra* as being part of the autism community, to educators using *Minecraft* and *Pokémon GO* in the classroom, to disability led innovation in creating or adapting games to be accessible to students with physical and learning disabilities, as well as mental disorders all around the world (China, Australia, United Kingdom and USA) (Granic et al., 2014). On this regard, Minecraft (an off-the-shelf block-based game which involves constructing different buildings and figures) may enable these students to self-learn various subjects or skills within the game such as writing and reading with some support from the teacher (Stam, 2014). It is a commercial off-the-shelf block-based sandbox game which involves constructing different buildings and figures. Minecraft Education Edition is an alternative version of the game developed specifically for use in educational settings, suitable to encourage teamwork and non-linear gameplay (Andersen, Rustad, 2022).

The reason why Minecraft can help people with autism, for example, is due to the order and control that they crave in real life and thus assists the players in becoming at ease with each other (Porter, 2013). Students that are usually seen as problematic and disruptive in class transform into regular students ("Minecrafters") when they get into the game, acting on the level of other students in the same class and responding positively to the teacher figure. That's why Minecraft and other types of videogames reveal to be useful tools to students often isolated and excluded from classroom dynamics while creating a virtual safe space (thanks to the teacher who maintains the game control) to explore critical topics (Petrov A., 2014).

In synthesis, serious games aiming to foster social inclusion in the contemporary digital and diverse societies may be divided into three groups according to the specific sub-goal they want to reach:

1. Supporting disengaged and disadvantaged learners and enhancing employability, e.g.: games helping people with learning disabilities, games that support low-level training.
2. Promoting health and well-being, e.g.: games aim at raising awareness about certain physical and mental health issues, promote health and well-being either as part of prevention, or in support of those that are dealing with health problems.
3. Fostering civic participation and community-building, e.g.: games raising awareness about political and governmental topics, games supporting participatory community planning.

Concerning serious game outcomes, literature is rich in studies adopting very differentiate perspectives and not always convergent, but it is possible to affirm that a common trait of all of them is the general positive effect of serious games on learning processes and users' motivation.

Sitzmann (2011) conducted a meta-analysis of 65 studies on serious games and found that individuals trained through games improved their actual tasks more than did those trained with traditional approaches. These findings were confirmed by Wouters, van Nimwegen, van Oostendorp, and Spek (2013).

Alonso-Fernandéz et al. (2019) tried to fill the gap in the literature about serious games results by providing data-based evidence on game learning outcomes for serious games, giving an example of some specific experiences. What makes interesting this study is that each game was used in real-world educational scenarios and not only limited to experiments in controlled environments. The serious game *Conectado* is used by the teachers in the classroom to address bullying and cyberbullying with the aim to arise awareness (Calvo-Morata et al., 2018), while the serious game *DownTown* is designed for promoting independence by training skills in using the subway to users with intellectual disabilities (Cano et al., 2018).

Concerning the learning outcome associated to serious game, Boyle et al. (2016), with their systematic review on 143 papers, although revealing the difficulty to generalize results on serious games efficacy in specific domains due to the wide heterogeneity of studies, they give empirical evidence about the positive impacts and outcomes of games on learning processes in general. The most occurring outcome reported for games for learning was knowledge acquisition. study designs were used to address different outcomes. RCTs were used most frequently in studies of knowledge acquisition and perceptual and cognitive outcomes; quasi-experimental designs were used to study all the different learning outcomes, but especially knowledge acquisition, physiological and perceptual and cognitive outcomes; correlational designs were used most frequently with affective, social, and soft skills and behavior change, while survey designs were used most with knowledge acquisition, affective and behavior change outcomes.

A series of papers defined "serious games" were identified in the current review than in the previous ones, suggesting that the term has entered the mainstream in recent years. However, the term is used interchangeably with games-based learning.

There was some evidence that games were successfully used for skill acquisition in health planning and for behavior change in substance abuse, as well as supporting collaborative interactions, soft skills, and empathy. Games for learning are usually addressed to healthy eating, triage training, sustainability, operations management, and advanced life support retraining.

3. RESEARCH AGENDA AND CONCLUSIONS

3.1. Research Agenda

As organizations increasingly recognize the value of incorporating game-based learning into educational and training initiatives, the potential for leveraging this approach in sustainability-oriented studies and fostering diversity in companies becomes evident. This research agenda aims to outline (at least) four main avenues for future studies that offer practical implications, both on the managerial and social perspective.

At first, can be noted as the enhancement of learner-centric approaches may help to investigate the effectiveness of assigning e-learning games as project assignments to groups, focusing on sustainability, diversity, and inclusive education. More specifically, it might be conducted a longitudinal study to assess the impact of game-based projects on students' understanding of social challenges and thus fostering the sensibility to the issues such those promoted by the UN 2030 Agenda. In this discussion we have already discussed some of these targets (see also 2.1. Gaming and the promotion of the SDG agenda), but a broader and more articulate review would certainly be helpful in fostering this debate. This perspective can better examine the transferability of skills developed through game-based projects to real-world problem-solving scenarios in the organizations. Furthermore, on the managerial side, it potentially helps to identify best practices for integrating game-based projects into educational programs, enabling educators and managers to foster creativity, analytical thinking, and problem-solving skills among learners. In our perspective, the development of a strategic integration of education plans for the integration of the divers could be combined with the development of the transferable soft skills within the organization.

A second stream of literature can be associated with a broader mapping of the spread of the phenomena of serious games for sustainability education. This literature review perspective could be the best for evaluating the educational contribution of serious games in sustainability, thus considering logical categories that may help to group logical categories such as for example: the game characteristics, design, the target audience, teaching exclusivity, etc. Furthermore, it could be hypothesized the proposal of a logical framework for evaluating the effectiveness of serious games, considering game philosophy, design elements, and the (potential or expected) educational outcomes. In terms of managerial implications, it is supposed to provide to educators and decision-makers a framework for selecting and designing serious games that align with specific sustainability education goals, fostering a more informed integration of serious games into curricula and education strategies.

The potential third stream could be linked to the promotion of videogame-based programs focusing on the target of digital native audiences. Further studies could explore the advantages and challenges of using videogames in courses and training programs to engage digital native students and employees in a technology-driven and sustainability-oriented context. More specifically these studies may investigate the driving factors that make video-games powerful educational tools for digital native learners.

The analysis of the role of videogames may expand the imagination and worldview of individuals in technology-driven environments and avoid the 'digital divide' of education processes thanks to the effective update of learning processes. Furthermore, this assessment might be able to appreciate the impact of videogames on promoting empathy, decision-making, and responsibility among learners, thus the inclusion of the 'diverse' in organizations also on the emotional side. With refers to the managerial impact, it provides insights into the design and implementation of video game-based educational programs to effectively reach and engage digital native audiences, helping organizations tailor training initiatives for the modern workforce.

In addition, we suggest investigating the complexities, costs, and challenges associated with developing serious games for educational purposes, with an innovative focus on sustainability and diversity. Further research may explore the key features that can effectively contribute to the success of serious games for holistic learning. More specifically, we suppose that can be suggested to firms and on-purpose strategies to address the challenges and enhance the development of effective educational games. Consequently, it could be provided actionable insights for organizations considering the development of serious games for educational purposes, helping them navigate challenges and maximize the impact of game-based learning initiatives.

In summary, this research agenda aims to bridge existing gaps in understanding the potential of game-based perspectives for sustainability-oriented studies and diversity integration, offering practical recommendations for educators and organizational leaders.

Finally, we also suggest that in future studies practical applications and case studies with primary data and from 'on field' investigations should be developed that promote the development of a greater sustainability orientation. This empirical extension of this first theoretical stage of the analysis, could also consider different or additional topics than those currently analyzed, further enriching the presented logic model.

3.2. Conclusions

Without claiming to be an extensive and comprehensive review of the literature, this contribution seeks to foster the debate for the promotion of a culture linked to the principles of sustainable development in both the educational and corporate spheres. With reference to this study, three prevalent and related themes among the literatures related to gaming, management, and sustainable development were traced and grouped into the following themes: (2.1.) gaming and the promotion of the SDG agenda, (2.2.) gaming and the education for an effective communication, (2.3.) gaming to sensitize toward inequalities and disability on the job.

To sum up, in this context, it is emphasized that the progressive dissemination of the principles of sustainability must take place through the widespread integration of several disciplines, research areas and through an increase in methodologies and processes in favor of an interdisciplinary approach to complex problems (Pineda-Martínez et al., 2023). With this in mind, it is argued that already at an individual development stage, even during training or educational projects, one can contribute to the development and dissemination of a culture in the corporate and working environment that also benefits from such a holistic and multidimensional approach. Specifically discussed was the role of gamification in promoting the goals identified by the 17 SDGs proposed by United Nations, for a more effective communication capacity and effective reduction of inequalities. This study suffers from the following limitations. It does not retrace the gaming-related debate in a continuous and systematic way, but merely retraced the most impactful contributions in the non-gaming (and efficiency driven working environments and) context(s), with in mind that it would have been used to promote sustainability-oriented behaviors. as a result, it emerges how further studies can broaden the scope of investigation and insight, both by increasing the issues involved and by interpolating these with the different types of gaming design proposed.

RESEARCH FUNDING

The author(s) received no financial support for the research, authorship, and/or publication of this article.

REFERENCES

Ainscow, M. (2020). Promoting inclusion and equity in education: Lessons from international experiences. *Nordic Journal of Studies in Educational Policy*, 6(1), 7–16. DOI: 10.1080/20020317.2020.1729587

Alonso-Martínez, D., Jiménez-Parra, B., González-Álvarez, N., Godos-Díez, J. L., & Cabeza-García, L. (2019). Taking advantage of students' passion for apps in sustainability and CSR teaching. *Sustainability (Basel)*, 11(3), 779. DOI: 10.3390/su11030779

Amory, A., & Seagram, R. (2003). Educational game models: conceptualization and evaluation: the practice of higher education. *South African Journal of Higher Education*, 17(2), 206–217.

Andersen, R., & Rustad, M. (2022). Using Minecraft as an educational tool for supporting collaboration as a 21st century skill. *Computers and Education Open*, 3, 100094. Advance online publication. DOI: 10.1016/j.caeo.2022.100094

Annan-Diab, F. A., & Molinari, C. (2017). Interdisciplinarity: Practical approach to advancing education for sustainability and for the Sustainable Development Goals. *International Journal of Management Education*, 15(2), 73–83. DOI: 10.1016/j.ijme.2017.03.006

Bernstein, R. S., Bulger, M., Salipante, P., & Weisinger, J. Y. (2020). From diversity to inclusion to equity: A theory of generative interactions. *Journal of Business Ethics*, 167(3), 395–410. DOI: 10.1007/s10551-019-04180-1

Berzosa, A., Bernaldo, M. O., & Fernández-Sanchez, G. (2017). Sustainability assessment tools for higher education: An empirical comparative analysis. *Journal of Cleaner Production*, 161, 812–820. DOI: 10.1016/j.jclepro.2017.05.194

Bešić, E., Paleczek, L., Ladenstein, J., & Gasteiger-Klicpera, B. (2023). Reaching the 'Hard to Reach': Implementing "Education for All" by Participative Action Research and Students' Voices. In Shaping Tomorrow Today–SDGs from multiple perspectives (pp. 141-160). Wiesbaden: Springer Fachmedien Wiesbaden. DOI: 10.1007/978-3-658-38319-0_7

Blanco-Portela, N., Benayas, J., Pertierra, L. R., & Lozano, R. (2017). Towards the integration of sustainability in Higher Education Institutions: A review of drivers of and barriers to organisational change and their comparison against those found of companies. *Journal of Cleaner Production*, 166, 563–578. DOI: 10.1016/j.jclepro.2017.07.252

Boyle, E. A., Hainey, T., Connolly, T. M., Gray, G., Earp, J., Ott, M., Lim, T., Ninaus, M., Ribeiro, C., & Pereira, J. (2016). An update to the systematic literature review of empirical evidence of the impacts and outcomes of computer games and serious games. *Computers & Education*, 94, 178–192. DOI: 10.1016/j.compedu.2015.11.003

Calvo-Morata, A., Rotaru, D. C., Alonso-Fernández, C., Freire-Morán, M., Martínez-Ortiz, I., & Fernández-Manjón, B. (2018). Validation of a cyberbullying serious game using game analytics. *IEEE Transactions on Learning Technologies*, 13(1), 186–197. DOI: 10.1109/TLT.2018.2879354

Corbett, J. (2001). Teaching approaches which support inclusive education: A connective pedagogy. *British Journal of Special Education*, 28(2), 55–59. DOI: 10.1111/1467-8527.00219

Council of European Union. (2004). Joint report by the Commission and the Council on social inclusion 7101/04.

Cox, T. (1994). *Cultural diversity in organizations: Theory, research and practice*. Berrett-Koehler Publishers.

Cox, T. H., & Blake, S. (1991). Managing cultural diversity: Implications for organizational competitiveness. *The Academy of Management Perspectives*, 5(3), 45–56. DOI: 10.5465/ame.1991.4274465

Davies, H. (2016). The Growing Pervasiveness of Games and Play. *Digital Games Research Association (DiGRA) Australia Queensland Symposium*.

Deterding, S., Dixon, D., Khaled, R., & Nacke, L. (2011). From game design elements to gamefulness: defining "gamification". In Proceedings of the 15th international academic MindTrek conference: Envisioning future media environments (pp. 9-15). DOI: 10.1145/2181037.2181040

Dicheva, D., Dichev, C., Agre, G., & Angelova, G. (2015). Gamification in education: A systematic mapping study. *Journal of Educational Technology & Society*, 18(3), 75–88.

Douglas, B. D., & Brauer, M. (2021). Gamification to prevent climate change: A review of games and apps for sustainability. *Current Opinion in Psychology*, 42, 89–94. DOI: 10.1016/j.copsyc.2021.04.008 PMID: 34052619

Ebron, K. T., Luzynski, C., & Nath Komanski, C. S. (2023). Leave No One Behind: How systemic racism impacts Sustainable Development Goals. *International Journal of Public Leadership*, 19(1), 31–44. DOI: 10.1108/IJPL-02-2022-0010

Ellis, K., Leaver, T., & Kant, M. (2023). Gaming Disability. Disability Perspective on Contemporary Videogames. Routledge.

Fabricatore, C., & Lopez, X. (2012). Sustainability learning through gaming: An exploratory study. *Electronic Journal of e-Learning*, 10(2), 209–222.

Fritzsche, D. J., Leonard, N. H., Boscia, M. W., & Anderson, P. H. (2014). Simulation Debriefing Procedures, Development Business Simulation Experience Learning Process Annuary ABSEL Conference, 31(0).

Gatti, L., Ulrich, M., & Seele, P. (2019). Education for sustainable development through business simulation games: An exploratory study of sustainability gamification and its effects on students' learning outcomes. *Journal of Cleaner Production*, 207, 667–678. DOI: 10.1016/j.jclepro.2018.09.130

Georgeac, O. A., & Rattan, A. (2023). The business case for diversity backfires: Detrimental effects of organizations' instrumental diversity rhetoric for underrepresented group members' sense of belonging. *Journal of Personality and Social Psychology*, 124(1), 69–108. DOI: 10.1037/pspi0000394 PMID: 35679195

Göbel, S., Wendel, V., Ritter, C., & Steinmetz, R. (2010). Personalized, adaptive digital educational games using narrative game-based learning objects. In *Entertainment for Education. Digital Techniques and Systems* (pp. 438–445). Springer. DOI: 10.1007/978-3-642-14533-9_45

Granic, I., Lobel, A., & Engels, R. M. (2014). The benefits of playing video games. *The American Psychologist*, 69(1), 66–78. DOI: 10.1037/a0034857 PMID: 24295515

Griffin, R. W., Phillips, J. M., & Gully, S. M. (2020). Organizational behavior: Managing people and organizations. CENGAGE Learning.

Harteveld, C., Javvaji, N., Machado, T., Zastavker, Y. V., Bennett, V., & Abdoun, T. (2020). Gaming4All: Reflecting on Diversity, Equity, and Inclusion for Game-Based Engineering Education. 2020 IEEE Frontiers in Education Conference (FIE), 1-9. DOI: 10.1109/FIE44824.2020.9274176

Heras-Saizarbitoria, I., Urbieta, L., & Boiral, O. (2022). Organizations' engagement with sustainable development goals: From cherry-picking to SDG-washing? *Corporate Social Responsibility and Environmental Management*, 29(2), 316–328. DOI: 10.1002/csr.2202

Hunt, V., Layton, D., & Prince, S. (2015). Diversity matters. McKinsey & Company.

Janakiraman, S., Watson, S. L., & Watson, W. R. (2018). Using Game-based Learning to Facilitate Attitude Change for Environmental Sustainability. *Journal of Education for Sustainable Development*, 12(2), 176–185. DOI: 10.1177/0973408218783286

Jean, S., Medema, W., Adamowski, J., Chew, C., Delaney, P., & Wals, A. (2018). Serious Games as a catalyst for boundary crossing, collaboration and knowledge co-creation in a watershed governance context. *Journal of Environmental Management*, 223, 1010–1022. DOI: 10.1016/j.jenvman.2018.05.021 PMID: 30096742

Jungmin, K., & Youngsun, L. (2016). Serious games for the job training of persons with developmental disabilities. *Computers & Education*, 95, 328–339. DOI: 10.1016/j.compedu.2016.02.001

Kim, P., Hong, J. S., Bonk, C., & Lim, G. (2011). Effects of group reflection variations in project-based learning integrated in a Web 2.0 learning space. *Interactive Learning Environments*, 19(4), 333–349. DOI: 10.1080/10494820903210782

Kraus, S., Schleich, M., Tröster, A., & Roig-Tierno, N. (2019). Cultural diversity in large enterprises: A qualitative analysis from the Alpine Rhine Valley. *Journal of Promotion Management*, 25(5), 640–663. DOI: 10.1080/10496491.2019.1585570

Lavander, T. (2011). Video Games as Change Agents—The Case of Homeless: It's No Game | The Homeless Hub, McMaster. *Journal of Communication*, 7(1), 13–36.

Lavoué, E., Monterrat, B., Desmarais, M., & George, S. (2019). Adaptive Gamification for Learning Environments, in IEEE Transactions on Learning Technologies, 12(1), 16-28. .DOI: 10.1109/TLT.2018.2823710

Marquart-Pyatt, S. T. (2016). Environmental trust: A cross-region and cross-country study. *Society & Natural Resources*, 29(9), 1032–1048. DOI: 10.1080/08941920.2016.1164265

Meya, J. N., & Eisenack, K. (2018). Effectiveness of gaming for communicating and teaching climate change. *Climatic Change*, 149(3-4), 319–333. DOI: 10.1007/s10584-018-2254-7

Michael, D., & Chen, S. (2006). *Serious games: Games that educate, train, and inform.* Thomson Course Technology.

Modarelli, G. (2023). The "gaming society" between homologation and diversity: Trends, evolutions, perspectives and critical aspects of the fragmented self in organized and hyperlinked relations. *Journal of Organizational Culture Communications and Conflict*, 27(S3), 1–4.

Nah, F. F. H., Zeng, Q., Telaprolu, V. R., Ayyappa, A. P., & Eschenbrenner, B. (2014). Gamification of education: a review of literature. *HCI in Business: First International Conference, HCIB 2014, Held as Part of HCI International 2014, Heraklion, Crete, Greece, June 22-27, 2014Proceedings*, 1, 401–409.

Nguyen, C. T. (2017). Philosophy of games. Philosophy Compass, 12(8), e12426.
Noemí, P.M., & Máximo, S.H. (2014). Educational games for learning. *Universal Journal of Educational Research*, 2(3), 230–238.

Noemí, P. M., & Máximo, S. H. (2014). Educational games for learning. *Universal Journal of Educational Research*, 2(3), 230–238. DOI: 10.13189/ujer.2014.020305

Oblinger, D. G. (2004). The Next Generation of Educational Engagement. *Journal of Interactive Media in Education*, 8(1), 1–18. DOI: 10.5334/2004-8-oblinger

Patrick, H. A., & Kumar, V. R. (2012). Managing workplace diversity: Issues and challenges. *SAGE Open*, 2(2), 2158244012444615. DOI: 10.1177/2158244012444615

Pedersen, C., Togelius, J., & Yannakakis, G. N. (2010). Modeling player experience for content creation. *IEEE Transactions on Computational Intelligence and AI in Games*, 2(1), 54–67. DOI: 10.1109/TCIAIG.2010.2043950

Peng, W., Lee, M., & Heeter, C. (2010). The Effects of a Serious Game on Role-Taking and Willingness to Help. *Journal of Communication*, 60(4), 723–742. DOI: 10.1111/j.1460-2466.2010.01511.x

Peterková, J., Repaská, Z., & Prachařová, L. (2022). Best Practice of Using Digital Business Simulation Games in Business Education. *Sustainability (Basel)*, 14(15), 8987. DOI: 10.3390/su14158987

Petrov, A. (2014), Using Minecraft in Education: A Qualitative Study on Benefits and Challenges of Game-Based Education, TSpace Repository OISE, Master of Teaching Research Project, University of Toronto, https://hdl.handle.net/1807/67048

Pineda-Martínez, M., Llanos-Ruiz, D., Puente-Torre, P., & García-Delgado, M. Á. (2023). Impact of Video Games, Gamification, and Game-Based Learning on Sustainability Education in Higher Education. *Sustainability (Basel)*, 15(17), 13032. DOI: 10.3390/su151713032

Ponomareva, Y., Uman, T., Bodolica, V., & Wennberg, K. (2022). Cultural diversity in top management teams: Review and agenda for future research. *Journal of World Business*, 57(4), 101328. DOI: 10.1016/j.jwb.2022.101328

Porter, G. G. (2013). Minecraft for children with autism. Retrieved from Autism Key: https://www.autismkey.com/minecraft-for-children-with-autism/

Prado, A. M., Arce, R., Lopez, L. E., García, J., & Pearson, A. A. (2020). Simulations Versus Case Studies: Effectively Teaching the Premises of Sustainable Development in the Classroom. *Journal of Business Ethics*, 161(2), 303–327. DOI: 10.1007/s10551-019-04217-5

Rodela, R. (2013). The Social learning discourse: Trends, Themes and interdisciplinary influences in current research. *Environmental Science & Policy*, 25, 157–166. DOI: 10.1016/j.envsci.2012.09.002

Rosati, F., & Faria, L. G. D. (2019). Business contribution to the Sustainable Development Agenda: Organizational factors related to early adoption of SDG reporting. *Corporate Social Responsibility and Environmental Management*, 26(3), 588–597. DOI: 10.1002/csr.1705

Schrader, C. (2023). Serious games and game-based learning. In *Handbook of Open, Distance and Digital Education* (pp. 1255–1268). Springer Nature Singapore. DOI: 10.1007/978-981-19-2080-6_74

Seaborn, K., & Fels, D. I. (2015). Gamification in theory and action: A survey. *International Journal of Human-Computer Studies*, 74, 14–31. DOI: 10.1016/j.ijhcs.2014.09.006

Selwyn, N., & Facer, K. (2007). Beyond the digital divide: Rethinking digital inclusion for the 21st century.

Shliakhovchuk, E. (2018). Using Video Games in Intercultural, Diversity and Inclusive Education. *11th Annual International Conference of Education, Research and Innovation*, 10326–10336. DOI: 10.21125/iceri.2018.0946

Sinicropi, S., & Cortese, D. (2021). (Re) Thinking diversity within sustainable development: A systematic mapping study. *Corporate Social Responsibility and Environmental Management*, 28(1), 299–309. DOI: 10.1002/csr.2050

Stanitsas, M., Kirytopoulos, K., & Vareilles, E. (2019). Facilitating sustainability transition through serious games: A systematic literature review. *Journal of Cleaner Production*, 208, 924–936. DOI: 10.1016/j.jclepro.2018.10.157

Tanner, C., Schmocker, D., Katsarov, J., & Christen, M. (2022). Educating moral sensitivity in business: An experimental study to evaluate the effectiveness of a serious moral game. *Computers & Education*, 178, 104381. Advance online publication. DOI: 10.1016/j.compedu.2021.104381

Toda, A. M., Valle, P. H., & Isotani, S. (2017). The dark side of gamification: An overview of negative effects of gamification in education. In *Researcher links workshop: higher education for all* (pp. 143–156). Springer International Publishing.

United Nations. (2018). The World's Future – A Sustainable Development Goals Game that highlights the interlinkages among the SDGs and targets. Available at: https://sdgs.un.org/partnerships/worlds-future-sustainable-development-goals-game-highlights-interlinkages-among-sdgs

Waldman, D. A., & Sparr, J. L. (2023). Rethinking diversity strategies: An application of paradox and positive organization behavior theories. *The Academy of Management Perspectives*, 37(2), 174–192. DOI: 10.5465/amp.2021.0183

Walsh, D. (2009, April). Wii can do it: Using co-design for creating an instructional game. In *Proceedings of the CHI 2009*, Boston, MA DOI: 10.1145/1520340.1520722

Williams, D. A., & Wade-Golden, K. C. (2023). *The chief diversity officer: Strategy structure, and change management*. Taylor & Francis.

Wouters, P., van Nimwegen, C., van Oostendorp, H., & van der Spek, E. D. (2013). A meta-analysis of the cognitive and motivational effects of serious games. *Journal of Educational Psychology*, 105(2), 249–265. DOI: 10.1037/a0031311

Zichermann, G., & Cunningham, C. (2011). *Gamification by design: Implementing game mechanics in web and mobile apps*. O'Reilly Media, Inc.

Zimmerman, E., & Chaplin, H. (2013, September 9). Manifesto: The 21st century will be defined by games. Retrieved from: https://kotaku.com/manifesto-the-21st-century-will-be-defined-by-games-1275355204

Zyda, M. J. (2005). From visual simulation to virtual reality to games. *Computer*, 38(9), 25–32. DOI: 10.1109/MC.2005.297

ENDNOTE

1 Although the term serious game is widely used, European Commission (2012) proposes to substitute it with the other one *special-purpose games* referring to games developed for a particular purpose beyond entertainment. According to European experts, this option would allow to overcome the idea that traditional commercial games are not able to produce learning outcomes nor engagement.

Chapter 3
Gamification Against Inequalities at Work: A Systematic Literature Review

Valentina Toscano
https://orcid.org/0009-0008-9076-0535
University of Milano-Bicocca, Italy

ABSTRACT

The chapter investigates the potential of gamification as a tool for enhancing employees' well-being, inclusion, and equality in corporate environments. A systematic literature review was performed according to the PRISMA methodology, and 348 documents from the Scopus database and 262 from Web of Science were screened, resulting in 12 studies that met the criteria for inclusion. The results suggest that gamification can positively impact businesses by enhancing employee engagement, discussion, motivation, and performance, thus contributing to a more inclusive and equal work environment. Nonetheless, it highlights the need for more robust empirical research to validate the positive effects of gamification and guide its practical implementation in workplaces, also considering its relevance in pursuing the Sustainable Development Goals of 2030 Agenda, in particular SDG 8: Decent Work and Economic Growth.

1. INTRODUCTION

According to the literature, employee well-being concerns the positive feelings, perceptions, and sentiments that arise in employees during their working activities. It takes the form of personal satisfaction derived from the job, which leads to a good mood, cognitive assessment, meaningful work, and involvement (Molnár et

DOI: 10.4018/979-8-3693-1172-1.ch003

al., 2024). Rajashekar and Jain (2024) analyzed the concept of holistic wellbeing, showing how it is composed of five different dimensions: physical wellbeing, social wellbeing, financial wellbeing, spiritual wellbeing, and psychological wellbeing, the latter in turn composed of mental and emotional wellbeing. All of the previous dimensions are very significant for employees, and organizations must be able to put appropriate actions in place for them all to be promoted and achieved. Indeed, management literature highlights how workers' holistic well-being is essential for firms to increase their productivity and revenues, ensuring subsequent company success, economic growth, and resilience (Park et al., 2022; Rajashekar & Jain, 2024).

Social well-being directly affects the relationships between employees. In order to achieve this, companies need to encourage employee bonding by fostering interactions among them, offering team-building activities, and encouraging mutual support and inclusion (Rajashekar & Jain, 2024). To this end, organizations are called upon to introduce emotional management approaches based on reciprocal respect that effectively foster employee cooperation (Mayr & Teller, 2024). In particular, this can be achieved through socialization activities organized and facilitated by managers with the support of the workforce itself, which can also be effective for including workers with disabilities (Sanclemente et al., 2024). Inclusion also turns out to be a key element not only for its positive influence on employee engagement and productivity, but also because it fosters the exchange of ideas and the development of innovative approaches to managing and solving problems (Groenewald, 2024). Although, however, a commitment on behalf of businesses in this area has been detected, it is evident that achieving this well-being and inclusion is still a significant challenge for them, which even now daily interface with issues of work-life balance, discrimination, or inequality (Bapuji et al., 2024; Feagin & Eckberg, 1980; Hebl et al., 2020; Triana et al., 2021).

These concerns have also been emphasized in the United Nations 2030 Agenda. As a matter of fact, they have been included in the Sustainable Development Goals (SDGs) being pursued globally, particularly in SDG 8 - *Promote sustained, inclusive, and sustainable economic growth, full and productive employment, and decent work for all.* In detail, this SDG aims, among other goals, to ensure fair treatment and pay equity for all employees doing equal work: women and men, including young people and people with disabilities. In order to pursue this goal, companies are therefore called upon to adopt a diversity management policy - targeting women, young people, and disadvantaged groups - to ensure equal development and career opportunities for the entire workforce. It is, therefore, essential for companies to train their Human Resources departments on issues of anti-discrimination and promoting inclusion, so that hiring evaluations or the definition of contractual aspects transcend factors such as gender, age, geographic origin of the worker, and, more generally, any personal and non-professional characteristics (United Nations General Assembly, 2015).

However, it is still very complex for businesses to tackle those issues (Ligorio et al., 2023) even though they have started implementing several policies (Gazzola et al., 2020; Mariappanadar, 2024) in order to improve diversity and inclusion within their workplaces (Anand & Winters, 2008). In this concern, there are many ways in which these goals could be achieved, and among them, the use of gamification can be identified (Modarelli, 2023; Tomé Klock et al., 2024). Games allow for a different - more playful - approach to serious and complex topics and can be used in various contexts, whether educational or not (Meshcheryakova & Hemmert, 2023). Therefore, the potential of gamification can also be exploited within business contexts, where it can be introduced to address contemporary problems, such as inclusion and diversity (Oprescu et al., 2014).

In the managerial literature, gamification is a relatively young field of research (Rauschenberger et al., 2019). In particular, the topic is addressed mainly from the perspective of education, where the game is intended as a tool that is capable of improving the cognitive and learning process, both for employees and students of all ages, including those with disabilities (Afyouni et al., 2017; Arias Aranda et al., 2016; Cardona-Reyes et al., 2021; Lier & Breuer, 2020; Lyons et al., 2023; Rauschenberger et al., 2019). However, it almost lacks an analysis of gamification in the corporate context for pursuing sustainability goals, particularly those related to employee well-being, equality, and inclusion (Owen, 2017). This research is set in this context, and its objective is to understand how, in the academic literature, gamification as a tool to achieve employee inclusion and workers' well-being in the corporate context has already been analyzed, studied, and discussed.

The chapter is structured as follows: after outlining the theoretical background of using gamification in the business context in section 2, the research methodology is presented in section 3. The results of the performed systematic literature review are treated in section 4. Finally, section 5 contains a discussion of the collected results, the conclusions of the research, and some ideas for further studies on the topic.

2. THEORETICAL BACKGROUND

Gamification can be defined as the application of game-design elements and game principles in non-game contexts (Timbó et al., 2019). It represents a relatively novel concept and can be used in different social and business settings to influence individual behaviors and skills (Buckley et al., 2019). Indeed, by using game-based learning, it is possible to spread specific knowledge to new learners who actively participate in the game (Pellicone et al., 2022), who are proven to have with this method higher understanding levels of concepts (Dixit et al., 2018). Gamification can also be used as a means of inclusion and to decrease environmental barriers, thanks to the easier accessibility of games for people with disabilities (Sousa, 2020). Digitalization and gamification can also be implemented for the pursuit of the SDGs for the education and dissemination of computational thinking (Soboleva et al., 2021), first and foremost among those who are in charge of preparing strategies and putting in place actions aimed at the achievement of sustainability goals (Mylonas et al., 2023). The prominence given to these issues at the international level should increase awareness regarding their seriousness, both on the part of citizens and businesses, in order to emphasize the need to adopt an active collaborative approach and identify appropriate solutions (Capellán-Pérez et al., 2019) to those "wicked" problems (Morini et al., 2022). Indeed, given the magnitude and relevance of the SDGs, a joint collective action to achieve them, involving the entire community, is essential. Therefore, awareness of sustainability issues and learning through games must be extended to the entire society, comprehending the public sector, companies, and private citizens (Chen & Ho, 2022). Previous studies have also shown how gamification systems can effectively motivate individuals to achieve specific goals, improving their ability to carry out certain tasks (Stefan et al., 2019).

Thus, the benefits of using games are manifold. Focusing on the business context, they can be summarized in efficient recruitment (Siala et al., 2020), improved customer service offerings (Calandra et al., 2024), employee training and education, including sustainability, and support for inclusion and skill enhancement, such as collaborative and cooperative work (Aggrawal & Boowuo, 2023; Pineda-Martínez et al., 2023). In particular, they can be used to sensitize employees of different ages, backgrounds, biographies, and characteristics to tolerance of differences and to build a peaceful, stimulating, and sustainable work environment. Gamification, because of its characteristics, thus turns out to be a tool that can be used in the pursuit of SDG 8, which aims precisely at ensuring equity and inclusion of employees (Brauner & Ziefle, 2022; Modarelli et al., 2024).

However, the introduction of gaming within the business organization requires not only a high economic investment but also a radical change in processes, with investment in e-tools aimed at innovation (Hjalager et al., 2022) and corporate mindset (Ligorio et al., 2023). Indeed, for the implementation of a gamification platform to be effective, all the components of the organization must be willing to cooperate and have active cognitive, emotional, and behavioral involvement. It is relevant, therefore, in order to achieve the common goal, that these individuals are mentally and actively engaged as they actually believe in what is required (Dyer, 2021). Gamification can also help balance intrinsic and extrinsic motivational drivers, which is essential for pursuing business, economic, social, and environmental goals (Haque et al., 2024).

However, companies can also encounter some difficulties in applying gamification in their context, particularly among experienced workers, pre-retirement-age employees, and pensioners, who are reluctant to introduce gaming methods into their professional activities. Indeed, they are used to carrying out their work activities systematically without using technology and are sometimes averse to change (Liang et al., 2011). Moreover, given the little empirical work already done regarding the benefits of applying gamification in business settings, there is still little recognition of its validity and efficiency (Seaborn & Fels, 2015).

3. METHODOLOGY

To achieve the research aim, it was decided to perform a systematic literature review, following the instructions and checklists disclosed in the PRISMA (Preferred Reporting Items for Systematic Reviews and Meta-Analyses) Statement (Page et al., 2021). This methodology is considered appropriate for achieving the research objective because it "*can provide syntheses of the state of knowledge in a field, from which future research priorities can be identified*" (Page et al., 2021: 1). The literature review includes the documents collected on the Scopus database, owned by Elsevier, and on Web of Science, owned by Thomson Reuters, selected because they include international documents published in numerous indexed scientific journals, which are evaluated through peer-review processes and published for their rigor and relevance for the scientific community (Ayala et al., 2020). To determine the relevant documents for the present study – the ones that offer contributions that deal with the sustainable topics of inclusion, diversity, disability, and fighting inequalities in the work environment using gamification - the following query was used on the databases:

TITLE-ABS-KEY ("Sustainable Development Goals" OR "SDG*" OR "divers*" OR "disabilit*" OR "inequalit*" OR "inclusi*") AND TITLE-ABS-KEY ("gamification" OR "game-bas*" OR "game bas*") AND TITLE-ABS-KEY ("work*" OR "business*" OR "organis*" OR "organiz*")

The results obtained from the Scopus database search were limited to documents published in the subject areas of "Social Sciences" and "Business, Management & Accounting" and written in English. The result of the query is 348 documents. Instead, concerning Web of Science, results were limited to the Social Sciences Citation Index (SSCI) Core collection and written in English, resulting in 262 documents. The 610 documents were screened to identify and analyze more in-depth only those that consistently deal with the research aim of this work, according to the following process.

After excluding 79 duplicate items, the first step related to screening involved reading the remaining 531 abstracts. Only the papers whose abstracts contained references to the conduct of a study on the use of gaming in work settings to increase the well-being, inclusion, and equality of employees passed the screening process. Therefore, papers with studies that analyzed gamification's effects on student learning were excluded. Learning was considered only concerning the corporate context, long-life learning was excluded, as well as documents examining the use of gamification in dealing with external parties, such as stakeholders. Given the few documents identified, all sources (journal articles, books, book chapters, or conference proceedings) were considered.

The first screening phase resulted in 39 documents being assessed for eligibility and subjected to full-paper screening. The inclusion criteria remained the same. Again, 27 papers were excluded because the research they reported was not deemed valid to answer the research question. Specifically, two papers dealt only partially with gamification; two did not have employees as the subject of the study; five did not refer to the business context; and 18 did not focus on gamification to ensure employees' inclusion or equality. This resulted in 12 studies, which were included in the literature review.

The inclusion process just described is summarized and depicted in Figure 1.

Figure 1. PRISMA 2020 flow diagram for systematic reviews (Page et al., 2021)

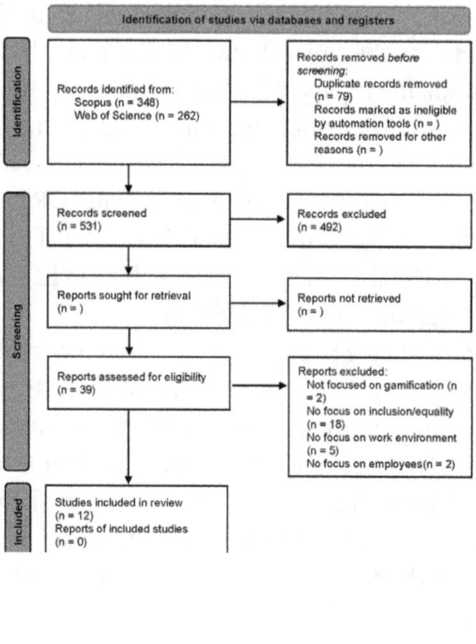

4. RESULTS

Table 1 represents the list of studies included in the review, including their authors, and places of publication. What emerges is that 2 of them were published in conference proceedings, while the rest were included in journals from different disciplines: one from education, one from human-centered IT, two from innovation, four from management, and two from engineering.

Table 1. Included studies

Title	Authors	Place of publication
Best practices for deploying digital games for personal empowerment and social inclusion	(Bleumers et al., 2013)	Proceedings of the 7th European Conference on Games Based Learning, ECGBL 2013
Designing mini-games as micro-learning resources for professional development in multi-cultural organizations	(Arnab et al., 2021)	Electronic Journal of e-Learning
Escaping generational conflict: using gamification to examine intergenerational communication & problem-solving	(Richards et al., 2024)	Review of Managerial Science
Gamification and resource pooling for improving operational efficiency and effective management of human resources: A case study with an ecommerce company	(Prasad et al., 2019)	International Journal of Management
Gamification in Dutch Businesses: An Explorative Case Study	(Van der Heijden et al., 2020)	SAGE Open
Gamification in for-profit organizations: A mapping study	(Szendrői et al., 2020)	Business: Theory and Practice

continued on following page

Table 1. Continued

Title	Authors	Place of publication
Gamification in Management: analysis and research directions	(Wanick & Bui, 2019)	International Journal of Serious Games
Gamification of query-driven knowledge sharing systems	(Van Toorn et al., 2022)	Behavior & Information Technology
Improving Inclusivity of Digitalization for Employees in Emerging Countries Using Gamification	(Behl et al., 2022)	IEEE Transactions on Engineering Management
Leveling up in corporate training: Unveiling the power of gamification to enhance knowledge retention, knowledge sharing, and job performance	(Capatina et al., 2024)	Journal of Innovation & Knowledge
Organizing employee-driven innovation (EDI) through game-based formats: Understanding participation	(Mosleh et al., 2024)	Creativity and Innovation Management
Tackling implicit and explicit bias through games that teach workplace diversity	(Himmelstein & Gopalakrishnan, 2017)	Proceedings of the 11th European Conference on Games Based Learning, ECGBL 2017

Source: Elaboration by the author

Moreover, the trend of documents published per year depicted in Figure 2 shows that the number of scientific publications regarding the present research topic is decidedly meager. The trend is not constant, and it can be noticed that for several years there was no publication on the theme (years 2014-2018, except for 2018), demonstrating how the theme was not yet considered relevant by the scientific community. As of 2019, the number of publications appears to have increased slightly, with the maximum number reached in 2024, being 3.

Figure 2. Number of published documents per year (Elaboration by the author)

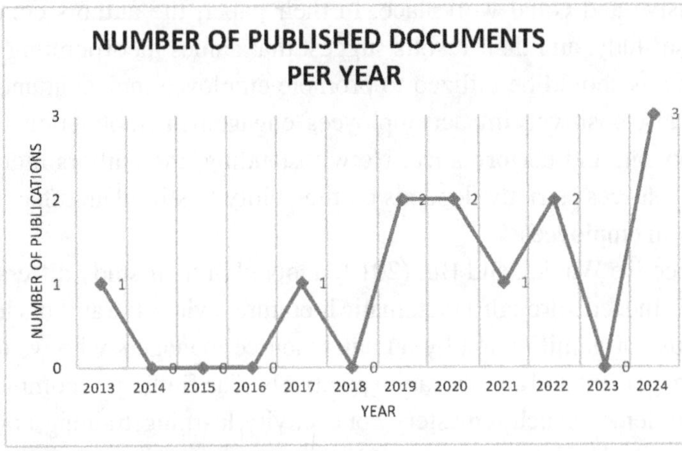

The contents and contributions of the 12 studies included in the systematic literature review are outlined in the following paragraphs.

In their research, Bleumers et al. (2013) examine the use of digital games for personal empowerment and social inclusion, emphasizing the necessity of balancing enjoyment, learning, and usability in game design. Through the analysis of seven projects representing different application domains of empowerment and inclusion, the authors affirm that digital games could effectively promote inclusion and equality among employees. Indeed, applying gamification in workplaces can boost engagement, motivation, and productivity, foster a sense of achievement, collaboration, and skill development, and improve employees' job satisfaction. According to the authors, the introduction of games could have a positive impact on an organization in terms of support for migrant integration, for marginalized young people, and for improving the quality of life of older people.

A few years later, Himmelstein and Gopalakrishnan (2017) performed a study focused on promoting the dialogue between employees about diversity and inclusion to increase them through the exchange of opinions. According to the authors, this could be realized by developing and testing game prototypes designed to stimulate employee discussions, encouraging them to explore different viewpoints and confront issues such as implicit bias, workplace conflicts, and disability. Indeed, workers can speak or behave freely during games in ways that are not always socially acceptable under other circumstances, increasing the discussion quality. Iterative prototyping and playtesting were employed in this research to gain insights into users' mental models and attitudes and develop game concepts.

According to Prasad et al. (2019), implementing gamification techniques in a working environment increases employee engagement and contributes to creating a more inclusive and equal workplace. In their paper, the authors conducted an empirical case study, and their results suggest that games incorporating challenge and fun elements should be utilized to promote employee inclusion and equality. Games could also positively impact employees' engagement, motivation, teamwork, skill development, and performance. Notwithstanding, the authors highlight that gamification's success strictly depends on the ability to stimulate effective behavioral changes in employees.

The perspective Wanick and Bui (2019) adopted in their study differs from the previous ones. Indeed, through a systematic literature review, the authors investigate the possible use of gamification by human resource managers who want to affect employee engagement and collaboration positively. The findings recommend incorporating game elements such as mastery, connectivity, learning, training, competition, rewards, points, and badges to boost employee inclusion and equality. For workers, gamification can lead to higher job satisfaction, enjoyment, skill development, and recognition opportunities.

Instead, Van der Heijden et al. (2020) focus on achieving employee career sustainability. The authors conducted an exploratory case study highlighting the connection between gamification theory and its possible practical applications. They suggest that gamification can enhance employees' satisfaction and career potential by fulfilling their psychological needs for competence in the workplace. They emphasize that managers should use games to match individual employee needs and preferences, to promote a supportive environment that provides ample resources to increase the workers' health, happiness, and productivity (i.e., their career sustainability).

Similarly, Szendrői et al. (2020) focus on the broader impacts of gamification in human resource management. The authors conducted a systematic mapping study to gather their results and affirm that gamification in the workplace can offer numerous benefits, including increased employee motivation, performance and learning outcomes, improved business processes, more efficient recruitment, and better job satisfaction and well-being.

Arnab et al. (2021) highlight the positive impact of using gamification by designing mini-games as micro-learning resources for addressing cultural risks in multicultural organizations. These mini-games facilitate reflection, practice, and self-assessment, aiding employees in developing critical competencies for practical work in diverse environments. The authors conducted a two-step testing process to gather feedback on the interactive resources complementing the online educational platform. They suggest that more straightforward yet interactive mini-games, such as quizzes or word cluster games, should be employed in working environments to promote inclusion and equality. According to the authors, gamification in the workplace can improve teamwork, problem-solving skills, and overall job satisfaction while providing a more enjoyable and interactive skill and knowledge acquisition method, consequently enhancing performance and productivity.

In their research, Behl et al. (2022) focus on how gamification can improve employee satisfaction, motivation, and engagement in digital transformation. The authors conducted a cross-sectional study using data collected by administering questionnaires to retail firm employees. They propose the use of gamification as a form of digitalization. Through their study, they show how gamification offers several benefits in working environments: it enhances employee motivation and engagement; it fosters a learning culture by identifying and addressing knowledge gaps and streamlining repetitive training programs; it supports team building, collaboration, and inclusion; it helps alleviate stress and pressure; it leads to better job performance and increased employees' satisfaction and wellbeing.

Instead, Van Toorn et al. (2022) analyze the applicability of gamification for improving knowledge reuse in Query-Driven knowledge-sharing systems (QKSS), which are knowledge repositories that gather domain expertise from an organization's data sources and provide relevant commentary. Through an experiment organized in collaboration with a Sydney-based data analytics firm, the authors showed that using social gamification elements can substantially improve the effective use of data analytics systems. Moreover, in using games, the authors noted that participants reduce information barriers, increase positive knowledge-sharing behavior, and create a feeling of connectedness between them. This behavior favors inclusion and well-being and helps foster a sense of organizational identity.

Richards et al. (2024) conducted content and thematic analysis to examine the impact of gamification on intergenerational team dynamics. They suggest that gamification can be used for training in workplaces with intergenerational diversity to enhance team communication and performance. In particular, they used escape room games to verify the increase in employee inclusion and equality. According to the authors, incorporating gamification in the workplace can provide several benefits for both companies and employees because it facilitates communication and collaboration between workers, reinforces the effectiveness of diversity training, helps understand generational preferences and different communication styles, and leads to more effective inclusion and engagement.

Capatina et al. (2024) also address the issue of knowledge sharing through gaming in their research. In particular, by applying a mixed-methods approach – which involved collecting quantitative data from surveys conducted with learners who attended gamified training sessions, and qualitative insights from experimental research based on eye-tracking technology - the authors studied the effectiveness of gamification techniques in corporate training. The results show how gamification promotes active engagement in the learning process and facilitates deeper assimilation of information, which is crucial for long-term knowledge retention. In addition, the social interactions that occur during the game lead employees to better engage with each other and increase mutual trust. Reflected in the working context, this fosters employee rapprochement and greater inclusion.

Lastly, Mosleh et al. (2024) analyzed the use of game-based formats to enhance employee participation in innovation and strategy-making. They perform a qualitative study based on coding, condensation, and interpretation of empirical material concerning a large European IT organization. Through this research, the authors proved that organizations could use games to foster employee collaboration and teamwork. Moreover, they can be considered a relevant tool to increase trust and communication amongst team members, increase employee inclusion and well-being, and lead to more effective collaboration and problem-solving across the organization.

The contributions of the 12 selected documents on increasing equality and diversity in workplaces through gamification are summarized in Table 2.

Table 2. Contribution of the included studies

Title	Authors	Contribution
Best practices for deploying digital games for personal empowerment and social inclusion	(Bleumers et al., 2013)	The introduction of digital games could have a positive impact on an organization in terms of support for migrant integration, for marginalized young people, and for improving the life quality of older people.
Designing mini-games as micro-learning resources for professional development in multi-cultural organizations	(Arnab et al., 2021)	Gamification in the workplace can improve teamwork, problem-solving skills, and overall job satisfaction while providing a more enjoyable and interactive skill and knowledge acquisition method, consequently enhancing performance and productivity.
Escaping generational conflict: using gamification to examine intergenerational communication & problem-solving	(Richards et al., 2024)	Incorporating gamification in the workplace can facilitate communication and collaboration between workers, reinforce the effectiveness of diversity training, help understand generational preferences and different communication styles, and lead to more effective inclusion and engagement.
Gamification and resource pooling for improving operational efficiency and effective management of human resources: A case study with an ecommerce company	(Prasad et al., 2019)	Games incorporating challenge and fun elements can positively impact employees' engagement, motivation, teamwork, skill development, performance, inclusion, and equality.
Gamification in Dutch Businesses: An Explorative Case Study	(Van der Heijden et al., 2020)	Gamification can enhance employees' satisfaction and career potential by fulfilling their psychological needs for competence in the workplace. Their use promotes a supportive environment that can increase the workers' health, happiness, and productivity (i.e., career sustainability).
Gamification in for-profit organizations: A mapping study	(Szendrői et al., 2020)	Gamification in the workplace can increase employee motivation, performance, and learning outcomes and improve business processes, recruitment, job satisfaction, and well-being.
Gamification in Management: analysis and research directions	(Wanick & Bui, 2019)	Incorporating game elements such as mastery, connectivity, learning, training, competition, rewards, points, and badges boosts employee inclusion and equality.

Title	Authors	Contribution
Gamification of query-driven knowledge sharing systems	(Van Toorn et al., 2022)	In using games, participants reduce information barriers, increase positive knowledge-sharing behavior, and create a feeling of connectedness. This favors inclusion and well-being and helps foster a sense of organizational identity.
Improving Inclusivity of Digitalization for Employees in Emerging Countries Using Gamification	(Behl et al., 2022)	Gamification offers several benefits in working environments: it enhances employee motivation and engagement; it fosters a learning culture; it supports team building, collaboration, and inclusion; it helps alleviate stress and pressure; it leads to better job performance and increased employees' satisfaction and wellbeing.
Leveling up in corporate training: Unveiling the power of gamification to enhance knowledge retention, knowledge sharing, and job performance	(Capatina et al., 2024)	The social interactions that occur during games lead employees to better engage with each other and increase mutual trust. This fosters rapprochement among employees and greater inclusion.
Organizing employee-driven innovation (EDI) through game-based formats: Understanding participation	(Mosleh et al., 2024)	Games can be used in organizations to foster collaboration and teamwork among employees. They can also be considered a relevant tool to increase trust and communication amongst team members, increase employee inclusion and well-being, and lead to more effective collaboration and problem-solving across the organization.
Tackling implicit and explicit bias through games that teach workplace diversity	(Himmelstein & Gopalakrishnan, 2017)	Game prototypes can stimulate employee discussions because workers perceive higher freedom of expression during games. This can encourage them to explore different viewpoints and confront issues such as implicit bias, workplace conflicts, and disability, increasing the discussion quality.

Source: Elaboration by the author

5. DISCUSSION AND CONCLUSION

In the current chapter, a systematic literature review was performed to outline state of the art in scientific literature on the topic of increasing inclusion and equality in working environments through the use of gamification. The result of the paper screening process led to the identification of only 12 papers that answered the research question, published between 2013 and July 2024 (Figure 2). Notably, it is evident that the analyzed topic is still underexplored, with the total number of scholarly publications concerning it being low. However, the academic community's interest in this topic seems to have been increasing since 2019, when annual publications have risen. In addition, the study shows that the maximum number of papers on the topic was published in 2024. This data is very interesting, especially since, at the time of writing this chapter, 2024 is still in the course; therefore, this data could change positively by the end of the year.

Furthermore, it is also worth pointing out that the reviewed studies are heterogeneous. The documents span various disciplines, including management, education, engineering, IT, and innovation, and are published mainly in academic journals and partially in conference proceedings. This diversity underscores the multidisciplinary interest in gamification and highlights a fragmented study approach. Moreover, the reviewed studies varied significantly in their focus, methodologies, and depth of analysis, making it challenging to cluster the findings into cohesive themes. Indeed, although all studies support the thesis that gamification positively affects employee inclusion, equality, and well-being, the approaches that are used to make that contribution and the perspectives analyzed differ significantly.

In particular, Wanick & Bui (2019) and Szendrői et al. (2020) conducted literature reviews focusing on the relevance of the role played by human resource managers in increasing employee inclusion and well-being through the use of gaming. In detail, in the first case, the authors investigate which elements must necessarily be included in games for them to be effective for this purpose; in the second, instead, the authors focused on identifying the benefits that gamification can provide in the business context.

The remaining ten studies adopted an empirical approach, and their contributions were derived from conducting practical research. In particular, the study by Van der Heijden et al. (2020) shows how gaming can be considered a tool that positively affects the psychological well-being of the employee individually, as it allows him or her to understand what his or her needs actually are, and to suggest the most effective actions to be implemented in order to achieve his or her goals. By contrast, the one by Bleumers et al. (2013) is the only included study to specifically emphasize the relevance of gamification as a tool that increases ethnic and minority inclusion in the corporate setting.

On the other hand, the theme most discussed among the papers included in the review is the use of gaming to enable moments of constructive dialogue and exchange among employees, which allows for increased inclusion and the consequent higher well-being of workers. In this regard, Himmelstein and Gopalakrishnan (2017) highlight how discussion is an indispensable tool for ensuring inclusion in the corporate context but that it is often limited because of people's fear of judgment from others. Therefore, gaming, during which participants can feel more freedom to express themselves, can be used to address this limitation. The same concept is supported by Van Toorn et al. (2022), who point out that gamification allows for lowering information barriers and increasing opportunities for discussion and connection among employees. According to Richards et al. (2024), moreover, employees who collaborate, compare, and communicate to achieve a common goal during the game are more likely to recreate the same dynamic when performing work activities. This is also confirmed by Arnab et al. (2021), according to which games can be used to facilitate confrontation and interaction among employees, positively influencing their inclusion, and by Capatina et al. (2024), according to whom the social interaction that takes place during the game allows employees to apprehend others' opinions better, lowering communication barriers.

Behl et al. (2022) and Mosleh et al. (2024) do not place gaming at the center of their studies, but nonetheless, they cross-over highlight the benefits of its use in the workplace context. Indeed, in the first case, the authors see gamification as a tool that is part of an organization's broader and necessary digitization process. It is seen as a means offered to employees that allows them to learn more efficiently and dynamically, with less effort, thus achieving the desired results faster and with greater satisfaction, thereby generating positive emotions and increasing well-being. The second study, on the other hand, does not consider gamification as a process directly aimed at inclusion, but as a tool to encourage employee dialogue and exchange of ideas to generate innovation. However, this collaboration positively influences employee relations, leading to achieving a higher level of inclusion within the organization.

Finally, Prasad et al. (2019) through their study emphasize the strong limitation that gamification has in pursuing the goal of greater inclusion and well-being: the ability to change workers' mindsets and behavior, so that they are more predisposed to discussion, dialogue, and creating a positive and inclusive working environment.

The existing studies, albeit scarce, collectively suggest that gamification can positively impact businesses by enhancing employee engagement, discussion, motivation, and performance, thus contributing to a more inclusive and equal working environment (Mayr & Teller, 2024; Park et al., 2022; Rajashekar & Jain, 2024). Gamification can thus be seen as a valuable and innovative tool for the pursuit of the SDGs of the 2030 Agenda, particularly SDG 8 (Brauner & Ziefle, 2022; Modarelli et al., 2024; Soboleva et al., 2021).

Notwithstanding, one notable gap that emerges from the current study is the scarce attention given to the use of gaming to pursue greater inclusion of people with disabilities in working contexts. As a matter of fact, despite the recognized potential of gamification to foster inclusivity, particularly for individuals with disabilities (Sanclemente et al., 2024), none of the reviewed studies specifically addressed this issue, which could represent an important area for future research.

Moreover, considering that the positive findings obtained are primarily based on theoretical discussions, case studies, and preliminary empirical evidence, a need for more robust empirical research could be highlighted to validate these claims and advance the understanding and implementation of gamification in corporate settings. Future research could indeed explore the managerial and organizational roles that gaming can play, study the dynamics, and best practices of gamification in working environments, and document case studies that illustrate its effectiveness (or eventual ineffectiveness). Additionally, a greater emphasis on longitudinal studies could offer insights into the long-term impacts of gamification on employee well-being and workplace equality.

The contribution of this chapter lies in providing an overview of the current state of the art in literature on the use of gamification to improve workers' well-being and reduce inequalities. Altogether, from the systematic literature review conducted, it emerges that the application of gamification in the corporate context for enhancing

REFERENCES

Afyouni, I., Rehman, F. U., Qamar, A. M., Ghani, S., Hussain, S. O., Sadiq, B., Rahman, M. A., Murad, A., & Basalamah, S. (2017). A therapy-driven gamification framework for hand rehabilitation. *User Modeling and User-Adapted Interaction, 27*(2), 215–265. Advance online publication. DOI: 10.1007/s11257-017-9191-4

Aggrawal, S., & Boowuo, H. (2023). Enhancing Teamwork Through Games: A Systematic Literature Review. *Proc. Front. Educ. Conf. FIE*. DOI: 10.1109/FIE58773.2023.10343284

Anand, R., & Winters, M.-F. (2008). A Retrospective View of Corporate Diversity Training From 1964 to the Present. *Academy of Management Learning & Education*, 7(3), 356–372. DOI: 10.5465/amle.2008.34251673

Arias Aranda, D., Bustinza Sánchez, O. F., & Djundubaev, R. (2016). Effects of gamified business simulations on entrepreneurial attitude at high school level. *Revista de Educacion, 2016*(371), 126–149. *Scopus*. Advance online publication. DOI: 10.4438/1988-592X-RE-2015-371-311

Arnab, S., Walaszczyk, L., Lewis, M., Kernaghan-Andrews, S., Loizou, M., Masters, A., Calderwood, J., & Clarke, S. (2021). Designing mini-games as micro-learning resources for professional development in multi-cultural organisations. *Electronic Journal of e-Learning*, 19(2), 44–58. DOI: 10.34190/ejel.19.2.2141

Ayala, I., Cuenca-Amigo, M., & Cuenca, J. (2020). Examining the state of the art of audience development in museums and heritage organisations: A Systematic Literature review. *Museum Management and Curatorship*, 35(3), 306–327. DOI: 10.1080/09647775.2019.1698312

Bapuji, H., Ertug, G., Soundararajan, V., & Shaw, J. D. (2024). Invisible Inequalities: Barriers, Challenges, and Opportunities. *Journal of Management*, 50(3), 835–848. DOI: 10.1177/01492063231205294

Behl, A., Pereira, V., Sindhwani, R., Bhardwaj, S., Papa, A., & Hassan, Y. (2022). Improving Inclusivity of Digitalization for Employees in Emerging Countries Using Gamification. *IEEE Transactions on Engineering Management*, 1–15. Advance online publication. DOI: 10.1109/TEM.2022.3216553

Bleumers, L., Mariën, I., Looy, J. V., Stewart, J., Schurmans, D., & All, A. (2013). Best practices for deploying digital games for personal empowerment and social inclusion. *Eur. Conf. Game. Base. Learn., 1*, 53–61. https://www.scopus.com/inward/record.uri?eid=2-s2.0-84893696104&partnerID=40&md5=9af6dc0cd58bff46acb2e3d169531943

Brauner, P., & Ziefle, M. (2022). Beyond playful learning – Serious games for the human-centric digital transformation of production and a design process model. *Technology in Society*, 71, 102140. Advance online publication. DOI: 10.1016/j.techsoc.2022.102140

Buckley, P., Noonan, S., Geary, C., MacKessy, T., & Nagle, E. (2019). An empirical study of gamification frameworks. *Journal of Organizational and End User Computing, 31*(1), 22–38. Advance online publication. DOI: 10.4018/JOEUC.2019010102

Calandra, D., Oppioli, M., Sadraei, R., Jafari-Sadeghi, V., & Biancone, P. P. (2024). Metaverse meets digital entrepreneurship: A practitioner-based qualitative synthesis. *International Journal of Entrepreneurial Behaviour and Research, 30*(2–3), 666–686. Advance online publication. DOI: 10.1108/IJEBR-01-2023-0041

Capatina, A., Juarez-Varon, D., Micu, A., & Micu, A. (2024). Leveling up in corporate training: Unveiling the power of gamification to enhance knowledge retention, knowledge sharing, and job performance. *Journal of Innovation & Knowledge*, 9(3), 100530. Advance online publication. DOI: 10.1016/j.jik.2024.100530

Capellán-Pérez, I., Álvarez-Antelo, D., & Miguel, L. J. (2019). Global sustainability crossroads: A participatory simulation game to educate in the energy and sustainability challenges of the 21st century. *Sustainability (Basel)*, 11(13), 3672. Advance online publication. DOI: 10.3390/su11133672

Cardona-Reyes, H., Trujillo-Espinoza, C., Arevalo-Mercado, C., & Muñoz-Arteaga, J. (2021). Training of Drone Pilots through Virtual Reality Environments under the Gamification Approach in a University Context. *Interaction Design and Architecture*, 49(49), 64–83. DOI: 10.55612/s-5002-049-004

Chen, F.-H., & Ho, S.-J. (2022). Designing a Board Game about the United Nations' Sustainable Development Goals. *Sustainability (Basel)*, 14(18), 11197. Advance online publication. DOI: 10.3390/su141811197

Dixit, R. K., Nirgude, M., & Yalagi, P. S. (2018). Employ gamification to make "I&CS" more interesting. *Journal of Engineering Education Transformations*, 32(2), 55–60.

Dyer, R. (2021). Gamified Emissions Through the Wisdom of Crowds. In A. Spanellis & J. T. Harviainen (Eds.), *Transforming Society and Organizations through Gamification* (pp. 129–150). Springer International Publishing. DOI: 10.1007/978-3-030-68207-1_8

Feagin, J. R., & Eckberg, D. L. (1980). Discrimination: Motivation, Action, Effects, and Context. *Annual Review of Sociology*, 6(1), 1–20. DOI: 10.1146/annurev.so.06.080180.000245

Gazzola, P., Pezzetti, R., Amelio, S., & Grechi, D. (2020). Non-Financial Information Disclosure in Italian Public Interest Companies: A Sustainability Reporting Perspective. *Sustainability (Basel)*, 12(15), 6063. DOI: 10.3390/su12156063

Groenewald, E. S. (2024). *Inclusive Workplaces: The Key Strategies for Sustainable Diversity Practices*. DOI: 10.5281/ZENODO.11032466

Haque, S., Panda, D., & Ghosh, A. (2024). Gamifying sustainability with self-efficacy: Motivating green behaviours in large industrial firms. *International Journal of Organizational Analysis, 32*(11), 74–93. Advance online publication. DOI: 10.1108/IJOA-08-2023-3951

Hebl, M., Cheng, S. K., & Ng, L. C. (2020). Modern Discrimination in Organizations. *Annual Review of Organizational Psychology and Organizational Behavior*, 7(1), 257–282. DOI: 10.1146/annurev-orgpsych-012119-044948

Himmelstein, J., & Gopalakrishnan, G. (2017). Tackling implicit and explicit bias through games that teach workplace diversity. In *Proc. Eur. Conf. Games Based Learn., ECGBL* (pp. 244–252). Academic Conferences and Publishing International Limited. https://www.scopus.com/inward/record.uri?eid=2-s2.0-85036460892&partnerID=40&md5=bd35599d1451282b4607d3f0b17fa705

Hjalager, A.-M., Graakjær Smed, S., & Jensen, J. F. (2022). E-Tools for Tourism Innovation Management: A New Typology. In *Handb. Of e-Tourism* (pp. 1465–1489). Springer International Publishing; DOI: 10.1007/978-3-030-48652-5_79

Liang, X., Chen, M., & Leung, V. C. M. (2011). A game-theoretic approach for relay assignment over distributed wireless networks. *IWCMC - Int. Wirel. Commun. Mob. Comput. Conf.*, 1557–1562. DOI: 10.1109/IWCMC.2011.5982770

Lier, L. M., & Breuer, C. (2020). The motivating power of gamification: Does the inclusion of game elements increase the effectiveness of worksite health promotion programs? *International Journal of Workplace Health Management, 13*(1), 1–15. Advance online publication. DOI: 10.1108/IJWHM-04-2019-0055

Ligorio, L., Venturelli, A., Rosato, P., & Campo, R. (2023). Fostering sustainable development goals through gamification. *Journal of Management & Organization*, 1–22. Advance online publication. DOI: 10.1017/jmo.2023.54

Lyons, R. M., Fox, G., & Stephens, S. (2023). Gamification to enhance engagement and higher order learning in entrepreneurial education. *Education and Training. Education + Training*, 65(3), 416–432. Advance online publication. DOI: 10.1108/ET-05-2022-0204

Mariappanadar, S. (2024). Improving Quality of Work for Positive Health: Interaction of Sustainable Development Goal (SDG) 8 and SDG 3 from the Sustainable HRM Perspective. *Sustainability (Basel)*, 16(13), 5356. DOI: 10.3390/su16135356

Mayr, K., & Teller, C. (2024). The ethical edge: Unveiling the power of virtuousness in retailing from employees' perspectives. *Journal of Retailing and Consumer Services*, 81, 104025. DOI: 10.1016/j.jretconser.2024.104025

Meshcheryakova, A. O., & Hemmert, F. (2023). Tales from the Future: Exploring Game Design Strategies for Creativity and Play. In *Lect. Notes Educ. Technol.* (pp. 565–574). Springer Science and Business Media Deutschland GmbH. DOI: 10.1007/978-981-99-0942-1_59

Modarelli, G. (2023). Editorial: Combining CSR, public-private policies, inclusiveness and complex challenges for integral well-being by reciprocity relations — An agenda for global governance. *Corporate and Business Strategy Review*, 4(2), 4–6. DOI: 10.22495/cbsrv4i2editorial

Modarelli, G., Rainero, C., & Amelio, S. (2024). Games, diversity and occupation: A bidimensional CSR perspective for adaptive organisations. *Social Responsibility Journal*, 20(9), 1787–1808. DOI: 10.1108/SRJ-07-2023-0390

Molnár, C., Csehné Papp, I., & Juhász, T. (2024). Organizational strategies and tools of employee well-being as perceived by employees. *Management & Marketing*, 19(2), 336–361. DOI: 10.2478/mmcks-2024-0015

Morini, L., Chen, Y.-F., Adefila, A., Mahon, D., Dawson, M., Mohamad, F., Minoi, J. L., & Schwartz, G. (2022). Playful Participatory Mapping: Co-creating Games to Foster Systems Thinking. In Costa C. (A c. Di), *Proc. European Conf. Games-based Learn.* (pp. 387–395). Dechema e.V. https://www.scopus.com/inward/record.uri?eid=2-s2.0-85141169336&partnerID=40&md5=fa24c927511ab71026d9a80bad4cd1b3

Mosleh, W., Bäckstroem, I., Manfrini, C., & Leue-Bensch, C. (2024). Organizing employee-driven innovation (EDI) through game-based formats: Understanding participation. *Creativity and Innovation Management*, caim.12625. Advance online publication. DOI: 10.1111/caim.12625

Mylonas, G., Hofstaetter, J., Giannakos, M., Friedl, A., & Koulouris, P. (2023). Playful interventions for sustainability awareness in educational environments: A longitudinal, large-scale study in three countries. *International Journal of Child-Computer Interaction, 35.International Journal of Child-Computer Interaction*, 35, 100562. Advance online publication. DOI: 10.1016/j.ijcci.2022.100562

Oprescu, F., Jones, C., & Katsikitis, M. (2014). I PLAY AT WORK—Ten principles for transforming work processes through gamification. *Frontiers in Psychology*, 5. Advance online publication. DOI: 10.3389/fpsyg.2014.00014 PMID: 24523704

Owen, P. (2017). How gamification can help your business engage in sustainability. In *How Gamification Can Help Your Business Engage in Sustainability* (p. 77). Taylor and Francis. DOI: 10.4324/9781351275606

Page, M. J., McKenzie, J. E., Bossuyt, P. M., Boutron, I., Hoffmann, T. C., Mulrow, C. D., Shamseer, L., Tetzlaff, J. M., Akl, E. A., Brennan, S. E., Chou, R., Glanville, J., Grimshaw, J. M., Hróbjartsson, A., Lalu, M. M., Li, T., Loder, E. W., Mayo-Wilson, E., McDonald, S., & Moher, D. (2021). The PRISMA 2020 statement: An updated guideline for reporting systematic reviews. *BMJ (Clinical Research Ed.)*, (71), n71. Advance online publication. DOI: 10.1136/bmj.n71 PMID: 33782057

Park, J., Montiel, I., Husted, B. W., & Balarezo, R. (2022). The Grand Challenge of Human Health: A Review and an Urgent Call for Business–Health Research. *Business & Society*, 61(5), 1353–1415. DOI: 10.1177/00076503211073519

Pineda-Martínez, M., Llanos-Ruiz, D., Puente-Torre, P., & García-Delgado, M. Á. (2023). Impact of Video Games, Gamification, and Game-Based Learning on Sustainability Education in Higher Education. *Sustainability (Basel)*, 15(17), 13032. Advance online publication. DOI: 10.3390/su151713032

Prasad, K. D. V., Mruthyanjaya Rao, M., & Vaidya, R. (2019). Gamification and resource pooling for improving operational efficiency and effective management of human resources: A case study with an ecommerce company. *International Journal of Management, 10*(6), 76–87. Advance online publication. DOI: 10.34218/IJM.10.6.2019.008

Rajashekar, S., & Jain, A. (2024). A Thematic Analysis on "Employee Engagement in IT Companies from the Perspective of Holistic Well-being Initiatives". *Employee Responsibilities and Rights Journal*, 36(2), 165–187. DOI: 10.1007/s10672-023-09440-x

Rauschenberger, M., Willems, A., Ternieden, M., & Thomaschewski, J. (2019). Towards the use of gamification frameworks in learning environments. *Journal of Interactive Learning Research*, 30(2), 147–165.

Richards, M. B., Becker, K. L., & Stollings-Holder, J. (2024). Escaping generational conflict: Using gamification to examine intergenerational communication & problem-solving. *Review of Managerial Science, 18*(6), 1597–1616. Advance online publication. DOI: 10.1007/s11846-023-00669-2

Sanclemente, F. J., Gamero, N., Medina, F. J., & Mendoza-Denton, R. (2024). A multilevel model of job inclusion of employees with disabilities: The role of organizational socialization tactics, coworkers social support, and an inclusive team context. *Applied Psychology*, 73(3), 887–909. DOI: 10.1111/apps.12390

Seaborn, K., & Fels, D. I. (2015). Gamification in theory and action: A survey. *International Journal of Human Computer Studies, 74*, 14–31. Advance online publication. DOI: 10.1016/j.ijhcs.2014.09.006

Siala, H., Kutsch, E., & Jagger, S. (2020). Cultural influences moderating learners' adoption of serious 3D games for managerial learning. *Information Technology and People, 33*(2), 424–455. Advance online publication. DOI: 10.1108/ITP-08-2018-0385

Soboleva, E. V., Suvorova, T. N., Zenkina, S. V., & Bocharov, M. I. (2021). Developing Computational Thinking of Specialists of the Future Through Designing Computer Games for Educational Purposes. *European Journal of Contemporary Education, 10*(2), 462–475. Advance online publication. DOI: 10.13187/ejced.2021.2.462

Sousa, C. (2020). Empowerment and ownership in intellectual disability gaming: Review and reflections towards an able gaming perspective (2010-2020). *International Journal of Film and Media Arts, 5*(1), 14–23. Advance online publication. DOI: 10.24140/ijfma.v5.n1.02

Stefan, I. A., Stefan, A., Goldbach, I. R., & Hamza-Lup, F. (2019). Exploring the use of gamified systems in training and work environments. In *eLearning Softw. Educ. Conf.* (pp. 11–19). National Defence University - Carol I Printing House. DOI: 10.12753/2066-026X-19-001

Szendrői, L., Dhir, K. S., & Czakó, K. (2020). Gamification in for-profit organisations: A mapping study. *Business: Theory and Practice, 21*(2), 598–612. Advance online publication. DOI: 10.3846/btp.2020.11864

Timbó, S., de Melo Bezerra, J., & Hirata, C. M. (2019). Supporting Gamified Experiences for Informal Collaborative Groups. In *Lect. Notes Bus. Inf. Process.* (Vol. 363, pp. 42–57). Springer Verlag. DOI: 10.1007/978-3-030-26169-6_3

Tomé Klock, A. C., Palomino, P. T., Rodrigues, L. A. L., Toda, A. M., Simanke, S., Spors, V., Santana, B. S., & Hamari, J. (2024). Gamification towards and alongside equity, diversity and inclusion: Looking back to move forward. *New Media and Society.New Media & Society*. Advance online publication. DOI: 10.1177/14614448241254028

Triana, M. D. C., Gu, P., Chapa, O., Richard, O., & Colella, A. (2021). Sixty years of discrimination and diversity research in human resource management: A review with suggestions for future research directions. *Human Resource Management*, 60(1), 145–204. DOI: 10.1002/hrm.22052

United Nations General Assembly. (2015). *Transforming Our World: The 2030 Agenda for Sustainable Development. Draft resolution referred to the United Nations summit for the adoption of the post- 2015 development agenda by the General Assembly at its sixty-ninth session.*

Van der Heijden, B. I. J. M., Burgers, M. J., Kaan, A. M., Lamberts, B. F., Migchelbrink, K., Van den Ouweland, R. C. P. M., & Meijer, T. (2020). Gamification in Dutch Businesses: An Explorative Case Study. *SAGE Open, 10*(4). *SAGE Open*, 10(4). Advance online publication. DOI: 10.1177/2158244020972371

Van Toorn, C., Kirshner, S., & Gabb, J. (2022). Gamification of query-driven knowledge sharing systems. *Behaviour & Information Technology*, 41(5), 959–980. DOI: 10.1080/0144929X.2020.1849401

Wanick, V., & Bui, H. (2019). Gamification in Management: Analysis and research directions. *International Journal of Serious Games, 6*(2), 57–74. Advance online publication. DOI: 10.17083/ijsg.v6i2.282

Section 3

Employability, Inclusion, and Game-Based-Driven Corporate Social Responsibility Actions

Chapter 4
Promoting Inclusivity:
Corporate Social Responsibility in Game-Based Learning and Professional Employment

Vaishali Deepak Sahoo
https://orcid.org/0009-0001-8118-2509
Vishwakarma University, India

Deepak Ranjan Sahoo
https://orcid.org/0000-0003-4013-2422
MIT Arts, Design, and Technology University, India

ABSTRACT

Corporate social responsibility (CSR) initiatives have expanded to encompass a wide array of endeavors aimed at fostering inclusivity across society. This chapter delves into the role of CSR in promoting inclusivity within the realms of game-based learning and professional employment. Through an examination of existing literature and case studies, this chapter underscores the significance of CSR endeavors in fostering a more inclusive environment for diverse populations, including individuals with disabilities, minorities, and marginalized groups. Game-based learning and professional employment stand out as domains with profound implications for social and economic impact. This thematic analysis explores the intersection of these two areas and their contributions to broader social and economic outcomes. By integrating methods of game-based learning with inclusive employment practices, businesses can play a pivotal role in advancing social equity while simultaneously enhancing organizational performance and fostering innovation.

DOI: 10.4018/979-8-3693-1172-1.ch004

1. INTRODUCTION

Corporate Social Responsibility (CSR) has become an integral aspect of modern business practices, with companies increasingly recognizing their role in contributing to social and environmental sustainability. In recent years, the focus of CSR has expanded to include efforts aimed at promoting inclusivity and diversity within the workforce and beyond. This chapter explores how CSR initiatives can support inclusivity in two interconnected domains: game-based learning and professional employment.

Game-based learning has emerged as a promising approach to education and training, leveraging the engaging and interactive nature of games to enhance learning outcomes. Similarly, fostering inclusivity in professional employment involves creating opportunities for individuals from diverse backgrounds to thrive in the workplace(*ECGBL 201711th European Conference on Game-Based Learning*, 2017). By examining the intersection of CSR, game-based learning, and professional employment, this chapter aims to provide insights into how businesses can drive positive social change while also benefiting their bottom line.

Research indicates that game-based learning bolsters engagement, critical thinking, and problem-solving, creating interactive learning spaces. It is linked to lowered training expenses and better information retention. Thematic analysis highlights its positive impact on job readiness and performance, suggesting transformative implications for workforce development and education strategies. The literature work broadly categorized on the below aspects:

- **Corporate Social Responsibility:** Corporate Social Responsibility (CSR) refers to the voluntary actions that businesses take to address social, environmental, and ethical concerns in their operations and interactions with stakeholders. CSR initiatives can take various forms, including philanthropy, environmental sustainability efforts, ethical sourcing practices, and diversity and inclusion initiatives(*What We Know and Don't Know About Corporate Social Responsibility: A Review and Research Agenda - Herman Aguinis, Ante Glavas, 2012*, n.d.). By integrating CSR into their business strategies, companies can enhance their reputation, build trust with stakeholders, and contribute to positive social impact.\
- **Inclusivity in Professional Employment:** Creating an inclusive workplace involves fostering a culture where individuals from diverse backgrounds feel valued, respected, and empowered to contribute their unique perspectives as mentioned by the (Arnab & Clarke, 2017) and talents. Inclusive employment practices encompass recruitment and hiring strategies, employee training and development programs, and organizational policies that promote diversity

and equity. Research has shown that companies with diverse workforces are more innovative, adaptable, and competitive in the global marketplace. By embracing inclusivity in hiring and retention practices, businesses can tap into a broader talent pool, enhance employee engagement and productivity, and better serve diverse customer bases as mentioned by the (de Souza Gandra Camilo, 2024). In addition to promoting social equity, inclusive employment practices can also lead to tangible business benefits, including increased profitability and improved organizational performance.

- **Inclusivity in Game-Based Learning:** Game-based learning involves the use of games, simulations, and interactive activities to facilitate learning and skill development. This approach has gained popularity in educational settings due to its ability to engage learners, promote critical thinking, and enhance retention of information (Angafor et al., 2020). Inclusivity in game-based learning refers to ensuring that educational games are accessible and beneficial to learners from diverse backgrounds, including those with disabilities, different learning styles, and cultural differences. Research has shown that incorporating principles of universal design and accessibility into game design can improve the overall learning experience for all students. For example, features such as adjustable difficulty levels, alternative control schemes, and multi-modal feedback can accommodate a wider range of learners and promote inclusivity in educational games as mentioned by the (Amran et al., 2021). Furthermore, game-based learning can also be used to address social issues and promote empathy and understanding among players.

In the realm of literary discourse, there exists a significant body of work dedicated to exploring the nuances of inclusivity within the realm of game-based learning (GBL). This discourse, informed by insights from educators, game artisans, and students alike, endeavors to craft narratives that are not only accessible but also captivating, tailored to the kaleidoscopic tapestry of player identities. Employing a tapestry woven from both primary anecdotes and secondary chronicles, including colloquies with vested parties and a delve into existing literary opuses, this endeavor embraces a participatory ethos. Its revelations contribute to the codification of inclusivity benchmarks for educators, paving the way for the creation of pedagogical marvels adept at embracing the multifarious needs of learners, as articulated by (Rye & Sousa, 2023).

Furthermore, this artistic endeavor reveals the potential to enhance communal engagement, self-governance, temporal acumen, and inclusivity for reticent souls. However, it concedes that pedagogical methodologies such as participatory modeling may not universally resonate and might necessitate tutelary patronage. Pedagogical constraints, degrees of engagement, cognitive styles, and prowess all impinge upon the efficacy of this framework. Nonetheless, the Territory Game framework offers a glimmer of hope in elucidating the intricacies of veterinary decision-making and nurturing the analytical faculties imperative for efficacious judgment calls. Subsequent inquiries should scrutinize its adaptability, expansiveness, and enduring impact across the variegated landscapes of education.

Within the literary panorama of veterinary scholarship, the crux of effective decision-making lies in a holistic grasp of the interwoven matrices of animal, societal, and environmental well-being. To instill a sense of systemic cognizance amongst veterinary practitioners, participatory modeling and ludic pedagogies have emerged as invaluable instruments. These pedagogical paradigms, encapsulating elements of play, pedagogy, and problem-solving, serve as conduits for skill honing. The present study, in particular, probes into the potential of a multiplayer ludic framework, notably the Territory Game, as a participatory apparatus to cultivate systemic ruminations within the ambit of a Master of Veterinary Medicine curriculum.

Through its assimilation into the pedagogical repertoire, this ludic endeavor exposes learners to convoluted decision-making conundrums, guiding them through the labyrinth of real-world complexities. A qualitative perusal of deliberations and responses unveils the pivotal role played by the game in nurturing systemic cogitation amongst veterinary scholars. Revelations posit that ludic pedagogy, embedded within a participatory scaffold, enriches participants' comprehension of the intricacies inherent in decision-making. The simulated milieu fosters a broadened vista and prompts contemplation of an array of factors germane to decision-making, as posited by (Irabor et al., 2023).

In conclusion, the exploration of gamification in higher education has shown promise in steering away from traditional asynchronous modes of engagement towards fostering synchronous interactivity and collaboration among all stakeholders involved in teaching and learning (Dacre et al., 2018). While previous research predominantly focused on integrating predefined game elements, thus reflecting an asynchronous approach to practice development, our investigation emphasizes the significance of co-creation. By embracing co-creation, wherein teaching and learning stakeholders engage in synchronous partnership, we uncover a profound shift in gamification-based learning development. Our findings underscore that a synchronous co-creation process cultivates a heightened sense of partnership and inclusivity among students, thereby enriching the educational experience. This signifies a pivotal step towards realizing the transformative potential of gamification in higher education.

2. CASE STUDIES ON GAME-BASED LEARNING

- **Microsoft Game-Based Learning:** Microsoft is committed to fostering inclusivity and accessibility in both its products and workplace culture. Through initiatives such as the Microsoft Disability Answer Desk and the Xbox Adaptive Controller, Microsoft has made significant strides in making technology more accessible to individuals with disabilities. In addition, the company has implemented inclusive hiring practices and diversity and inclusion training programs to create a more inclusive work environment for employees from diverse backgrounds.
- **Google Game-Based Learning:** Google is known for its commitment to diversity and inclusion, with initiatives aimed at promoting gender equality, racial and ethnic diversity, and LGBTQ+ rights. The company has implemented unconscious bias training for employees, launched programs to support underrepresented groups in technology, and established partnerships with community organizations to promote diversity and inclusion in the tech industry.
- **IBM Game-Based Learning:** IBM has a long history of promoting diversity and inclusion in the workplace, dating back to its pioneering efforts to hire women and people of color in the early 20th century. Today, IBM continues to prioritize diversity and inclusion through initiatives such as the IBM Equal Opportunity Policy, which prohibits discrimination based on factors such as race, gender, and sexual orientation. The company also offers diversity and inclusion training programs for employees and partners with organizations such as the National Society of Black Engineers and the Hispanic Heritage Foundation to support underrepresented groups in technology.

3. SOCIAL IMPACT OF GAME-BASED LEARNING AND PROFESSIONAL EMPLOYMENT

Game-based learning and professional employment are two domains that have significant implications for social impact. This thematic analysis delves into the ways in which these two areas intersect and contribute to broader social outcomes. Through the examination of existing literature and case studies, this analysis identifies key themes related to the social impact of game-based learning and professional employment, including accessibility, diversity, skill development, and economic empowerment(Fonseca et al., 2023). By exploring these themes, this analysis aims to shed light on the potential of game-based learning and professional employment to drive positive social change and foster inclusive societies.

Game-based learning and professional employment are increasingly recognized as powerful drivers of social impact, with the potential to address a wide range of social challenges and promote inclusive societies. (Glavas & Schuster, 2020)Game-based learning leverages the engaging and interactive nature of games to facilitate learning and skill development, while professional employment provides individuals with opportunities for economic empowerment and social inclusion. This thematic analysis explores the social impact of game-based learning and professional employment, examining key themes and implications for broader social outcomes.

3.1 Social Impact of Game-Based Learning and Professional Employment Thematic Analysis

Case studies illustrate the substantial social impact of game-based learning, enhancing critical thinking, teamwork, engagement, and knowledge retention. Likewise, gamification cultivates a vibrant workplace culture, motivating employees and advancing their skills. These approaches highlight the transformative influence of gaming elements in both educational and professional environments.

- **Accessibility:** Accessibility is a key theme that cuts across both game-based learning and professional employment(Glavas & Schuster, 2020). In the context of game-based learning, accessibility refers to the design of educational games and platforms to ensure that they are inclusive and beneficial for learners(Fonseca et al., 2023) from diverse backgrounds, including those with disabilities, different learning styles, and cultural differences. Features such as adjustable difficulty levels, alternative control schemes, and multimodal feedback can enhance accessibility and accommodate a wider range of learners. (Nadeem et al., 2023) for employees with disabilities, and fostering a culture of diversity and inclusion. By prioritizing accessibility in both game-based learning and professional employment, organizations can promote social equity and ensure that everyone has equal opportunities to learn and succeed.
- **Diversity:** Diversity is another prominent theme in the social impact of game-based learning and professional employment. In game-based learning, diversity refers to the representation of different cultures, identities, and perspectives in educational games and content. By incorporating diverse characters, storylines, and cultural references, game developers can create more inclusive and engaging learning experiences that resonate with a broader audience. Professional employment, diversity entails creating diverse and in-

clusive workplaces that reflect the full spectrum of human diversity, including differences in race, gender, ethnicity, sexual orientation, and disability. Research has shown that diverse teams are more innovative, adaptable, and competitive, as they bring together a variety of perspectives and ideas. By embracing diversity in hiring and retention practices, organizations can foster creativity, drive innovation, and enhance organizational performance.

- **Skill Development:** Skill development is a central theme in both game-based learning and professional employment, with implications for individual growth and social mobility. In game-based learning, educational games are designed to facilitate the acquisition of knowledge, skills, and competencies in various subject areas(Lai & Hwang, 2016), such as math, science, language arts, and critical thinking. Through interactive gameplay, learners can engage with complex concepts, practice problem-solving skills, and develop real-world competencies that are applicable in academic, professional, and personal contexts as mentioned by the (Sukhov, 2019) By gaining new skills and competencies, individuals can enhance their employability, advance their careers, and achieve economic independence. Moreover, investing in skill development can contribute to social mobility by providing individuals with pathways out of poverty and into higher-paying and more fulfilling jobs.
- **Economic Empowerment:** Economic empowerment is a key outcome of both game-based learning and professional employment, with implications for individual well-being and societal progress. In game-based learning(Thirumalesh Madanaguli et al., 2023), educational games can empower learners by equipping them with the knowledge, skills, and confidence to succeed academically and professionally. By improving educational outcomes and expanding opportunities for learning, game-based learning can help individuals break the cycle of poverty and achieve economic security, by providing opportunities for career advancement and upward mobility, professional employment can empower individuals to achieve their full potential and contribute to the economic growth and prosperity of society as a whole.

3.2 Case Studies on the Social Impact of Game-Based Learning and Professional Employment

- **Minecraft:** Minecraft, a popular sandbox video game, has been widely used as a tool for game-based learning in educational settings. Through its open-world gameplay and creative building mechanics(Titus & Ng'ambi, 2023), Minecraft allows students to explore, collaborate, and problem-solve in virtual environments. Teachers have leveraged Minecraft to teach subjects such as history, geography, mathematics, and computer science, fostering creativity, critical thinking, and collaboration among students.

- **Salesforce:** Salesforce, a leading cloud-based software company, has prioritized diversity and inclusion in its workforce and corporate culture. The company has implemented inclusive hiring practices, such as the Rooney Rule and the Equal Pay Assessment, to ensure that its workforce reflects the diversity of its customer base. Salesforce also offers employee resource groups, diversity(Titus & Ng'ambi, 2023) training programs, and mentorship opportunities to support underrepresented groups in technology and promote a culture of inclusion.
- **Codecademy:** Codecademy, an online platform for learning coding and programming skills, has democratized access to technical education and professional development. Through its interactive coding tutorials and projects(Sousa & Rocha, 2019), Codecademy enables individuals from diverse backgrounds to learn in-demand skills such as web development, data science, and cybersecurity. The platform offers free and paid subscription options, making it accessible to learners of all ages, backgrounds, and income levels.

Game-based learning and professional employment have significant implications for social impact, with the potential to drive positive change and foster inclusive societies. By prioritizing accessibility, diversity, skill development, and economic empowerment, organizations can leverage game-based learning and professional employment to address social challenges, promote social mobility, and empower individuals to reach their full potential. Through case studies of companies such as Minecraft, Salesforce, and Codecademy, this thematic analysis has illustrated the ways in which game-based learning and professional employment can contribute to broader social outcomes and create a more equitable and inclusive world.

3.3 Economic Impact of Game-Based Learning and Professional Employment Thematic Analysis

Game-based learning enhances engagement, critical thinking, and problem-solving skills. It fosters a more interactive learning environment, potentially reducing training costs and improving knowledge retention. Thematic analysis reveals positive correlations between game-based learning and professional employment, indicating increased job readiness and performance. This method has the potential to revolutionize strategies for workforce development and education. The following are the key aspects:

- **Workforce Development:** Workforce development is a central theme in the economic impact of both game-based learning and professional employment. In the context of game-based learning, educational games and simulations(Van Eck, 2006) provide learners with opportunities to acquire new skills, knowledge, and competencies that are relevant to the modern workforce(Calza-Perez et al., n.d.). By engaging with game-based learning platforms, individuals can develop critical thinking, problem-solving, and communication skills that are highly valued in today's job market.
- **Skill Acquisition:** Skill acquisition is another key theme in the economic impact of game-based learning and professional employment. Educational games and simulations are designed to teach specific skills and competencies in areas such as STEM (science, technology, engineering, and mathematics), digital literacy(de Souza Gandra Camilo, 2024), and problem-solving. By engaging with game-based learning platforms, individuals can acquire new skills and competencies that are in demand in today's knowledge-based economy.
- **Job Creation:** Job creation is a critical outcome of both game-based learning and professional employment. In the context of game-based learning, the development and implementation of educational games and simulations(Wirba, 2023) create employment opportunities for game designers, developers, educators, and instructional designers. The growing demand for game-based learning solutions has led to the emergence of a vibrant industry that supports job creation and economic growth as mentioned by (Salcedo & Alejandra, 2023).
- **Innovation:** Innovation is a driving force behind the economic impact of game-based learning and professional employment. Educational games and simulations encourage creativity, experimentation, and problem-solving, fostering a culture(Parker et al., 2022) of innovation among learners. By engaging with game-based learning platforms, individuals can develop the critical thinking and entrepreneurial skills needed to drive innovation and economic growth.

3.4 Case Studies Economic Impact of Game-Based Learning and Professional Employment

- **Khan Academy:** Khan Academy is an online platform that offers free educational resources and tutorials in subjects such as mathematics, science, and computer programming. Through its interactive videos, exercises, and games, Khan Academy has democratized access to high-quality education and fostered skill development among learners of all ages and backgrounds.

- **Google:** Google is known for its innovative workplace culture and commitment to employee development and empowerment. The company offers a wide range of professional development programs, including Google University, which provides employees with access to training and certification opportunities in areas such as data analytics, machine learning, and cloud computing.
- **Unity Technologies:** Unity Technologies is a leading provider of game development tools and platforms, including the Unity game engine. The company's platform enables game developers to create immersive and interactive experiences for a wide range of platforms, including mobile devices, consoles, and virtual reality headsets. By empowering game developers with tools and resources, Unity Technologies has fueled innovation and creativity in the game industry.

Game-based learning and professional employment have significant economic implications, with the potential to drive workforce development, skill acquisition, job creation, and innovation. By investing in game-based learning platforms, educational resources, and professional development opportunities, policymakers and stakeholders can support economic growth and prosperity in both developed and developing economies. Through case studies of companies such as Khan Academy, Google, and Unity Technologies, this thematic analysis has illustrated the ways in which game-based learning and professional employment can contribute to economic development and drive positive social change.

4. SUSTAINABLE IMPACT OF GAME-BASED LEARNING AND PROFESSIONAL EMPLOYMENT

Game-based learning and professional employment are integral components of sustainable development, with the potential to foster long-term social, economic, and environmental sustainability. This thematic analysis delves into the sustainable impact of game-based learning and professional employment, examining key themes such as education for sustainable development, green job creation, skills for the future, and corporate sustainability practices(Wirba, 2023). Through the synthesis of existing literature and case studies, this analysis aims to elucidate how investments in game-based learning and professional employment can contribute to sustainable development goals and promote a more equitable and resilient society.

4.1 Sustainable Impact of Game-Based Learning and Professional Employment Thematic Analysis

- **Education for Sustainable Development:** Education for sustainable development is a central theme in the sustainable impact of both game-based learning and professional employment. Game-based learning platforms and educational games provide opportunities for learners to engage with sustainability concepts, such as environmental conservation, social equity, and economic development. Through interactive gameplay and immersive experiences, learners can develop a deeper understanding of sustainability issues and explore solutions to real-world challenges.
- **Green Jobs:** Green jobs are another key theme in the sustainable impact of game-based learning and professional employment. Game-based learning platforms and educational programs can prepare individuals for careers in sustainability-related fields, such as renewable energy, environmental conservation, and green technology(Sukhov, 2019). By providing training and skill development opportunities, game-based learning can help individuals enter the growing green economy and pursue rewarding careers that contribute to environmental sustainability.
- **Skills for the Future:** Skills for the future are essential for addressing the complex challenges of the 21st century and building a more sustainable society. Game-based learning platforms and educational games can help individuals develop critical thinking(Parker et al., 2022), problem-solving, and digital literacy skills that are essential for success in the modern economy. By engaging with immersive and interactive learning experiences, learners can acquire the skills and competencies needed to thrive in a rapidly changing world.
- **Corporate Sustainability:** Corporate sustainability practices are critical for advancing sustainable development goals and promoting responsible business conduct. Game-based learning platforms and educational programs can raise awareness about corporate sustainability issues and inspire individuals to advocate for sustainability within their organizations(Kapralos et al., 2015). By integrating sustainability principles into educational curricula and training programs, game-based learning can empower individuals to become agents of change and drive sustainability initiatives in their workplaces.

Professional employment offers opportunities for individuals to contribute to sustainable development through their work and career paths. By integrating sustainability principles into business practices(Wang, 2022), professionals can drive positive change within their organizations and communities. Education for sustainable development equips individuals with the knowledge, skills(Titus & Ng'ambi, 2023), and values needed to address complex sustainability issues and build a more sustainable future for all.

5. DISCUSSION ON THE GAME-BASED LEARNING AND PROFESSIONAL EMPLOYMENT THEORIES

Given the evolving challenges to conventional employment structures, notably the global competition for location-independent professional roles, the Higher Education sector faces escalating pressure to facilitate smoother transitions for graduates into the workforce. This study delves into Bourdieu's concept of practice and the cultivation process to examine how personal behaviors and attributes, extending beyond mere academic knowledge and employability qualifications typically associated with a university degree, can be applied. Of particular interest is the impact of the shared service center model on the displacement, automation, and outsourcing of traditional entry-level tasks that historically served as stepping stones into professional careers. Empirical evidence suggests that cultivating these behaviors could confer an advantage in securing graduate employment by demonstrating readiness for the workplace. The chapter advocates for a more innovative approach from management educators, employers, government entities, and professional organizations, emphasizing the importance of nurturing student behaviors and attributes through work-based learning, without neglecting the development of intellectual abilities and subject expertise.

The widespread integration of modern technologies in our society underscores the importance and utility of incorporating practical activities into education. This necessity is particularly evident in engineering disciplines, such as cybersecurity, data science, and artificial intelligence. Furthermore, in the context of distance education, these practical activities gain even greater significance. They offer distinct advantages, including the promotion of critical thinking and the enhancement of students' abilities and skills relevant to their future careers.

Various options exist for integrating practical activities into education, including remote and virtual laboratories, virtual reality environments, and game-based platforms. This chapter focuses on the development of a novel cloud-based educational platform with a game-based approach, characterized by a modular and flexible architecture utilizing lightweight containers. This architecture facilitates interactive features, monitoring services, and transparent data storage. Leveraging gamification, the platform seamlessly integrates gaming elements into the instructional process.

In the context of professional employment and game-based learning, corporate social responsibility, or CSR, refers to the process by which businesses and organizations integrate social, ethical, and environmental factors into their operations. This strategy not only improves society but also draws in talent, develops employee satisfaction, and improves brand reputation. Here are some examples of real-world applications for CSR:

- **Development of Ethical Games:** By making sure their games uphold moral ideals and avoid damaging stereotypes, game creation companies may embrace CSR concepts. For instance, a business might create instructional games that encourage inclusion and diversity or teach environmental awareness.
- **Community Engagement:** Through game-based learning programs, businesses can interact with their local communities. For example, a game developer could collaborate with educational institutions or nonprofits to create instructional games that address community needs, such boosting health awareness or teaching financial literacy.
- **Employee Volunteering:** As part of CSR initiatives, employers can encourage staff members to donate their time and expertise to charitable causes. For instance, a gaming company might plan volunteer activities where staff members use their knowledge of game production to make educational games or material for youngsters from disadvantaged backgrounds.
- **Sustainable Practices:** Using eco-friendly materials, cutting down on waste, and consuming less energy are just a few examples of how game development studios may make their operations more sustainable. This dedication to sustainability not only lessens its negative effects on the environment but also provides a good example for workers and clients.
- **Equality in Hiring Procedures**: CSR also includes encouraging inclusion and diversity in the workplace. To ensure workforce diversity, game development companies might adopt inclusive hiring procedures. For instance, aggressively seeking out members of underrepresented groups and offering them equal chances to progress. Ensuring equitable compensation, benefits, and working environments for workers is a fundamental aspect of corporate social responsibility. It is important for game development companies to respect labor laws and put their employees' welfare first. This entails offering chances for career advancement and maintaining a positive work-life balance.
- **Accountability and Transparency:** Businesses need to take responsibility for their activities and be open about their CSR initiatives. This entails keeping stakeholders informed about CSR initiatives on a regular basis, reporting on developments, and fixing any errors.

Companies can benefit their business and employees while simultaneously making a beneficial influence on society by incorporating CSR ideas into game-based learning and professional employment.

5.1 Case Studies Sustainable Impact of Game-Based Learning and Professional Employment

Case studies show how game-based learning has a long-lasting effect on professional career. They demonstrate improved critical thinking, problem-solving, and engagement skills among students. Positive relationships are highlighted by theme analysis, suggesting enhanced job preparedness and performance. These results demonstrate the transformative potential of game-based learning in fostering sustainable workforce development.

- **EcoRise:** EcoRise is a nonprofit organization that empowers K-12 teachers and students to create a sustainable future for all. Through its curriculum and professional development programs, EcoRise integrates sustainability education into schools and classrooms, inspiring students to become environmental stewards and change-makers in their communities.
- **Interface:** Interface, a global flooring company, is committed to sustainability and environmental stewardship. The company has implemented a comprehensive sustainability strategy, Mission Zero, which aims to eliminate negative environmental impacts from its operations by 2020. Interface has pioneered innovations in sustainable manufacturing, product design, and supply chain management, demonstrating that businesses can be profitable while also prioritizing environmental sustainability.
- **Patagonia:** Patagonia, an outdoor apparel company, is known for its commitment to environmental and social responsibility. The company invests in sustainable materials, fair labor practices, and environmental activism, aligning its business operations with its values and mission.(Wirba, 2023) Patagonia's approach to corporate sustainability has earned it a loyal customer base and recognition as a leader in responsible business conduct.

Game-based learning and professional employment have significant potential to drive sustainable development and foster positive social, economic, and environmental outcomes. By integrating sustainability principles into educational curricula, workforce development programs, and corporate practices, stakeholders can empower individuals to become agents of change and build a more equitable, resilient, and sustainable society as articulated by (Fonseca et al., 2023). Through case studies of organizations such as EcoRise, Interface, and Patagonia, this thematic analysis has illustrated the ways in which investments in game-based learning and professional employment can contribute to sustainable development and advance global sustainability goals.

Corporate Social Responsibility (CSR) initiatives play a crucial role in promoting inclusivity in game-based learning and professional employment. By embracing diversity and equity in their operations, businesses can create positive social impact while also driving innovation and competitiveness as articulated by (Wirba, 2023). Through case studies of companies such as Microsoft, Google, and IBM, this chapter has demonstrated the importance of CSR in fostering inclusivity and highlighted best practices for creating more inclusive workplaces and educational environments.

Moving forward, businesses must continue to prioritize CSR efforts that promote inclusivity and diversity, both internally and externally. By investing in accessible and inclusive technologies, implementing inclusive hiring practices, and fostering a culture of diversity and equity, companies can contribute to a more inclusive society while also reaping the benefits of a diverse and engaged workforce.

6. MODEL FOR PROMOTING INCLUSIVITY: CORPORATE SOCIAL RESPONSIBILITY IN GAME-BASED LEARNING AND PROFESSIONAL EMPLOYMENT

Promoting inclusivity through corporate social responsibility (CSR) initiatives in game-based learning and professional employment is crucial for fostering economic and social development. This model presents a comprehensive approach to promoting inclusivity that addresses both economic and social dimensions. It encompasses strategies for enhancing diversity, equity, and inclusion in recruitment, training, and workplace culture, as well as leveraging game-based learning platforms to promote accessible education and skill development. By integrating CSR principles into organizational practices and educational initiatives, stakeholders can create more equitable opportunities for individuals from diverse backgrounds and contribute to sustainable economic and social progress as mentioned by (Amran et al., 2021).

Promoting inclusivity through corporate social responsibility (CSR) initiatives is essential for building equitable and sustainable societies. In the context of game-based learning and professional employment, inclusivity is crucial for ensuring that individuals from diverse backgrounds have equal opportunities to access education, develop skills, and pursue meaningful careers.(Pineda-Martínez et al., 2023) articulated the comprehensive model outlines strategies for promoting inclusivity that address both economic and social dimensions, with a focus on leveraging CSR principles to create positive impact in game-based learning and professional employment settings.

6.1 Understanding the Context

Before implementing strategies to promote inclusivity, it is essential to understand the context in which game-based learning and professional employment operate. This involves conducting a thorough assessment of the demographic composition of the target audience, identifying barriers to inclusivity, and understanding the social and economic factors that influence access to education and employment opportunities. (Van Eck, 2006) mentioned in the article that by gaining insights into the unique challenges faced by diverse communities, stakeholders can tailor their initiatives to address specific needs and promote equitable outcomes.

6.2 Enhancing Diversity and Inclusion in Recruitment

A key aspect of promoting inclusivity is ensuring that recruitment processes are inclusive and bias-free. Organizations can achieve this by implementing diversity-focused recruitment strategies, such as targeted outreach to underrepresented groups, using diverse hiring panels, and incorporating inclusive language in job postings as articulated by (Glavas & Schuster, 2020). Additionally, leveraging technology, such as blind resume screening and algorithm-based recruitment tools, can help mitigate unconscious biases and ensure that candidates are evaluated based on their qualifications and skills rather than demographic characteristics.

6.3 Providing Accessible Education and Training

In the realm of game-based learning, promoting inclusivity involves creating accessible and inclusive learning environments that cater to the diverse needs of learners. This may include designing educational games with built-in accessibility features, such as customizable controls, alternative input methods, and audio descriptions. Moreover, providing training and support for educators on inclusive teaching practices and Universal Design for Learning (UDL) principles can help ensure that all learners have equal opportunities to succeed.

6.4 Fostering Inclusive Workplace Cultures

In professional employment, fostering inclusive workplace cultures is essential for attracting, retaining, and advancing diverse talent. Organizations can promote inclusivity by implementing diversity and inclusion training programs, establishing employee resource groups, and providing mentorship and sponsorship opportunities for underrepresented employees. Moreover, creating policies and practices that support work-life balance, flexible scheduling, and remote work can help accommodate the needs of diverse employees and promote a culture of inclusion and belonging as mentioned by the (Arnab & Clarke, 2017).

6.5 Leveraging Game-Based Learning for Skill Development

Game-based learning platforms offer unique opportunities to promote inclusivity by providing accessible and engaging educational experiences for learners from diverse backgrounds. Organizations can leverage game-based learning to develop essential skills and competencies, such as critical thinking, problem-solving, and digital literacy, that are in demand in the modern workforce.(Angafor et al., 2020) designing educational games that address diverse learning styles and preferences, stakeholders can ensure that all learners have equal opportunities to acquire relevant skills and knowledge.

6.6 Promoting Equitable Career Advancement Opportunities

In professional employment, promoting inclusivity also involves providing equitable career advancement opportunities for employees from underrepresented groups. This may include implementing transparent promotion processes, establishing mentorship programs, and providing leadership development opportunities for diverse talent. Moreover, creating pathways for career progression and skill development, such as tuition reimbursement programs and on-the-job training initiatives, can help employees overcome barriers to advancement and achieve their full potential as mentioned by (Nadeem et al., 2023).

6.7 Measuring and Monitoring Progress

Finally, measuring and monitoring progress is essential for evaluating the effectiveness of inclusivity initiatives and identifying areas for improvement. Organizations can track key diversity metrics, such as representation rates, turnover rates, and promotion rates, to assess the impact of their efforts over time. Additionally, gathering feedback from employees and stakeholders through surveys, focus groups, and interviews can provide valuable insights into the experiences and perceptions of diverse individuals within the organization. (Nadeem et al., 2023) articulated that by regularly reviewing and analyzing data on inclusivity outcomes, stakeholders can make informed decisions and continuously refine their strategies to promote inclusivity effectively.

7. ANALYTICAL MODEL ON GAME-BASED LEARNING AND EMPLOYMENT

An analytical model of game-based learning and working involves breaking down the various components, processes, and outcomes associated with using games for educational purposes and professional development. This model aims to provide a systematic framework for understanding how game-based learning intersects with working environments, highlighting key factors that influence effectiveness and impact. Here's an outline of an analytical model:

Figure 1. Factors of game based learning and employment (Own Contribution)

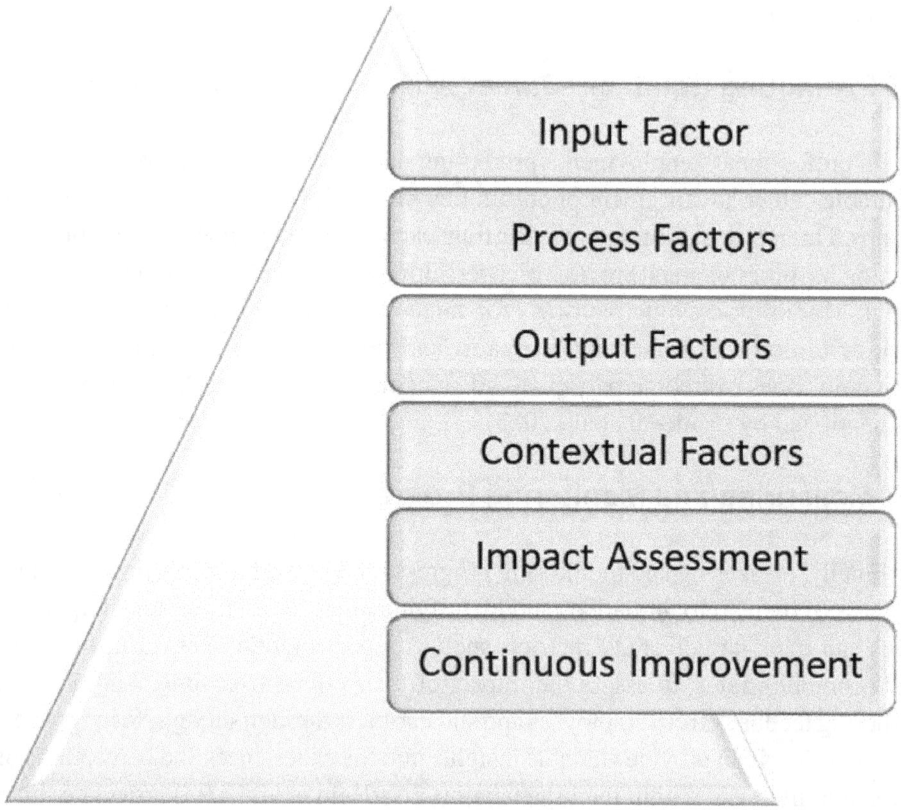

- **Input Factor**
    - **Game Design:** Analyze the design elements of educational games, including mechanics, dynamics, aesthetics, and narrative, to understand how they facilitate learning.
    - **Learning Objectives:** Identify the educational goals and desired learning outcomes that inform the development of game-based learning experiences.
    - **User Characteristics**: Consider the characteristics of the target audience, such as age, background, prior knowledge, and learning preferences, to tailor game-based learning experiences accordingly.
- **Process Factors:**
    - **Engagement:** Assess the level of engagement and immersion that learners experience while interacting with game-based learning environments.
    - **Interactivity:** Examine the degree to which learners can actively engage with and manipulate elements within the game to drive their learning experience.
    - **Feedback Mechanisms:** Evaluate the effectiveness of feedback mechanisms in providing timely and relevant feedback to learners, facilitating learning progression and skill development.
    - **Adaptively:** Explore how game-based learning environments adapt to individual learner needs and performance levels, providing personalized learning experiences.
- **Output Factors:**
    - **Knowledge Acquisition:** Measure the extent to which learners acquire new knowledge, skills, and competencies through game-based learning experiences.
    - **Skill Development:** Assess the development of specific skills and competencies targeted by the game-based learning intervention, such as problem-solving, critical thinking, and collaboration.
    - **Transferability:** Evaluate the transferability of learning outcomes from the game-based learning environment to real-world contexts, assessing the practical applicability of acquired knowledge and skills.
    - **Motivation and Engagement:** Gauge the impact of game-based learning on learner motivation, engagement, and attitudes towards learning and working.
- **Contextual Factors:**
    - **Educational Context:** Consider the broader educational context in which game-based learning is implemented, including curriculum alignment, institutional support, and teacher involvement.

- Workplace Environment: Explore the organizational culture, policies, and practices that influence the integration of game-based learning into professional development and training initiatives.
    - **Technological Infrastructure:** Assess the availability and accessibility of technology resources, such as devices, platforms, and internet connectivity, to support game-based learning and working activities.
- **Impact Assessment:**
    - **Quantitative Metrics:** Use quantitative measures, such as pre- and post-test scores, learning analytics data, and performance indicators, to assess the impact of game-based learning on learning outcomes and working performance.
    - **Qualitative Feedback:** Gather qualitative feedback from learners, instructors, and employers through surveys, interviews, and focus groups to capture nuanced insights into the effectiveness and utility of game-based learning in working environments.
    - **Long-Term Effects:** Consider the long-term effects of game-based learning on individual career development, organizational productivity, and workforce innovation, examining its sustainability and scalability over time.
- **Continuous Improvement:**
    - **Iterative Design**: Emphasize the iterative design and development of game-based learning interventions, incorporating feedback from stakeholders and ongoing evaluation to refine and improve learning experiences.
    - **Professional Development:** Provide opportunities for educators, trainers, and instructional designers to enhance their knowledge and skills in designing, implementing, and evaluating game-based learning initiatives through professional development programs and communities of practice.
    - **Organizational Support**: Foster a culture of innovation and experimentation within organizations, encouraging collaboration, knowledge sharing, and risk-taking to drive continuous improvement in game-based learning and working practices.

By employing this analytical model, stakeholders can systematically evaluate and optimize the design, implementation, and impact of game-based learning initiatives in working environments, ultimately enhancing learning outcomes, professional development, and organizational performance.

8. CONCLUSION

Promoting inclusivity through Corporate Social Responsibility (CSR) initiatives in game-based learning and professional employment is paramount for advancing economic and social development. This holistic approach addresses the importance of diversity, equity, and inclusion across recruitment, training, and workplace culture, while harnessing the potential of game-based learning platforms to enhance accessible education and skill development.

In conclusion, this chapter has delved into the multifaceted intersection of Corporate Social Responsibility (CSR), inclusivity promotion, game-based learning (GBL), and professional employment. Through an analytical review of existing literature and case studies, we have elucidated the pivotal role of CSR initiatives in fostering inclusivity within the realms of GBL and professional employment. The integration of CSR practices, particularly those leveraging GBL methodologies, has been underscored as a potent means to create more inclusive workplace environments. By examining various input, process, output, contextual factors, and impact assessment metrics, we have provided a comprehensive framework for stakeholders to evaluate and optimize the design, implementation, and impact of GBL initiatives in professional employment settings.

Furthermore, the chapter has emphasized the importance of continuous improvement, iterative design, professional development, and organizational support to drive sustained advancements in GBL practices and their societal impacts. As we move forward, it is imperative for organizations to embrace CSR-driven inclusivity efforts, leverage GBL methodologies, and collaborate across sectors to foster a more equitable, innovative, and prosperous future for all.

REFERENCES

Amran, A., Jalil, H. A., Muhamad, M., & Nasharuddin, N. A. (2021). Factors Contributing to Collaborative Game-Based Learning (CGBL) Effectiveness. *Asian Social Science, 17*(11). DOI: 10.5539/ass.v17n11p1

Andreoni, V., & Richard, A. (2023). Exploring the interconnected nature of the sustainable development goals: The 2030 SDGs Game as a pedagogical tool for interdisciplinary education. *International Journal of Sustainability in Higher Education*, 25(1), 21–42. DOI: 10.1108/IJSHE-11-2022-0378

Angafor, G. N., Yevseyeva, I., & He, Y. (2020). Game-based learning: A review of tabletop exercises for cybersecurity incident response training. *Security and Privacy*, 3(6), e126. DOI: 10.1002/spy2.126

Arnab, S., & Clarke, S. (2017). Towards a trans-disciplinary methodology for a game-based intervention development process. *British Journal of Educational Technology*, 48(2), 279–312. DOI: 10.1111/bjet.12377

Calza-Perez, M., Perez-Ruiz, P., Enri-Peiró, S., Martínez-Climent, C., & Sánchez-García, J. (n.d.). Key factors influencing knowledge acquisition through game-based learning. *Psychology & Marketing*. DOI: 10.1002/mar.21966

Chee, Y. S. (2007). Embodiment, embeddedness, and experience: Game-based learning and the construction of identity. *Research and Practice in Technology Enhanced Learning*, 02(01), 3–30. DOI: 10.1142/S1793206807000282

de Souza Gandra Camilo, V. Y. (2024). *Articulations of inclusivity within in-game concerts: A comparative multi-case study* [MRes, University of Glasgow]. https://theses.gla.ac.uk/84035/

ECGBL 2017 11th European Conference on Game-Based Learning. (2017). Academic Conferences and publishing limited.

Fonseca, I., Caviedes, M., Chantré, J., & Bernate, J. (2023). Gamification and Game-Based Learning as Cooperative Learning Tools: A Systematic Review. *International Journal of Emerging Technologies in Learning*, 18(21), 4–23. DOI: 10.3991/ijet.v18i21.40035

Glavas, C., & Schuster, L. (2020). Design principles for electronic work integrated learning (eWIL). *The Internet and Higher Education*, 47, 100760. DOI: 10.1016/j.iheduc.2020.100760

Herodotou, C., Rienties, B., Hlosta, M., Boroowa, A., Mangafa, C., & Zdrahal, Z. (2020). The scalable implementation of predictive learning analytics at a distance learning university: Insights from a longitudinal case study. *The Internet and Higher Education*, 45, 100725. DOI: 10.1016/j.iheduc.2020.100725

Hwang, G.-J., Chiu, L.-Y., & Chen, C.-H. (2015). A contextual game-based learning approach to improving students' inquiry-based learning performance in social studies courses. *Computers & Education*, 81, 13–25. DOI: 10.1016/j.compedu.2014.09.006

Interdisciplinary Design of Game-based Learning Platforms: A Phenomenological Examination of the Integrative Design of Game, Learning, and Assessment | SpringerLink. (n.d.). Retrieved January 27, 2024, from https://link.springer.com/book/10.1007/978-3-030-04339-1

Kapralos, B., Fisher, S., Clarkson, J., & van Oostveen, R. (2015). A course on serious game design and development using an online problem-based learning approach. *Interactive Technology and Smart Education*, 12(2), 116–136. DOI: 10.1108/ITSE-10-2014-0033

Lai, C.-L., & Hwang, G.-J. (2016). A self-regulated flipped classroom approach to improving students' learning performance in a mathematics course. *Computers & Education*, 100, 126–140. DOI: 10.1016/j.compedu.2016.05.006

Lopes, A. P., & Soares, F. (2018). Perception and performance in a flipped Financial Mathematics classroom. *International Journal of Management Education*, 16(1), 105–113. DOI: 10.1016/j.ijme.2018.01.001

Nadeem, M., Oroszlanyova, M., & Farag, W. (2023). Effect of Digital Game-Based Learning on Student Engagement and Motivation. *Computers, 12*(9). https://doi.org/ DOI: 10.3390/computers12090177

Pineda-Martínez, M., Llanos-Ruiz, D., Puente-Torre, P., & García-Delgado, M. Á. (2023). Impact of Video Games, Gamification, and Game-Based Learning on Sustainability Education in Higher Education. *Sustainability, 15*(17). DOI: 10.3390/su151713032

Pivec, M. (2004). *Guidelines for Game-based Learning*. Pabst Science Publishers.

Qian, M., & Clark, K. R. (2016). Game-based Learning and 21st century skills: A review of recent research. *Computers in Human Behavior*, 63, 50–58. DOI: 10.1016/j.chb.2016.05.023

Salcedo, P., & Alejandra, A. (2023). *Enhancing Students' Motivation in the EFL Classroom Through Life is Strange: A Digital Game-Based Learning Scenario Proposal*. https://diposit.ub.edu/dspace/handle/2445/200580

Salido, P. S., & Breviescas, B. D. (2024). Unlocking Potential: Best Practices for Promoting Independence and Life Skills in Intellectual Disability Learners of Special Education Class of Alubijid Central School. *Best Practices in Disability-Inclusive Education, 3*(1). https://publication.seameosen.edu.my/index.php/diebook/chapter/view/395

Sierra, J., & Rodríguez-Conde, M.-J. (2021). The Microfinance Game: Experiencing the dynamics of financial inclusion in developing contexts. *International Journal of Management Education*, 19(3), 100540. DOI: 10.1016/j.ijme.2021.100540

Skillman, A. (2023). An Analysis of Gamification and Game-Based Learning as Strategies for Anti-Oppressive Education. *Social Justice and Community Engagement Major Research Papers*. https://scholars.wlu.ca/sjce_mrp/12

Sousa, M. J., & Rocha, Á. (2019). Leadership styles and skills developed through game-based learning. *Journal of Business Research*, 94, 360–366. DOI: 10.1016/j.jbusres.2018.01.057

Sukhov, A. (2019). Ethical issues of simulation video games. *Proc. European Conf. Games-Based Learn., 2019-October*, 705–712. DOI: 10.34190/GBL.19.060

Sun, Z., & Xie, K. (2020). How do students prepare in the pre-class setting of a flipped undergraduate math course? A latent profile analysis of learning behavior and the impact of achievement goals. *The Internet and Higher Education*, 46, 100731. DOI: 10.1016/j.iheduc.2020.100731

Thirumalesh Madanaguli, A., Dhir, A., Kaur, P., Mishra, S., & Srivastava, S. (2023). A systematic literature review on corporate social responsibility (CSR) and hotels: Past achievements and future promises in the hospitality sector. *Scandinavian Journal of Hospitality and Tourism*, 23(2–3), 141–175. DOI: 10.1080/15022250.2023.2221214

Titus, S., & Ng'ambi, D. (2023). Digital Gaming for Cross-Cultural Learning: Development of a Social Constructivist Game-Based Learning Model at a South African University. *International Journal of Game-Based Learning*, 13(1), 1–20. DOI: 10.4018/IJGBL.331995

Van Eck, R. (2006). Digital Game-Based Learning: It's Not Just the Digital Natives Who Are Restless. *EDUCAUSE Review*, 41(2), 16–30.

Wang, R. T.-C. (2022). Investigating the contribution of role-plays for social sustainability: Designing a role-play game for CSR Communication. *Developments in Business Simulation and Experiential Learning: Proceedings of the Annual ABSEL Conference, 49*. https://absel-ojs-ttu.tdl.org/absel/chapter/view/3322

What We Know and Don't Know About Corporate Social Responsibility: A Review and Research Agenda—Herman Aguinis, Ante Glavas, 2012. (n.d.). Retrieved January 27, 2024, from https://journals.sagepub.com/doi/10.1177/0149206311436079

Wirba, A. V. (2023). Corporate Social Responsibility (CSR): The Role of Government in promoting CSR. *Journal of the Knowledge Economy*, 15(2), 7428–7454. Advance online publication. DOI: 10.1007/s13132-023-01185-0

Section 4
Game-Based-Learning Approaches: A Strategy for Enlarging Stakeholder Plethora

Chapter 5
Digital Game-Based Learning as a Tool for Intercepting Stakeholders' Tendencies

Andrea Fontanella
https://orcid.org/0000-0001-8173-4716
University of Pisa, Italy

ABSTRACT

This conceptual chapter proposes an innovative way for organisations to engage new stakeholders through video games. This concept requires an explanation of the psychological mechanisms that permit an effective learning process through games and video games. In the educational field, simulation-based video games are effective learning tools because they motivate gamers-learners through an immersive virtual experience to improve themselves in competitive challenges. Shifting to the organisational dimension, video games can be used to upgrade primary stakeholders. An organisation is interested in establishing new relationships with new stakeholders and enhancing the relationships with existing stakeholders. Nowadays, stakeholders want to feel closer to organisations and prefer to establish relationships with those organisations which reflect their values and ethical principles. Thus, organisations must intercept these values and principles to engage existing and new stakeholders, and video games can contribute to helping the organisation achieve this goal.

DOI: 10.4018/979-8-3693-1172-1.ch005

INTRODUCTION

This chapter aims to propose an innovative way to use digital game-based learning in the organisational dimension, proposing the subject as a tool to improve the interrelation (by engagement) with all of its stakeholders, internal and external. On the internal side, DGBL can be used as it is used in the educational field. At the same time, for what concerns the external stakeholders, it could be a useful way to intercept their tendencies and values by making them participate in a virtual version of the organisation. These purposes can be obtained by relying on the intrinsic characteristics of video games and the effects they have on human minds and behaviours.

The notion of stakeholder emerged in management and organisational debate during the 1980s (Freeman, 1984). From that, stakeholder theory became important in the scientific literature, organisations' dynamics, and the business world.

Nowadays, the formalisation of a stakeholder engagement plan is an important help for organisations because it identifies their stakeholders and concerns (Bruce & Shelley, 2010). Organisations must create relationships once their stakeholders are identified, adopting the best approach for every stakeholder category. Organisations aim not only to establish relationships with new stakeholders but also to enhance the relationships with existing ones. Literature shows that managers of those organisations that continuously need to update their employees sometimes resort to digital game-based learning. This approach uses video games as educational tools.

The use of games and video games for educational purposes is a topic that has a central role in the scientific debate.

The industry of video games has become one of the most prolific in the world, competing to the one of movies (Wang et al., 2008). Video games can create a very immersive environment that motivates gamers to continue playing and improve themselves to win challenges and overcome obstacles, being motivated by success (Prensky, 2003).

According to Yee (2006), people play video games for three main reasons: relationships created with other gamers, achievement of in-game objectives and competition, and the identification gamers have with virtual reality. The same reasons motivate the educational properties of video games. Video games enhance learning through visualisation, experimentation, and creativity (Betz, 1995), all elements fed by the intrinsic motivation in video games.

Regarding the educational aspect of video games, it is important to establish the learning goals and choose the proper typology of video games. For example, managerial games are the most used in business and accounting education (Dickinson & Faria, 1997) because of the faithful reality they can build for gamers.

The same principle is used in organisations that need their employees constantly updated (Ismail & Klischewski, 2020). Using DGBL, primary stakeholders learn faster than traditional approaches and observe increased motivation, improving their engagement and performance (Drucker, 2002; Ahmad et al., 2005).

The organisation does not only have the "duty" of keeping its stakeholders motivated and updated but also the need to intercept new stakeholders in the environment. To satisfy this need, the organisation can use different strategies to approach different categories of stakeholders.

About these strategies, this chapter proposes an innovative approach to engage new stakeholders (and the existing ones, too). Using simulation-based video games in the form of business games, the organisation could realise a video game in which the stakeholder-gamer is the organisation's CEO. Because of the immersive and motivational reality (Yee, 2006), the stakeholder-gamer will probably personalise the organisation by reflecting his values and ethical principles (Sicart, 2011). By analysing the various decisions, the organisation can have a faithful representation of some characteristics of its stakeholders, eventually being able to intercept some potential new ones. Moreover, as a side effect, playing a business game similar to reality could also erudite the stakeholders, making them more aware of an organisation's reality and functioning.

This chapter has been realised by consulting important contributions of great scholars, which helped to define key concepts rigorously. The chapter is structured in paragraphs and subparagraphs and is carried out as follows. Paragraph 1.1 illustrates the methodology adopted for developing this chapter. Paragraph 1.2 describes digital game-based learning by proposing a process that starts from the psychological basis of the playing activity and culminates with the debate about using video games as educational tools. The work then proceeds with a description of the characteristics that an educational video game should have. Subparagraph 1.2.1 focuses on managerial and simulation-based business games, the typology of video games most used in accounting and business studies (Faria et al., 2009). The video games are described in detail, also reporting the psychological implications that playing these video games could have on the player as, for example, the personalisation of the virtual business, which leads the gamer-learner to transfer his values into the virtual environment (Sicart, 2011). The first paragraph also has a second subparagraph, 1.2.2, which describes the MMORPBGs, which can be considered the potential evolution of simulation-based business games. Precisely, this category of video games provides a more immersive and engaging experience because gamers develop a virtual avatar who will start at a low level (avatars start as employees in some businesses or run a small activity) to become, by winning challenges and improving itself, a top manager. The third subparagraph, 1.2.3, proposes the limitations of the DGBL under both the educational and the psychological approaches.

Paragraph 1.3 introduces stakeholders. The concept is explained from its origins, from the definitions to the early interpretations of great scholars. The paragraph also provides the importance of the relationships between organisations and stakeholders, focusing on the importance of establishing an interrelation between the two subjects. This paragraph presents two subparagraphs. The first, 1.3.1, introduces digital game-based learning for upgrading primary stakeholders in organisations that need to update their employees continuously. Furthermore, the subparagraph shows how the learning process can engage stakeholders, enhancing the relationship they have with the organisation and, by doing so, increasing the organisation's competitive advantage (Drucker, 2002).

The second subparagraph, 1.3.2, is focused on the stakeholder engagement issue. Even if this process was briefly introduced in subparagraph 1.3.1, it is analysed more deeply. In the last paragraph, 1.3.3, the conceptual model of using video games as a tool to intercept stakeholders' values and principles, aiming at their engagement, is described. The choice of putting the chapter's core in the last section is because it is the conclusion of a process that merges the two crucial topics of digital game-based education (including all its psychological implications) and stakeholder engagement, giving value to the relation that links them and highlighting the methodological setting of this research.

Methodology

This chapter has been realised as a conceptual chapter. As conceptual papers do, this conceptual chapter needs to provide more data because it focuses on proposing a new perspective by relying on existing knowledge (Gilson & Goldberg, 2015). Adopting this framework means starting to develop a theory. "*A conceptual framework, which is simply a less developed form of a theory, consists of statements that link abstract concepts to empirical data. Theories and conceptual frameworks are developed to account for or describe abstract phenomena that occur under similar conditions.*" (Rudestam & Newton, 2014, p. 6). By doing this, it is possible to organise or structure ideas (even abstract ones) when data or contributions are not available.

This methodological approach has been chosen for multiple reasons. First, no contributions or case studies in the literature demonstrate or illustrate that organisations use video games to intercept stakeholders' values and tendencies and, starting from those, elaborate their competitive strategy (as regularly happens when organisations develop a market analysis for the same purposes). At the same time, there is much evidence about gamers' tendency to play some kind of video game by personalising their avatar or actions as a consequence of the high-immersive context in which they are inserted (Yee, 2006). Second, a practical experiment aiming to collect empirical evidence has not been conducted or organised, so relying on empirical or other data sources is impossible. Although this can be seen as a limitation of this research, this gap could be fulfilled in future works. Third, the literature provides many contributions to DGBL and its usefulness in education for both the scholar and, more important for this research's purpose, the organisational level. This means that the organisational dimension already uses the video game approach. Still, it just has a different goal from the one individuated for this chapter, making it possible, through the conceptual framework, to hypothesise the consequences of using it as a tool to intercept stakeholders' values and tendencies and increase their engagement with the organisation.

Digital Game-Based Learning

Since childhood, playing games has been part of the growth of every human being, and it is an activity that accompanies people for a considerable amount of their lives, also being an important part of their social, intellectual and mental development (Rieber, 1996; Amory et al., 1999). Even if the activity of playing is usually related to childhood and adolescence (youth in general), extensive research on play with adults in anthropology, psychology, and education suggests that play is an important tool to socialise and learn throughout life (Yawkey & Pellegrini, 1984; Provost, 1990; Blanchard, 1995; Rieber, 1996). Moreover, Blanchard (1985) argues that play appears to be a universally accepted mode of learning, enforcing the role that playing has over people's lives.

With the rise of technology, computer-based games appeared in the market, proposing several categories of games: simulation, first-person adventures, sports, strategy and lots more; there is a game for the needs of everyone, needs which pushed the video game industry so hard that it has become a multibillion-dollar industry that rivals that of the movies (Wang et al., 2008). All these games offer players many immersive and different experiences, also enhanced by technological improvements of the digital systems that make it possible to create more sophisticated software for experiences so deep to be considered real. "Immersion" is a keyword in the video games industry. Software houses focus on the engagement element, trying to provide more challenging and engaging products to gamers, who experience joy and satisfaction when they achieve an objective and are increasingly motivated to overcome obstacles when they fail (Prensky, 2003). According to Yee (2006), there are three main reasons gamers play:

- The satisfaction of the *relationships* created while interacting with other gamers (especially in the case of online video games);
- *Immersion*, which is defined as the identification with game characters and living in the fantastic world of the game;

- The *achievement*, the result of overcoming challenges and becoming more powerful than before, is an element which stimulates and motivates the gamer to continue playing.

Even if some scholars argue that the activity of gaming affects cognitive functions and motivation and detaches gamers from reality (McKee, 1992; Billen, 1993), it appears instead that games motivate gamers to measure themselves against virtual challenges of crescent difficulty by stimulating their curiosity (Thomas & Macredie, 1994). By having their curiosity stimulated, gamers search for information to satisfy it. When a gamer finds missing information or *learns*, for example, the exact timing for avoiding a boss' attack or the combination of commands to use, they learn something new. The activity of learning, stimulated by the game's difficulty (or challenging, which is one of the elements that make the game entertaining), poses a question to education and psychology scholars: *Can video games be used as a tool for learning?*

According to Lepper & Cordova (1992), funny learning seems more effective than "traditional" learning. Moreover, motivation plays an important role in learning (Prensky, 2003). In fact, according to social cognitive theory (SCT), motivation results from an interaction between personal, behavioural and environmental determinants (Bandura, 1986), which are stimulated by the gaming activity. This perspective suggests that learning by gaming should be effective because it would be a fun activity with an intrinsic motivation to improve oneself, aiming to win a challenge (with, in this case, obvious educational purposes). Moreover, another element which usually characterises video games is fantasy (Malone, 1980, 1981a, 1981b), which can be very important in creating motivating environments (Ebner et al., 2007). Amory et al. (1999) suggest that gaming and learning are closely associated; in fact, video games enhance learning through visualisation, experimentation and creativity (Betz, 1995) and sometimes include situations in which, to find a solution, the development of critical thinking oriented towards logical steps to obtain a concrete solution is required (Huntington, 1984). Focusing on learning through visualisation, Thomson & Ridding (1990) and Tversky et al. (2002) argue that animation is more effective than comparable graphics when it presents fine-grained actions that static graphics cannot represent.

Digital Game-Based Learning (DGBL) is used in several sectors, including education (All et al., 2015), a field in which the debate about the usefulness of DGBL is still open but in which the phenomenon is arising, especially in some countries in the world. For example, "education" is one of the busiest and most competitive industry sectors in the Thai Google Play Store and App Store (Vate-U-Lan, 2014). One strength of video games is interactivity, an element that students appreciate and that is increasingly used in education (Barnabè et al., 2023). Combining interactivity, learning and video games by attributing the interactivity factor exclusively to video games is imprecise. Interactivity, the ability to respond to the learner's actions between teachers and students, is crucial for a good learning experience (Beauchamp & Kennewell, 2010). The difference between the interactivity teachers-students and the interactivity gamers-single-player-video games is that in the second case, the gamers are just interacting with their abilities and knowledge about the situation the software proposes; there is no one with whom to interact. Another strength point is the video game's power to intrinsically motivate gamers to engage in their activities (Ryan & Deci, 2000). This element would be important for a good learning experience because gamers-learners would be motivated to engage in an educational activity without external coercion (All et al., 2014), resulting in a potentially better outcome than the one provided by other approaches.

Moreover, with the rise of the Internet, the multiplayer game experience has been harshly improved. Before, the multiplayer experience was limited to the capacity of a single device to manage more controllers. Nowadays, it is possible to play the same video game with hundreds of gamers around the world. Thanks to this possibility, which is translated, especially into online video games, into the possibility of building teams, cooperation and socialisation in video games are improved, incrementing the benefits of the potential use of video games as instruments for learning (Mann et al., 2002).

Of course, software developed for educational purposes, even if it is a video game, has certain characteristics to be effective. The most important of these, which is also the one from which the entire software is thought and consequently built, is the attainment of the learning goals decided. Learning goals make the developer aware of the typology of the game they will build (e.g., a simulation video game or an adventurous one with some educational problems to be solved to proceed in the game). Then, the educational video game must reflect the characteristics of the others: the learner must find the activity intrinsically motivating (Kinzie & Sullivan, 1989; Kinzie, 1990; Lepper & Malone, 2021). Moreover, educational video games should be like the largest part of video games, so:

- Challenging;
- Curiosity-stimulator;
- Fantastic;
- Controllable (Malone, 1981a; Malone & Lepper, 2021; Lepper & Malone, 2021).

As said, fantasy is an element which can push a learner's motivation towards persisting in their attempts to overcome the challenging obstacles of the game. The challenge is intertwined with curiosity and closely conforms to the Piagetan equilibration process[1], as Rieber (1996) underlined.

When the gamer-learner faces a problem without an immediate solution (challenge), they will seek a solution (curiosity is triggered and, in the case of DGBL, this is the phase during which the gamer-learner is effectively learning, so this is the educational phase of the game) and, if the environment is stimulating enough (fantasy), they will be motivated not only in finding the solution to the actual problem but also to continue in measuring themselves in challenges more difficult than the previous one. Of course, motivation must be protected. Challenges must not be too easy or difficult; otherwise, motivation could decrease, and the video game's engagement capacity would harshly decrease.

According to Chen & O'Neill et al. (2005), the effectiveness of DGBL can be defined regarding three parameters:

- Intensity and longevity of engagement with a video game;
- The commercial success of a video game;
- Acquisition of knowledge and skills resulted in the video game's implementation as an instructional tool.

The third point regards the transfer of knowledge to learners. Its achievement can be observed by identifying eventual changes between the situation before the implementation of the video game and the one after that, referring to applying the learning content to real-world situations (Korteling et al., 2011). As said, several typologies of video games could be chosen for educational and learning purposes. Another element that should be considered while defining the learning goals is the subject, which is meant to be taught through the video game. For example, simulation games have had the strongest presence in accounting and business (digital) education (Faria et al., 2009).

Business Games for Accounting and Business Education

Even if DGBL research on video games in the accounting and business field is not rich (Carenys & Moya, 2016), it is not able to provide a consistent number of publications which can help to explain the phenomenon, as highlighted in the previous paragraph, DGBL finds a fertile ground. Management games in managerial education have gained increasing importance in the educational scenario (Dickinson & Faria, 1997; Martin, 2000): in the US, 97,5% of the AACSB[2] members use them during their courses (Baldissin et al., 2007). The scholars argue that, in addition to classic management game logic, the MMORPG[3] logic can be declined into management games to make them a more useful tool for learning by gaming. In this typology of video games, gamers are immersed in a reality in which they compete against other gamers to overcome challenges and become increasingly powerful by increasing their resources (even financially, because to buy powerful items, money is necessary, and money is obtained by overcoming challenges). Moreover, MMORPGs appear to have all four virtual features of virtual worlds: interactivity (with other gamers, especially the members of the same team), physicality, persistence and safety (Delwiche, 2006). Nowadays, simulation games are the most used in DGBL for social sciences, including accounting and business education (Faria et al., 2009). Before describing and defining simulation video games and their potential as tools for entertainment and learning, it is useful to focus on the meaning of the word "simulation". According to Alessi & Trollip (1984), a simulation is any attempt to mimic a real or imaginary environment or system and usually pursues two purposes: scientific or educational. Focusing on the educational aspect, it appears that simulations aim to teach someone about a phenomenon by observing the consequences of actions or decisions generated by the simulation at different speeds of time (simulation can be real-time, slowed or accelerated, depending on the users' needs). Learning by using simulations is becoming widely established within medical education (Dankbaar et al., 2016) because of the provision of learning tasks and instruction in a realistic and engaging computer-based environment (Sitzmann, 2011) in which learners can practice on delicate issues without the eventuality of harming the patient.

There are several definitions for simulation games and video games.

According to De Freitas & Oliver (2006), simulation games are evolving open-ended situations of specific realities that can be social or physical and in which the participants play roles with both responsibilities and constraints. Ranchhod et al. (2014) provide a definition that embraces the learning purpose of this category of games and video games because they define simulation games as simplified and dynamic representations of reality structured as interactive games intended to enhance experimental learning.

Simulation video games present some relevant characteristics, which Gredler (2013) outlined. A good simulation video game present:

- A model which permits the interaction between students and complex situations;
- A defined role and task for each gamer;
- An environment which allows gamers to learn different strategies.

Defined the characteristics of a simulation video game, it is interesting to analyse how this software can be used in business and accounting education. The learning video games market offers many management games structured as simulation games.

Simulation management video games can be seen as a representation of the reality in which the gamer can improvise himself, for example, as the CEO of an airline company, choose the routes and the air fleet, and operate on fares, aiming to make the business grow and win against competitors.

One of simulation video games' most interesting and useful characteristics is the possibility of making choices in a challenging and immersive environment and observing their consequences, permitting gamers to learn how to improve their strategy (Kiili, 2005; Huang et al., 2010). This characteristic of simulation video games, which intrinsically requires the gamers' learning activity, is crucial for utilising a video game as a tool for learning.

Simulation video games are part of the serious games category, a typology of video games that does not have a clear definition but is recognised as those video games "*used for training, advertising, simulation or education that are designed to run on personal computers or video games consoles*" (Susi et al., 2007, p. 3).

Serious video games are not limited to providing gamers with a benefit; they are just an immersive and engaging gaming experience. However, they provide more benefits because of their goal to solve problems by training or investigating (Abt, 1987). Thus, there is an intrinsic attempt to enrich gamers' knowledge and sharpen their skills. Because of the characteristics of simulation video games that create a protected environment, gamers can be free to commit mistakes without paying any consequence in the real world, making them free to learn from them. Because gamers face real-life situations using specific knowledge to achieve various goals, it is possible to state that serious games go beyond mere entertainment (Baldissin et al., 2013).

Even if this still represents an innovation, serious games are used in the DGBL context in secondary schools and universities, especially in the social sciences field.

Analysing and applying the DGBL to accounting and business results in the so-called business games being the most used (and the most suited for) teaching and learning. Faria et al. (2009) listed some of the learning outcomes derived from using these kinds of games as educational tools:

- Learning outcomes and objectives;
- Improving decision-making skills;
- Improving the ability of strategy production;
- Learning how to work in a team with a scheduled deadline;
- Gaining experience.

The introduction of such a new subcategory of video games implies two questions. The first is, of course, "What is a business game?" while the second is about the characteristics that permit this typology of video games to be the most suited for educational purposes: "Why business games?".

Greenlaw et al. (1962) defined business games in a way that can still be useful in defining their digital evolution: "*a sequential decision-making exercise structured around a model of business operation, in which participants assume the role of managing the simulated operation*" (p. 14). This definition partially embeds the answer to the second question; the business game is structured as a business simulation in which gamers must decide about several business operations. Consequently, the virtual environment is not open but limited to the commands gamers can input, observing their consequences and learning even from the worst ones. This consideration explains *why business games* are suitable as educational tools in the context of DGBL. A closed environment does not give gamers, who are limited to deciding among the commands they can input to make their managerial decisions, too much freedom of action. This standardises gamers-learners' actions, making it easier to evaluate them and make them aware and learn from their own decisions than a business game structured as an MMORPG (as, for example, *IndustryPlayer®* and *Perfectcompetition®* are).

Defined the business games, it is possible to focus on the characteristics of this software.

During a business game session, one or more gamers assume the role of a manager and, by consulting their teammates, they decide on the strategy and input their decisions, which will be elaborated by the software that will produce a scenario. Because business games involve competition with other gamers, the software will elaborate on every decision, and the consequent scenario will consider the effects of the different strategies. Predicting other competitors' strategies becomes crucial for winning the business game, so there is a double learning phase. On the one hand, a team must learn the best strategy to run their virtual business; on the other, they must learn competitors' strategies to react properly.

Another interesting fact is that gamers can reflect on their visions and values while playing video games and business games (Sicart, 2011). This possibility makes possible the virtual business's personalisation, reflecting on various parameters, the leading principles of the gamer-manager. Indicators such as brand reputation and environmental sustainability impact the overall performance of the business, but, at the same time, they are in-game achievements which can be pursued, such as a good return on equity (ROE) and return on investment (ROI).

The Evolution of Business Games: MMORPBG

The last paragraph described the most used typology of business games, characterised as simulation video games, in which there is a closed environment in which gamers make their decisions, and the system elaborates and crosses with competitors' before giving a simulation of the results.

This paragraph will describe a typology of video games, which can be seen as the evolution of business games. The structure is that of an MMORPG, so it is an internet-based game in which a large number of gamers play at the same time. Unlike simulation video games, MMORPBG[4] has a good level of realism because of real-time playing (Baldissin et al., 2013). MMORPBGs introduce characteristics of business games into the dynamic and progressive logic of MMORPGs. Thus, gamers will start from the bottom of their entrepreneurial career and, by experience, compete against each other to become the market leader with the best business. The more gamers play, the more perfect the market becomes (Wellington et al., 2017). Adopting an MMORPG requires the implementation of an evolved graphic interface because gamers are not just making decisions. However, through their avatars, they are living the virtual reality with competitors and teammates.

This approach, by giving a more real experience (Baldissin et al., 2013) than the one offered by the simulation-based business games, presents some other advantages regarding simulation-based business games:

- The whole experience happens in real time. In MMORPBGs, there is no need to wait for the elaboration of the software, but all the gamers' decisions have immediate consequences;
- Gamers undergo a process of evolution. They start their experience at the lowest levels, trying to improve their positions through an effective and efficient business strategy. In contrast, in simulation-based business games, every gamer starts his experience as a top manager of an international business, so there is no phase during which gamers learn how to become a top manager starting from the bottom of the business;
- The possibility to communicate in real-time with teammates and competitors. In simulation-based business games, communication about the team's decision and the results given by the software is limited.

Adopting such a category of business games as an educational tool has different learning outcomes. If simulation-based business games promote experiential learning (Petersen & Ekambaram, 2016), MMORPGBs promote explorative learning.

This category of business games may also present some criticalities. In such a free environment, it takes work to establish definite learning goals and evaluate which strategy is better than the others.

In conclusion, it appears interesting to observe how different categories of video games may be useful in a crucial process of life as learning and, more in general, how something that is usually related exclusively to the fun dimension may discover itself as an interdimensional tool, capable of creating value by pursuing different purposes.

Limitations of DGBL

Previous paragraphs showed the qualities and advantages of using DGBL in education, describing how it can influence the learning (and teaching) practice. Although several shreds of evidence support this educational approach, the debate on DGBL is actual and open.

Many scholars, in fact, highlight the limits of this practice, which are oriented towards several dimensions.

Starting from the educational perspective, DGBL may make it difficult for teachers to establish a precise task completion deadline (Cojocariu & Boghian, 2014). In fact, learning by playing video games requires learners to win the game, and, for the intrinsic characteristics of video games, for being challenging, it must be adequately difficult. Moreover, the difficulty of a video game may discourage gamers, who will not continue playing and will not achieve their learning goal.

Adopting such educational methodology may cause the reduction of classroom interrelations (Keesee, 2012) due to different reasons. First, serious games (as seen, the most used for educational purposes) do not provide a social dimension. In fact, considering business games as an example, the action of playing is to make decisions and wait for their consequences. So, even if the context is to compete against other people in the same market, there is no direct interaction with them. Second, even if a video game would provide a social interface, it would be a text-to-text chat. So also, in this second case, direct social contact would need to be included. To avoid this situation, teachers may introduce some moments to involve their students-gamers and make them confront their experiences.

Regarding the psychological dimension, a serious limitation of using video games for educational purposes can be found in the video games' capacity to create dependence (Griffiths & Davies, 2005; Rehbein et al., 2010; Weinstein, 2010).

Dunne (2014) argues that video games are focused on creating an immersive environment, making gamers feel lost in another reality from which they do not want to exit, coming back to reality. According to the scholar, this situation may lead to gamers' alienation.

Organisations and Stakeholders

"A stakeholder in an organisation is any group or individual who can affect or is affected by the achievements of the organisation's objectives" (Freeman, 1984, p. 46).

At its enunciation, the stakeholder concept was relatively new for business economics and organisation. The word stakeholder itself is inspired by "stockholder", so all those interested in a business' decision-making process because they possess some shares of the business itself. Stakeholder means that there are other people and groups (employees, customers, creditors, competitors, communities and governments) who have a "stake" in the decision-making process of an organisation (Goodpaster, 1991).

Scholars have discussed the utility of stakeholders, trying to define why they are important for business life. Friedman (1962) stated that supporting stakeholders' interests is about capitalism. The economist sustained that stakeholders are just one of the elements necessary for maximising profit, the ultimate objective of every business. In contrast, recent literature sustains that stakeholders (considered individuals or groups) are crucial for a business and its reputation (Matuleviciene & Stravinskiene, 2015). Precisely, Neville et al. (2005) argue that the relationships between stakeholders and businesses are based on the dependency on some resources which are fundamental for the organisations and the eventual loss of them "*may place its* [the organisation] *survival in jeopardy*" (p. 1187). Stakeholder theory puts the concept of relationship at the centre. According to Attanasio et al. (2022), stakeholder theory is useful to achieve several goals:

- Resolve the needs of a broad group of stakeholders (Harrison et al., 2010);
- To shape relationships, making them more suitable for creating value for all the stakeholders (Freeman, 1984);
- To assess potential damages and benefits to broad groups or individuals (Post et al., 2002; Phillips, 2003; Sisodia et al., 2007).

Stakeholders theory acquires importance because businesses live in an environment where they must find an equilibrium to survive and thrive. Often, as a stakeholder's element of importance, organisations cannot produce all the necessary resources to complete their production cycle. So, they must retrieve them from other subjects, who become business stakeholders, creating a relationship with them. A business must protect and enhance the precious relationship it and the stakeholders created; otherwise, in case of interruption of the relationship, the business would lack resources and be put in potential danger.

Stakeholders are important not only as subjects that help businesses supply resources but also, especially nowadays, are crucial in increasing corporate reputation. This dimension has assumed a central role in the organisation's environment, especially in recent years. Corporate reputation can be considered as the interrelation between stakeholders and the organisation (Roberts & Dowling, 2002; Helm, 2007; Puncheva, 2008; Omar, 2009; Siano et al., 2010; Peloza et al., 2012; Matuleviciene & Stravinskiene, 2015). Interrelation means reciprocity, an active participation of both subjects in creating value for each other. Neville et al. (2005) and Bruce & Shelley (2010) sustain that a good interrelation between stakeholders and organisations may have positive effects not only from the corporate reputation perspective but also from the financial and social ones, increasing the value the organisation can create. As a cost, the corporate reputation and financial performance may be compromised when the interrelation stops and becomes a one-directional relation.

Once stakeholders and their importance for organisations have been described, it is useful to analyse them and briefly identify some different typologies of stakeholders. As said, stakeholders are those individuals or groups of people who have some interest in a specific organisation's achievement of its objectives. However, what are stakeholder groups and which characteristics distinguish every group from the others? According to Matuleviciene & Stravinskiene (2015), although there are many stakeholder groups, scientific literature (Freeman, 1984; Argandoña, 1998; Biscaccianti, 2003; Freeman et al., 2004; Verdeyen et al., 2004; Lozano, 2011) focuses only on a small part of them, the same that will be described here:

- Internal groups: all those individuals interested in the organisation's activities and financial performances;
- External groups: all those individuals not directly interested in the organisation's activities but who can be affected by the consequences. External stakeholders may be interested in financial support, ethics, values, satisfaction and other similar parameters (Florea, 2013).

Because of the undiscussed value created by stakeholders, one goal of every business is to attract stakeholders, create relationships and keep them. In recent years, also because of a more intense sensibility about important events, such as climate change, people became aware of the impact not only their actions have on the environment and society but also the impact on the same dimensions that the organisations with which they have a relationship have. This fact enhanced the role of business ethics, and organisations might seek to engage their stakeholders by acting on morals and ethical principles (Noland & Phillips, 2010). To "engage" means to look for and build a relationship which involves recognising some basic principles and, more importantly, recognising that every action one of the subjects involved takes has a direct (or indirect) impact on the surrounding reality, including the subjects themselves. Stakeholder engagement is defined as "*the interaction between an organisation and those individuals and groups that are impacted by, or influence, the organisation*" (Bruce & Shelley, 2010, p. 2).

Stakeholders now want not just to be in a relationship for value and interest with a certain organisation but to be partners in a reality which reflects their social values and ethics. Because of this, organisations must consider two crucial elements:

- The organisation's values and ethical principles must be declared and communicated, aiming to make stakeholders identify with them and make them more confident in keeping the interrelation with the organisation;
- The organisation's values and ethical principles must be reflected in every operation of the organisation itself. It is not sufficient for the organisation to declare to be aware of some social and ethical issues. However, the organisation must act concretely to concretise them by, for example, participating in social events and taking distances from people, movements, and other organisations far from the organisation's values (and those of its stakeholders).

These (social) activities aim to create and increase consensus among the various stakeholders.

Consensus is, in fact, a strong element for creating new relationships with potential stakeholders and enhancing the existing relationships with actual stakeholders.

According to Orlandini & Amelio (2022), an organisation aiming to engage more stakeholders can act to convince them through the adoption of some managerial models:

- Authoritarian, in which consensus is imposed (this model is frequently adopted in the relationships between an organisation and its employees);
- Persuasive, in which it is possible to appreciate a non-stop dialogue between the organisation and its stakeholders, aiming to make stakeholders participate in the decisions about some parts of the organisation's strategies;
- Manipulative. This is a model in which the organisation uses the relationships of trust previously created with its stakeholders to avoid critiques;
- Emulative, a managerial model in which the organisation starts to emulate its stakeholders' behaviour (but also other organisations' behaviour that has realised an increase of the consensus among its stakeholders), aiming to increase consensus among them;
- Antagonist, in which the relationships between the organisations and the stakeholders are built around contractual agreements. This approach is common in relationships between businesses and workers (Coda, 1995).

Stated this, it appears clear that, for an organisation, it is crucial to intercept potential stakeholders' and stakeholders' values and ethical principles for adopting the best managerial model to establish and keep strong the interrelation with them and obtain a condition of competitive advantage in the market (Drucker, 2002).

To engage stakeholders efficiently, an organisation must adopt an effective social practice. Elaborating an effective social practice requires the adoption of some actions. The first (among the most important) is a deep and accurate analysis of the external and internal environment (Orlandini & Amelio, 2022), aiming to individuate potential criticalities and opportunities. With the information retrieved from the environmental analysis, the organisation can create an accurate map of some characteristics of potential stakeholders. Consequently, the organisation must understand how stakeholders could influence its decisions. If, in addition to all the variables that could affect this process, the abovementioned elements about ethics and values are considered too, the process of engaging stakeholders is complex and requires intense effort to be completed.

Stakeholders and Video Games

As said in the conclusion of the previous chapter, the process of engaging stakeholders is complex and, especially nowadays, complicated by some elements, such as people's ethics and values, which intensify the organisation's efforts.

Another element that must be considered is the overall stakeholders' knowledge and preparation about the organisation and those elements that are of interest for establishing an interrelation with the organisation.

This phase requires a specification about the categorisation of stakeholders. In the previous paragraph, external stakeholders have been distinguished from internal ones. For a better understanding of the contents of this paragraph, it is useful to adopt a different categorisation of stakeholders by referring to the one that divides stakeholders into primary and secondary (McIntosh et al., 1998; Lindfelt, 2002). Both categories present two subcategories in which the various primary or secondary stakeholders are divided into social or non-social stakeholders, considering all those non-human stakeholders (except environmental pressure groups and animal welfare organisations, considered secondary non-social stakeholders) as non-social.

Even if this is an element that should be considered a major concern of every stakeholder, especially for primary ones, it is necessary to be constantly updated because of the extreme dynamism of the market and the environment. Focusing on primary stakeholders, it is clear that employees are identified as primary stakeholders under both the normative and the instrumental perspectives (Mitchell et al., 1997; Phillips, 1999). Updating employees and, in general, primary stakeholders can be reconducted to a teacher-student relationship, in which some employees of an organisation (students) must obtain improved information, knowledge and know-how through learning from other employees (teachers) who will instruct them. The learning process embedded in the organisational processes made scholars question the utility of using DGBL to update primary stakeholders.

Research about the use of DGBL in organisational logic is scarce, but it provides some evidence about using DGBL as an educational tool inside organisations. An example is provided by a study carried out by Ismail & Klischewski (2020). The scholars analysed the possibility of increasing the maturity of SMEs' stakeholders through implementing DGBL to make them learn Information Technology. The tool was chosen because of its fundamental characteristics, affordance and scalability. Gamification[5] of the organisation can be useful to engage and motivate people to achieve their goals (Burke, 2014). As said, video games stimulate, by challenging, people's motivation, making them more focused on the activity of learning. DGBL helped solve organisational issues, such as technological illiteracy, employee lack of motivation and many others (Baxter et al., 2017; Ismail & Klischewski, 2020; Larson, 2020; Friedrich et al., 2020). Moreover, there is positive evidence about using DGBL as a useful tool for all those managers who need to constantly improve their employees' knowledge (Kapp, 2012), a methodology usually utilised in SMEs. This evidence is important because it is not limited to all the elements described in previous paragraphs about using video games but also introduces another quality: speed.

Those managers adopt DGBL because of a continuous need for updates for their employees, so the process must be carried on fast. DGBL, in this sense, appears to be not only the best-suited tool from the learning perspective but also under the efficiency one if "efficiency" is considered the capacity to deliver the best possible learning path in less time consumption.

This capacity can be explained by referring to some characteristics of gamification. According to Kapp (2012), gaming uses humans' psychological predisposition to be motivated to challenge and achieve objectives, making them perform activities that they ordinarily (and out of a game context) consider not stimulating. While playing video games, people receive continuous stimuli to continue playing, so they are motivated to concentrate on that activity (Ryan & Deci, 2000), improving their performances (Kiili, 2005; Huang et al., 2010) and, by doing so, acquiring new knowledge and competencies, so learning.

This is a way through which it is possible to engage primary stakeholders. Keeping them updated and useful has several consequences on their feeling of engagement. Firstly, and most importantly, it engages them by keeping active the interrelation between the organisation and its employees (as said, if establishing relationships with stakeholders is important for an organisation from several points of view, keeping it active and enhancing it is even more important); secondly, it engages them by keeping them motivated and immersed in a dynamic environment (Hitt et al., 2001). Keeping primary stakeholders motivated and engaging them positively affects their performance and, consequently, the organisation's performance. Engagement can be considered a boost for employees because it makes them feel useful, important, and responsible for the importance of their work, so they will be motivated to perform better.

The most adopted typology of video games used in organisational contexts is serious games, which organisations built according to their needs to improve their primary stakeholders' soft skills (Ekambaram & Petersen, 2017). The utility of serious games in the organisational dimension is in the game's mechanics: when a player learns by playing a game, then the player applies that learning immediately in the game and moves on to learning new skills (Gee, 2003).

In conclusion, research suggests that DGBL can be useful for engaging primary stakeholders by acting on their psychological characteristics of being motivated to achieve particular objectives while involved in competition and challenges. However, organisations' objective is to keep the interrelation with their stakeholders (primary and secondary) active and engage new stakeholders. Aiming to this objective, the following paragraph will provide a possible innovative use of video games for engaging stakeholders.

Stakeholder Engagement Through Digital Game-Based Learning

The last paragraph described the importance of engaging stakeholders, proposing the fundamental concept of "relationship" (which assumes the connotations of interrelation because of the bivalence of the relationship between the organisation and all its stakeholders).

Focusing on the link between the concept of "engagement" and the concept of "stakeholder", Lerbinger (2006) states that engagement is about *developing* and *sustaining* relationships between stakeholders. The concept of engagement can be seen as the term that identifies all the organisation's efforts to intercept stakeholders' beliefs to involve those people in its activities and decisions (Bruce & Shelley, 2010). Moreover, the engagement of stakeholders gives the impression of corporate responsibility (Greenwood, 2007). Being accountable to its stakeholders makes the organisation responsible, and the organisations that act responsibly towards their stakeholders concretise the belief around which corporate responsibility is built.

While regarding new stakeholders (or potential ones), the concept of developing relationships has different meanings. According to the first distinction presented in the previous paragraph, stakeholders can be divided into internal and external. Analysing the external category and creating a relationship requires different approaches. Establishing a relationship with a supplier is different from establishing a relationship with a customer: with the firsts, the interrelation is about the provisioning of raw materials and, generally, resources; with the seconds, the interrelation can assume a more articulate form, focusing on a high quality of the product or the service provided, the value for money and, as said in the previous paragraphs, even on the common values between the organisation and the customer, ethical principles, environmental sustainability and others.

According to this, engaging new stakeholders is a process that requires intense efforts on several dimensions, especially under the personal values and characteristics of potential stakeholders. This process usually requires a multi-phase approach, during the first of which the environment is deeply analysed, as happens while adopting marketing strategies for placing a new product on the market (Blythe, 2006).

Nowadays, it is possible to use social media to analyse potential stakeholders' sentiments and opinions to elaborate a more precise strategy for engaging them, so use communication to engage them. Scientific literature illustrates that National Sports organisations widely utilise the so-called relationship market (RM) to create a bond with potential stakeholders (Abeza & O'Reilly, 2014). By using communication through social media, it is possible to establish interrelations with stakeholders, who interact with the organisation and create value from the very beginning of the relationships. On social media, it is possible to intercept people's values and observe their reactions to the organisation's initiatives and competitors'. By reacting to content, stakeholders create useful data for organisations, which can structure their communicative strategy to engage them. In this sense, stakeholders' reactions to the organisations' communications on social media channels can be considered a cooperative approach because, on the one hand, the organisation uses social media to promote its product and spread its communicative strategy; on the other, stakeholders explicit their sentiments and opinion about it, providing useful feedbacks to the organisation's strategies. Collaboration is a helpful factor in stakeholder engagement (Lozano, 2007). However, even if the reaction on social media can be considered a collaborative process between the organisation and its stakeholders, the process appears chaotic because an organisation has to analyse every reaction, deconstruct it and keep only the useful ones.

Moreover, people's reactions happen only when they respond to an external stimulus, which is the publication of the content by the organisation. Collaboration is not only the result of the reaction on social media but can be stimulated by using other tools. Collaborative platforms provide a useful example in this sense. Collaborative platforms are a concept introduced recently in the scientific debate. They are defined as "[...] *an organisation or program with dedicated competencies, institutions, and resources for facilitating the creation, adaptation and success of multiple or ongoing collaborative projects or networks.*" (Ansell & Gash, 2018, p. 20). Collaborative platforms motivate people to pursue a common or shared interest or to find a compromise when individual interests are not collimating; in fact, using this tool when adopted for collaborative governance (Lee, 2023) makes it possible to overcome obstacles (in the early stages of the whole process) by adapting structures and developing common purposes (which assume the connotations of compromises when the original individual interests are not shared). Even if collaborative platforms motivate people to collaborate (as said, collaboration is helpful for engaging stakeholders), they appear not to be the best-suited tool to help organisations engage their stakeholders. In fact, according to the definition provided by Ansell & Gash (2018), the organisation is the subject deputed to provide resources, competencies, institutions, and the other elements described in the definition to stakeholders. A process like this appears similar to the relationship created on social media in which the stakeholders react to the organisation's content or proposal.

This chapter explained several concepts about different topics. By considering all the contents, it is possible to identify some focal points:

- Learning is an interactive activity;
- Video games motivate people to improve themselves and their abilities for winning challenges, overcoming obstacles, and achieving objectives. To do this, gamers learn;
- Because of the previous point, some video games are appropriately structured as educational tools. For this purpose, in the category of serious games, simulation-based video games appear to be the most used for business and accounting studies;
- Stakeholders create more value when their relationship with the organisation is an interrelation, so both actors act considering each other. The organisation must engage its existing and potential new stakeholders to achieve this objective.

Starting from these, engaging stakeholders using simulation-based video games could be possible, as Hitt et al. (2001) illustrated when investigating stakeholders' engagement through their learning-to-upgrade process, and Fleming et al. (2020) described how serious games can engage stakeholders in managing risks and emergencies.

Fleming et al. (2020) argue that serious games can engage stakeholders in risk management and disaster management. Even if this is not the topic of this chapter, this is an interesting contribution which demonstrates that video games can engage stakeholders. Furthermore, Fleming et al.'s contribution, like Ekambaram & Petersen (2017) and Gee (2003), describe that serious games can be adapted to different contexts and topics, depending on the organisation's needs.

Thus, an organisation could develop a simulation-based video game (which would assume the characteristics of a business game because of the topics offered) where the gamer can improvise as the organisation's CEO. While playing, the stakeholder-gamer will be immersed in a challenging environment where he will compete against other stakeholder-gamers to become the market leader. Even if this business game is not for educational purposes (differently from those specifically used for that), the activity of learning, even if it is still present, does not have a central role; it is important to have real people as opponents instead of artificial intelligence or algorithms for multiple reasons. First, artificial opponents cannot create value for the organisation because they are not real stakeholders but just part of the virtual environment; they are part of the video game. The organisation needs to create interrelations with stakeholders, so humans. Second, "*when participants have their own goals, it is challenging to generate shared motivation*" (Lee, 2023, p. 806). As said in previous paragraphs, according to the SCT, gaming stimulates and motivates gamers to continue playing by acting on particular factors (Bandura, 1986). Being opponents of each other motivates stakeholder-gamers not only through the video game itself but also through the chance to be the best CEO of the organisation and perform better than all the opponents.

Using a video game to engage stakeholders does not only have positive consequences related to the intrinsic capacity of a video game to stimulate motivation in gamers (Wang et al., 2008). As CEOs of the organisation, stakeholder-gamers may play by personalising the organisation itself because of the high level of immersion the gaming experience offers (Yee, 2006). This would mean that they would reflect their ethical principles and values (Sicart, 2011), one of the most important characteristics that, nowadays, act in establishing (and conserving) a good relationship between stakeholders and organisations. Furthermore, the immersive experience offered by the simulation could make the stakeholder-gamer feel more included in the organisation's dynamics, increasing their sense of belonging and engagement.

Of course, it is still being determined if stakeholders-gamers will play to win or personalise their experience as CEOs of the organisation. Thus, the organisation could extract data from the video game (simply retrieving all the choices made by stakeholder-gamers), aggregate them and retrieve information about the strategies implemented and, more importantly, for engaging stakeholders, which are the values and the more frequent principles, so the most shared by stakeholders.

This need to intercept stakeholders' values and principles through video games can be fulfilled at its best using a simulation-based serious game.

The reasons that justify this choice are the same, for which the same typology of video games was preferred, for example, to MMORPGs for developing DGBL programs. Although MMORPGs offer a more immersive gaming experience than simulation-based video games and more freedom of choice (which means an extremely higher degree of personalisation), this could be counterproductive for the achievement of the organisation's goal (the interception of stakeholders' values and principles for a better action of engagement) because, with such high personalisation, there is the eventuality of registering choices so different and about so many dimensions of the organisation that extracting data would be a difficult process (and potentially useless). Simulation-based video games, instead, offer a less free environment because they let gamers act freely but only by using pre-set commands. This characteristic makes it easier to extract data because the difference is only to be found in different approaches and choices about a list of pre-determined topics (for example, it is possible to observe gamers who prefer to maximise ROI and other ones who prefer to reduce their profit in favour of selling a high quality good to a lower price aiming to increase the ethical values of the organisation). This helps the organisation determine who its stakeholders are and what their concerns are (Bruce & Shelley, 2010).

Integrating this approach with the existing ones, organisations could increase their capacity to engage stakeholders by enhancing the existing relationships through motivation (Hitt et al., 2001) and try to engage new stakeholders (keeping the existing ones) by intercepting their values and principles expressed during the gaming experience.

How Organisations Can Intercept Stakeholders' Tendencies and Values Through Video Games: A Conceptual Framework

"Stakeholder analysis is an approach, a tool or a set of tools for generating knowledge about actors, individuals and organisations for understanding their behaviour, intentions, interrelations and interests" (Brugha & Varvasovszky, 2000; Varvasovszky & Brugha, 2000, p. 338).

Developing a stakeholder analysis is a multi-phase process. According to Schmeer (1999), a stakeholder analysis is composed of eight steps, of which the fourth and the fifth are particularly interesting for this chapter. In fact, after the preliminary phases of the process, developing the stakeholder analysis requires the collection of data. According to its objectives and the results of the previous phases, it develops the set of questions that will be administered to stakeholders. Then, it starts to interview stakeholders. The final phases regard the elaboration of data and the production of the information.

This technique highlights the organisation's active role and the stakeholders' passive role. It is possible to define the organisation as active because it analyses the environment, prepares the interviews, chooses the questions, and asks stakeholders to answer them. Stakeholders have a passive role instead because they have to answer the organisation's questions.

Adopting the methodological tool of stakeholder analysis has some limitations. Varvasovszky & Brugha (2000) individuated some of them:

- The eventual relationship with other stakeholders may affect the stakeholder's willingness to participate in the interview;
- If too many stakeholders participate, the map processing may result in something too complex;
- Pre-selecting stakeholders may exclude potentially useful stakeholders from the selection (Fottler et al., 1989).

Paragraph 1.3.2 illustrates how video games' intrinsic characteristics may make stakeholders act by personification while they play with them. Moreover, the paragraph anticipated a key concept: "The organisation could extract data from the video game" by processing gamers' choices and strategies. How do it?

Simulation-based business games are the most suitable games for achieving the goal because of their characteristic of being designed for learning and training (Susi et al., 2007). This quality also depends on business games not being structured to measure gamers' coordination or speed in composing a combination of commands but to measure gamers' ability to make decisions about their virtual organisation's strategy, forecasting rivals' ones, using a system of pre-set options. In fact, every option is available, in the same way, to all the gamers involved in the game, making it easy for the game master (in the educational field, the teacher) to track every gamer's strategy.

By relying on these simulation-based business game characteristics, the organisations could act as the game master and obtain precious information about their stakeholders' (or potential ones') strategies, eventually focusing on particular variables such as ethical, environmental, or sustainability values.

Adopting this approach, which is different from stakeholder analysis, makes the stakeholder gamer act no more passively but actively. In fact, the organisation sets and proposes the simulation-based business game, and the stakeholders play with it, competing against each other to win the challenge and, at the same moment, they produce precious data for the organisation.

Figure 1. How the organization intercepts stakeholders' values and tendencies by using a business game

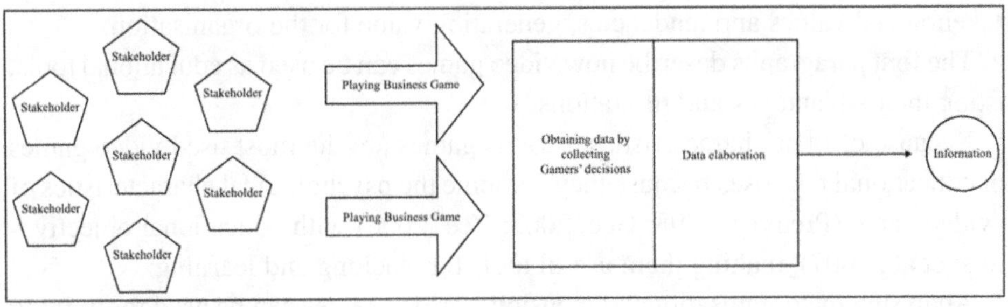

Source: own elaboration

Figure 1 shows how this system acts. Stakeholders play the organisation's business game. Because of the structure of a business game, it is easy for the organisation to retrieve stakeholders' choices and strategies, aggregating and elaborating them to produce information which can be used to create value and competitive advantage.

This approach avoids stakeholder analysis limitations because, without an interview, so without direct questions to which to answer, eventual relationships are irrelevant. Furthermore, the numerosity of stakeholders is irrelevant because video games propose a set of possible options that are the same for every player, so there is no eventuality of results being too personalised. Finally, there is no need to pre-select stakeholders, avoiding sampling biases.

This approach has some limitations:

- The business game provides a pre-set of possible options. Gamers could not find the option or the combination of options that reflected their values, so the information produced may not be accurate;
- Gamers could play opportunistically or casually without personalising their gaming experience. Even in this eventuality, the information produced may not be accurate;
- To be motivated to start playing seriously, stakeholder gamers could need a prize. This may increase costs for the organisation.

This approach is an element of novelty in the scientific literature because even if scholars brought evidence about using serious games to engage stakeholders (Gee, 2003; Ekambaram & Petersen, 2017; Fleming, 2020), to the best of our knowledge, there are no contributions about planning the stakeholder strategy on collecting stakeholders' values and tendencies using a simulation-based business game.

CONCLUSIONS AND DISCUSSION

This chapter aims to describe DGBL and propose it as a tool useful to intercept stakeholders' values and tendencies, generating value for the organisation.

The first paragraphs describe how video games can be used as educational tools, listing their advantages and limitations

Because of their characteristics, serious games are the most used video games for educational purposes because they combine the psychological characteristics of a video game (Prensky, 2003; Gee, 2003; Yee, 2006) with educational objectives (Susi et al., 2007), making them useful tools for teaching and learning.

Analysing the organisational dimension, serious games can be used for training human resources in dynamic contexts, which requires quick learning processes (Hitt et al., 2001). Moreover, scholars argue that this typology of videogames is able to engage stakeholders in different contexts, topics and disciplines (Gee, 2003; Ekambaram & Petersen, 2017).

By analysing the literature, this chapter proposes a conceptual approach for engaging stakeholders through simulation-based business games.

Stakeholder gamers, by personalising their gaming experience, will play the business game following their values. The organisation can collect gamers' choices and strategies, intercept gamers' values, and elaborate an effective stakeholder analysis.

This chapter contributes to the scientific literature by proposing an element of novelty and originality in the stakeholders analysis field and in the DGBL debate. This concept is the first in the literature to adopt video games as tools for developing a stakeholder analysis that overcomes the biases and limitations of classic stakeholder analysis methodologies. Of course, this concept has its advantages and limitations, which are listed and described in paragraph 1.3.3.

However, this chapter presents some limitations.

Although the conceptual framework is a recognised and widely used methodological approach (Gilson & Goldberg, 2015), there is a lack of empirical evidence.

However, this gap can be filled with future research by proposing a practical experiment, building a business game for an organisation and observing how stakeholders interact with it. After the collection and the elaboration of data retrieved, it will be possible to compare those results with the ones obtained by developing a classical stakeholder analysis.

List of Abbreviations Used

CEO: *Chief Executive Officer.*

DGBL: *Digital Game-Based Learning.*

MMORPG: *Massively Multiplayer Online Role-Playing Game.*

MMORPBG:*Massively Multiplayer Online Role-Playing Business Game.*
RM:*Relationship Market.*
ROE:*Return On Equity.*
ROI:*Return On Interests.*
SCT:*Social Cognitive Theory.*
SME:*Small and Medium Enterprises.*

REFERENCES

Abeza, G., & O'Reilly, N. (2014). Social media platforms' use in building stakeholder relationships: The case of national sport organizations. *Journal of Applied Sport Management*, 6(3), 10.

Abt, C. C. (1987). *Serious games*. University Press of America.

Ahmad, S. J., O'Regan, N., & Ghobadian, A. (2005). Leadership, decision making and internal stakeholder engagement. *International Journal of Management and Decision Making*, 6(3-4), 345–358. DOI: 10.1504/IJMDM.2005.006559

Alessi, S. M., & Trollip, S. R. (1984). *Computer-based instruction: Methods and development*. Prentice-Hall, Inc.

All, A., Castellar, E. P. N., & Van Looy, J. (2014). Measuring effectiveness in digital game-based learning: A methodological review. *International Journal of Serious Games*, 1(2). Advance online publication. DOI: 10.17083/ijsg.v1i2.18

All, A., Castellar, E. P. N., & Van Looy, J. (2015). Towards a conceptual framework for assessing the effectiveness of digital game-based learning. *Computers & Education*, 88, 29–37. DOI: 10.1016/j.compedu.2015.04.012

Amory, A., Naicker, K., Vincent, J., & Adams, C. (1999). The use of computer games as an educational tool: Identification of appropriate game types and game elements. *British Journal of Educational Technology*, 30(4), 311–321. DOI: 10.1111/1467-8535.00121

Ansell, C., & Gash, A. (2018). Collaborative platforms as a governance strategy. *Journal of Public Administration: Research and Theory*, 28(1), 16–32. DOI: 10.1093/jopart/mux030

Argandoña, A. (1998). The stakeholder theory and the common good. *Journal of Business Ethics*, 17(9/10), 1093–1102. DOI: 10.1023/A:1006075517423

Attanasio, G., Preghenella, N., De Toni, A. F., & Battistella, C. (2022). Stakeholder engagement in business models for sustainability: The stakeholder value flow model for sustainable development. *Business Strategy and the Environment*, 31(3), 860–874. DOI: 10.1002/bse.2922

Baldissin, N., De Toni, A. F., & Nonino, F. (2007). Evolution of the management games: Towards the massive multiplayer online role-playing game. *Learning with Games*, 9-16.

Baldissin, N., De Toni, A. F., & Nonino, F. (2013). What is a Business Game? Historical background and evolution of business games in serious games context. *Business game-based learning in management education, 3.*

Bandura, A. (1986). *Social foundations of thought and action.*

Barnabè, F., Armenia, S., Nazir, S., & Pompei, A. (2023). Critical Thinking Skills Enhancement through System Dynamics-Based Games: Insights from the Project Management Board Game Project. *Systems*, 11(11), 554. DOI: 10.3390/systems11110554

Baxter, R. J., Holderness, D. K.Jr, & Wood, D. A. (2017). The effects of gamification on corporate compliance training: A partial replication and field study of true office anti-corruption training programs. *Journal of Financial Accounting Research*, 2(1), A20–A30. DOI: 10.2308/jfar-51725

Beauchamp, G., & Kennewell, S. (2010). Interactivity in the classroom and its impact on learning. *Computers & Education*, 54(3), 759–766. DOI: 10.1016/j.compedu.2009.09.033

Betz, J. A. (1995). Computer games: Increase learning in an interactive multidisciplinary environment. *Journal of Educational Technology Systems*, 24(2), 195–205. DOI: 10.2190/119M-BRMU-J8HC-XM6F

Billen, A. (1993). Could it be the end for Super Mario? *The Observer*, *27*, 51.

Biscaccianti, A. (2003). Business ethics and profit-The impact of corporate social responsibility programs on corporate strategic planning. *Cahiers du CEREN*, 5, 14–27.

Blanchard, K. (1995). *The anthropology of sport: An introduction.* ABC-CLIO.

Blythe, J. (2006). *Fondamenti di marketing*. Pearson Italia Spa.

Bruce, P., & Shelley, R. (2010). Assessing stakeholder engagement. *Communication Journal of New Zealand*, 11(2), 30–48.

Burke, B. (2014). *Gartner Redefines Gamification*. Gartner Blog Network.

Carenys, J., & Moya, S. (2016). Digital game-based learning in accounting and business education. *Accounting Education*, 25(6), 598–651. DOI: 10.1080/09639284.2016.1241951

Coda, V. (1995). Dilemmas of Business Ethics. *Economia Aziendale*, 14, 7–14.

Cojocariu, V. M., & Boghian, I. (2014). Teaching the relevance of game-based learning to preschool and primary teachers. *Procedia: Social and Behavioral Sciences*, 142, 640–646.

Dankbaar, M. E., Alsma, J., Jansen, E. E., van Merrienboer, J. J., van Saase, J. L., & Schuit, S. C. (2016). An experimental study on the effects of a simulation game on students' clinical cognitive skills and motivation. *Advances in Health Sciences Education : Theory and Practice*, 21(3), 505–521. DOI: 10.1007/s10459-015-9641-x PMID: 26433730

De Freitas, S., & Oliver, M. (2006). How can exploratory learning with games and simulations within the curriculum be most effectively evaluated? *Computers & Education*, 46(3), 249–264. DOI: 10.1016/j.compedu.2005.11.007

Delwiche, A. (2006). Massively multiplayer online games (MMOs) in the new media classroom. *Journal of Educational Technology & Society*, 9(3), 160–172.

Dickinson, J. R., & Faria, A. J. (1997). A random strategy criterion for validity of simulation game participation. *Simulation & Gaming*, 28(3), 263–275. DOI: 10.1177/1046878197283003

Drucker, P. F. (2002). They're not employees, they're people. *Harvard Business Review*, 80(2), 70–77. PMID: 11894680

Dunne, D. J. (2014). Brechtian alienation in videogames. *Press Start*, 1(1), 79–99.

Ebner, M., & Holzinger, A. (2007). Successful implementation of user-centered game based learning in higher education: An example from civil engineering. *Computers & Education*, 49(3), 873–890. DOI: 10.1016/j.compedu.2005.11.026

Ekambaram, A., & Petersen, S. A. (2017). Enhancing Stakeholder Management Competences in Construction Projects using Serious Games. In *Proceedings of the 9th Nordic Conference on Construction Economics and Organization.*

Faria, A. J., Hutchinson, D., Wellington, W. J., & Gold, S. (2009). Developments in business gaming: A review of the past 40 years. *Simulation & Gaming*, 40(4), 464–487. DOI: 10.1177/1046878108327585

Fleming, K., Abad, J., Booth, L., Schueller, L., Baills, A., Scolobig, A., & Leone, M. F. (2020). The use of serious games in engaging stakeholders for disaster risk reduction, management and climate change adaption information elicitation. *International Journal of Disaster Risk Reduction*, 49, 101669.

Florea, R., & Florea, R. (2013). Stakeholders interests analyse and harmonization-starting point of strategic approach. *Economy Transdisciplinarity Cognition*, 16(1), 130.

Fottler, M. D., Blair, J. D., Whitehead, C. J., Laus, M. D., & Savage, G. T. (1989). Assessing key stakeholders: Who matters to hospitals and why? *Journal of Healthcare Management*, 34(4), 525–546.

Freeman, R. E. (1984). *Strategic Management: A Stakeholder Approach Pitman Publishing Inc.*

Freeman, R. E., Wicks, A. C., & Parmar, B. (2004). Stakeholder theory and "the corporate objective revisited". *Organization Science*, 15(3), 364–369. DOI: 10.1287/orsc.1040.0066

Friedman, M. (1962). *Capitalism and freedom. Friedman*. The University of Chicago.

Friedrich, J., Becker, M., Kramer, F., Wirth, M., & Schneider, M. (2020). Incentive design and gamification for knowledge management. *Journal of Business Research*, 106, 341–352. DOI: 10.1016/j.jbusres.2019.02.009

Gilson, L. L., & Goldberg, C. B. (2015). Editors' comment: So, what is a conceptual paper? *Group & Organization Management*, 40(2), 127–130.

Goodpaster, K. E. (1991). Business ethics and stakeholder analysis. *Business Ethics Quarterly*, 53–73.

Gredler, M. E. (2013). Games and simulations and their relationships to learning. In *Handbook of research on educational communications and technology* (pp. 571–581). Routledge.

Greenlaw, P. S., Herron, L. W., & Rawdon, R. H. (1962). Business simulation in industrial and university education.

Greenwood, M. (2007). Stakeholder engagement: Beyond the myth of corporate responsibility. Journal of Business Ethics, 74, 315–327.

Griffiths, M. D., & Davies, M. N. (2005). Does video game addiction exist. Handbook of computer game studies, 359, 372.

Harrison, J. S., Bosse, D. A., & Phillips, R. A. (2010). Managing for stakeholders, stakeholder utility functions, and competitive advantage. *Strategic Management Journal*, 31(1), 58–74. DOI: 10.1002/smj.801

Helm, S. (2007). One reputation or many? Comparing stakeholders' perceptions of corporate reputation. *Corporate Communications*, 12(3), 238–254. DOI: 10.1108/13563280710776842

Hitt, M. A., Ireland, R. D., & Hoskisson, R. E. (2009). *Strategic Management: Concepts & Cases Competitiveness and Globalization* (8th ed.). South-Western Cangage Learning.

Huang, W. H., Huang, W. Y., & Tschopp, J. (2010). Sustaining iterative game playing processes in DGBL: The relationship between motivational processing and outcome processing. *Computers & Education*, 55(2), 789–797. DOI: 10.1016/j.compedu.2010.03.011

Huntington, F. (1984). The Learning Machine: Thinking Is an Adventure. *InCider*, 2(10), 33–36.

Ismail, M. S., & Klischewski, R. (2020). BP-IT alignment in SMEs: a game-based learning approach to increase stakeholders' maturity. *Business Process Management: 18th International Conference, BPM 2020, Seville, Spain, September 13–18, 2020 Proceedings, 18*, 400–416.

Kapp, K. M. (2012). *The gamification of learning and instruction: game-based methods and strategies for training and education*. John Wiley & Sons.

Keesee, G. S. (2012). Educational games. Teaching and learning resources. http://teachinglearningresources. pbworks. com/w/page/35130965/Educational% 20Games.

Kiili, K. (2005). Digital game-based learning: Towards an experiential gaming model. *The Internet and Higher Education*, 8(1), 13–24. DOI: 10.1016/j.iheduc.2004.12.001

Kinzie, M. B. (1990). Requirements and benefits of effective interactive instruction: Learner control, self-regulation, and continuing motivation. *Educational Technology Research and Development*, 38(1), 5–21. DOI: 10.1007/BF02298244

Kinzie, M. B., & Sullivan, H. J. (1989). Continuing motivation, learner control, and CAI. *Educational Technology Research and Development*, 37(2), 5–14. DOI: 10.1007/BF02298286

Korteling, J. E., Helsdingen, A. S., Sluimer, R. R., Van Emmerik, M. L., & Kappé, B. (2011). *Transfer of Gaming: Transfer of training in serious gaming*. TNO.

Lee, H. (2023). Collaborative governance platforms and outcomes: An analysis of Clean Cities coalitions. *Governance: An International Journal of Policy, Administration and Institutions*, 36(3), 805–825. DOI: 10.1111/gove.12702

Lepper, M. R., & Cordova, D. I. (1992). A desire to be taught: Instructional consequences of intrinsic motivation. *Motivation and Emotion*, 16(3), 187–208. DOI: 10.1007/BF00991651

Lepper, M. R., & Malone, T. W. (2021). Intrinsic motivation and instructional effectiveness in computer-based education. In *Aptitude, learning, and instruction* (pp. 255–286). Routledge.

Lerbinger, O. (2006). *Corporate public affairs: Interacting with interest groups, media, and government.* Routledge. DOI: 10.4324/9781410617262

Lozano, R. (2007). Collaboration as a pathway for sustainability. *Sustainable Development (Bradford)*, 15(6), 370–381. DOI: 10.1002/sd.322

Lozano, R. (2011). Addressing stakeholders and better contributing to sustainability through game theory. *Journal of Corporate Citizenship*, 2011(43), 45–62. DOI: 10.9774/GLEAF.4700.2011.au.00004

Malone, T. (1981, May). What makes computer games fun? In *Proceedings of the Joint Conference on Easier and More Productive Use of Computer Systems (Part-II): Human Interface and the User Interface-Volume 1981* (p. 143).

Malone, T. W. (1980). *What makes things fun to learn? A study of intrinsically motivating computer games*. Stanford University.

Malone, T. W. (1981a). Toward a theory of intrinsically motivating instruction. *Cognitive Science*, 5(4), 333–369.

Malone, T. W., & Lepper, M. R. (2021). Making learning fun: A taxonomy of intrinsic motivations for learning. In *Aptitude, learning, and instruction* (pp. 223–254). Routledge.

Mann, B. D., Eidelson, B. M., Fukuchi, S. G., Nissman, S. A., Robertson, S., & Jardines, L. (2002). The development of an interactive game-based tool for learning surgical management algorithms via computer. *American Journal of Surgery*, 183(3), 305–308. DOI: 10.1016/S0002-9610(02)00800-0 PMID: 11943132

Martin, A. (2000). The design and evolution of a simulation/game for teaching information systems development. *Simulation & Gaming*, 31(4), 445–463. DOI: 10.1177/104687810003100401

Matuleviciene, M., & Stravinskiene, J. (2015). The importance of stakeholders for corporate reputation. *The Engineering Economist*, 26(1), 75–83.

McKee, V. (1992). Out of sight—and out of mind. *Life and Times, The Times*, *22*, 5–22.

Mitchell, R. K., Agle, B. R., & Wood, D. J. (1997). Toward a theory of stakeholder identification and salience: Defining the principle of who and what really counts. *Academy of Management Review*, 22(4), 853–886. DOI: 10.2307/259247

Neville, B. A., Bell, S. J., & Mengüç, B. (2005). Corporate reputation, stakeholders and the social performance-financial performance relationship. *European Journal of Marketing*, 39(9/10), 1184–1198. DOI: 10.1108/03090560510610798

Noland, J., & Phillips, R. (2010). Stakeholder engagement, discourse ethics and strategic management. *International Journal of Management Reviews*, 12(1), 39–49. DOI: 10.1111/j.1468-2370.2009.00279.x

O'Neil, H. F., Wainess, R., & Baker, E. L. (2005). Classification of learning outcomes: Evidence from the computer games literature. *Curriculum Journal*, 16(4), 455–474. DOI: 10.1080/09585170500384529

Omar, M., Williams, R. L.Jr, & Lingelbach, D. (2009). Global brand market-entry strategy to manage corporate reputation. *Journal of Product and Brand Management*, 18(3), 177–187. DOI: 10.1108/10610420910957807

Orlandini, P., & Amelio, S. (2022). *Un percorso aziendale verso la sostenibilità.* Giappichelli.

Peloza, J., Loock, M., Cerruti, J., & Muyot, M. (2012). Sustainability: How stakeholder perceptions differ from corporate reality. *California Management Review*, 55(1), 74–97. DOI: 10.1525/cmr.2012.55.1.74

Petersen, S. A., & Ekambaram, A. (2016, October). Interaction, Experience, Reflection: Enhancing Project Management Training using Serious Games. In European Conference on Games Based Learning (p. 521). Academic Conferences International Limited.

Phillips, R. (1999). On stakeholder delimitation. *Business & Society*, 38(1), 32.

Phillips, R. (2003). *Stakeholder theory and organizational ethics*. Berrett-Koehler Publishers.

Post, J. E., Preston, L. E., & Sachs, S. (2002). Managing the extended enterprise: The new stakeholder view. *California Management Review*, 45(1), 6–28. DOI: 10.2307/41166151

Prensky, M. (2003). Digital game-based learning. *Computers in Entertainment*, 1(1), 21–21. DOI: 10.1145/950566.950596

Provost, J. A. (1990). Work, play, and type: Achieving balance in your life.

Puncheva, P. (2008). The role of corporate reputation in the stakeholder decision-making process. *Business & Society*, 47(3), 272–290. DOI: 10.1177/0007650306297946

Ranchhod, A., Gurău, C., Loukis, E., & Trivedi, R. (2014). Evaluating the educational effectiveness of simulation games: A value generation model. Information Sciences, pp. 264, 75–90.

Rehbein, F., Psych, G., Kleimann, M., Mediasci, G., & Mößle, T. (2010). Prevalence and risk factors of video game dependency in adolescence: Results of a German nationwide survey. *Cyberpsychology, Behavior, and Social Networking*, 13(3), 269–277.

Roberts, P. W., & Dowling, G. R. (2002). Corporate reputation and sustained superior financial performance. *Strategic Management Journal*, 23(12), 1077–1093. DOI: 10.1002/smj.274

Rudestam, K. E., & Newton, R. R. (2014). Surviving your dissertation: A comprehensive guide to content and process. Sage publications.

Ryan, R. M., & Deci, E. L. (2000). Intrinsic and extrinsic motivations: Classic definitions and new directions. *Contemporary Educational Psychology*, 25(1), 54–67. DOI: 10.1006/ceps.1999.1020 PMID: 10620381

Schmeer, K. (1999). Stakeholder analysis guidelines. *Policy Toolkit for Strengthening Health Sector Reform, 1*, 1-35.

Siano, A., Kitchen, P. J., & Confetto, M. G. (2010). Financial resources and corporate reputation: Toward common management principles for managing corporate reputation. *Corporate Communications*, 15(1), 68–82. DOI: 10.1108/13563281011016840

Sicart, M. (2011). *The ethics of computer games*. MIT Press.

Sisodia, R., Wolfe, D., & Sheth, J. N. (2003). *Firms of endearment: How world-class companies profit from passion and purpose*. Pearson Prentice Hall.

Sitzmann, T. (2011). A meta-analytic examination of the instructional effectiveness of computer-based simulation games. *Personnel Psychology*, 64(2), 489–528. DOI: 10.1111/j.1744-6570.2011.01190.x

Susi, T., Johannesson, M., & Backlund, P. (2007). Serious games: An overview.

Thomas, P., & Macredie, R. (1994). Games and the design of human-computer interfaces. *Educational & Training Technology International*, 31(2), 134–142. DOI: 10.1080/0954730940310208

Varvasovszky, Z., & Brugha, R. (2000). A stakeholder analysis. *Health Policy and Planning*, 15(3), 338–345.

Vate-U-Lan, P. (2014). Redesign principles of game-based learning: expectations from stakeholders in a developing country. Paper presented at the 8th European Conference of Game-based Learning (ECGBL2014).

Verdeyen, V., Put, J., & van Buggenhout, B. (2004). A social stakeholder model. *International Journal of Social Welfare*, 13(4), 325–331. DOI: 10.1111/j.1468-2397.2004.00328.x

Wang, C. K. J., Khoo, A., Liu, W. C., & Divaharan, S. (2008). Passion and intrinsic motivation in digital gaming. *Cyberpsychology & Behavior*, 11(1), 39–45. DOI: 10.1089/cpb.2007.0004 PMID: 18275311

Weinstein, A. M. (2010). Computer and video game addiction—A comparison between game users and non-game users. *The American Journal of Drug and Alcohol Abuse*, 36(5), 268–276.

Wellington, W. J., Hutchinson, D. B., & Faria, A. J. (2017). Measuring the impact of a marketing simulation game: Experience on perceived indecisiveness. *Simulation & Gaming*, 48(1), 56–80. DOI: 10.1177/1046878116675103

Yawkey, T. D., & Pellegrini, A. D. (Eds.). (2018). *Child's play: Developmental and applied* (Vol. 20). Routledge. DOI: 10.4324/9781315099071

Yee, N. (2006). The psychology of MMORPGs: Emotional investment, motivations, relationship formation, and problematic usage. *Avatars at work and play: Collaboration and interaction in shared virtual environments, 34*, 187–207.

ENDNOTES

1 According to the Swiss psychologist, the continuous adaptation between accommodation and assimilation always creates new equilibria in which phases are identifiable in different stages.

2 Association to Advance Collegiate Schools of Business.

3 Massively Multiplayer Online Role-Playing Game.

4 Massive Multiplayer Online Role Playing Business Game.

5 "*The use of gameplay mechanics for non-game application*" (Kapp, 2012, p. 10)

Section 5
Game-Based-Learning Applications in Business and Management Area

Chapter 6
Game-Learning in Action: A Serious Board Game on Human Capital Reporting

Selena Aureli
https://orcid.org/0000-0002-2169-1694
University of Bologna, Italy

Monica Bartolini
https://orcid.org/0000-0002-1833-1014
University of Bologna, Italy

Giorgia Moschini
University of Bologna, Italy

ABSTRACT

Human capital (HC) plays an important role in organizations, serving as a primary source of innovation and competitiveness. Assessment and disclosure of how HC is managed and enhanced are fundamental elements of every sustainability report. However, companies and consultants might not be prepared for HC disclosure. Accounting practitioners did not learn about sustainability and HC reporting during their university career, nor are they familiar with procedures to draw up and audit ESG reports. Hence, this chapter aims to enhance education in sustainability and HC reporting through an engaging and active teaching approach, called game-based learning, designed to improve learners' performance by boosting both engagement and motivation. The authors propose a team-based board game incorporating serious game elements, which blends innovative contents on the role of HC (D&I included) in value creation and sustainability disclosure. The game was tested and applied with international university students.

DOI: 10.4018/979-8-3693-1172-1.ch006

1. INTRODUCTION

Human capital (HC) plays an important role in an organization as it is connected to personnel`s knowledge, competencies, experiences, attitudes, and abilities that are considered the main indicators and sources of innovation and competitiveness. Being aware of the impact of HC practices on companies' strategy achievements and profitability (Cormier et al., 2009; Samudhram et al., 2014), investors and other stakeholders are increasingly demanding HC disclosure as part of the wider corporate practice of sustainability reporting (Kolk, 2003; Chicchiello *et al.*, 2023).

Whether it be voluntary or mandatory, sustainability reporting requires organizations to assess and disclose the stock of HC and how it is managed and enhanced, using specific Key Performance Indicators (KPIs). Therefore, several frameworks and guidelines have been issued by standard setters to help companies measure and report HC. For example, both the reporting framework issued by the SASB (2017) and the IIRC framework (issued in 2013 and recently revised in 2021) identify HC as a key capital that creates company value. Worldwide renowned, the GRI has a long history in setting guidelines for reporting social aspects related to employees and has recently issued dedicated standards (i.e., the GRI 401 on Employment, the GRI 402 on Labour relations, the GRI 403 on Health and safety, the GRI 404 on Training and education, the GRI 405 on Diversity and equal opportunity, and the GRI 406 on Non-discrimination).

Policies to improve the practice of accounting for HC can be dated to the 70s (Vithana et al., 2021); however, only recently there have been legislative interventions that strictly mandate non-financial reporting to corporations, including HC and D&I topics (Oelrich et al., 2024). In Europe, both the previous Non-Financial Reporting Directive (NFRD) came into force on 5th December 2014 and the latest Corporate Sustainability Reporting Directive (CSRD) published in January 2023 commit public entities to report on "Social responsibility and treatment of employees", "Respect for human rights", and "Diversity on company boards (in terms of age, gender, educational and professional background)". In the USA, in 2020, the Securities and Exchange Commission revised HC disclosure rules to improve shareholders' understanding of how HC management contributes to corporate value and strategy, and aspects of D&I are the most frequently added areas of HC reporting (Batish *et al.*, 2021).

Despite such legislative requirements and stakeholder pressures for more disclosure on HC (Elbannan, 2016), the accounting and finance departments – usually in charge of company reporting – are not always prepared for this challenge (Özsözgün Çalişkan, 2014). Accounting practitioners did not learn about sustainability and integrated reporting, nor about human capital reporting, during their university career (Showalter, 2022). The staff of accounting and finance departments is not fully aware of its role in proving metrics, developing procedures, and disclosing information to draw up ESGs reports, first, and audit them, after.

When IIRC guidelines were issued in 2013, an interesting debate on its implications for accounting curricula flourished (Owen, 2013; Correa Ruiz, 2013; Kamp-Roelands, 2013). However, only a few authors have attempted to analyse how sustainability can be really incorporated into accounting curricula proposing action research studies (Haigh and Hazelton, 2010) or other methods (Rodrigues and Morais (2021). As a result, despite strong external pressures to incorporate sustainability into accounting curricula (Senaratne *et al.*, 2022; Del Baldo and Baldarelli, 2017), current professional accounting education programs do not seem to properly embed social and environmental matters (Sharma and Kelly, 2014; Boulianne et al., 2018; Venturelli et al., 2021).

Given the previous premises, this chapter aims to contribute to education in the field of sustainability and HC reporting by proposing an engaging and active teaching approach that uses games to improve learning. This teaching strategy, called game-based learning, is designed to improve learners' performance (Isabelle, 2020) by boosting both engagement and motivation.

More in detail, we propose a board game to be played in teams that has the main features of a serious game. Its design combines the teaching of innovative contents on the role of HC (D&I included) in value creation and sustainability disclosure with modern and engaging teaching methods and material.

The game was tested and consecutively applied to international university students over four semesters. However, two key features make the game also applicable to adult education and the business context, especially when companies start their journey toward sustainability and have to set project teams for acculturating employees and devising which HC policies are in line with the company strategy. First, the fact that the game does not require previous deep knowledge about the topic (neither of sustainability reporting standards nor of HC management). Second, the game strongly fosters teambuilding, communication, collaboration and, therefore, contributes to further develop team management and problem-solving. These skills are extremely important within the workplace.

The chapter is organized as follows. Next section summarizes the theoretical background of our project, while section 3 describes the game developed; together with its main purpose and learning objectives. The game design and its steps are also discussed. Finally, in section 4 we present some preliminary findings/feedback from learners and discuss the implications of game-based learning in our teaching experience. Finally, we report conclusive comments and limitations of our study.

2. LITERATURE BACKGROUND

2.1 Concept and Relevance of Human Capital and D&I Policies for Organizations

Human Capital Definition and Development in the Business Domain

Since the early academic rationalization of the term Human Capital (HC) by Becker (2009) in the Sixties, companies have recognized the importance of investing in HC, that has been defined as employees' education and training to improve the quality of the labour force, which in turn contributes to profitability and growth. Yet, this early notion of HC as a company productive factor has been further developed over the decades, mainly thanks to the transition from the traditional economy, which is based on productive process, to the knowledge economy, which requires maximizing human potential. One of the most used definitions of HC in the field of accounting and reporting is the one provided by the IIRC guidelines in 2013, that includes "people's competencies, capabilities and experience, and their motivations to innovate, including their: alignment with and support for an organization's governance framework, risk management approach, and ethical values; ability to understand, develop and implement an organization's strategy; loyalties and motivations for improving processes, goods and services, including their ability to lead, manage and collaborate".

With the advent of more humanistic connotations (Bourdieu, 1986) of HC, that emphasize the role of social relations, companies have begun to consider their employees' well-being and therefore, have started implementing a large variety of policies for HC development, not limited to training and salaries, but focusing on employees' physical and social security, work-life balance, human rights and personal development too. So, today, especially after the Covid-19 pandemic (Arthi and Parman, 2021), companies investing in HC often focus on employees' well-being, which spans from material and economic terms to reach all levels of a person's wellness, including the mental, social and physical sides (Modarelli, 2023). The search for well-being at the workplace implies giving employees the possibility to enjoy a favourable context, to carry out interpersonal relations, to benefit from an adequate work-life balance, standard of living and welfare. When these conditions are met, the competencies and experiences of all employees, regardless of their different backgrounds, beliefs, and social characteristics, can be deployed within organizations in full. Therefore, greater attention to the diversity of employees and their inclusion in the workplace is rising, which are considered a cornerstone of HC and key indicators of sustainable HC management.

D&I in the Business

In literature, 'diversity' refers to a range of different characteristics among people, which include -but not limited to-: gender and gender identity, race and ethnicity, age and generation, culture, religion and belief system, culture, socio-economic status, language and accent, disability, mental health, education, work experience, thinking and personality type, etc (Mazur, 2010; O'Reilly et al., 1998). With the term 'inclusion', we define instead "a dynamic state of operating in which diversity is leveraged to create a fair, healthy, and high-performing organization or community. An inclusive environment ensures equitable access to resources and opportunities for all. It also enables individuals and groups to feel safe, respected, engaged, motivated, and valued, for who they are and for their contributions toward organizational and societal goals" (O'Mara and Richter, 2011, p.1).

The implementation of D&I policies (i.e. that welcome diversity and embrace it in the workplace) by companies has never been as important as it is nowadays, given the several positive impacts that are attributed to them (Ely and Thomas, 2020). Cox and Blake already reported in 1990 several benefits that a diverse work team provides: *cost advantages*, in terms of lower turnover and absenteeism rates; *increased human resources acquisition*, due to the attractiveness of an inclusive company attentive to diversity; *marketing benefits*, as a better reputation favour relationships with all types of stakeholders; *creativity*, the most innovative companies have heterogeneous teams so that they think "out of the box" and have multiple points of view; *problem-solving*, the more different backgrounds you have in a group, the greater the number of solutions to the same problem; and *system flexibility*, due to different approaches and cognitive systems.

In recent years, academic emphasis has been on how diversity enhances the functioning of both organizational and top-management teams (Harrison et al., 2007). It avoids group thinking in the workforce, which hinders innovation. In the board room, it allows decision makers to recognize different environmental signals, because a diverse group has a greater capacity to understand different stakeholders' needs and bring in a multiple-perspective analysis of the problem. Attention to different group interests can lead to higher quality decisions than those made under a uniform board, and therefore to better performance (Adeabah et al., 2019; Maxfield *et al.*, 2018; Birindelli *et al.*, 2018). Therefore, greater diversity leads to greater innovation, knowledge, competitiveness, growth, and ultimately greater profitability as demonstrated by many academic studies (Cox and Blake, 1991; Ely and Thomas, 2001; DiTomaso *et al.*, 2007; Herring, 2009; Pieterse *et al.*, 2013). Company policies aiming to enhance D&I in the workplace are usually labelled as 'diversity management' (Gilbert *et al.*, 1999); a concept that generally refers to a range of practices and policies devoted to build a greater and better inclusion of people who possess different characteristics (of various kinds) to the traditional corporate workforce population (Aureli, 2008; Lorbiecki and Gavin, 2000). The main purpose of such policies is thus to make workplaces richer in different talents, ways of thinking and interacting, and to improve, through effective and deep inclusion, the well-being and harmony of workers. Also, diversity policies seek to avoid organizations from applying discrimination against employees based on their gender, race, religion or national origin (Herring, 2009). As a consequence, diversity management (Flood and Romm, 1996; Gilbert *et al.*, 1999) mainly deals with leadership education: managers are asked "to teach themselves and others within their organizations to value multicultural differences in both associates and customers so that everyone is treated with dignity" (Mazur, 2010, p. 5).

Over the years the concepts of diversity and diversity management have acquired more and more meanings and included different aspects. Starting from cultural diversity (Cox and Blake, 1990), an increasing number of studies have appeared on gender diversity and gender pay gap (Blau and Kahn, 2007; Francoeur *et al.*, 2008; Bear *et al.*, 2010; Badal and Harter, 2014; Adeabah *et al.*, 2019). In recent years, relevant topics previously neglected, such as sexual and affective orientation and LGBTQ+ rights (Hossain *et al.*, 2020), age discrimination (Neumark, 2021), and empowerment of people with disabilities (Khan *et al.*, 2019) have been gaining ground.

Also external institutional expectations and normative pressures demand businesses to take action on D&I (Cole and Salimath, 2013) as demonstrated by the United Nations 2030 Agenda, which includes SDGs that deal specifically with D&I, such as: Goal 4 - Ensure inclusive and equitable quality education and promote lifelong learning opportunities for all; Goal 5 - Achieve gender equality and empower all women and girls; Goal 8 - Promote sustained, inclusive and sustainable economic growth, full and productive employment and decent work for all; Goal 9 - Build resilient infrastructure, promote inclusive and sustainable industrialization and foster innovation; Goal 10 - Reduce inequality within and among countries; Goal 16 - Promote peaceful and inclusive societies for sustainable development, provide access to justice for all and build effective, accountable and inclusive institutions at all levels (United Nations, 2015).

Similarly, the Corporate Sustainability Reporting Directive (CSRD) requires more transparency on social aspects with special attention to policies on D&I to be reported under all the Social European standards ESRS sub-topics. In particular, the new disclosure requirement DR S1-9 mandates the application of diversity indicators to prepare a more comprehensive and effective disclosure.

2.2 The Disclosure of HC and D&I Policies and its Integration in University Curricula

D&I Reporting

D&I is considered part of a company's social responsibility strategy and as such it is included in sustainability, ESG and integrated reports (IRs) by corporations (Oelrich et al., 2024). Therefore, D&I disclosure is compulsory for companies that are obliged to prepare a sustainability or non-financial report (in Europe the obligation regards all listed medium- and large-sized companies starting from year 2024). Even when not mandatory, D&I reporting has become a "must-have" corporate practice for companies worldwide (Hofer-Bonfin et al., 2023). D&I disclosure is important for signalling a company's commitment to societal values and rules to stakeholders. D&I disclosure enhances a company's reputation and, as demonstrated by the great attention of investors on ESG aspects in general, and D&I dimensions in particular (Bax, 2023), it contributes to risk management and market-value stability (McMillan-Capehart *et al.*, 2010).

Academia also demonstrates that reporting these aspects has a positive impact on corporate financial performance (Williams and O'Reilly, 1998; Florida and Gates, 2001; Ryan *et al.*, 2002; Taliento et al., 2019).

Over the past decades, companies have found themselves adopting and reporting D&I-related policies for three main reasons: i) *regulatory*, which have gradually pushed corporate management policies to be aligned with changing regulatory framework on equal opportunity and social sustainability; ii) *economic*, related to the expectation of economic benefits; and iii) *ethical*, to make evident the application of CSR policies adopted for ethical (Buemi *et al.*, 2015). Whatever the case, companies are now looking for the most appropriate D&I policies to adopt and the best way to report their D&I investments to the market. GRI standards, SABS standards, and IIRC guidelines are the most widespread frameworks applied by companies for reporting to investors who are paying close attention to how companies incorporate these initiatives into their business (Bloomberg, 2019). And the ESRS (European Sustainability Reporting Standards) recently issued by the EFRAG will play a fundamental role soon.

Differences among existing national and international reporting standards are now converging due to continuing calls for harmonization (Tschopp and Nastanski, 2014; Afolabi *et al.*, 2022; Adams and Abhayawansa, 2022; Zaid and Issa, 2023). However, sustainability managers and accountants still struggle to select the best framework KPIs to properly cover all the several dimensions that must be reported. Chomsky (2023) states that understanding and implementing key sustainability metrics and indicators is like navigating in an unfamiliar and unclear area. This is the reason why accountants and managers need to be trained on sustainability metrics.

The Inclusion of D&I Disclosure in University Programs and Other Forms of Training

The increased attention to D&I has raised a debate in the accounting discipline and among accounting educators that shall prepare future professionals, consultants, and managers. *Can accountants contribute to D&I? Are accountants well-equipped to effectively contribute to D&I-related goals?* These are just examples of questions that permeate accounting journals (Egan, 2021). For sure, if both HC and D&I issues are integrated into education programs, these themes will become more prominent in the backgrounds of future managers and professionals who contribute to strategic choices (Hambrick and Mason, 1984). The same is true for education on sustainability and integrated reporting.

According to Showalter (2022), accounting practitioners currently working in businesses did not learn enough about HC and D&I during their university career and are not always aware of their role in reporting metrics and developing procedures and controls to draw up and audit ESG reports. Only recently, we started feeling pressures to incorporate sustainability reporting (in general) into university accounting curricula (Senaratne *et al.*, 2022; Del Baldo and Baldarelli, 2017) and to review professional accounting education programs to increasingly incorporate social and environmental matters (Sharma and Kelly, 2014; Boulianne et al., 2018; Venturelli et al., 2021). The debate on the implications for accounting curricula associated with HC reporting flourished when the IIRC guidelines were issued in 2013 (Owen, 2013; Correa Ruiz, 2013; Kamp-Roelands, 2013). The IIRC guidelines assign HC a key role as one of the six capitals that allow a company to create value in the short and long term. However, only a few authors have attempted to analyse how these topics can be really incorporated into accounting curricula (Haigh and Hazelton, 2010; Rodrigues and Morais, 2021).

Given this lack of current educational practices on HC and D&I reporting, we have questioned on how teachers shall approach this theme in class with their students. Since accounting and reporting are perceived as 'boring' (this has driven initiatives focused on repackaging the accounting profession as vibrant and exciting -Andon et al., 2010), teachers are prompt to adopt engaging learning techniques that motivate students. In this regard, serious games represent an interesting approach to explore as described in the following section.

2.3 Game-Based Learning

The Use of Games to Enhance Engagement and Learning

Teaching and training are more effective when educational activities apply certain gaming principles that favour users' engagement. Game-based learning is a learning model that incorporates game features and game use strategies (Zainuddin *et al.*, 2020) in a 'non-game contexts' (Deterding et al., 2011), like training and educational programs. According to many researchers, game-based approaches have greater efficacy than traditional learning (Earp et al., 2014): by engaging learners, this approach encourages desired behaviour and desired outcomes among them.

Literature analysis reveals that game-based learning is mostly employed in high school and university education: Fabricatore and Lopez (2012) report that 40% of games in the domain of sustainability address schools.

However, also companies are applying and benefiting from the use of games in the business. More than 10 years ago, Werbach and Hunter (2012) demonstrated that game thinking can motivate employees and customers; it can be used in many business areas, from marketing and sales to production and R&D. HR departments greatly adopt game-based learning to enhance employees' training and development (Abuladze, 2023; Amstrong and Landers, 2018; Larson, 2020).

This learning model is based on constructivist learning (York and DeHaan, 2018), which foresees the necessity of experience learning through social interactions with the environment and other subjects like classmates or colleagues. It is a teaching strategy that promotes enjoyable learning so that learners change their behaviour and decide to engage in worthwhile learning activities. Since many teaching approaches are not seen as communicative, learners frequently feel bored and lack interest in the content they are studying. This lack of interest may have a negative impact on students' learning results by preventing them from actively participating in their education (Isabelle, 2020).

Motivation to learn is therefore positively affected by games that increase the attention and effort that students dedicate to the learning activity (Chebotareva *et al.*, 2020; Hamari and Koivisto, 2013). Jones (2009), who has mostly analysed the use of games in the academic environment, says that students' motivation – intended as a "goal-directed physical or mental activity" – "is not important in and of itself, but rather it is important because motivated students tend to engage in activities that help them learn and achieve highly in academic settings" (p. 272). In short, motivation is considered a *sine qua non* of successful learning (Prensky, 2003). This positive influence of games on students' motivation is mainly grounded in the Theory of Gamified Learning (Landers, 2014; 2017). Today, game-based learning is considered to be a motivating pedagogical approach (Isabelle, 2020) which is more effective than traditional methods of teaching (Westera, 2019). Games motivate students in many settings, and they are very useful also in collaborative problem-based learning experiences (Jones, 2013).

The Design and Structural Elements of Serious Games

In the latest years, game-based learning has widely relied on digital technologies (Fu et al., 2016; Fotidias and Sigala, 2015), but computers and ICTs are not always necessary. Game-based learning "does not necessarily involve the use of an actual game or information technology. Rather, it involves the integration of design elements or activity patterns traditionally found in games into educational contexts" (Buckley and Doyle, 2016, p. 1163).

Serious games are a specific category of games that serve an educational purpose rather than being purely entertaining (Susi et al., 2007). The concept of serious games is closely linked to "edutainment" (education through entertainment), which aims to educate students while also entertaining them. Serious games can range from quizzes to simulation or adventure games, and more. Prensky (2001) emphasizes that games should be fun first, then they should encourage learning, while Michael and Chen (2006, p.21) define serious games as "games that do not have entertainment, enjoyment, or fun as their primary purpose".

These games have become a popular tool integrated into various academic courses (Zhonggen, 2019) because they present several benefits as they can support the development of different skills such as analytical skills, strategic thinking, learning capabilities, planning, communication and collaboration, visual selective attention, group decision-making, etc. (Wang et al., 2016; Mitchell and Savill-Smith, 2004; Kirriemuir & McFarlane, 2004; Squire & Jenkins, 2003).

Previous literature on serious games (Blumberg et al., 2012; Riemer and Schrader, 2015; Landers, 2014; Landers et al., 2017) emphasizes that, despite not being designed for entertainment, these games are highly useful in engaging students. Yet, to achieve engagement and enhance motivation, serious games must incorporate engaging and immersive aspects (as in the case of computer games) together with targeted educational material (Malone, 1980). The challenge lies in blending these two components seamlessly to maintain the learner's interest and attention (Prensky, 2003).

Several authors have investigated the design elements that shall be integrated in a serious game to active game-based learning (Bezanilla et al., 2014; Nicholson, 2015; Buckley and Doyle, 2016). Since the work of Abt (1970), who theorized the structural components of a serious game design, researchers agree on the following elements for modelling a serious game:

a) Clearly defined objectives and goals;
b) Rules useful to determine the order, rights, and responsibilities of players, as well as intermediate goals to achieve;
c) Challenges, which are problems to face;
d) Interaction, arising from the game mechanics and dynamics, which also includes the result of immediate feedback and evidence of progress towards the goals.

The first element – goals attainment – is considered a very critical component. According to Malone (1980; 1981), it must be uncertain to create a challenging environment (which is connected to point c). Four methods exist for making goal attainment uncertain, applicable to a diverse range of individuals or even the same person at varying times: a) *variable difficulty level*, including search and effort required to reach the goal, b) *multiple level goals*, taking advantage in terms of cognitive motivation, c) *hidden information*, provoking curiosity and contributing to the challenge of the game, d) *randomness*, used to increase interest. All of them creates challenges that favor motivation as suggested by cognitive theories (Malone, 1981).

In addition, objectives and rules shall be carefully designed and connected to make the challenges feasible and create a positive competitive dynamic (Bezanilla et al., 2014; Nicholson, 2015; Buckley and Doyle, 2016). The latter can be favoured by the introduction of a reward system for achieving goals or targets.

Finally, an important ingredient in any serious game is the aesthetic of the learning experience, which is a matter of emotions perceived by learners (like joy, thrill, frustration, victory, anxiety, fulfilment, excitement, etc.). This aspect should be central during the design of a game (Hunicke et al., 2004). Even if serious games are oriented to education or skills training, student learning becomes enjoyable because amusement when playing the game is designed for learning purposes (Koster, 2004). Serious games can also create immersive learning experiences by modelling real-life situations in an imaginary world. This captivates the player's full attention and helps them retain knowledge (Michael and Chen 2006).

The Use of Games in Accounting and Reporting

When talking about game-based learning, the subject learned is material. Among the many disciplines and fields of education where game-based learning has been applied (e.g. mathematics, foreign languages, computer science, engineering), sustainability and CSR are new areas. Previous research reports the use of games to teach students how to reduce energy use, improve transportation and air quality, manage waste, conserve water and manage other environmental or social aspects (Redman et al., 2021; Fabricatore and Lopez, 2012). As confirmed by Douglas and Brauer (2021), the application of games mainly refers to sustainability-related management decisions, while reporting about sustainability and non-financial aspects is still unexplored.

Sustainability reporting is a more technical aspect and belongs to the domains of accounting and accountability. Application of game-based learning in accounting and reporting is limited to some small experiences: the game named DEBORAH -Double Entry Bookkeeping or Accounting History- by Malaquias et al. (2018), the Cost Accounting Game by Cho and Park (2011), and a Job Cost Simulation by Lippincott and Pergola (2009). Finally, Brown and Kohlbeck (2017) propose, as far as we know, the only instructional case study about non-financial sustainability reporting but with a focus on assurance provision.

Given this gap in the educational literature, this study aims to contribute to the field of game-based learning applied to sustainability matters, by developing a new game on HC and D&I reporting and then exploring its impact on students' learning (Tinti *et al.*, 2023).

3. GAME DESCRIPTION

The serious board game developed, titled "Human Capital Disclosure within Integrated Reporting - Fashion4You - Create your Report", represents an example of game-based learning in action. It combines the teaching of innovative contents on the role of HC (D&I included) in value creation and sustainability disclosure with modern and engaging teaching methods and materials. The game has been developed within an EU-funded project and the tools developed to set up the game are freely available[1].

It has been designed in line with literature's suggestions for a serious game (Abt, 1970); so, it unfolds through dedicated activities and involves a set of rules and actions in a cohesive manner, motivating teams to compete with each other (Oliveira and Petersen, 2014). Competitiveness is reinforced by the fact that at the end of the game a winning team is identified. The game elements have been planned to satisfy the criteria highlighted by Bezanilla et al. (2014), Nicholson (2015) and Buckley and Doyle (2016) for a 'meaningful' serious game. This combination of elements is supposed to bring out from the players their intrinsic motivation to learn while getting immersed in the game.

The game must be played in teams (composed of a minimum of 3, up to a maximum of 6 members). Having a team to draft the report reflects what usually happens inside organizations, where the CEO appoints a project team to prepare the sustainability or IR. In business contexts, this team usually includes the CFO and/or someone from the accounting department, the audit function, the investor relator, and external consultants from accountancy and audit firms. The mission of the game is to design a section of the IR of a company operating in the high-end fashion industry; more precisely, participants are asked to focus on the HC disclosure section including all its different aspects: diversity and inclusion, employment and remuneration, health and safety, labour practices, human rights, skills and knowledge, training and education.

Although referring to the drafting of an IR, the game focuses on HC only. This choice is grounded on several reasons. First, given the breadth of the topic (IR), a choice was necessary to make the mission feasible for a game with teaching purposes. Second, HC, together with social and relational issues, is very often underexplored and still underdeveloped, both in practice and in theoretical frameworks, compared to other forms of capitals and issues (e.g., the environmental ones). Nevertheless, the social dimension of sustainability is gaining relevance in recent studies; in this context, D&I issues are receiving increasing attention. Third, the choice of HC was also due to the importance and the strategic role played by this typology of capital in small- and medium-sized enterprises (SMEs) that represent the economic backbone of EU countries. A deep awareness and understanding of this capital and its value are then required to properly support both the measurement and management of a company's HC.

The next sections describe the learning objectives of the game developed, as well as the different steps to play it.

3.1 Learning Objectives of the Game

The game is organized in three steps (Figure 1). Each step requires learners to achieve a specific goal. Objectives and goals (point a, according to the design elements theorised by Abt in 1970) are clearly stated by the case study text, the toolkit provided to students, and the instructions provided by the teacher in class. During the first step, the main team's goal is to design the section of the IR about HC, while in the second step each team makes a self-assessment of the overall quality of the work done through a series of checklists and questions raised by the instructor. Finally, during the third step, team members are pushed to suggest improvements to overcome the limitations highlighted during the self-assessment phase. Each step mimics similar project phases that companies set up in the real context.

Through this game, learners train several abilities, pursuing the following learning objectives:

- Implement the theory on IR and HC to a real business case,
- Adapt the concept of HC to a specific context/industry,
- Implement the theory on performance measurement systems and KPIs,

- Implement the guidelines and tools for IR and sustainability reporting and experience their limitations,
- Practice their soft skills, since at its different stages the game requires the implementation of a wide range of abilities, from leadership and negotiation skills to teamworking and problem-solving, to time management and creativity, without neglecting adaptability, critical thinking, and communication.

As it should typically happen in a game-learning context, learners are not explicitly told what the teaching objectives are. The latter are reflected in the design instead and are reached or monitored too. However, our game very explicitly communicates to students what game goals they are asked to achieve, even without mentioning specific learning goals. For a game to be engaging, in fact, learning objectives should be substituted by game goals from the learners' perception. Such different perceptions can deeply change the game and learning experiences: no awareness of study efforts but, instead, a combination of pleasure, motivation, and an experience of being able to do something new.

From the learning performance point of view, the game leads learners along a progressive cognitive learning scale, reaching all its intermediate steps of proficiency. According to the revised version of Bloom's Taxonomy (Anderson *et al.*, 2001), there are six levels of cognitive learning, namely: remembering, understanding, applying, analysing, evaluating, and creating. Each level is conceptually different and progressively implemented in the game (Figure 1).

Figure 1. The cognitive learning scale along the steps of the game

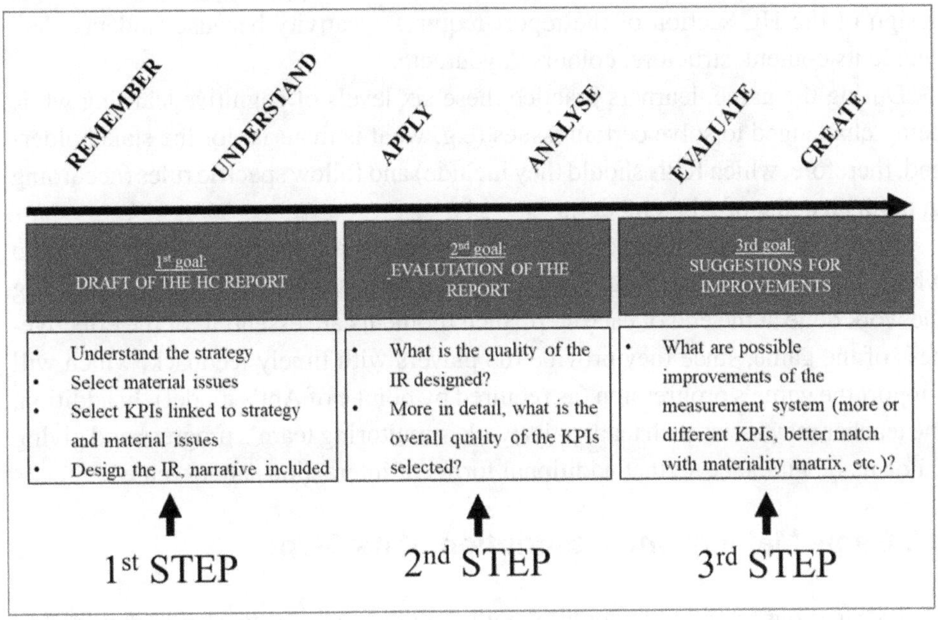

Remembering means retrieve, recall, or recognize relevant knowledge from long-term memory. For example, in the game learners shall remember the meaning of HC in order to be able to disclose it in an IR; they should also recall the accounting principles for reporting (like objectivity, reliability, verifiability etc.).

Understanding, instead, implies being able to demonstrate comprehension through one or more forms of explanation. The game requires students to compare alternative reporting practices and understand the different impacts and relationships associated to the choice of KPIs.

Applying indicates the ability to use information or skills in new contexts. In this case, students implement IR principles to a new case with its peculiar characteristics (a SME, working in the fashion industry, family-owned and international in scope).

Analysing is about breaking concepts and topics into their constituent parts and determining how the parts relate to one another and/or to an overall structure or purpose. In our game, students analyse the relationship between the company's competitive pillars and HC elements; they also must classify KPIs by topic and sub-dimension to understand whether and how they relate or overlap.

Evaluating is when learners make judgments based on criteria and standards. For example, students shall consider the materiality matrix when choosing KPIs among the long list of available metrics provided by the game toolkit, based on the GRI guidelines.

Finally, *creating* involves putting elements together to form a new coherent or functional whole, by reorganizing elements into a new pattern or structure. The design of the HC section of the report requires creativity because students shall decide its content, structure, colours, layout, etc.

During the game, learners practice these six levels of cognitive learning while being challenged to solve certain issues (e.g. what is material for the stakeholders and, therefore, which KPIs should they include) and follow specific rules (according to points b and c of Abt's model).

Finally, it should be mentioned that each step of the game has a time limit within which students must carry out their activity. There is also a moment for checking the work done at the end of each step. Such moments are essential for the effectiveness of the game, since they provide the players with timely feedback, which will support the game's progression (as required by point c of Abt's model). In addition, the teacher may assist each team in its work, monitoring team's progress and giving tailor-made guidance so that additional forms of interactions are executed.

3.2 Game Material and Description of its Steps

To carry out the game, a toolbox with the necessary kit to play is provided to each team. Figure 2 describes the box content, which includes for the first step: a description of the case study; a list of required outputs step by step; the materiality matrix of the company, as well as a zoom on the matrix quadrant with the most relevant topics; a brief recap of the IIRC's principles; an intuitive recap of the most important characteristics that effective KPIs should have; a folder with tens of KPI labels to be selected (and customized) as HC measures: flipcharts and markers to create the report.

To run the second step, instead, the toolkit is enriched by four checklists, that respectively concern: (1) the HC aspects disclosed, (2) the cost of the metrics selected, (3) the assessment of the current performance of each aspect measured, and finally (4) the reliability of the selected metrics, as well as their timing. These checklist's elements can be referred to as any metric, since the associated label describes all the aspects mentioned above.

Figure 2. The toolkit provided to students

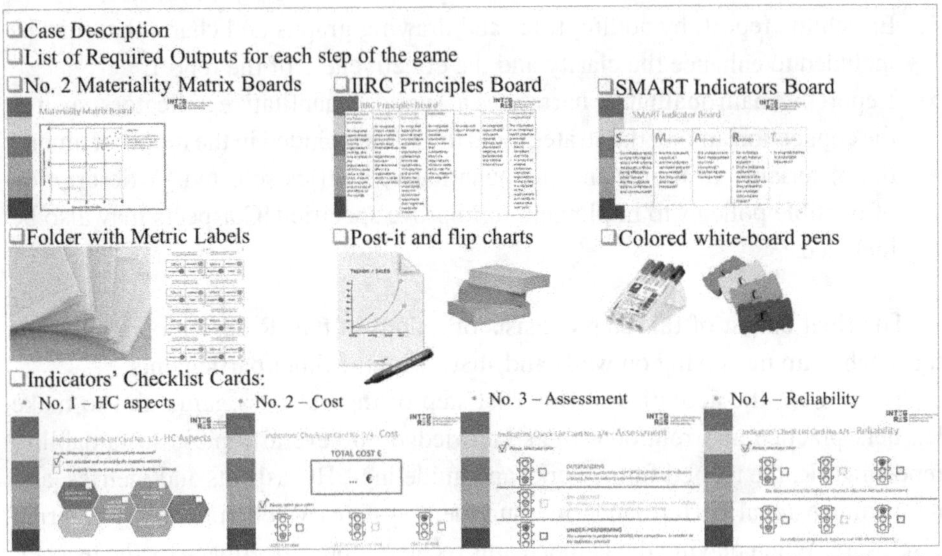

Furthermore, a video clip showing game moments and outputs is available at this link https://youtu.be/bRh1SihEI3M. Finally, a complete set of open-source materials to prepare the toolkit and to run the game is available here https://www.integres.eu/results-outcomes/io1-teaching-materials/ (Course 3: Integrated Reporting and Human Capital for SMEs) and here https://www.integres.eu/results-outcomes/io2-ebook/ (Get the book).

Step 1/3

After an introduction to the business game by the teacher who explains instructions, game goals, and tasks' timing, learners are asked to draft the HC section of an IR according to the following indications.

1) Tailor the HC section of the IR (i.e., the output of the game) to the characteristics of the business case. For this, the game provides them with a company profile and a brief description of its business model pillars, also based on the dynamics of the industry, as well as on its most critical capitals. Furthermore, a materiality matrix is provided to identify the key issues to be disclosed;
2) Select the best bundle of KPIs from a list provided by the teacher, created by combining GRI and SASB's metrics for HC disclosure (D&I included). Learners should achieve the best match with the profile of the company and the industry dynamics. During this first step, learners should care only about the issues covered by any KPIs (D&I, employment and remuneration, health and safety, labour practices, human rights, skills and knowledge, training and education);

3) Customize the KPIs and add metrics, if necessary, that can be considered more material and appropriate for the industry and the company's business;
4) Enrich the report, by adding titles and drawing graphs and charts that may be included to enhance the clarity and the effectiveness of the report;
5) Report the main qualitative narratives to support quantitative indicators, such as the connection among the strategy and the KPIs included in the report or among the materiality of topics and the quantitative metrics selected. A description of possible policies to implement to improve specific HC aspects may also be included.

The final output of this step consists of a draft of the IR design on a flipchart that each team must hang on walls and share with the other participants.

To sum up, the activities of this first step of the business game aim to make learners practice and reinforce their knowledge on several topics: sustainability reporting, IR, the related frameworks and guidelines, HC aspects and metrics, and multi-dimensional performance measurement systems when supporting external disclosure. When playing the game, teams receive support/feedback by the teacher.

The soft skills involved in this step are several, i.e., leadership, negotiation, teamworking, problem-solving, creativity, time management, adaptability, and communication.

Step 2/3

While the activities of the first step are intended to enable learners to design their report tailored to the business case characteristics, in the second step new game tools (cards and checklists) are used to make learners implement some key principles for IR and performance measurement, while assessing the quality of the selected metrics and the connected narratives.

In detail, through checklists provided by the teacher, learners self-assess the work done. Several dimensions or aspects regarding the report designed and the KPIs selected shall be evaluated by learners. Many dimensions under scrutiny are linked to sustainability reporting principles, therefore helping learners to concretely apply such accounting principles. The self-assessment refers to:

1) the balance between conciseness vs. completeness of the report;
2) the balance between costs vs. benefits of the report designed by teams;
3) the balance between positive vs. negative impacts of the company's activities regarding the issues described by the metrics selected;
4) the compliance of the reports designed by teams with the IIRC principles;

5) the identification of the HC elements to be improved, given the current performance of the company concerning any of them.

As said, learners use additional information cards and checklists associated with any metric selected to perform the self-assessment phase. Such additional information is included in the game toolkit, but it is handed over to students only at the start of the second step. Information regards KPIs' characteristics that would emerge when the company puts into action the designed reporting. Such characteristics concern: (1) comprehensiveness (i.e., whether they cover all the relevant aspects of HC, D&I included), (2) cost of measurement and hence its affordability, (3) assessment of company's current performance on the aspects measured, (4) reliability and accountability of measurement, (5) timeliness of measures. To assess the overall quality of the reporting designed, the indicators' checklist provides a score for each characteristic, classifying the results according to a traffic light rating system.

This self-assessment activity is also due to the challenging nature of the leaning goals to be achieved. As theorized by Malone (1980; 1981), in fact, goals attainment must be uncertain to create a challenging environment. So, this game adopts a multiple level goals strategy, taking advantage in terms of cognitive motivation and, consequently, requires moment to evaluate the work done.

This step of the game encourages the use of several soft skills, like critical thinking, time management, problem-solving, and adaptability.

Step 3/3

As a natural consequence of previous steps, during this last phase of the game learners are asked to provide a presentation of the work done and the results of the self-assessment activity, as well as recommendations for future improvements based on the limitations highlighted during the second step. In fact, the checklists may highlight:

1) strengths and weaknesses of the report proposed;
2) suggestions and next improvements to overcome the limitations checked and better support the drafting of the IR (like investments in ICT, training, assurance/auditing, analytical skills reinforcement, improvement of internal and external databases, etc.);
3) new indicators (based on what is currently not reported but important), always paying attention to the balance between costs and benefits and the other aspects assessed through the checklists.

During this last step, learners realise the connection between the activities performed so far and the learning goals underlying the game design (not explicitly declared before). This final step is then necessary to make students aware of what they have learned, and it helps them perceive how they can apply it in a different context.

Furthermore, also step 3 implies the use of soft skills, like negotiation, teamworking, problem-solving and lateral thinking, time management, creativity, and adaptability. Finally, by presenting the work done to the lecturer, team members also practice communication and leadership skills.

To recap, the following table (Table 1) summarizes the elements of our game matching the key elements of a serious game as ascribed by the literature.

Table 1. The key elements of our serious game

Key elements of a serious game	Characteristics of our game
Objectives	▪ goals and targets for each step ▪ preparatory/introductory material on theoretical aspects, to submit before the game
Set of rules	▪ rules provided by the instructor at the beginning of the game ▪ time schedule for step progression
Interaction	▪ step by step feedback by the teacher ▪ self-assessment of the work done in steps 2 and 3 ▪ final feedback provided by other teams
Suitable challenges	▪ challenges to face in each step ▪ challenges connected to learning outcomes ▪ multiple level goals strategy
Competitive dynamics and reward system	▪ uncertain level of goals attainment ▪ competitive game with a winning team identified by the teacher
Aesthetic of the experience	▪ simulation of a real-life context (company case) ▪ autonomy of teams ▪ coloured and easy-to-use tool kit to facilitate the activities and generate pleasure/amusement in playing the game

4. RESULTS

The game was tested first and submitted in different classes subsequently, over four semesters, to international university students attending Italian, Irish, Dutch, French, and Belgian degree programs (involving intra- and extra-UE students, from 35 different countries). This diversity of geographical origins has not hindered engagement. Having heterogeneous students has enriched the outputs created at the end of the game, which have benefitted from a more extensive spectrum of backgrounds, cultures, and experiences. The international scope better reflected real-world context, where businesses shall interact with investors and stakeholders from many countries; at the same time, it allows to state that the activities required by the game can be applied in different geographical contexts.

A survey was conducted to find out the level of appreciation of the game as a measure of success (Gatian, 1994) and quality assessment. In detail, the survey focused on students' engagement, which is related to motivation, and perceived learning. The latter is our measure of students' performance and game's effectiveness. The survey is made by closed-ended questions (students are required to express their level of agreement or disagreement on a Likert scale) and open text boxes for comments.

The survey was submitted online through the Qualtrics platform, on a voluntary basis and completely anonymously, with no impact on students' grades. About 75% of students who played the game responded to the survey. In total 164 valid and complete responses have been collected.

The characteristics of the final sample of 164 students are described in Table 2. About 57% of respondents were attending a master's degree program, while the remaining 43% a bachelor's one.

Table 2. Sample description

	Data	N.	%
Gender	Female	119	72.6
	Male	45	27.4
Program Level	Master's/Two Years Degree	94	57.3
	Bachelor's Degree	70	42.7
Did you already play games in your previous university courses?	Yes	42	25.6
	No	122	74.4
Did you already have a work experience (e.g. internship, your own business)?	Yes	123	75.0
	No	41	25.0
Did you already attend a seminar, lecture, or course about sustainability and/or integrated reporting before playing the game (not just having read about the topic)?	Yes	90	54.9
	No	74	45.1

Students have highly welcomed the game, recognizing the importance of both the topic and the proposed learning-method, as well as its effectiveness and contribution to their degree program's contents. Figure 3 reports the perceived usefulness and several open comments confirm they appreciation of the game design: *"Great game, it definitely improved my knowledge of reporting, very well organized"* (example of a student's comment in the open text box).

Figure 3. Using the game is important and useful (1-I strongly disagree/5-I fully agree)

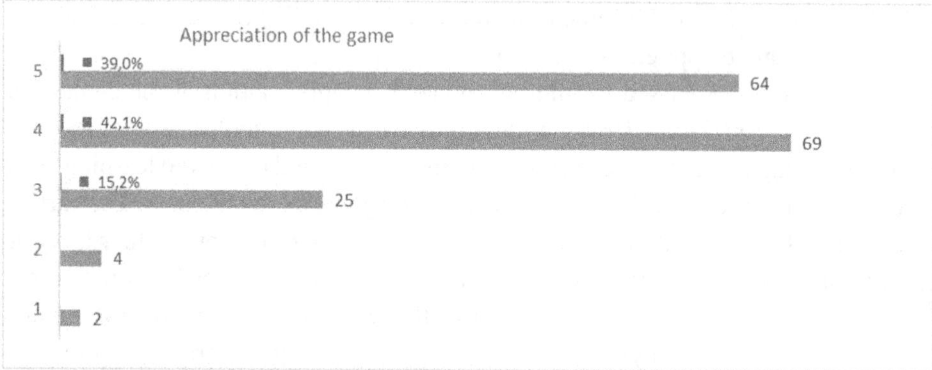

The survey further confirms the game's ability to foster learning by increasing engagement, as also supported by some students' comments: *"I really appreciated the professor for giving us this project. I learned better this way and I thought it was a very interesting way to apply the knowledge I obtained during the course"*. They appreciated the opportunity to enrich their technical and practical knowledge and strengthen their skills, in the light of their future career: *"It was more engaging and practical as it would be in the real world"*.

Another aspect to highlight involves the emotional responses evoked in students during the implementation of the game, which has elicited situational and individual interest. Both Figures 4 and 5 report aspects of engagement and comments explain how entertainment is important is this context. A student wrote: "*The game was fun and original!"*. Another one reported*: "I think playing games is fun and a useful experience, not only to improve teamworking skills but also to revise the materials collected during the courses"*.

Figure 4. As a user, I think the game's experience is fun (1-I strongly disagree/5-I fully agree)

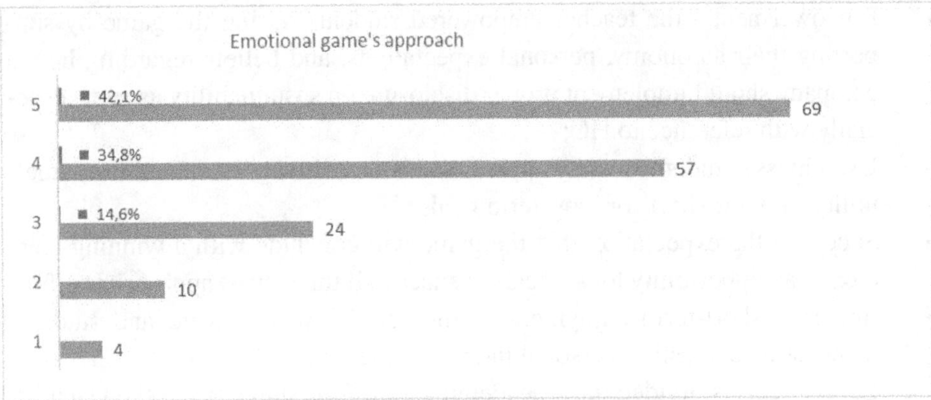

Figure 5. As a user, I think the game's experience is interesting (1-I strongly disagree/5-I fully agree)

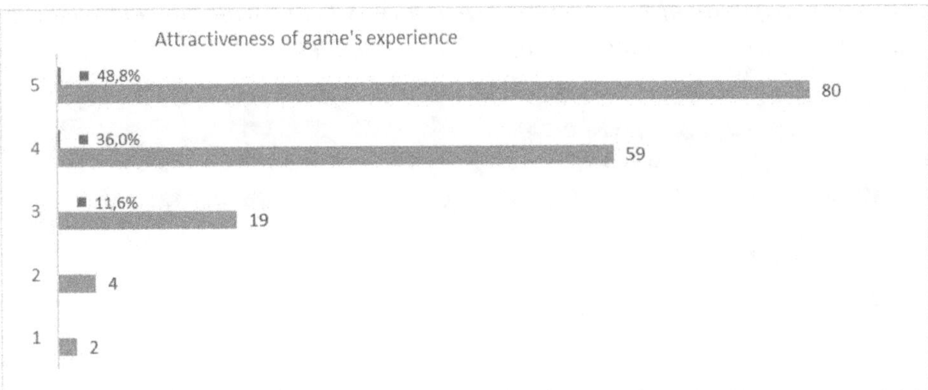

Finally, from the survey, there is evidence of the ease of use of the game despite the challenges posed. For example, a student said "*I really enjoyed the game activity. It was challenging, but this is part of any work*". Another one said, "*Great game, definitely improved my knowledge of reporting, very well organised and with clear objectives that facilitated the flow of activities*". Also, the high-quality performance of the learning experience is important. Figure 6 shows student's appreciation for the quality of the learning experience, which can intensify academic motivation, as highlighted by Jones (2009, 2013), based on five key elements: empowerment, usefulness, success, interest, and caring. More in detail:

- Empowerment - the teacher empowered students during the game by supporting their autonomy, personal expectations, and beliefs regarding how a company should implement proper disclosure on sustainability aspects, especially with reference to HC;
- Usefulness - students widely appreciated and positively evaluated the game's utility for their short- or long-term goals;
- Success - the expectation that the game will conclude with a winning team creates an opportunity for students to succeed if they invest appropriate effort;
- Interest - short-term enjoyment of the activity was evident, and students demonstrated a lasting personal interest in the topic;
- Caring - this is divided into "academic caring", as students felt the teachers' dedication and personal interest in providing new and different knowledge, and "personal caring", as students perceived that the teacher cares about their well-being.

Figure 6. The quality of the learning experience is better with the game than in traditional classes (1-I strongly disagree/5-I fully agree)

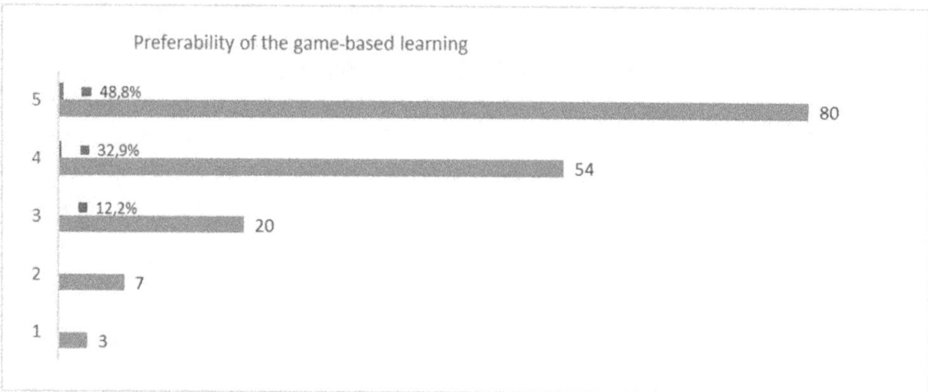

Based on the above results, we unveiled a high level of students' satisfaction with the overall learning experience. They also enjoyed much more it compared with the traditional learning approach of frontal lectures used in all countries where we administered the game.

5. CONCLUSIONS AND LIMITATIONS

Research has extensively demonstrated the positive consequences of a company's greater attention to D&I in terms of talent attraction and employee retention rate. Today, also 'work-life balance' and 'flexibility' represent key challenges for companies that can be addressed with the introduction of specific training and education programs on D&I issues. In fact, D&I is closely related to the entire person's journey within the enterprise. Despite the importance of D&I, many business leaders and managers lack knowledge and awareness on the topic, while investors and other stakeholders place a great emphasis on D&I policies and their outcomes. To satisfy their information needs, external reporting on D&I aspects has become a must-have corporate practice for companies worldwide (Hofer-Bonfin et al., 2023), even when reporting is not mandatory by law. As a consequence, managers as well as consultants that support businesses should start learning about HC and D&I reporting. Also, university students, which are the leaders and professionals of the future, should become familiar with these topics. Teachers are therefore required to enrich their academic programs to fully integrate HC and D&I reporting. With specific regard to business and economics degrees, accounting disciplines should deeply encompass such emerging topics.

In this context, the contribution of our study is twofold. First, it provides to teachers and trainers a learning tool specifically tailored to improve HC and D&I knowledge in a field where a gap still exists. It can positively contribute to understand what HC and D&I are, as well as how to measure them for disclosure and management purposes, both in educational and work environments. In fact, although tested in university context so far, our game is designed as a serious game useful for different kinds of learners (such as students, professionals, managers, and other employees). It focuses on key aspects connected to human resources: D&I, employment and remuneration, health and safety, labour practices, human rights, skills and knowledge, training, and education. Key issues and core concepts about measurement are implemented to develop awareness and understanding of such elements and to support their monitoring, which is the pre-requisite for both external disclosure and internal management. In other words, measurement enables control that supports decision making in turn.

A second contribution of our game has a methodological nature, since it enriches the existing scant literature on the impacts of game-based learning on sustainability and reporting aspects (Tinti et al., 2023). Our game has been designed as a serious game, increasingly recognized as an effective mean of improving learning outcomes and helping learners to concentrate on the targeted topic (Wang et al., 2016; Zhonggen, 2019; Guillén-Nieto and Aleson-Carbonel, 2012).

A survey has been conducted to test the appreciation of our game at a university level and investigate students' perceptions. Being aware that the survey does not objectively measure students' learning achievements, we believe that the findings are still important and of practical interest to teachers and trainers. In fact, our study confirms that using serious games can significantly increase learning engagement and has the potential to enhance the overall learning performance.

Furthermore, consistently with previous literature (Guillén-Nieto and Aleson-Carbonell, 2012; Garneli et al., 2017; Zhonggen, 2019), our survey revealed important indicators of satisfaction and effectiveness in the use of serious games, such as perceived usefulness, ease of use, and goal clarity. This is consistent with the idea that a careful planning of game design elements is fundamental when developing educational material at all levels (Malone, 1980; 1981).

Under these conditions, students feel more likely to focus on the contents of the game and experience a sense of enjoyment. These findings confirm that serious games have remarkable potential as educational tool.

Limitations of This Study and Future Research Directions

The present study is not without limitations. First, our findings rely on a self-administered survey that reports students' perceived learning. A more objective measurement of the games' learning effectiveness could be obtained by assessing future participants' knowledge both before and after the game.

Another major limitation concerns the fact that the game was applied only in the university setting. Therefore, our investigation fails to provide conclusive evidence regarding the game effectiveness in a work context. However, we believe that it can potentially enhance learning outcomes in the context of business education and training too, because we introduced specific factors also designed to business settings, in line with Guillén-Nieto and Aleson-Carbonel (2012): instructional content, game cycle, debriefing, perceived educational value, transfer of learned skills, and intrinsic motivation.

Furthermore, our game implementation focused on young generations (bachelor and master students), while its extension across all age groups may generate different results. For example, elderly demographic may respond in a different way to the challenges of our game.

These limitations represent fertile areas for future research activity that could involve businesses and, therefore, help them develop increased awareness of sustainability topics among managers and employees, as well as more D&I oriented policies.

Future implementation of the game could also address professional accountants and auditors, in the light of the challenges posed to them by the evolution of company reporting towards sustainability, as a result of both voluntary and regulatory pressing forces.

REFERENCES

Abt, C. C. (1970). *Serious Games*. Viking Press.

Abuladze, L. (2023). Use of Gamification in Employee Training and Development. DOI: 10.53465/EDAMBA.2022.9788022550420.1-10

Adams, C. A., & Abhayawansa, S. (2022). Connecting the COVID-19 pandemic, environmental, social and governance (ESG) investing and calls for 'harmonisation'of sustainability reporting. *Critical Perspectives on Accounting*, 82, 102309. DOI: 10.1016/j.cpa.2021.102309

Adeabah, D., Gyeke-Dako, A., & Andoh, C. (2019). Board gender diversity, corporate governance and bank efficiency in Ghana: A two-stage data envelope analysis (DEA) approach. Corporate Governance. *Corporate Governance (Bradford)*, 19(2), 299–320. DOI: 10.1108/CG-08-2017-0171

Afolabi, H., Ram, R., & Rimmel, G. (2022). Harmonization of sustainability reporting regulation: Analysis of a contested arena. *Sustainability (Basel)*, 14(9), 5517. DOI: 10.3390/su14095517

Anderson, L. W., & Krathwohl, D. R. (Eds.). (2001). *A Taxonomy for Learning, Teaching, and Assessing: A Revision of Bloom's Taxonomy of Educational Objectives*. Addison Wesley Longman, Inc.

Andon, P., Chong, K. M., & Roebuck, P. (2010). Personality Preferences of Accounting and non-Accounting Graduates Seeking to Enter the Accounting Profession. *Critical Perspectives on Accounting*, 21(4), 253–265. DOI: 10.1016/j.cpa.2010.01.001

Armostrong, M. B., & Landers, R. N. (2018). Gamification of employee training and development. *International Journal of Training and Development*, 22(2), 162–169. DOI: 10.1111/ijtd.12124

Arthi, V., & Parman, J. (2021). Disease, downturns, and wellbeing: Economic history and the long-run impacts of COVID-19. *Explorations in Economic History*, 79, 101381. DOI: 10.1016/j.eeh.2020.101381 PMID: 33162564

Aureli, S. (2008). *La gestione delle differenze culturali nell'attività di impresa*. Giappichelli.

Badal, S., & Harter, J. K. (2014). Gender diversity, business-unit engagement, and performance. *Journal of Leadership & Organizational Studies*, 21(4), 354–365. DOI: 10.1177/1548051813504460

Batish, A., Gordon, A., Kepler, J. D., Larcker, D. F., Tayan, B., & Yu, C. (2021). Human Capital Disclosure: What Do Companies Say About Their 'Most Important Asset'? Rock Center for Corporate Governance at Stanford University Working Paper Forthcoming.

Bax, K. (2023). Do diverse and inclusive workplaces benefit investors? An Empirical Analysis on Europe and the United States. *Finance Research Letters*, 52, 103509. DOI: 10.1016/j.frl.2022.103509

Bear, S., Rahman, N., & Post, C. (2010). The impact of board diversity and gender composition on corporate social responsibility and firm reputation. *Journal of Business Ethics*, 97(2), 207–221. DOI: 10.1007/s10551-010-0505-2

Becker, G. S. (2009). *Human capital: A theoretical and empirical analysis, with special reference to education*. University of Chicago press.

Bezanilla, M., Arranz, S., Rayn, A., Rubio, I., Menchaca, I., Guenaga, M., & Aguilar, E. (2014). A proposal for generic competence assessment in a serious game. *Journal of New Approaches in Educational Research*, 3(1), 42–51. DOI: 10.7821/naer.3.1.42-51

Birindelli, G., Dell'Atti, S., Iannuzzi, A., & Savioli, M. (2018). Composition and activity of the board of directors: Impact on ESG performance in the banking system. *Sustainability (Basel)*, 10(12), 1–10. DOI: 10.3390/su10124699

Blau, F. D., & Kahn, L. M. (2007). The gender pay gap. *The Economists' Voice*, 4(4). Advance online publication. DOI: 10.2202/1553-3832.1190

Bloomberg. (2019). Accelerating D&I is essential to remain competitive and attract a new generation of investors. Retrieved from https://www.bloomberg.com/professional/blog/accelerating-di-essential-remain-competitive-attract-new-generation-investors/

Blumberg, F. C., Almonte, D. E., Anthony, J. S., & Hashimoto, N. (2012). *Serious Games: What are they? What do they do? Why should we play them? The Oxford Handbook of Media Psychology*. Oxford University Press.

Boulianne, E., Keddie, L. S., & Postaire, M. (2018). (Non) coverage of sustainability within the French professional accounting education program. Sustainability Accounting. *Management and Policy Journal*, 9(3), 313–335.

Bourdieu, P. (2011). The forms of capital (1986). Cultural theory: An anthology, 1(81-93), 949.

Buckley, P., & Doyle, E. (2016). Gamification and student motivation. *Interactive Learning Environments*, 24(6), 1162–1175. DOI: 10.1080/10494820.2014.964263

Buemi, M., Guazzo, G., & Conte, M. (2015). *Il Diversity Management per una crescita inclusiva: strategie e strumenti*. FrancoAngeli.

Campbell, J. L. (2007). Why would corporations behave in socially responsible ways? An institutional theory of corporate social responsibility. *Academy of Management Review*, 32(3), 946–967. DOI: 10.5465/amr.2007.25275684

Chebotareva, I., Pashutina, O., & Makhova, V. (2020, May). Digital Gamification as a Leading Factor in the Educational and Learning Process of Law Students. In 6th International Conference on Social, economic, and academic leadership (ICSEAL-6-2019) (pp. 228-234). Atlantis Press. DOI: 10.2991/assehr.k.200526.034

Cho, H. J., & Park, J. I. (2011). Cost accounting game model for education and operating method. *Advanced Materials Research*, 199, 1667–1670. DOI: 10.4028/www.scientific.net/AMR.199-200.1667

Chomsky, R. (2023), Measuring Sustainability in Business. Sustainability Review. Retrieved from: https://sustainablereview.com/measuring-sustainability-in-business/

Cicchiello, A. F., Marrazza, F., & Perdichizzi, S. (2023). Non-financial disclosure regulation and environmental, social, and governance (ESG) performance: The case of EU and US firms. *Corporate Social Responsibility and Environmental Management*, 30(3), 1121–1128. DOI: 10.1002/csr.2408

Cole, B. M., & Salimath, M. S. (2013). Diversity identity management: An organizational perspective. *Journal of Business Ethics*, 116(1), 151–161. DOI: 10.1007/s10551-012-1466-4

Cormier, D., Aerts, W., Ledoux, M. J., & Magnan, M. (2009). Attributes of social and human capital disclosure and information asymmetry between managers and investors. Canadian Journal of Administrative Sciences/Revue Canadienne des Sciences de l'Administration, 26(1), 71-88.

Correa Ruiz, C. (2013). A commentary on 'integrated reporting: A review of developments and their implications for the accounting curriculum'. *Accounting Education*, 22(4), 360–362. DOI: 10.1080/09639284.2013.817800

Cox, T. H., & Blake, S. (1991). Managing cultural diversity: Implications for organizational competitiveness. *The Academy of Management Perspectives*, 5(3), 45–56. DOI: 10.5465/ame.1991.4274465

Del Baldo, M., & Baldarelli, M. G. (2017). Educating for sustainability: Perspectives and critical notes on accounting scholars' role in higher education. *Scientific Annals of Economics and Business*, 64(4), 411–422. DOI: 10.1515/saeb-2017-0032

Deterding, S., Dixon, D., Khaled, R., & Nacke, L. (2011, September). From game design elements to gamefulness: defining" gamification". In Proceedings of the 15th international academic MindTrek conference: Envisioning future media environments (pp. 9-15).

DiTomaso, N., Post, C., & Parks-Yancy, R. (2007). Workforce diversity and inequality: Power, status, and numbers. *Annual Review of Sociology*, 33(1), 473–501. DOI: 10.1146/annurev.soc.33.040406.131805

Douglas, B. D., & Brauer, M. (2021). Gamification to prevent climate change: A review of games and apps for sustainability. *Current Opinion in Psychology*, 42, 89–94. DOI: 10.1016/j.copsyc.2021.04.008 PMID: 34052619

Earp, J., Ott, M., Popescu, M., Romero, M., & Usart, M. (2014). Supporting human capital development with serious games: An analysis of three experiences. *Computers in Human Behavior*, 30, 715–720. DOI: 10.1016/j.chb.2013.09.004

Egan, M. (2021). Diversity, Inclusion, and the Opportunities for Accounting Research [D]. *Social and Environmental Accountability Journal*, 41(3), 201–207. DOI: 10.1080/0969160X.2021.1986088

Elbannan, M. A. (2016). IFRS adoption, legal systems and the voluntary disclosure of human capital: Cross-country evidence from the banking industry. *Accounting and Finance Research*, 5(4), 30–48. DOI: 10.5430/afr.v5n4p30

Ely, R. J., & Thomas, D. A. (2001). Cultural diversity at work: The effects of diversity perspectives on work group processes and outcomes. *Administrative Science Quarterly*, 46(2), 229–273. DOI: 10.2307/2667087

Ely, R. J., & Thomas, D. A. (2020). Getting serious about diversity. *Harvard Business Review*, 98(6), 114–122.

Fabricatore, C., & Lopez, X. (2012). Sustainability Learning through Gaming: An Exploratory Study. *Electronic Journal of e-Learning*, 10(2), 209–222.

Flood, R. L., & Romm, N. (1996). Diversity management. Critical Systems Thinking, 81-92.

Flood, R. L., & Romm, N. R. (1996). Contours of diversity management and triple loop learning. *Kybernetes*, 25(7/8), 154–163. DOI: 10.1108/03684929610149747

Florida, R., & Gates, G. (2001). *Technology and Tolerance: The Importance of Diversity to High-Technology Growth*. The Brookings Institution.

Fotiadis, A. K., & Sigala, M. (2015). Developing a framework for designing an Events Management Training Simulation (EMTS). *Journal of Hospitality, Leisure, Sport and Tourism Education*, 16, 59–71. DOI: 10.1016/j.jhlste.2015.03.001

Francoeur, C., Labelle, R., & Sinclair-Desgagné, B. (2008). Gender diversity in corporate governance and top management. *Journal of Business Ethics*, 81(1), 83–95. DOI: 10.1007/s10551-007-9482-5

Fu, K., Hainey, T., & Baxter, G. (2016, October). A systematic literature review to identify empirical evidence on the use of computer games in business education and training. In European Conference on Games Based Learning (p. 232). Academic Conferences International Limited.

Garneli, V., Giannakos, M., & Chorianopoulos, K. (2017). Serious games as a malleable learning medium: The effects of narrative, gameplay, and making on students' performance and attitudes. *British Journal of Educational Technology*, 48(3), 842–859. DOI: 10.1111/bjet.12455

Gartner Says By 2015, More Than 50 Percent of Organizations That Manage Innovation Processes Will Gamify Those Processes. (2011). Gartner Newsroom. Retrieved November 7, 2013, from https://www.gartner.com/newsroom/id/1629214

Gatian, A. W. (1994). Is user satisfaction a valid measure of system effectiveness? *Information & Management*, 26(3), 119–131. DOI: 10.1016/0378-7206(94)90036-1

Gilbert, J. A., Stead, B. A., & Ivancevich, J. M. (1999). Diversity management: A new organizational paradigm. *Journal of Business Ethics*, 21(1), 61–76. DOI: 10.1023/A:1005907602028

Guillén-Nieto, V., & Aleson-Carbonell, M. (2012). Serious games and learning effectiveness: The case of It'sa Deal! *Computers & Education*, 58(1), 435–448. DOI: 10.1016/j.compedu.2011.07.015

Haigh, M., & Hazelton, J. (2010). Incorporating Sustainability into Accounting Curricula. *Accounting Education*, 19(1&2), 159–178.

Hamari, J., & Koivisto, J. (2013, June). Social Motivations To Use Gamification: An Empirical Study Of Gamifying Exercise. In ECIS (Vol. 105, No. 5, pp. 18-19). https://aisel.aisnet.org/ecis2013_cr/105

Hambrick, D. C., & Mason, P. A. (1984). Upper echelons: The organization as a reflection of its top managers. *Academy of Management Review*, 9(2), 193–206. DOI: 10.2307/258434

Harrison, D., & Klein, K. (2007). What's the difference? Diversity constructs as separation, variety, or disparity in organizations. *Academy of Management Review*, 32(4), 1199–1228. DOI: 10.5465/amr.2007.26586096

Herring, C. (2009). Does diversity pay?: Race, gender, and the business case for diversity. *American Sociological Review*, 74(2), 208–224. DOI: 10.1177/000312240907400203

Hofer-Bonfim, B., Savych, Z., & Schnitzer, J. (2023). Comparing Diversity & Inclusion (D&I) disclosures across nine countries. In Diversity and Inclusion across languages (pp. 83-108). Frank & Timme, Berlin.

Hossain, M., Atif, M., Ahmed, A., & Mia, L. (2020). Do LGBT workplace diversity policies create value for firms? *Journal of Business Ethics*, 167(4), 775–791. DOI: 10.1007/s10551-019-04158-z

Hunicke, R., LeBlanc, M., & Zubek, R. (2004). MDA: A formal approach to game design and game research. *Proceedings of the AAAI Workshop on Challenges in Game AI*, 4(1).

Isabelle, D. (2020). Gamification of Entrepreneurship Education. *Decision Sciences Journal of Innovative Education*, 18(2), 203–223. DOI: 10.1111/dsji.12203

Itam, U., & Bagali, M. M. (2019). Diversity and inclusion management: a focus on employee engagement. In Gender and Diversity: Concepts, Methodologies, Tools, and Applications (pp. 1771-1788). IGI Global. DOI: 10.4018/978-1-5225-6912-1.ch093

Jones, B. D. (2009). Motivating students to engage in learning: The MUSIC model of academic motivation. *International Journal on Teaching and Learning in Higher Education*, 21(2), 272–285.

Jones, B. D., Epler, C. M., Mokri, P., Bryant, L. H., & Paretti, M. C. (2013). The effects of a collaborative problem-based learning experience on students' motivation in engineering capstone courses. *The Interdisciplinary Journal of Problem-Based Learning*, 7(2), 2. DOI: 10.7771/1541-5015.1344

Kamp-Roelands, N. (2013). A commentary on 'Integrated reporting – a review of developments and their implications for the accounting curriculum'. *Accounting Education*, 22(4), 357–359. DOI: 10.1080/09639284.2013.817799

Khan, N., Korac-Kakabadse, N., Skouloudis, A., & Dimopoulos, A. (2019). Diversity in the workplace: An overview of disability employment disclosures among UK firms. *Corporate Social Responsibility and Environmental Management*, 26(1), 170–185. DOI: 10.1002/csr.1669

Kirriemuir, J., & McFarlane, A. (2004). Literature review in games and learning: https://telearn.hal.science/hal-00190453/document

Kolk, A. (2003). Trends in sustainability reporting by the Fortune Global 250. *Business Strategy and the Environment*, 12(5), 279–291. DOI: 10.1002/bse.370

Koster, R. (2004). *Theory of Fun for Game Design*. O'Reilly Media.

Landers, R. N. (2014). Developing a Theory of Gamified Learning: Linking Serious Games and Gamification of Learning. *Simulation & Gaming*, 45(6), 752–768. DOI: 10.1177/1046878114563660

Landers, R. N., Armstrong, M. B., & Collmus, A. B. (2017). How to use game elements to enhance learning: Applications of the theory of gamified learning. In *Serious games and edutainment applications* (pp. 457–483). Springer. DOI: 10.1007/978-3-319-51645-5_21

Larson, K. (2020). Serious games and gamification in the corporate training environment: A literature review. *TechTrends*, 64(2), 319–328. DOI: 10.1007/s11528-019-00446-7

Lippincott, B., & Pergola, T. M. (2009). Use of a job cost simulation to engage gen Y students. *Journal of the International Academy for Case Studies*, 15(1), 107.

Lorbiecki, A., & Gavin, J. (2000). Critical turns in the evolution of Diversity Management. *British Journal of Management*, 11(s1), 11. DOI: 10.1111/1467-8551.11.s1.3

Malaquias, R. F., Malaquias, F. F. D. O., Junior, D. M. B., & Zambra, P. (2018). The use of a serious game and academic performance of undergraduate accounting students: An empirical analysis. *Turkish Online Journal of Distance Education*, 19(2), 117–127. DOI: 10.17718/tojde.415825

Malone, T. W. (1980). *What makes things fun to learn? A study of intrinsically motivating computer games*. Stanford University.

Malone, T. W. (1981). Toward a theory of intrinsically motivating instruction. *Cognitive Science*, 5(4), 333–369.

Maxfield, S., Wang, L., & Magaldi de Sousa, M. (2018). The effectiveness of bank governance reforms in the wake of the financial crisis: A stakeholder approach. *Journal of Business Ethics*, 150(2), 485–503. DOI: 10.1007/s10551-016-3116-8

Mazur, B. (2010). Cultural diversity in organisational theory and practice. Journal of intercultural management, 2(2), 5-15.

McMillan-Capehart, A., Aaron, J. R., & Cline, B. N. (2010). Investor reactions to diversity reputation signals. *Corporate Reputation Review*, 13(3), 184–197. DOI: 10.1057/crr.2010.20

Michael, D. R., & Chen, S. L. (2005). *Serious games: Games that educate, train, and inform*. Muska & Lipman/Premier-Trade.

Mitchell, A., & Savill-Smith, C. (2004). The use of computer and video games for learning. A review of the literature, 88(10), 1397-1399.

Modarelli, G. (2023). Combining CSR, public-private policies, inclusiveness and complex challenges for integral well-being by reciprocity relations—An agenda for global governance. *Corporate and Business Strategy Review*, 4(2), 4–6. DOI: 10.22495/cbsrv4i2editorial

Nederveen Pieterse, A., Van Knippenberg, D., & Van Dierendonck, D. (2013). Cultural diversity and team performance: The role of team member goal orientation. *Academy of Management Journal*, 56(3), 782–804. DOI: 10.5465/amj.2010.0992

Neumark, D. (2021). Age discrimination in hiring: Evidence from age-blind vs. non-age-blind hiring procedures. *The Journal of Human Resources*.

Nicholson, S. (2015). A recipe for meaningful gamification. In *Gamification in education and business* (pp. 1–20). Springer. DOI: 10.1007/978-3-319-10208-5_1

O'Mara, J., & Richter, A. (2011). Global diversity and inclusion benchmarks: Standards for organizations around the world. O'Mara and Associates.

O'Reilly, C. A.III, Williams, K. Y., & Barsade, S. (1998). Group demography and innovation: Does diversity help? In Gruenfeld, D. H. (Ed.), *Composition* (pp. 183–207). Elsevier Science/JAI Press.

Oelrich, S., Siebold, N., & Ketelhut, K. (2024). Diversity at work: Firms' strategic responses to mandatory diversity disclosure. *Accounting Horizons*, 38(1), 123–138. DOI: 10.2308/HORIZONS-2022-083

Oliveira, M., & Petersen, S. (2014). The choice of serious games and gamification. In *International Conference on Serious Games Development and Applications*. Springer. DOI: 10.1007/978-3-319-11623-5_18

Owen, G. (2013). A rejoinder to commentaries on 'integrated reporting: A review of developments and their implications for the accounting curriculum'. *Accounting Education*, 22(4), 363–365. DOI: 10.1080/09639284.2013.817801

Özsözgün Çalişkan, A. (2014). How accounting and accountants may contribute in sustainability? *Social Responsibility Journal*, 10(2), 246–267. DOI: 10.1108/SRJ-04-2012-0049

Prensky, M. (2001). Fun, play and games: What makes games engaging. Digital game-based learning, 5(1), 5-31.

Prensky, M. (2003). Digital game-based learning. Computers in entertainment (CIE), 1(1), 21-21.

Redman, A., Wiek, A., & Barth, M. (2021). Current practice of assessing students' sustainability competencies: A review of tools. *Sustainability Science*, 16(1), 117–135. DOI: 10.1007/s11625-020-00855-1

Riemer, V., & Schrader, C. (2015). Learning with quizzes, simulations, and adventures: Students' attitudes, perceptions and intentions to learn with different types of serious games. *Computers & Education*, 88, 160–168. DOI: 10.1016/j.compedu.2015.05.003

Rijamampianina, R., & Carmichael, T. (2005). A pragmatic and holistic approach to managing diversity. *Problems and Perspectives in Management*, (1), 109–117.

Rodrigues, M. A. B., & Morais, A. I. (2021). How to challenge university students to work on integrated reporting and integrated reporting assurance. *Sustainability (Basel)*, 13(19), 10761. DOI: 10.3390/su131910761

Ryan, J., Hawdon, J., & Branick, A. (2002). The political economy of diversity: Diversity programs in fortune 500 companies. *Sociological Research Online*, 7(1), 26–40. DOI: 10.5153/sro.702

Samudhram, A., Stewart, E., Wickramanayake, J., & Sinnakkannu, J. (2014). Value relevance of human capital based disclosures: Moderating effects of labor productivity, investor sentiment, analyst coverage and audit quality. *Advances in Accounting*, 30(2), 338–353. DOI: 10.1016/j.adiac.2014.09.012

SASB. (2017) Sustainability Accounting Standard Board-Conceptual framework, Retrieved from: https://sasb.org/wp-content/uploads/2020/02/SASB_Conceptual-Framework_WATERMARK.pdf

Senaratne, S., Gunarathne, N., Herath, R., Samudrage, D., & Cooray, T. (2022). Institutional pressures and responses to the introduction of integrated reporting into accounting curricula: The case of Sri Lankan universities. *Accounting Education*, 31(5), 536–566. DOI: 10.1080/09639284.2022.2032775

Sharma, U., & Kelly, M. (2014). Students' perceptions of education for sustainable development in the accounting and business curriculum at a business school in New Zealand. *Meditari Accountancy Research*, 22(2), 130–148. DOI: 10.1108/MEDAR-12-2012-0042

Showalter, D. S. (2022) The Role of Accounting in ESG Reporting: A Q&A with D. Scott Showalter. Retrieved from NC state university: https://mac.ncsu.edu/news/2023/03/02/the-role-of-accounting-in-esg-reporting-a-qa-with-d-scott-showalter/

Squire, K., & Jenkins, H. (2003). Harnessing the power of games in education. *Insight (American Society of Ophthalmic Registered Nurses)*, 3(1), 5–33. PMID: 12703249

Susi, T., Johannesson, M., & Backlund, P. (2007). Serious games: An overview: https://www.diva-portal.org/smash/get/diva2:2416/FULLTEXT01.pdf

Taliento, M., Favino, C., & Netti, A. (2019). Impact of environmental, social, and governance information on economic performance: Evidence of a corporate 'sustainability advantage' from Europe. *Sustainability (Basel)*, 11(6), 1738. DOI: 10.3390/su11061738

Tschopp, D., & Nastanski, M. (2014). The Harmonization and Convergence of Corporate Social Responsibility Reporting Standards. *Journal of Business Ethics*, 125(1), 147–162. DOI: 10.1007/s10551-013-1906-9

United Nations. (2015). Transforming our world: the 2030 Agenda for Sustainable Development: https://documents-dds-ny.un.org/doc/UNDOC/GEN/N15/291/89/PDF/N1529189.pdf?OpenElement

Venturelli, A., Fasiello, R., & Pizzi, S. (2021). CSR education in economia aziendale curricula: An overview. *Administrative Sciences*, 11(4), 137. DOI: 10.3390/admsci11040137

Vithana, K., Soobaroyen, T., & Ntim, C. G. (2021). Human resource disclosures in UK corporate annual reports: To what extent do these reflect organisational priorities towards labour? *Journal of Business Ethics*, 169(3), 475–497. DOI: 10.1007/s10551-019-04289-3

Wang, Y., Rajan, P., Sankar, C. S., & Raju, P. K. (2016). Let them play: The impact of mechanics and dynamics of a serious game on student perceptions of learning engagement. *IEEE Transactions on Learning Technologies*, 10(4), 514–525. DOI: 10.1109/TLT.2016.2639019

Werbach, K., & Hunter, D. (2012). *For the Win: How Game Thinking Can Revolutionize Your Business*. Wharton Digital Press.

Westera, W. (2019). Why and How Serious Games can Become Far More Effective: Accommodating Productive Learning Experiences, Learner Motivation and the Monitoring of Learning Gains. *Journal of Educational Technology & Society*, 22(1), 59–69.

Williams, K. Y., & O'Reilly, C. A. (1998). Demography and diversity in organizations: A review of 40 years of research. *Research in Organizational Behavior*, 20(20), 77–140.

York, J., & DeHaan, J. W. (2018). A constructivist approach to game-based language learning: Student perceptions in a beginner-level EFL context. *International Journal of Game-Based Learning*, 8(1), 19–40. DOI: 10.4018/IJGBL.2018010102

Zaid, M. A., & Issa, A. (2023). A roadmap for triggering the convergence of global ESG disclosure standards: lessons from the IFRS foundation and stakeholder engagement. Corporate Governance: The International Journal of Business in Society.

Zainuddin, Z., Chu, S. K. W., Shujahat, M., & Perera, C. J. (2020). The impact of gamification on learning and instruction: A systematic review of empirical evidence. *Educational Research Review*, 30, 100326. DOI: 10.1016/j.edurev.2020.100326

Zhonggen, Y. (2019). A meta-analysis of use of serious games in education over a decade. *International Journal of Computer Games Technology*, 2019, 2019. DOI: 10.1155/2019/4797032

KEY TERMS AND DEFINITIONS

Diversity & Inclusion (D&I): Is a movement that focuses on acknowledging and valuing differences among individuals in various settings, like workplaces or communities. Diversity includes characteristics such as gender, race and ethnicity, age, sexual orientation, disability, and more. While Inclusion aims to create an environment where diverse individuals are actively empowered and included. The main goal of D&I is to build an equitable and harmonious environment in both society and organizations, by embracing human differences, fostering acceptance and collaboration, and, specifically in organizations, enhancing creativity, innovation, and overall well-being.

Engagement: Refers to the state of being actively involved, committed, or interested in a particular activity or task, marked by enthusiasm, dedication, and emotional investment. Educational engagement it pertains to the extent of participation, attention, and interest that students exhibit in the learning process, influencing their understanding and retention of information.

Game-Based Learning: Is an educational approach to learning and teaching based on gamification, which consists of behavioral simulation, experiential, and computer games. This approach allows both students and employees to acquire knowledge, skills, and techniques that can significantly impact their careers.

Human Capital (HC): Is the collective stock of skills, attributes, knowledge, and expertise of employees, which play an integral role in increasing the productivity and sustainability of an organization. Put simply, HC refers to qualities that human beings have or learn that make them more productive

Integrated Reporting (IR): An IR aims to provide insights on the resources and relationships used and influenced by an organization – these are collectively referred to as "the capitals" in the IR Framework, provided by the Integrated Reporting Council (IIRC).

Motivation: Refers to the level of enthusiasm and participation that students demonstrate in their learning. It plays a crucial role in determining their willingness to engage in educational activities. Employing effective teaching strategies can empower and enhance students' motivation, ultimately contributing to a positive and productive learning experience.

Serious Games: Involve a set of rules and actions in a cohesive manner and it motivates players to compete with others; in fact, serious games usually elect a winner. Moreover, a serious game includes elements such as play, exposition, choice, information, engagement, and reflection. These elements facilitate the game in promoting intrinsic motivation and deep engagement in the learning process.

ENDNOTE

1 The open-source material is available here https://www.integres.eu/results-outcomes/io1-teaching-materials/ (Course 3: Integrated Reporting and Human Capital for SMEs) and here https://www.integres.eu/results-outcomes/io2-ebook/ (Get the book).

Chapter 7
Transformative Learning in Higher Education:
Unveiling the Impact of Innovative Teaching Strategies Through the Games of Marketing

Tamara Guerrero Gómez
Universidad de Granada, Spain

Juan Miguel Alcántara Pilar
https://orcid.org/0000-0002-8112-6152
Universidad de Granada, Spain

Álvaro J Rojas Lamorena
https://orcid.org/0000-0001-5102-6954
Universidad de Granada, Spain

Eugenia Rodríguez López
Universidad de Granada, Spain

ABSTRACT

Higher education is undergoing a transformation towards student-centered approaches, moving away from traditional methods to embrace innovative methodologies that encourage active student participation in learning. This chapter explores the benefits of adopting non-conventional teaching methodologies to enhance student engagement and socialization across various subjects, as well as their acquisition of relevant knowledge and skills. A specific activity within the "Games of Marketing" project is detailed, which has been implemented over five academic years with high student approval. In summary, this chapter highlights the shift towards student-

DOI: 10.4018/979-8-3693-1172-1.ch007

centered learning in higher education and the exploration of innovative teaching methodologies through the "Games of Marketing" project. It emphasizes the project's adaptability, its impact on student engagement, and its potential to enhance learning outcomes across diverse educational settings.

1. INTRODUCTION

Currently, higher education requires a transformation that allows a more active participation of the student, moving from conventional teaching methods to new tools and methodologies that facilitate such activation of students, assuming a greater role in their own learning (González-Lizárraga, Becerra-Traver and Yáñez-Diaz, 2016; Núñez, Penelas and Cuesta, 2014; Whitehead, 2008). In this reality, there are a series of competencies on the part of students resulting from integrating, mobilizing and having different cognitive, affective, and psychomotor skills, in addition to knowledge (Boni and Lozano, 2007; Said et al., 2023), which allow the student to face with guarantees of success the resolution of different problems in the academic, professional or social field (Royal Decree 1393, 2007).

Referring to the previous paragraph, this chpater aims to show the advantages of incorporating non-conventional teaching methodologies, in favor of obtaining a greater involvement and socialization of students in the development of various subjects and in the acquisition of knowledge and skills related to the subject. For this purpose, the activity within the project called Games of Marketing will be detailed below. This work is totally descriptive since the evaluation surveys answered by the students, they usually evaluate not only this activity but all those that make up the project, so our contribution with this work is to describe an activity that we have been doing for 5 academic years, with a great acceptance among students and that can be transferred to any educational center and to any teaching area. It is worth mentioning that without rigor in teaching and training, we have looked for the exact moments to include this type of activities, always related to the subject itself.

Therefore, the aim of this chapter is to deepen in the structure of one of the activities of the project that captures the attention of students because it brings together students from different courses who have to work in teams. In addition, we explain the two modalities, describing in more detail one of the six missions. Finally, a behavioral model is proposed with confirmation and subjective learning as antecedents, satisfaction as mediator and recommendation as final variable. The aim is to analyze the moderating effect of participating or not in Games of Marketing in this proposed model. In addition, the aim is to arouse curiosity in other colleagues to apply similar activities.

2. THEORETICAL FRAMEWORK.

2.1. Innovation and Teaching Methodologies in the Teaching Within the EHEA

The consolidation of the EHEA has necessitated a transformation in the role of teaching (Rodríguez-Gómez and Gairín Sallán, 2015), demanding the cultivation of a holistic development of students by integrating diverse skills, abilities, and values (Fandos, Jiménez, Orús, Peligero, and Pina, 2015). This paradigm shift underscores the imperative for universities to innovate their teaching methodologies to facilitate learning and skill acquisition among students (Pagés et al., 2016). Central to this process is the concept of transformative learning, as articulated by Mezirow (1991), wherein individuals engage in critical reflection on their assumptions, beliefs, and perspectives. "Transformative learning" is a process through which individuals critically reflect on their assumptions, beliefs, and perspectives, leading to a fundamental shift in their understanding of themselves and the world around them. This shift often results in changes in behavior, attitudes, and values, enabling individuals to respond more effectively to complex situations and engage in more meaningful ways with others (Mezirow, 1991; Jost, 2011; Tilak et al., 2020). This transformative learning journey empowers students to transition from passive recipients of knowledge to active participants in their own education, engaging in a variety of activities such as games, research, and debates (van Diepen, Stefanova, and Miranowicz, 2009; Orús et al., 2016). Its application in the academic context holds significant potential for addressing the evolving needs and preferences of young consumers within higher education. This potential stems from the inherent capacity of transformative learning to foster critical reflection and deep engagement with course content and tools, thereby facilitating meaningful personal and intellectual growth among students. By integrating transformative learning principles into pedagogical approaches, universities can create learning environments that are conducive to the development of essential skills such as critical thinking, problem-solving, and adaptability (Cranton, 2016; Sacavarelli et al., 2021).

One key reason for the wider discussion of transformative learning application in academia is its ability to enhance the relevance and applicability of course content to real-world contexts. By encouraging students to critically examine their assumptions and perspectives, transformative learning enables them to connect theoretical concepts with practical experiences, thereby fostering a deeper understanding of subject matter. This process not only enhances student engagement and motivation but also equips them with the skills and knowledge necessary for success in their future careers (Sacavarelli et al., 2021).

Furthermore, the application of transformative learning in academia can contribute to the creation of inclusive and diverse learning environments. By encouraging students to explore and challenge their own beliefs and perspectives, transformative learning promotes empathy, understanding, and respect for differing viewpoints. This not only fosters a sense of belonging and acceptance within the academic community but also prepares students to navigate the complexities of an increasingly diverse and interconnected world (Achnepfleitner et al., 2021; Taylor, 2007).

Additionally, the evolving nature of higher education demands a reevaluation of traditional teaching methods and approaches. As universities strive to meet the changing needs and preferences of students, there is a growing recognition of the importance of student-centered learning experiences. Transformative learning offers a framework for designing curricula and instructional strategies that prioritize student engagement, empowerment, and agency. By incorporating elements of transformative learning into their teaching practices, educators can create dynamic and interactive learning environments that encourage active participation and collaboration among students (Mezirow, 2000; Goller & Rieckmann, 2022).

The application of transformative learning in the academic context warrants wider discussion due to its potential to enhance student learning outcomes, promote inclusivity and diversity, and adapt to the evolving needs of higher education. By embracing transformative learning principles, universities can better prepare students to thrive in an increasingly complex and interconnected world (Slavich & Zimbardo, 2012)

These teamwork activities require collaboration among students, fostering communication and socialization, in addition to greater interaction with the subject and the teacher, which allows the acquisition of skills and competencies difficult to acquire with traditional teaching methodologies (Exley and Dennick, 2007; Núñez et al., 2014), as it improves the processing of the subject (Blasco-Arcas, Buil, Hernández-Ortega and Sesé, 2013). This allows the improvement of students' academic results and performance at the university level (García-Martin and Cantón-Mayo, 2019; Halpern, Piña and Ortega-Gunckel, 2020; Lee, 2011) while affecting their perception of their own learning. Teaching innovation favors student involvement in classes, facilitating the acquisition of competencies and improving the student's perception of teaching, seeing it as more satisfactory than the traditional one and at the same time enriching (Orús et al., 2014).

In our case, within a broader teaching innovation project, we focus on explaining the purpose of one of its activities called "Games of Marketing", with which we try to improve the training of students through a series of practical activities, bringing them closer to the professional reality to which they will access as graduates, and facilitating the acquisition of transversal competencies. For this purpose, we will rely on two types of learning, project-based and problem-based:

- Project-based learning will be evident when the activity requires the direct involvement of students in the configuration of a result to be presented.
- Problem-based learning, on the other hand, is present when, starting from a reality (problem), a cognitive conflict arises in the context of the student, which will lead him/her to make decisions.

The teaching methodologies employed for the development of experiences, as well as the support resources utilized, can be adapted to any subject, regardless of the field to which it belongs, thus subject to the creativity and problem-solving abilities of the instructor.

For active learning based on competencies, it is essential to consider constructivism as a support for learning. Constructivism, which is a current of psychological and educational research, is based on the consideration that previous knowledge generates new knowledge, experiences shape the subject's mental structures, and learning is neither passive nor objective, but subjective in light of individual experiences (Curay and Ramón, 2021; Lee and Fanguy, 2022). Moreover, when there is an interaction between the social environment and subject, one's mental schemas are compared with those of others, giving rise to social constructivism. Cognitive conflict triggers students to internalize and transform new information, creating new learning and facing diverse situations, which may or may not be similar to reality (Sasson, Yehuda and Miedijensky, 2022). Based on Vygotski's social constructivism theory, social learning is born, in which students interact to help each other (Almuhailib and Al-Ahdal, 2021; Al-Smadi, 2014; Taber, 2020).

On the other hand, game-based learning consists of the use of games as a tool to support learning, thus, board or role-playing games are adaptable to the educational context for the achievement of objectives (Krath, Schürmann and Korflesch, 2021; Perez-Manzano and Almela-Baeza, 2018). To speak of Gamification, it is necessary that the use of games brings with it a planned structure of mechanics and dynamics with the aim of increasing motivation (Danielli, 2015; Toribio and Robles, 2021; Fraga, Vila and Matínez, 2021; Wardaszko, 2016). Gamification is the application of game design elements and principles in non-game contexts to engage users and enhance their experience, motivation, and learning outcomes (De Oliveira y Mayer, 2014; Deterding et al, 2011; Polo-Peña et al., 2024). Thus, point systems, achievements, rankings, time, levels, challenges, and rewards are mechanics that develop socialization, acceptance, status, attention, physical activity, integration, etc (Loureiro, Bilro and Aires, 2020; Su, 2016).

The elements expressed in the previous paragraphs related to teaching innovation, and in particular, with gamification as an element to include a novelty in the classes to motivate and involve students, are found in the activity called "Games of

Marketing", within a teaching innovation project organized by the authors of this work. The structure of this project is explained below.

2.2. Teaching Methodology: Structure of the Games of Marketing Activity

Games of Marketing are developed under a cooperative learning method, in which the teacher poses the problem, ensures that the groups are balanced, distributes roles, and makes sure that everyone participates. It is a structured activity in which the progress of the group depends on everyone's contribution.

Games of Marketing (MgM) have been changing and improving throughout the life of the teaching innovation project, developing in two models. One is called basic level, where a series of consecutive group tests are carried out in the form of a gymkhana. Once the group has finished a test, it goes to the next one, without the option to choose from a range of options. On the other hand, the veteran level where students choose the tests to perform according to their strategy. Both types of games are usually set in a series or well-known movies such as The Hunger Games, The Squid Games or Game of Thrones. Next, we will explain the development of each of the levels or modalities.

2.2.1. Basic Level

Games of Marketing Basic Level is a competition of a playful nature in which teams of students must overcome a set of missions along a route (also called "gymkhana").

All groups perform the same type of missions, but in different order in a linear fashion (see Table 1).

Table 1. Example of mission sequencing by group.

	0	1	2	3	4	5
Group 1	Mission 0	Mission 1	Mission 3	Mission 5	Mission 2	Mission 4
Group 2	Mission 0	Mission 1	Mission 4	Mission 5	Mission 3	Mission 2
Group 3	Mission 0	Mission 1	Mission 2	Mission 4	Mission 5	Mission 3
Group 4	Mission 0	Mission 1	Mission 4	Mission 5	Mission 3	Mission 2
Group 5	Mission 0	Mission 1	Mission 5	Mission 2	Mission 3	Mission 4

Source: Own elaboration

Route and Points

As in any gymkhana, the tests or missions are developed sequentially along a route, giving the activity dynamism due to the changes of scenery. In Games of Marketing Basic Level, the route is made up of six points: a starting point that coincides with the end point, and five intermediate points. The details of these are shown in the following table (see Table 2).

Table 2. Points that make up the game route

Item designation	Brief explanation
Exit point or Classroom 0	At this point is where the opening scene is made and where the Mission Zero (M0), which consists of the market orientation table, is handed out. The students, in groups, are given an envelope with different versions of the tables. Once they fill it in, they hand it in and receive the M1.
Intermediate points or teachers' offices (P1, P2, P3, P4, P5).	These points are the teachers' offices where the student arrives and hands in the Mission. The teacher who receives it, must check that the student has not made a mistake in the delivery point and then: The students are given a type test that they have to answer. Once returned by the participants, they are given the next Mission.
Arrival point or Classroom 0	They hand in the M5, which is the last one, and it is recorded in which position they have arrived since it influences the final score. The group must stay in the starting classroom.

Source: Own elaboration

Other unavoidable parts of the game are the library and the copy shop. In the library the students find the manuals with which to find the answer to the Mission "consult the manual", and in the copy shop the students pick up a Mission from the copy shop employee. These places are mere passing points for students to discover the University Campus facilities.

In Table 3, the example of the sequence of missions and tour is presented.

Table 3. Example of mission sequencing and tour by groups.

	Classroom 0	Teacher's office 1	Teacher's office 2	Teacher's office 3	Teacher's office 4	Teacher's office 5	Classroom 0
Group 1	Mission 0	Mission 1	Mission 3	Mission 5	Mission 2	Mission 4	G1
Group 2	Mission 0	Mission 1	Mission 4	Mission 5	Mission 3	Mission 2	G2
Group 3	Mission 0	Mission 1	Mission 2	Mission 4	Mission 5	Mission 3	G3
Group 4	Mission 0	Mission 1	Mission 4	Mission 5	Mission 3	Mission 2	G4
Group 5	Mission 0	Mission 1	Mission 5	Mission 2	Mission 3	Mission 4	G5

For example, Group 1, once they have completed Mission 0 in the exit classroom, receives Mission 1, which they take to the office of teacher 1, to whom they must give the Mission already solved, after which they must take a 10-question test provided by the teacher, and once solved, they will receive Mission 2. Figure 1 shows an outline of the process.

Figure 1. Sequential output process and first mission (Own elaboration)

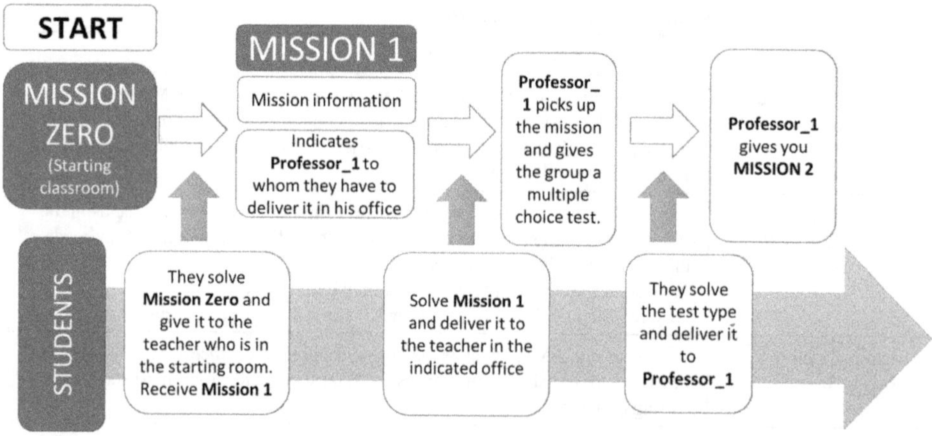

Thus, at the intermediate points (teachers' offices), the students must hand in the missions they have already solved, take a multiple-choice test, and pick up a new Mission. In this case, when the students pick up Mission 4, they must go to the Exhibition Hall, solve the test there and deliver the result to Professor 3's office.

The students, once they pick up Mission 4, must go to the Exhibition Hall, solve the test there and deliver the result to teacher 3's office.

In each Mission received and delivered by the teacher, there are codes to check that the origin and destination are correct. The Group of the Mission also appears, and a section for them to promote the activity in the different social networks that the project has.

Figure 2. Presentation of a mission (deliverable to the student) (Own elaboration)

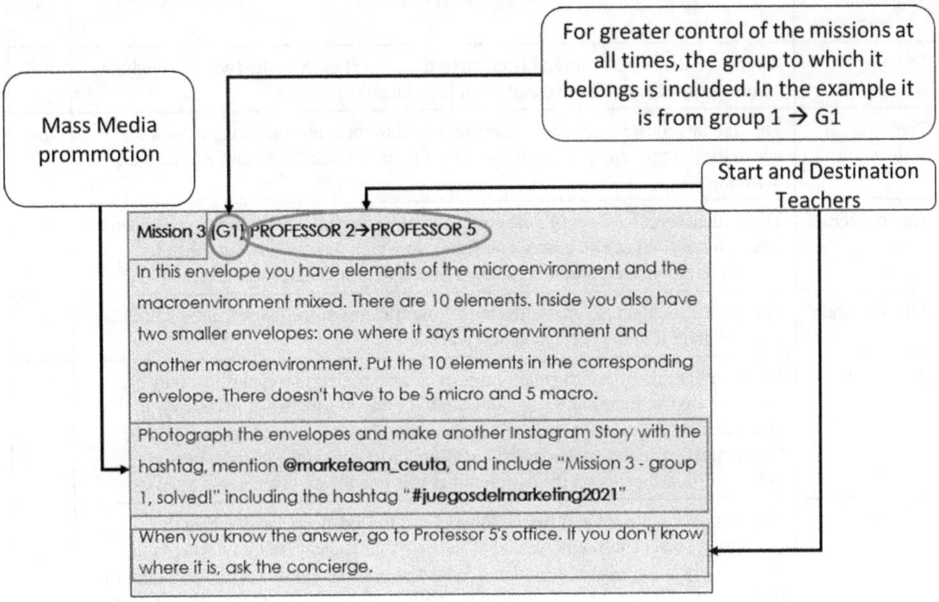

To facilitate the explanation of this activity, we will assume a Marketing Games - basic, where there are five Groups (G1, G2, G3, G4 and G5), and where 5 teachers participate (P1, P2, P3, P4 and P5), since material will be provided to understand the activity subject to these parameters.

Types of Tests and Evaluation

Several types of tests were proposed. Table 4 below shows the seven types of exercises that the teams will have to solve, which correspond to the "missions" of the game, as well as the valuation that each one of them has in the final score of each team in the game up to a maximum of 10 (100%). However, it should be noted that the time factor plays a fundamental role and students will also receive an extra grade determined by the order in which they reach the finishing point.

Table 4. Types of mission in games of marketing basic level and scoring

Mission Name	Description	%
Mission cero	This is the output mission that consists of filling in the gaps in a table containing the key aspects of the different types of market orientation (competition, assumptions, efforts).	10%

continued on following page

Table 4. Continued

Mission Name	Description	%
Test	It consists of 10 questions and is given to the team at each of the five intermediate points of the course. The average of all tests taken is counted.	50%
Consultation in the book	The students must respond to a question posed to them by consulting a book for which they are provided with all the details to locate it in the library and arrive at the answer.	10%
Macro-micro puzzle	The students receive a set of notes on macroenvironmental and microenvironmental situations, as well as two empty envelopes, in which they should put the notes classified into macroenvironmental and microenvironmental situations.	10%
Alphabet soup	The word search puzzle was collected by the students at the Copy Center and they had to deliver it to the corresponding teacher.	10%
Pregunta libre	These are questions that the team finds in an unexpected place, and that they can answer thanks to their knowledge or search for the information if necessary. In the example case, 3 questions were left in the exhibition room (see Figure 3). Each Group must solve the question that corresponds to it and take it to the person indicated (this appears on the Mission that was previously given to the team).	10%
Box test	This test has two purposes: firstly, for students to find a code with which they can open a secret chest, and secondly, for first-year students to know where the teachers' pigeonholes are located and in turn to become familiar with the names of the teachers. The teachers' pigeonholes (mailboxes) are numbered by default with two digits. Figure 4 explains how students obtain the key to open the box where the macro-microenvironment missions are stored.	

Source: Own elaboration

Figure 3. Posters with "free questions" (Own elaboration)

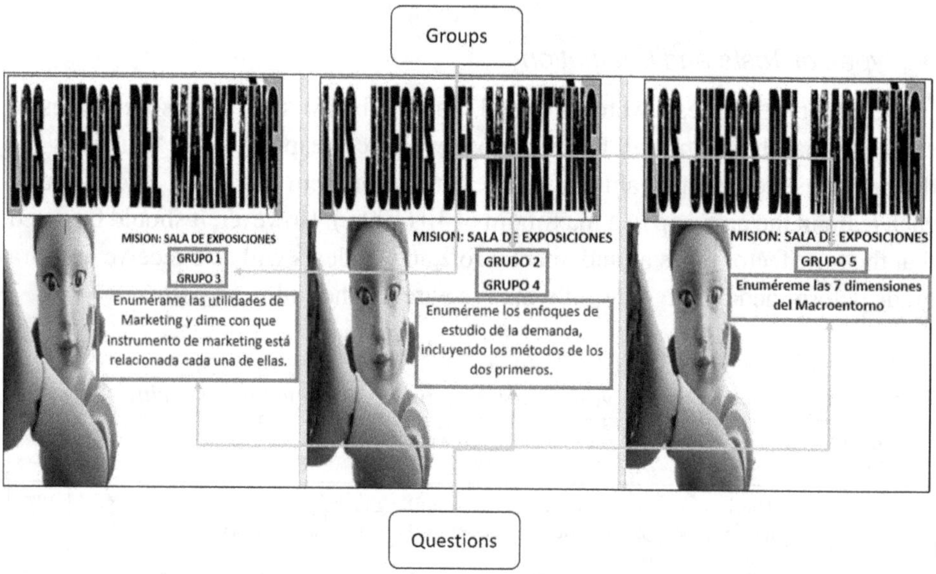

Figure 4. Explanation of how to obtain the code that opens the chest (Own elaboration)

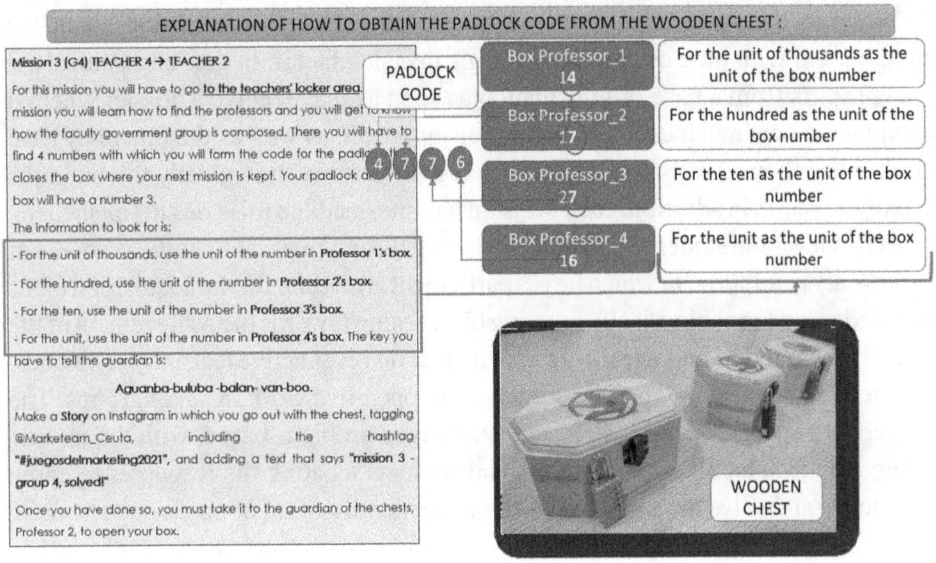

Special Setting Conditions: The Case of the "Squid Game"

Games of Marketing carry with them a thematic setting, referring to television series with great impact at the time of their development. This is incorporated in the decoration, design of the resources used, and even the organization's clothing. For example, the basic and veteran games developed in the 2019-2020 academic year were based on the science fiction and adventure series The Hunger Games and the medieval fantasy series Game of Thrones, respectively. In the 2021-2022 course, Games of Marketing Basic Level, have been set in the controversial TV series The Squid Game, a thriller whose premiere broke audience records on Netflix in October 2021 (El Español, 2021). For the aforementioned edition of Games of Marketing, the organization counted on the participation of several students playing the role of "soldiers". The soldiers, spread out in different areas of the University Campus, will be able to shout to the participants: "red light!" (the participant must stop), or "green light!" (the participant may continue on his way). The player who does not stop must turn in his player card, which will penalize his team.

2.2.2. Veteran Level

While in the basic level, the student had no previous information about the missions and with time as the only strategic decision factor, in the veteran level the student starts from a base of information as soon as they receive a dossier where it is explained how much each of the missions is worth, as well as the time they have to complete them. They must select between 6 missions strategically to obtain the maximum score, in addition, each Mission has intermediate missions to finish them.

In this level the student investigates to solve the enigmas, activating a process of uncertainty resolution, in which he is a participant at all times of the acquisition of his knowledge, and capable of self-directing his learning towards the achievement of the objective. Therefore, it is a learning activity that involves active learning techniques, centered on the student, and that stimulates cooperative work in small groups. The cooperative environment prevails, and learning is problem-based, with the teacher acting only as a facilitator and guide, and students locating the resources to apply knowledge and solve the problem, through the identification of needs and research.

Figure 5. Material handed out to students (photographic archive of the team)

The students, in their dossier, only have the start of each Mission. They are also given Mission ZERO, which, unlike Games of Marketing - Basics, they must solve correctly in order to exit, and a paper with codes (see Figure 6) that will serve them for the Mission to hire the fleet of ships.

Figure 6. Codes given to students together with the Dossier and the mission ZERO (Own elaboration)

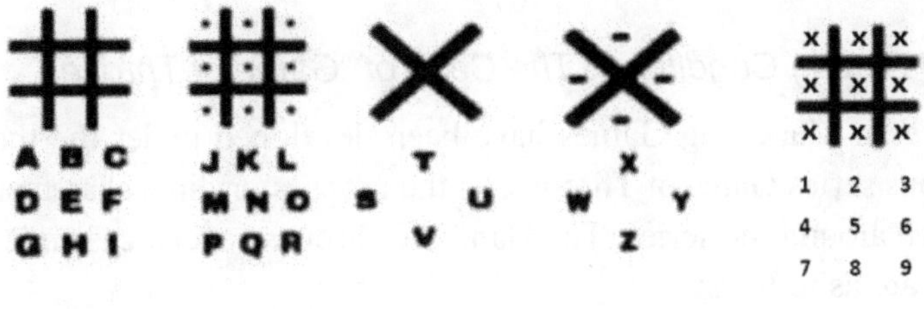

Types of Tests

- Search for answers in the library: A classroom is used as a library, where the books that the students will need are left. They must go and look for the solution to the question posed in one of the missions.
- PERT realization: develop a PERT diagram, to obtain the critical path.
- Obtain a code. The numbers of pigeonholes (mailboxes) of faculty members, the solution of a multiple-choice test or a true-false test are used to give codes that are used to open chests that hide other missions.
    - o Example of true-false: If the solution is 2 true answers and 9 false answers, it would lead them to room 29. In the case of a multiple-choice test with 4 possible answers (a, b, c and d), the number of answers for each option would give a code for a padlock.
    - o Example of a multiple-choice test: A multiple-choice test exercise with only 4 options (a, b, c and d), after solving it, the students had to count how many a, b, c and d there were, and from there they would get the code. If the result of a multiple-choice test with 4 options out of 20 questions had:
        - 4 answers a
        - 7 answers b
        - 6 answers c
        - 3 answers d

The code given by this test is 4763.

- Alphabet soup: you have to find ten concepts of Marketing Management and Marketing Research in the alphabet soup.

- Free questions: questions from the subjects they are being tested on in the games in another modality; short answers, definitions, etc.

Special Setting Conditions: The Case of "Game of Thrones"

The Veteran Marketing Games have been developed under the theme of the world-famous series Game of Thrones, so the props, storyline, characters and missions revolve around the series. The Game of Thrones special case missions, with their score, are as follows:

1. get a dragon egg: with this Mission the Group can get between 5 and 6 points, as they do not know which dragon egg they are chasing. In the case of getting Drogon, they would get 6 points. In the case of getting Viserion or Rhaegal, they would get 5.
2. To get the Golden Company: 4 points.
3. To obtain the Unsullied: 4 points.
4. Hunt a wraith: 3 points.
5. Get the Army of the Savages: 2 points.
6. Obtain a vidriagon blade: 1 point.

In the same dossier they are told where each of the characters participating in the activity set in Game of Thrones are located (see Table 5).

Table 5. Characters and location.

	Character / City	Office / Classroom
1	Red Priestess	Office 31
2	Rumor Advisor	Office 28
3	Iron Bank	Classroom 25
4	House of the Maesters	Student Delegation
5	The Citadel Library	Video-conference seminar.
6	Night Guard	Teachers' lounge

Source: Own elaboration

In the following, to explain how a Mission would develop, we will use the example of "Getting a dragon egg". The text is as follows:

Initial text: *"To get a Dragon Egg, raise it and dominate ponent, you must visit the Red Priestess, Teacher's Name, and have her give you the keys to make the way. There are only three dragon eggs. The Group that reaches the 4th will have no prize."*

In the "Dossier of the Organizing Teacher" all the missions that make up each of the main missions are explained in detail, and the names of the teachers who participated in this activity have been changed to "Name of the Teacher" or "Name of the Teacher". When the dossiers are prepared for the activity, they should be changed to the teacher who represents the character.

When the students go to visit the Red Priestess, she gives them three missions to carry out, the results of which they must bring back to her. Below is the text:

> **Red Priestess Scene (teacher 4)**
> "To get a dragon egg you are going to invest a lot of time and perhaps sacrifice some lives. You will have to complete 3 missions for the next step. You can do them in a group or divide them among yourselves. It depends on the strategy you want to take.
> The first Mission is to know how to get to the west, since you will have to navigate. To do this, here is a challenge that you must overcome and show me that you can follow the navigation route that I give you.
> The second mission is based on finding a ship that will take you to Essos. To do this you have to visit the Rumor Advisor. There they will give you a Mission for which you will obtain a pass for the ship that will take you to Esso.
> The third mission has to do with your abilities to search for information. To do this, you must search for this book in The Citadel Library and bring me the answer that appears on this scroll.
> Once you have found the route of the first Mission, the pass to travel to Essos and you have found the answer to the scrolls, visit me again and I will give you the next step."

As we see, there are three missions:

- One given to him by the Red Priestess
- Another one that will be given to you by the Rumors Counselor.
- The third Mission that you will have to look for in the Library of The Citadel

The texts of the missions, although participating teachers are recommended not to read them, but rather to interpret them as closely as possible. It is then given to the students. Once the Group obtains the three tests and gives them to the teacher who represents the Red Priestess, she will tell them:

> *Very well, my daring adventurers. I see that you are capable of surpassing the missions that I have sent you and much more. Now you must visit the House of the Maester, and they can help you locate the dragon eggs after crossing the Narrow Sea.*

With this, the students must go to a new point, the House of the Masters, which will tell them:

> *Dragon eggs are a legend, and as such, they are difficult to find. I have to tell you that there are only 3 and you are not the only ones looking for them, and there are also three legends about where to find them. You must select one of the envelopes.*

You give the maester a choice between 3 envelopes, and without them knowing, depending on which one they take, they are looking for one of the dragons. It has as many envelopes as Groups finds, because everyone can try to get the dragon egg. Whoever is faster is the one who will get one of the three.

For example, the envelope for EGG 1 says the following: **DRAGON EGG - 1:**

"To get the key you must first be able to discover the following 4 codes where:
A: Number of marketing instruments that make up the Marketing-Mix.
B: The ten from the box of the vice dean of academic organization of the Faculty of Education, Economics and Technology.
C: Number of dimensions that the macro-environment has (according to the table in the marketing book).
D: The number of marketing instruments with which we can provide useful information.

Once you have obtained these codes, you can cross the Narrow Sea and look for the dragon egg in the study room. You must ask for the key:

SE03-BC

Replacing the BC with the numbers in the puzzle.
Inside you will find a chest with a padlock, use the 4-digit key with the padlock.
In it will be the dragon egg. Luck
NOTE: When you obtain the code as well as the number of the locker where it is kept, go ask the House of the Maestre, so that they can confirm that you have it correct. You can use the coins to get help. "

This Mission is important to explain. The dragon eggs are inside a chest, with a lock. The letters A, B, C and D are the 4 digits of the padlock. A is a teacher's locker number. The rest are marketing questions. When they had A, B, C and D, they had the possibility of asking the master if the code was correct, who told them yes or no, and if it was not, he only told them the figure that was wrong. Once they had the code, they would ask for the SE03-BC key to the locker, where B and C had already obtained it. With the code they would open the lock and see what dragon egg they had gotten. In Figure 7 you can see a diagram of this Mission.

Figure 7. Mission 1. Get a dragon egg (Own elaboration)

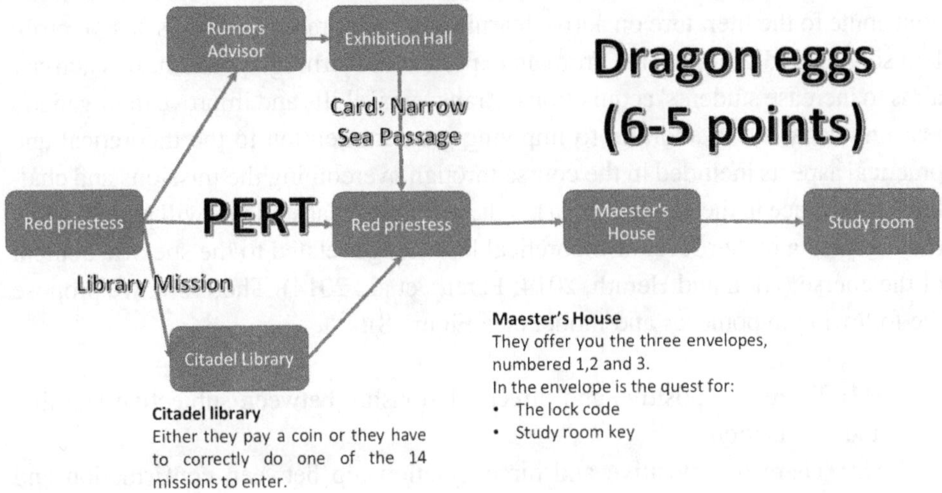

2.3. Proposed Model

Taking the theory of confirmation of expectations in consumer behavior (Oliver, 1980), adapted from the original theory, moving from the mixed pre/post consumption affirmation to a post-acceptance model (Bhattacherjee, 2001). The post-acceptance model tries to explain users' intention to continue using a systemba based on the assumption that users, after initial acceptance and a period of initial use, form an opinion about it. At the same time, users form an opinion about the benefits. After a period of use, a degree of confirmation and perceived usefulness develop, and both will influence users' perceived satisfaction, helping to explain users' willingness to continue using the system (Larsen et al., 2009). In our case, recommend the innovation project that we propose the confirmation variable that measures your opinion about its activities, experience and expectations. You can see the items used to measure it in Table 6. The statement that a higher level of confirmation in the use of a system will affect the satisfaction obtained with its use and that it will reinforce the users' intention to continue using them, with recommending it is indirectly supported by studies arguing that prior behavior (i.e., acceptance of features) is the most important antecedent of future behavior (i.e., continued use of features) (Bagozzi & Kimmel, 1995; Davis & Venkatesh, 2004).

To the model proposed by Lasen et al. (2009) we added the variable subjective learning as a background, through which we analyzed the effects of the role of students in several important aspects of learning. Specifically, this study proposes that students' participation in the project positively affects their subjective learning, satisfaction, and intention to recommend (Orus et al., 2016; Wang et al, 2024). We contribute to the literature on active learning by encouraging students' active problem solving and group work. From an experiential learning approach, this activity aims to increase students' acquisition of transversal skills and improve their general learning capacity, in addition to implying greater attention to the theoretical and practical aspects included in the course through overcoming the missions and challenges they face in the activity. As a result, we expect that students will perceive that they acquire a higher level of theoretical knowledge related to the specific content of the course (Alon and Herath, 2014; Pereira et al., 2014). Therefore, we propose the following hypotheses and model (see Figure 8):

> **H1:** There is a positive and direct relationship between subjective learning and satisfaction.
> **H2:** There is a positive and direct relationship between confirmation and satisfaction.
> **H3:** There is a positive and direct relationship between satisfaction and recommendation.

Figure 8. Proposed model (Own elaboration)

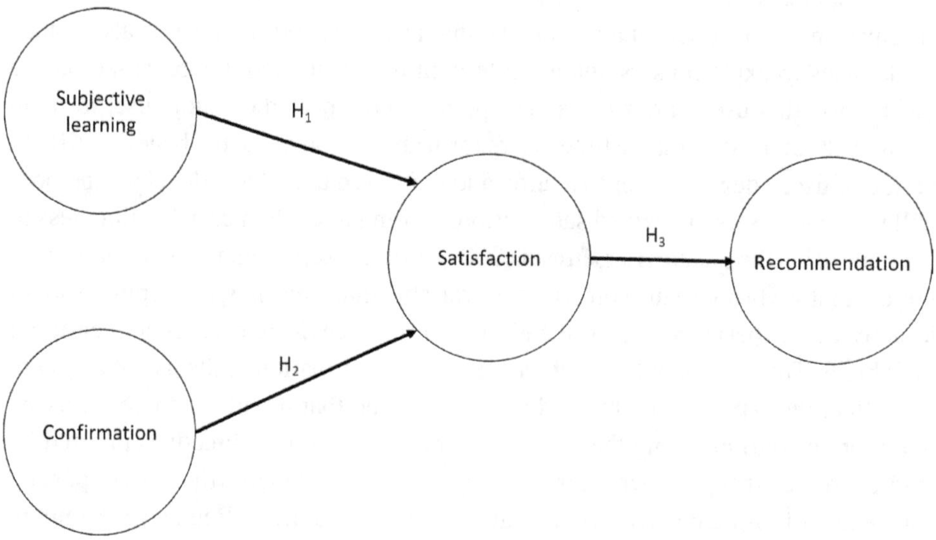

Furthermore, in this work we want to confirm that Games of Marketing activity has a positive effect on the proposed model. To do this, its moderating effect will be measured by comparing Group 1, students who have enjoyed the activity in their academic year versus those who have not, Group 2. Therefore, we propose the following hypothesis:

> **Hm:** The activity of Games of Marketing has a positive effect on the students, which is reflected in the fact that...
> **Hm1:** The direct relationship between confirmation and satisfaction will be different between Group 1 and Group 2.
> **Hm2:** The direct relationship between subjective learning and satisfaction will be different between Group 1 and Group 2.

3. METHODOLOGY

3.1. Sample Description

The sample was made up of 216 students of the Degree in Business Administration and Management, from the 1st, 2nd and 4th courses. This sample was divided into two groups. Group 1, made up of those students who had enjoyed Games of Marketing activity during their academic year, with a size of 111 individuals, compared to those who had not, Group 2, made up of a total of 105 individuals.

3.2. Scale Used and Validation

In Annex 1 you can see the scale used to measure the variables confirmation, subjective learning, satisfaction and recommendation. All goodness indicators are above the recommended values. In Table 6 it can be seen that the discriminant validity (Fornell and Larcker, 1981) is confirmed between all the variables in the two Groups except for the variable satisfaction and subjective learning, in Group 2. To assess this data, it was estimated the model by creating a dummy variable that united those two, and it was compared with the original. The chi-square of the original was significantly lower than that of the model with the dummy variable, so we accept the results in table 7, keeping both variables as different.

Table 6. Discriminant validity table

Groups	Group 1				Group 2			
Variable	**1**	**2**	**3**	**4**	**1**	**2**	**3**	**4**
Recomendation(1)	*0,89*				*0,83*			
Confirmation(2)	0,78	*0,90*			0,83	*0,80*		
Subjective learning (3)	0,84	0,74	*0,90*		0,70	0,77	*0,85*	
Satisfaction (4)	0,73	0,82	0,86	*0,87*	0,72	0,81	0,80	*0,75*

Source: Own elaboration

4. RESULS

In this section we will analyze the estimation of the multiGroups model, as well as its comparison. According to Figure 9, it can be seen that for Group 1, those individuals who did enjoy Games of Marketing, all the proposed relationships are confirmed. On the other hand, for students who did not enjoy the activity, H2 is not confirmed, that is, the direct effect between subjective learning and satisfaction, therefore, of the two antecedent variables proposed, only confirmation is found in the model, having a higher coefficient than in Group 1.

Figure 9. Results of the proposed model (Own elaboration)

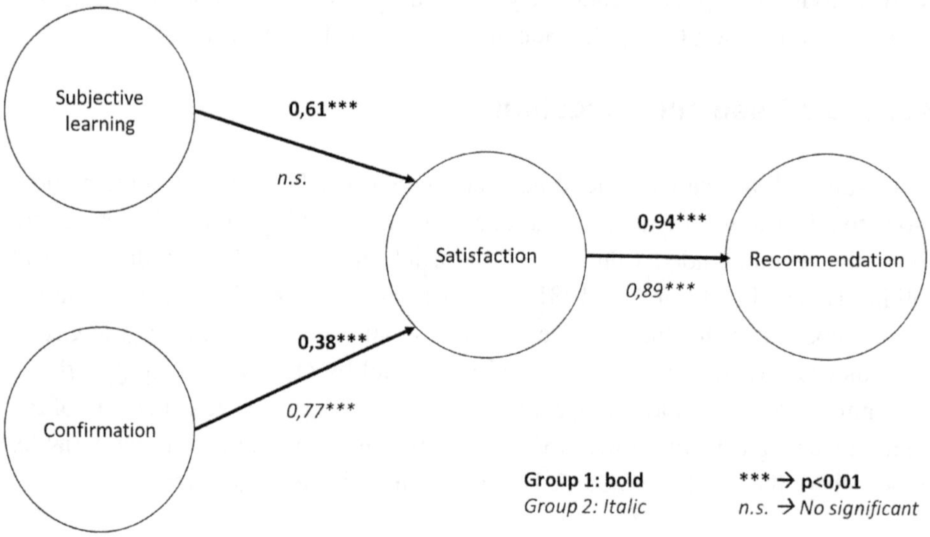

We also proposed the comparison between both Groups. We can see that there are significant differences. In the case of confirmation, the value is significantly higher for Group 2. Furthermore, for the relationship between subjective learning and satisfaction, significant differences are also seen but this time higher in Group 1. To finish the comparison, the relationship between satisfaction and recommendation do not show any difference between the Groups (see Table 7).

Table 7. Comparison between moderated relationships

Relationships to compare	Group 1		Group 2		t-valor	p-valor
	Coef. Est.	E.S.	Coef. Est.	E.S.		
Confirmation → Satisfaction	0,343	0,08	0,801	0,172	2,492	**0,013**
Subjective learning → Satisfaction	0,557	0,09	0,178	0,135	2,430	**0,016**
Satisfaction → Recomendation	1,004	0,10	0,949	0,133	0,339	0,735
Efectos totales						
Confirmation → Recomendation	0,345	0,008	0,760	0,023	17,497	**0,000**
Subjective learning → Recomendation	0,559	0,009	0,168	0,017	21,275	**0,000**

Source: Own elaboration

In summary, the analysis conducted in this section sheds light on the nuanced dynamics underlying the effects of engagement with marketing games on students' learning outcomes and satisfaction levels. Through the estimation of the multiGroups model and subsequent comparison between Group 1 and Group 2, we have uncovered valuable insights into the differential impact of enjoyment of marketing games on various aspects of student engagement and satisfaction.

Our findings highlight the importance of considering individual differences in the enjoyment of marketing games when assessing their educational efficacy. For students who derive enjoyment from these activities (Group 1), the proposed relationships between subjective learning, satisfaction, and recommendation are largely confirmed, with significant coefficients indicating a strong positive influence of engagement with marketing games on subsequent satisfaction and recommendation behavior. Conversely, for students who do not enjoy these activities (Group 2), the direct effect between subjective learning and satisfaction is not confirmed, suggesting a more complex relationship between engagement with marketing games and subsequent satisfaction levels.

Furthermore, the comparison between Group 1 and Group 2 reveals significant differences in the magnitude and nature of the relationships under investigation. While Group 1 demonstrates higher levels of confirmation and subjective learning, Group 2 exhibits a stronger relationship between subjective learning and satisfaction. These findings underscore the need for a nuanced understanding of the interplay between enjoyment of marketing games, learning outcomes, and satisfaction levels among students.

Moving forward, our research opens avenues for further investigation into the mechanisms underlying the differential effects of engagement with marketing games on student satisfaction and recommendation behavior. Future studies may explore the role of individual differences, contextual factors, and instructional design strategies in shaping students' experiences with marketing games and their subsequent educational outcomes.

In conclusion, our study contributes to the growing body of literature on the effectiveness of gamified learning approaches in educational contexts. By elucidating the complex dynamics at play in the relationship between engagement with marketing games, learning outcomes, and satisfaction levels, we provide valuable insights for educators, instructional designers, and researchers seeking to optimize the educational potential of gamified learning experiences

5. CONCLUSION

Next, we will analyze the results obtained in the comparison and we will conclude by explaining the results and conclusions that result from the use of this type of methodology, taking as reference the three fundamental pillars that support the teaching work: the teaching-learning process, the social value of teaching and teacher productivity in their career.

Based on the data collected, it is evident that the motivation of students who participated in the Games of Marketing within the innovation project is influenced by two antecedent variables examined in relation to satisfaction. Upon reviewing the utilized scale (refer to Annex 1), students perceive the activity to have exceeded their expectations, thus meeting their anticipated level of satisfaction, as indicated by the confirmation variable. Furthermore, the impact on satisfaction is greater than that of the internal variable, with students also reporting an enhancement in their knowledge and understanding of marketing, as reflected by the subjective learning variable.

Conversely, among the group that did not engage in the activity, satisfaction and subsequent recommendation are primarily based on confirmation, without a significant contribution from subjective learning. Although these students perceive the activity to be better and more positive than anticipated, and their expectations are exceeded, there is no discernible improvement in marketing knowledge and learning. This underscores the importance of considering motivating elements when designing course materials and activities.

With respect to teaching functions, in Games of Marketing the three teaching pillars are clearly seen: the teaching-learning process, the social value of teaching and the teacher's productivity in their career. With respect to the teaching-learning process, students are highly involved and motivated by this activity, preparing the subject about which they will be asked in sufficient time. Although it could be seen as a simply recreational activity, as it is a gymkhana set in imaginary worlds, for students it is not just that. Because we have been developing it for 5 academic years, in our faculty it is already an annual event to show who knows the most about marketing. Then, with respect to the social value of teaching, as said in previous paragraphs, the Groups are mixed by subjects. The activity includes several subjects that are taught in different years of the degree. With this, students interact with classmates with whom they do not have much confidence in passing tests. And with respect to the third pillar, the productivity of the teaching career, this activity is a commitment to teaching in an academic world where everything is research. The Group that makes up this project continues to teach classes with all the necessary rigor, but we look for time to be able to work and develop activities that enrich the student's teaching experience.

Regarding the limitations of the work, the main one is the sample of individuals, although the reality is that on the campus where the activity takes place, the classes are made up of 30-40 students, and within the entire sample is the entire population of 1st, 2nd and third year students. Another limitation could be seen in classifying the Groups and the indirect evaluation of Games of Marketing activity with a common questionnaire, but it is the only way to compare since we could not compare the students who did not enjoy the activity with those who did. another possible way.

While the integration of gaming into teaching and learning processes holds promise for enhancing engagement and motivation among students, particularly in digital-native populations, it is essential to recognize and address several limitations associated with this approach, especially in the context of adult education. One significant challenge is the potential mismatch between the preferences and learning styles of adult learners and the design and mechanics of educational games. Unlike traditional college-age students, adult learners may have different expectations, responsibilities, and time constraints that can impact their receptivity to gaming as a pedagogical tool.

Moreover, there are concerns regarding the effectiveness of gaming in facilitating deep learning and critical thinking skills, particularly in complex and specialized subject areas. While educational games may excel in promoting procedural knowledge and skill acquisition, they may fall short in promoting higher-order cognitive skills, such as analysis, synthesis, and evaluation, which are essential for academic success and professional development among adult learners.

Additionally, the successful adoption of gaming in educational settings relies heavily on the availability of appropriate technological infrastructure and support systems. Many adult learners may lack access to reliable internet connections, modern computing devices, or the technical proficiency required to navigate and engage with educational games effectively. Without adequate resources and support, the implementation of gaming in teaching and learning processes may exacerbate existing disparities in access and achievement among adult learners.

To overcome these limitations and ensure the success of game adoption in adult education, several conditions must be met. Firstly, educators must carefully select and design educational games that align with the learning objectives, preferences, and needs of adult learners. This may involve incorporating elements of authenticity, relevance, and practical applicability into game design to enhance engagement and promote meaningful learning experiences.

Furthermore, educators should provide comprehensive training and support to adult learners to familiarize them with the use of educational games and technology-enhanced learning environments. This may include workshops, tutorials, and ongoing technical assistance to build digital literacy skills and confidence among adult learners.

Moreover, the integration of gaming into teaching and learning processes should be complemented by a pedagogical approach that emphasizes active learning, collaboration, and reflection. By incorporating gaming as one of several instructional strategies within a broader educational framework, educators can leverage its strengths while mitigating its limitations, thereby maximizing its potential to enhance learning outcomes and student engagement among adult learners.

In conclusion, while the integration of gaming into teaching and learning processes offers exciting opportunities for enhancing engagement and motivation among adult learners, it is essential to recognize and address the limitations associated with this approach. By carefully considering the unique needs and challenges of adult learners and implementing appropriate strategies and support systems, educators can maximize the benefits of gaming in adult education and ensure its successful adoption in diverse learning environments.

Future lines of research related to the chapter could include exploring the sustained impact of innovative teaching strategies, such as the Games of Marketing, on students' learning outcomes, attitudes, and behaviors over time. Longitudinal studies could be conducted to assess the lasting effects of transformative learning experiences on students' personal and academic development.

Comparative analysis of different transformative learning approaches could provide valuable insights into the effectiveness of various pedagogical strategies in promoting student engagement, critical thinking, and transformative learning outcomes. By comparing the relative advantages and limitations of different transformative learning activities, researchers can identify best practices for designing and implementing transformative learning interventions in higher education settings.

Further research could delve into the factors influencing the success of transformative learning initiatives. This exploration may include investigating the design of learning activities, instructor support and guidance, student motivation and readiness, and institutional support structures. Understanding these factors could inform the development of effective strategies for promoting transformative learning in diverse higher education contexts.

The role of technology in facilitating transformative learning experiences is another area ripe for exploration. Researchers could investigate how digital technologies, such as gamification platforms, virtual reality simulations, and online collaborative tools, can enhance student engagement, promote critical reflection, and support the development of transformative learning outcomes. This research could shed light on the potential of technology-mediated learning environments to foster transformative learning in higher education.

Cross-cultural perspectives on transformative learning offer an opportunity to examine how cultural, social, and contextual factors shape the process and outcomes of transformative learning in diverse educational settings. By exploring cultural differences in students' perceptions, experiences, and outcomes of transformative learning activities, researchers can identify culturally sensitive approaches to promoting transformative learning in higher education. This research could contribute to the development of inclusive and culturally responsive teaching practices that enhance transformative learning experiences for all students.

REFERENCES

Al-Smadi, M. (2014). Gameducation: using gamification techniques to engage learners in online learning. *European Summit on Immersive Education*, 85-97.

Almuhailib, B., & Al-Ahdal, A. A. M. H. (2021). Learner-Centered Teaching in Saudi Context: Exploring the challenges from pre-service EFL teachers' perspective. *Journal of Positive Psychology and Wellbeing*, 5(4), 1170–1181.

Alon, I., & Herath, R. K. (2014). Teaching international business via social media projects. *Journal of Teaching in International Business, 25*(1), 44-59.

Bagozzi, R. P., & Kimmel, S. K. (1995). A comparison of leading theories for the prediction of goal-directed behaviours. *British Journal of Social Psychology*, 34(4), 437–461. DOI: 10.1111/j.2044-8309.1995.tb01076.x

Bhattacherjee, A. (2001). Understanding information systems continuance: An expectation–confirmation model. *Management Information Systems Quarterly*, 25(3), 351–370. DOI: 10.2307/3250921

Blasco-Arcas, L., Buil, I., Hernández-Ortega, B., & Sese, F. J. (2013). Using clickers in class. The role of interactivity, active collaborative learning and engagement in learning performance. *Computers & Education*, 62, 102–110. DOI: 10.1016/j.compedu.2012.10.019

Boni, A., & Lozano, J. F. (2007). The generic competences: An opportunity for ethical learning in the European convergence in higher education. *Higher Education*, 54(6), 819–831. DOI: 10.1007/s10734-006-9026-4

Cranton, P. (2016). *Understanding and promoting transformative learning: A guide to theory and practice*. Routledge.

Curay Correa, P., & Ramón, L. P. (2021). Storytelling in gamification: Planning an educational guide. *Revista de Ciencias Humanísticas y Sociales*, 6(2), 110–123.

Danelli, F. (2015). Implementing game design in gamification. In *Gamification in education and business* (pp. 67–79). Springer. DOI: 10.1007/978-3-319-10208-5_4

Davis, F., & Venkatesh, V. (2004). Toward pre-prototyping user acceptance testing of new information systems: Implications for software project management. *IEEE Transactions on Engineering Management*, 51(1), 31–46. DOI: 10.1109/TEM.2003.822468

De Oliveira Nunes, M., & Mayer, V. F. (2014). Mobile technology, games and nature areas: The tourist perspective. *Tourism & Management Studies*, 10(1), 53–58.

Deterding, S., Dixon, D., Khaled, R., & Nacke, L. (2011, September). From game design elements to gamefulness: defining" gamification". In Proceedings of the 15th international academic MindTrek conference: Envisioning future media environments (pp. 9-15).

Exley, K., & Dennick, R. (2007). *Teaching in small groups in Higher Education.* Narcea.

Fandos Herrera, C., Jiménez Martínez, J., Orús Sanclemente, C., Peligero Domeque, M., & Pina Pérez, J. M. (2015). Learning strategies, expectations and attitude: Do I like to act as a narrator or do I prefer to be told? In *XXVII Marketing Congress AEMARK 2015* (pp. 1239-1254). ESIC Editorial.

Fornell, C., & Larcker, D. (1981). Evaluating structural equation models with unobservable variables and measurement error. *JMR, Journal of Marketing Research*, 18(1), 39–50. DOI: 10.1177/002224378101800104

Goller, A., & Rieckmann, M. (2022). What do we know about teacher educators' perceptions of Education for Sustainable Development? A Systematic Literature Review. *Journal of Teacher Education for Sustainability*, 24(1), 19–34. DOI: 10.2478/jtes-2022-0003

Jost, M. (2011). Transformative learning and complex problem-solving among hospitality and tourism students. *Tourism & Management Studies*, 1025–1028.

Krath, J., Schürmann, L., & Von Korflesch, H. F. (2021). Revealing the theoretical basis of gamification: A systematic review and analysis of theory in research on gamification, serious games and game-based learning. *Computers in Human Behavior*, 125, 106963. DOI: 10.1016/j.chb.2021.106963

Larsen, T. J., Sørebø, A. M., & Sørebø, Ø. (2009). The role of task-technology fit as users' motivation to continue information system use. *Computers in Human Behavior*, 25(3), 778–784. DOI: 10.1016/j.chb.2009.02.006

Lee, K., & Fanguy, M. (2022). Online exam proctoring technologies: Educational innovation or deterioration? *British Journal of Educational Technology*, 53(3), 475–490. DOI: 10.1111/bjet.13182

Lee, Y. J. (2011). A study on the effect of teaching innovation on learning effectiveness with learning satisfaction as a mediator. *World Transactions on Engineering and Technology Education*, 9(2), 92–101.

Loureiro, S. M. C., Bilro, R. G., & de Aires Angelino, F. J. (2020). Virtual reality and gamification in marketing higher education: a review and research agenda. *Spanish Journal of Marketing-ESIC.*

Mezirow, J. (1991). *Transformative dimensions of adult learning*. Jossey-Bass.

Mezirow, J. (2000). Learning to think like an adult: Core concepts of transformation theory. In Mezirow, J. (Eds.), *Learning as transformation: Critical perspectives on a theory in progress* (pp. 3–33). Jossey-Bass.

Núñez Barriopedro, E., Penelas Leguía, A., & Cuesta Valiño, P. (2014). The development of web 3.0 as an innovation in teaching marketing and market research. *Caracciolos, revista digital de investigación en docencia, 2*(1).

Oliver, R. L. (1980). A cognitive model of the antecedents and consequences of satisfaction decisions. *JMR, Journal of Marketing Research*, 17(11), 460–469. DOI: 10.1177/002224378001700405

Orús, C., Barlés, M. J., Belanche, D., Casaló, L., Fraj, E., & Gurrea, R. (2014). Affective and objective consequences of using a YouTube channel to support teaching in marketing. National Marketing Congress AEMARK, 17-19 September, Elche (España).

Orús, C., Barlés, M. J., Belanche, D., Casaló, L., Fraj, E., & Gurrea, R. (2016). The effects of learner-generated videos for YouTube on learning outcomes and satisfaction. *Computers & Education*, 95, 254–269. DOI: 10.1016/j.compedu.2016.01.007

Pagés, T., Hernández, C., Abadía, A. R., Bueno, C., Ubieto-Artur, I., Márquez Cebrián, M., Sabaté Diaz, S., & Jorba Noguera, H. (2016). Innovation as a teaching competence at the university: Innovation aimed at improving learning. Aloma. *Revista de Psicologia i Ciències de l'Educació*, 34(1), 33–43.

Pereira, J., Echeazarra, L., Sanz-Santamaría, S., & Gutierrez, J. (2014). Student-generated online videos to develop cross-curricular and curricular competencies in nursing studies. *Computers in Human Behavior*, 31, 580–590. DOI: 10.1016/j.chb.2013.06.011

Polo-Peña, A. I., Fernández-Ruano, M. L., & Frías-Jamilena, D. M. (2024). The role of gamified environmental interpretation in boosting destination perceived value. *Tourism & Management Studies*, 20(2), 55–68. DOI: 10.18089/tms.20240205

Rodríguez-Gómez, D., & Gairín Sallán, J. (2015). Innovation, organizational learning and knowledge management in educational institutions. *Education*, 24(46), 73–90.

Royal Decree 1393/2007, of October 29, which establishes the organization of official university education. Recovered from: https://www.boe.es/buscar/pdf/2007/BOE-A-2007-18770-consolidado.pdf

Said, H., & Kamel, N. A. (2023). Linking e-leadership to innovative and proactive work behaviors in tourism higher education institutions: A moderated mediation model using SEM. *Tourism & Management Studies*, 19(4), 47–60. DOI: 10.18089/tms.2023.190404

Sasson, I., Yehuda, I., & Miedijensky, S. (2022). Innovative learning spaces: Class management and universal design for learning. *Learning Environments Research*, 25(3), 725–739. DOI: 10.1007/s10984-021-09393-8

Scavarelli, A., Arya, A., & Teather, R. J. (2021). Virtual reality and augmented reality in social learning spaces: A literature review. *Virtual Reality (Waltham Cross)*, 25(1), 257–277. DOI: 10.1007/s10055-020-00444-8

Schnepfleitner, F. M., & Ferreira, M. P. (2021). Transformative Learning Theory–Is It Tıme to Add A Fourth Core Element? *Journal of Educational Studies and Multidisciplinary Approaches*, 1(1), 40–49. DOI: 10.51383/jesma.2021.9

Slavich, G. M., & Zimbardo, P. G. (2012). Transformational teaching: Theoretical underpinnings, basic principles, and core methods. *Educational Psychology Review*, 24(4), 569–608. DOI: 10.1007/s10648-012-9199-6 PMID: 23162369

Su, C. H. (2016). The effects of students' motivation, cognitive load and learning anxiety in gamification software engineering education: A structural equation modeling study. *Multimedia Tools and Applications*, 75(16), 10013–10036. DOI: 10.1007/s11042-015-2799-7

Taber, K. S. (2020). Mediated learning leading development—the social development theory of Lev Vygotsky. In *Science education in theory and practice* (pp. 277–291). Springer. DOI: 10.1007/978-3-030-43620-9_19

Taylor, E. W. (2007). An update of transformative learning theory: A critical review of the empirical research (1999–2005). *International Journal of Lifelong Education*, 26(2), 173–191. DOI: 10.1080/02601370701219475

Tilak, S., Glassman, M., Kuznetcova, I., Peri, J., Wang, Q., Wen, Z., & Walling, A. (2020). Multi-User Virtual Environments (MUVEs) as alternative lifeworlds: Transformative learning in cyberspace. *Journal of Transformative Education*, 18(4), 310–337. DOI: 10.1177/1541344620932224

Toribio López, A., & Robles Rojas, E. (2021). *Gamification: An Educational Strategy to Improve the Commercial Training in the Sales Force*. Yearbook Faculty of Economics and Business Sciences.

Van Diepen, N. M., Stefanova, E., & Miranowicz, M. (2009). Mastering skills using ICT: An active learning approach. Research, Reflections and Innovations in Integrating ICT in Education, 226-233.

Wang, J., Kim, H. R., & Tran, T. B. H. (2024). Can shared leadership stimulate team members' proactive behaviour? Exploring through the bridge of psychological empowerment. *Tourism & Management Studies*, 20(2), 69–78. DOI: 10.18089/tms.20240206

Wardaszko, M. (2016). Building simulation game-based teaching program for secondary school students. *Simulation & Gaming*, 47(3), 287–303. DOI: 10.1177/1046878116635467

Whitehead, D. P. (2008). Thoughts on education and innovation. *Childhood Education, 85*(2), 105-B.

APPENDIX

Table 8. Scale and goodness adjustments

<table>
<tr><th rowspan="2">Variable</th><th rowspan="2">Ítems</th><th colspan="4">Group 1</th><th colspan="4">Group 2</th></tr>
<tr><th>Coef. Estand.(T-valor)</th><th>R²</th><th>FC</th><th>VE</th><th>Coef. Estand. (t-valor)</th><th>R²</th><th>FC</th><th>VE</th></tr>
<tr><td rowspan="3">Subjective learning (Orús et al., 2016)</td><td colspan="9">The activities of the teaching innovation project that I have completed have been useful for…</td></tr>
<tr><td>…improve my knowledge about marketing in general</td><td>0.864(*)</td><td>0,88</td><td rowspan="2">0,900</td><td rowspan="2">0,818</td><td>0,859 (*)</td><td>0,71</td><td rowspan="2">0,84</td><td rowspan="2">0,723</td></tr>
<tr><td>Better understand the marketing techniques, strategies and decisions followed by real companies.</td><td>0.943 (8,992)</td><td>0,75</td><td>0,842 (8,992)</td><td>0,53</td></tr>
<tr><td rowspan="4">Confirmation (Larsen et al., 2009)</td><td colspan="9">Regarding the activities developed…</td></tr>
<tr><td>…they were better than I expected.</td><td>0,929 (*)</td><td>0,86</td><td rowspan="3">0,928</td><td rowspan="3">0,812</td><td>0,756 (*)</td><td>0,57</td><td rowspan="3">0,845</td><td rowspan="3">0,723</td></tr>
<tr><td>…my experience has been more positive than I thought.</td><td>0,925 (8,475)</td><td>0,86</td><td>0,800 (8,475)</td><td>0,64</td></tr>
<tr><td>…they met my expectations.</td><td>0,847 (8,406)</td><td>0,72</td><td>0,858 (8,406)</td><td>0,74</td></tr>
</table>

continued on following page

Table 8. Continued

Variable	Ítems	Group 1				Group 2			
		Coef. Estand.(T-valor)	R^2	FC	VE	Coef. Estand. (t-valor)	R^2	FC	VE
Satisfaction (Orús et al., 2016)	Regarding marketing matters…								
	…I am satisfied with the teaching method applied in this course.	0,808 (*)	0,65	0,907	0,765	0,727 (*)	0,53	0,791	0,558
	…I am satisfied with the knowledge acquired in this course.	0,882 (7,116)	0,78			0,733 (7,116)	0,54		
	…The experience I have had in this course has been satisfactory.	0,926 (7,358)	0,86			0,770 (7,358)	0,59		
Recomendation (Larsen et al., 2009)	After having participated in the project…								
	I will tell other people positive aspects about the subject I have taken.	0,973 (*)	0,76	0,920	0,794	0,816 (*)	0,67	0,869	0,688
	I will recommend the subject to anyone who asks me for advice.	0,919 (9,399)	0,84			0,854 (9,399)	0,73		
	I will encourage you to participate in the activities developed in the subject.	0,879 (8,950)	0,77			0,818 (8,950)	0,67		

Chapter 8
Investigating the Potential of Maritime Serious Game Design in SIRE 2.0 Context: GAMESIRE 2.0

Süleyman Gürbüz
https://orcid.org/0000-0003-0670-3914
İstanbul Technical University, Turkey

Metin Celik
https://orcid.org/0000-0003-0107-1380
İstanbul Technical University, Turkey

ABSTRACT

Pre-vetting inspection is a critical process to enhance safety and environmental protection onboard tanker ships. The current study firstly proposes a serious game design model, namely GAMESIRE 2.0, for crew upskilling in tanker vetting requirements. This study considers recently updated requirements of Ship Inspection Report (SIRE 2.0) Programme of Oil Companies International Marine Forum (OCIMF). Using GAMESIRE 2.0 model, preliminary design of a serious game-based training is conducted in preparation for SIRE 2.0 Clause # 4.2.1, which focuses on navigational procedures on passage planning and execution. Further maritime studies might utilize GAMESIRE 2.0 model to design additional serious games in SIRE 2.0 context. In fact, scope of GAMESIRE 2.0 model can be extended through other maritime inspection regimes such as Chemical Distribution Institute (CDI), Tanker Management Self-Assessment (TMSA), Dry Bulk Management Standard (DRYBMS),

DOI: 10.4018/979-8-3693-1172-1.ch008

etc. Consequently, this study contributes to third-party standards on enhanced safety and environmental protection in tanker shipping industry.

INTRODUCTION

80% of the shipping accidents are mainly resulted from human error in spite of the updated regulations and systems with higher technology (Akyuz & Celik, 2018). Human error generates even higher risk on tanker ships considering their dangerous cargo. The Oil Companies International Marine Forum (OCIMF) started the Ship Inspection Report (SIRE) Programme in 1993 for minimizing the risk on tanker ships.

Within the scope of the SIRE Programme, tanker operators and owners conduct inspections for finding the non-conformities with OCIMF's SIRE Programme standards (Oil Companies International Marine Forum, 2023a). The Programme has a very large database of reports about tankers and barges. This database is accessible by OCIMF members and qualifying non-OCIMF members. SIRE reports are not mandatory but important indicators in the eyes of related maritime actors such as charterers, OCIMF members, terminal operators, and ship operators, as they are good indications for tanker quality. SIRE Programme is also in cooperation with International Maritime Organization (IMO) and port authorities to ensure safety of tanker shipping (OCIMF, 2021). SIRE Inspections can be conducted every six months (OCIMF, 2016).

The SIRE programme has been updated in January 2022 as SIRE 2.0. providing the SIRE programme with important advancements. Firstly, SIRE 2.0 has the potential to better investigate the future performances of tanker ships and crew through risk-based approach. SIRE 2.0 also improves the inspection criteria and procedures in a way to intensify the control over ships' safety procedures and equipment (Oil Companies International Marine Forum, 2023b).

SIRE inspections are conducted according to the SIRE 2.0 Question Library Part 1 and Part 2 (Version 1.0) documents issued in January 2022 (Oil Companies International Marine Forum, 2023c; Oil Companies International Marine Forum, 2023d). Part 1 of the document includes Chapters 1 to 7 while Chapters 8 to 12 are included in Part 2. For guiding the inspection process, these documents provides the SIRE clauses, objective of the clause, names of the related publications, industry guidance, suggested inspector actions, expected evidence as well as potential grounds for a negative observation.

In preparation for SIRE inspections, tanker ships currently perform detailed trainings namely "pre-vetting trainings" as well as working with consultant inspectors. However, non-conformities in SIRE inspections still persist (Christensen, 2013). Arslan et al. (2016) studied SIRE inspection non-conformities using the data from

2006-2015. They stated that non-conformities commonly stem from deficiencies in managerial skills, human factor and navigational skills. Navas de Maya et al. (2022) applied data mining technique for predicting future non-conformities of oil tankers. They explained that most non-conformities are caused by constructional problems, unsuccessful applications of operational safety, as well as human error such as insufficient maintenance, incorrect decisions and applying wrong procedures. In this regard, it is believed that effective training of officers on tanker ships are vital for eliminating the SIRE non-conformities and thus ensuring environmental protection as well as safety of tanker shipping.

International Convention on Standards of Training, Certification and Watchkeeping (STCW) 1978 as amended in 2010 (referred as STCW in this study), issued by International Maritime Organization (IMO), defines minimum competency standards of seafarers. Based on STCW, training of maritime students currently includes college-based education and training as well as practical training on board ship. Maritime institutions also provide practical training using land-based maritime simulators. However, it is put forward that there is an important gap between the competency level of young seafarers onboard ships and their required competency level (International Chamber of Shipping, 2020). It is regarded that cheaper and more flexible methods of practical training are needed in maritime domain and specifically for tanker shipping. Serious gaming, as a technology-enabled instructional method, offers an important potential not only for tanker shipping but also for the maritime domain in general (Nikitakos et al., 2017). In light of this, current chapter aims to propose and apply a serious game design model, namely GAMESIRE 2.0, for facilitating the design of maritime serious games in preparation for SIRE 2.0 inspections.

OBJECTIVES AND NEEDS OF THE STUDY

This study firstly aims to propose a serious game design model, which is specific to SIRE 2.0 inspections in the maritime domain. In this study, preliminary design of a maritime serious game is also conducted as a practical application of the proposed model, namely GAMESIRE 2.0. In general perspective, current study intends to provide valuable insight into gamification of SIRE 2.0 inspection trainings. We would like to emphasize that the research objective is closely rooted in the literature review of serious games and the industrial survey of serious gaming in the maritime domain. For this reason, it is believed that this study offers a theoretical contribution to the literature as well as a practical contribution to the maritime domain.

It is believed that this study is needed in the maritime serious gaming literature and maritime industry for two main reasons. Firstly, since the proposed GAMESIRE 2.0 model is specific to the maritime domain, it utilizes the learning theories which are particularly chosen to meet the demands of the maritime domain. For this reason, it is believed that GAMESIRE 2.0 model, compared to other models, has a more important potential to facilitate the design of more effective and useful serious games in preperation for the maritime SIRE 2.0 inspections. Secondly, GAMESIRE 2.0 model is regarded to be more successful than the majority of the reviewed serious game design models in providing practical and step-by-step guidance since most of the models explain the design process instead of guiding the researchers to design similar serious games.

LITERATURE REVIEW

Serious Games

The term "Serious Game" was first used in 1968 by Clark Abt and defined as "games having an explicit and carefully thought-out educational purpose and not intended to be played primarily for amusement" (Abt, 1970). It is also defined as games which are developed for educational purposes and engage players in significant learning experience (Djaouti et al., 2011).

Education and healthcare are among domains where serious games have been most commonly utilized. To start with, Koupritzioti and Xinogalos (2020) proposed a serious game for learning programming concepts. Moreover, Khan et al. (2022) developed a serious game for enhancing cyber security education. Fokides (2018) also utilized serious gaming perspective for teaching Math to primary school students and discovered that the students who played the game achieved better results on the test. Lee (2020) created an Augmented Reality (AR)-based mobile serious game for foreign language learning. Rodriguez (2022) put forward that serious games can successfully be used for engineering education. In addition, serious games are popular in healthcare domain as they create authentic training environments without causing any risk (Evans et al., 2015; Benkhedda & Bendella, 2019; Fusco et al., 2022). Serious gaming perspective are also applied in business (Nicholson, 2015; Fotiadis &Sigala, 2015; Fu et al., 2016; Loon et al., 2015), sports (Hamari & Sjöblom, 2017), social learning for sustainable development (Tribaldos & Schneider, 2021), music (Margoudi et al., 2016) and environmental protection (Nygren et al., 2022).

Game elements foster learning efficiency in various ways. To start with, serious games promote higher-order learning by increasing engagement and motivation (Landers, 2014; Gray et al., 2019; Zainuddin et al., 2020). Motivation is a psychological aspect which directs people into action by increasing energy, persistence, intention. Thus, motivation is commonly regarded as a primary determinant of enhanced learning (Ryan & Deci, 2000). During a game, players actively participate in exploration, problem solving, critical analysis, higher-order thinking (Westera, 2015; Westera, 2019). In addition, by enhancing engagement through gameplay scenario, games make the player involve in a questioning and sense making process (Bordwell, 1989). Game elements such as points, challenges, badges, and gaming goals are also explained to promote learning outcomes by improving participation in learning (Bai et al., 2020). In addition, serious games improve knowledge acquisition and optimize motivation and cognitive load (Ye et al., 2022). Besides, serious games promote goal setting (Yıldırım & Şen, 2019), improve critical thinking (Haruna et al., 2021; Turner et al., 2018), increase understanding and retention (Wang & Abbas, 2018), and foster attitude change (Chow et al., 2020).

Looking critically at serious gaming literature, it is discovered that the literature lacks approaches to promote the instructional aspects of serious games (Silva, 2020). Similarly, studies exploring the effects of game elements on serious game design are needed (Johnson et al., 2017). It is also reported that serious game studies mostly deal with the content to be taught (Laporte & Zaman, 2018) and pay less attention to design and development efforts (Korhonen et al., 2017). Moreover, allocation of limited resources (Chan & Zary, 2019) and design-related, administrative, and communicative challenges (Dimitriadou et al., 2020) are among main difficulties educators perceive while designing serious games. It is clear from the literature that additional research dealing with the design and development of serious games are needed.

MARITIME SERIOUS GAMING

Maritime Serious Gaming Literature

Serious gaming has become more popular in maritime literature in the last decade. Maritime literature has examples of serious games on STCW-based competency development. Firstly, Nikitakos et al. (2017) offered first version of the "Trader of the World" game for navigational safety training of seafarers, and reported that they acquired satisfactory feedback about the game. Bruzzone et al. (2013) also developed a serious game for crew's familiarization to operating procedures onboard ships. In addition, Sartini (2020) explained that serious gaming approach enhanced English speaking skills of maritime students. Türkistanlı and Kuleyin (2022) applied serious gaming perspective for improving decision-making skills of maritime students for collusion prevention and reported that the game enhanced students' decision-making skills.

Researchers also applied serious gaming approach for education and training outside the scope of STCW-based requirements. To start with, Philbin-Briscoe et al. (2017) proposed "The Seafarers-1" serious game for providing knowledge about seaborne trade mechanisms in the eastern Mediterranean during the Classical and Hellenistic periods. The study was funded by the European Union (EU)'s "iMare-Culture" Project. Poullis et al. (2019) introduced "The Seafarers-2" game as the second prototype of "The Seafarers-1" game. "The Seafarers-2" game also intends to increase engagement in learning the same topic with the first prototype.

Veronica and Calvano (2020) presented a serious game for enhancing children's knowledge about the ocean literacy and biodiversity. Steenbeek et al. (2020) utilized ecosystem modelling and serious gaming approaches together for increasing awareness of maritime spatial planning. Lastly, Pruyn (2023) offered a framework for using serious games in academic maritime education and applied the framework for teaching the students the link between maritime economics and technology as well as providing insight into ship production activities.

It is found out as a result of the literature review that most maritime serious games about the STCW-based competencies focus on developing hard skills. This being the case, it is regarded that more research is needed for education and training of maritime soft skills. It is also discovered that maritime serious gaming literature generally focuses on applications of specific serious games rather than serious game design. In this regard, it is believed that comprehensive and adaptable methodologies about design and development of maritime serious games are needed in a way to enable their effective utilization.

Maritime Serious Gaming Entrepreneurship Ecosystem

This section proposes an analysis of the maritime serious gaming entrepreneurship ecosystem. As a result of the analysis, 6 companies that are highly visible in the market providing commercially available maritime serious games are found. Table 1 presents information about these companies and the serious games they provide.

Table 1. Information about maritime serious game providers

Company	Location	Year	Number of SGs on Hard Skills	Number of SGs on Soft Skills	Technology Utilized in SGs	Domain of Products
A	USA	2020	<10	N/A	2D, 3D	Maritime
B	Türkiye	2011	<10	N/A	VR Simulation	Maritime
C	Greece	2006	4	N/A	VR Simulation	Maritime
D	Holland	2002	<10	N/A	VR Simulation	Maritime, Safety Training
E	Türkiye	2011	9	N/A	3D, VR Simulation	Maritime
F	USA	2000	4	N/A	3D, VR Simulation	Maritime, Various Training Applications

To start with, it is discovered that the number of companies providing commercially available maritime serious games is limited. 4 companies are found to be providing maritime serious games only in maritime domain while 2 other companies provide serious games for other domains in addition to the maritime domain. It is also found that all (6) companies offer various kinds of online maritime trainings such as video-based trainings and simulations in addition to serious games. Each of these companies offer less than 10 maritime serious games making the total number of commercially available games limited. Besides, these companies are founded after the year 2000 while all of their serious games are developed in the last decade. Although the number of games have increased in the last decade, it can be put forward that maritime serious gaming entrepreneurship is still in its infancy (Gurbuz & Celik, 2023).

Looking at the games, it is discovered that 5 of the 6 companies are utilizing VR technology in their serious games. In light of this, it might be proposed that companies tend to use advanced technology for developing their games, which might foster their effectiveness. In addition, all the games intend to develop hard (technical) skills of the players and it is concluded that games on maritime soft skills which facilitate application of hard skills in real life are also required (Gurbuz & Celik, 2023).

In addition to the companies, some projects also develop maritime serious games. Firstly, "Marine Litter in Europe Seas: Social Awareness and Co-Responsibility" (MARLISCO) project supported by the European Union was conducted between 2012 and 2015, proposing "Sea Dream Team" game for training players against marine littering (Marlisco, 2015). In addition, the "CREAMARE" project funded by European Union targets to develop 3D serious games to teach cultural heritage and promoting awareness of maritime pollution problem. The project continues from June 2022 to June 2025 with a total budget of 1.338 million Euro (Creamare, 2022). Additionally, not-for-profit "Deltares Institute" proposed "Port of the Future" serious game to foster port management and sustainable development of the ports (Deltares, 2018). The increasing number of similar projects can be regarded as a sign of their increasing popularity in the maritime entrepreneurship ecosystem.

Future Directions in Maritime Education and Training

The evolving nature of maritime operations cause the required maritime competencies and skills to change continuously. They are expected to become even more intricate as the concept of shipping continues to evolve. Utilization of ships with different autonomy levels such as manned, unmanned, shore-side control, semi-autonomous, fully autonomous etc. is anticipated to intensify the change in maritime concept and thus in required maritime skills. This being the case, different maritime actors such as faculties, shipping companies, simulator and technology providers, training centers etc. need to cooperate in ensuring that MET practices meet the evolving needs of the maritime domain (Sharma et al., 2021).

Simulator-based maritime training is a cost-effective and useful method for practical competency development (Hjelmervik et al., 2018). Simulator-based training enhances trainees' risk assessment and decision making skills in risky situations (Sanfilippo, 2017) and develops critical thinking through case-based learning (Bhardwaj & Pazaver, 2014). Shore-based simulators can also be used for generating realistic training scenarios without having to be onboard ships. Maritime shore-based simulators have allowed cadets to practice and develop their seafaring skills regardless of their time and place. However, time limitations might not allow maritime faculties to allocate enough time for all the students in simulator sessions.

In line with the enhancements in information technology, technology-enabled education and training methods are becoming increasingly available in maritime domain. In this regard, Virtual Reality (VR), Augmented Reality (AR), Mixed Reality (MR) as well as wearable technologies might enhance current MET practices by providing authentic training environments for developing practical maritime competencies. Considering that these technologies can be used on portable personal devices, they can offer affordable training solutions with higher availability to the users in comparison with land-based simulators (Mallam et al., 2019).

Despite the potential these technologies offer for the maritime domain, they should be well understood before their utilization with current MET practices. This means possible advantages, disadvantages as well as strengths and weaknesses should be thoroughly studied with close cooperation of academia and industry. Maritime literature should also research different types of technology-enhanced training methods focusing on specific competencies they might develop (Mallam et al., 2019). In this regard, this chapter aims to provide a research-based understanding about the design of serious games in SIRE 2.0 context as well as providing insight into maritime serious game design in general.

METHODOLOGY

Proposed GAMESIRE 2.0 Model

This chapter proposes GAMESIRE 2.0 serious game design model for designing serious games in preparation for SIRE inspections. GAMESIRE 2.0 model which is specific to SIRE inspections is an updated version of Serious Game Design for Maritime (SGDM) model proposed by Gurbuz (2021).

SGDM is a serious game design model which is developed for the maritime domain. SGDM has 8 steps for design of a maritime serious game (Gurbuz, 2021). These steps which are depicted in Figure 1 guide the designer from the beginning to the end of the design process.

Figure 1. SGDM model (Adapted from Gurbuz (2021))

In the first step of the SGDM model, the topic and target group of the training are defined. In Step-2, training objectives are to be defined based on the Knowledge, Understanding, and Proficiency column of the STCW. The objectives can also be defined based on another maritime convention as well as customized training requirements. In Step-3, the objectives are written as observable behaviors/abilities.

As per Step-4, behaviors/ abilities are to be assigned into one of the 4 quadrants of the Rigor& Relevance Educational Alignment Framework (ICLE, 2012) depending on their intricacy level. The Rigor Relevance Framework has 4 quadrants which are different combinations of Knowledge Taxonomy axis and Application Model axis. To start with, Quadrant A (Acquisition) depicts ability to learn knowledge and information with lower levels of cognitive function and to remember and understand this knowledge as it is without solving problem. Quadrant B (Application) depicts ability to use the obtained knowledge for problem solving. This quadrant includes solving even unpredictable real-world problems but still requires using lower level cognitive abilities (ICLE, 2012).

When we move to Quadrant C (Assimilation), cognitive skills which are used for creating solutions are changing from low-level to high-level. In this level, it is required to improve the bare knowledge with high-level cognitive skills, although there is no application of this process to solving real-world problems. Lastly, in Quadrant D (Adaptation) students are required not only to have high cognitive processing skills but also to use these skills to solve unexpected real-world problems. Students with Quadrant D level competency are expected to even further increase their skills with high cognitive ability to solve difficult problems no matter how confusing the problems are (ICLE, 2012). The assignment of the behaviors is conducted based on the cognitive competency level and application level of each behavior which are separately defined as high or low. The specific quadrant is defined by the combination of these two levels.

In Step-5, realistic scenarios are created starting from the Quadrant A behaviors/abilities and continue with the Quadrant B, C, and D. Scenarios for different quadrants will be in different levels of the game following the order of Quadrant A to Quadrant D. As per Step-6, hints and feedback are created. Corrective and more detailed feedback is to be provided after wrong answers/reactions so that the player can learn from their mistakes. Hints can also be added to the scenarios on a voluntarily basis in exchange for punishment score points. After that, succeeding/failing and assessment criteria are designed in Step-7. In this step, relative difficulties of the questions and their importance to real life competencies should be considered. Finally, in Step-8, the serious game design is reviewed and finalized.

The SGDM model has been utilized by Gurbuz and Celik (2022) for the preliminary design of a maritime serious game in preparation for SIRE 2.0 inspections. Gurbuz and Celik (2022) firstly developed a maritime gamified mentoring platform, namely "Maritime Gamentor". Using the SGDM model, they further designed a maritime serious game for task-based risk assessment training of the crew as the first module of the platform. Based on the experience acquired during this study, the SGDM maritime serious game design model is updated as GAMESIRE 2.0 in order to meet the specific needs of SIRE 2.0 context. GAMESIRE 2.0 model is depicted in Figure 2.

Figure 2. GAMESIRE 2.0 model

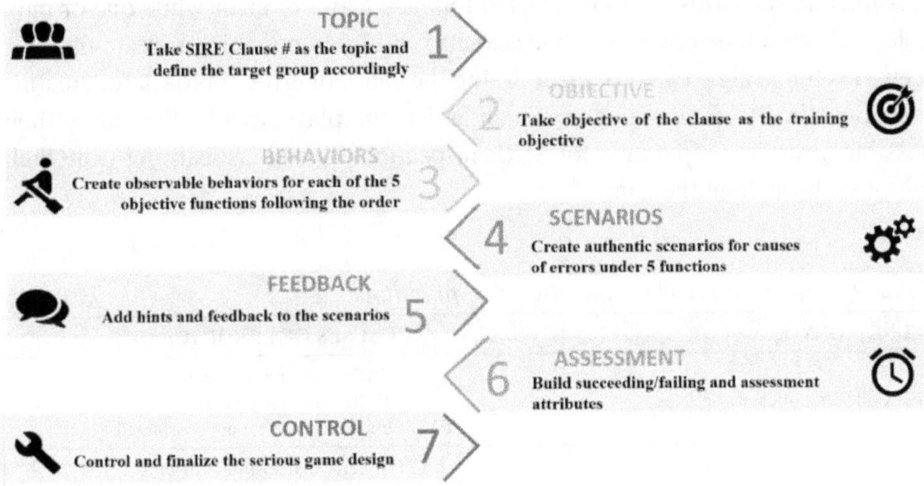

In Step-1 of the GAMESIRE 2.0 model, the target SIRE clause is taken as the topic of the serious game-based training. SIRE clauses can be found in SIRE 2.0 Question Library Part 1 and Part 2 (Version 1.0) documents issued in January 2022 by OCIMF (Oil Companies International Marine Forum, 2023c; Oil Companies International Marine Forum, 2023d) according to which SIRE inspections are conducted. Target group of the game is also defined in this step based on the explanation of the clause. As per Step-2, objective of the game is also defined based on the same documents, where objectives are clearly stated for each clause.

In Step-3, observable behaviors are created based on the objective of the game. For doing this, GAMESIRE 2.0 model utilizes 5 cognitive functions which are adapted from Whaley et al. (2016). These functions are collecting information, understanding/ sense-making, decision making, action and teamwork. It should be noted that the order of collecting information, understanding/sense-making, decision making and action functions are defined as 1 to 4 respectively. The order of the functions should be taken into account as their intricacy level increases in the given order. This means functions in higher order require higher level cognitive skills and enhanced ability to apply them in real life situations. However, the teamwork function can be used multiple times between any of other functions as cognitive flow of the teamwork function is dynamic and embedded in other functions. In order to create observable behaviors, the game objective should be decomposed into these functions and each function should be stated as specific behaviors or abilities in alignment with the game objective.

As per Step-4 of the model, authentic scenarios are created for the cognitive functions stated in Step-3. For facilitating scenario design, 3 causes of error (adapted from (Whaley et al.,2016)) are identified for each function and depicted in Table 2. Authentic scenarios are to be created for each cause of error while one or multiple of them can be covered in one scenario. It is also possible to create multiple scenarios for a single cause of error. Using the cause of error approach for creating scenarios aims to design a game which assists the players with eliminating their possible errors in preparation for SIRE inspections as well as learning from their mistakes throughout the game.

Table 2. Causes of error for the cognitive functions

FUNCTIONS (F)	CAUSES OF ERROR (C)
F1: Collecting Information	F1C1: Info not perceived F1C2: Info mis-perceived F1C3: Info perceived but not considered
F2: Understanding/ Sense-making	F2C1: Error in detecting problems F2C2: Error in identifying problems F2C3: Error in projecting future states
F3: Decision Making	F3C1: Incorrect goal or priority setting F3C2: Incorrect judgement of the situation F3C3: Incorrect simulation/evaluation of the options
F4: Action	F4C1: Failed to try required action F4C2: Executed the required action incorrectly F4C3: Timing error for the required action
F5: Teamwork	F5C1: Communication error F5C2: Leadership error F5C3: Collaboration and cooperation error

Last 3 steps of the GAMESIRE 2.0 model are applied in a similar way to those of the SGDM model. In Step-5 of the GAMESIRE 2.0 model, hints and feedback are added to the game. Feedback is of utmost importance for educational aspect of the game. In this regard, immediate feedback should be provided after all the answers or reactions (whether they are correct or wrong) of the player. Feedback should be in alignment with the scenarios so that the players can relate them with their game experience and retain the learned content longer. Feedback should be more detailed and corrective after wrong answers for enhancing the educational capability of the game in a way to facilitate learning from mistakes. Positive feedback should also be used after correct answers as they are important for fostering feeling of success and competence of the player. Hints should also be included in the game to increase the engagement of the players. Similarly, more hints should be provided to the players who are making more mistakes to promote their motivation and involvement in the game. Hints should fade out as the player continues in the game. Adaptive hints and feedback based on the answers of the players can also provide them with a more personalized learning experience.

In Step-6 of the model, succeeding/failing and assessment attribute of the game is built. Point values of the questions are defined taking into account the number of questions and their difficulties. The questions in later levels of the game should worth more points as they possibly require higher level abilities. Player can start the game with 0 points and earn point (s) for correct answers. Similarly, starting with 100 points, the player can lose point (s) for incorrect answers. The criteria for winning or losing the game are also to be defined in this step. Step-6 should also provide generalized assessment about the future training needs of the players considering their mistakes in the game. For instance, such an assessment might propose that the player needs urgent and corrective training on some specific topics or future trainings should be conservational rather than instructional. Finally, in Step-7 of the model, the overall game design is examined and finalized after making any necessary improvements.

Educational Theories Utilized in GAMESIRE 2.0 Model

Flow Theory

The Flow theory defines flow as a "holistic sensation that people feel when they act with total involvement" (Csikszentmihalyi, 1975, p. 36). Flow theory is considerably related to motivation and engagement as they all make people experience the activity for the sake of the activity itself, rather than a necessity or only reaching to the goal of the activity (Csikszentmihalyi, 2014). GAMESIRE 2.0 utilizes the flow theory as it structures the game design with an increasing difficulty through a pre-defined order of the cognitive functions from which the game scenarios are generated. This way, it is believed that the players will not be overwhelmed in the earlier parts of the game and can retain their involvement. Providing the players who make more mistakes with more hints is also advised in the model with the same purpose.

Self-Determination and Self-Efficacy Theories

Self-determination and self-efficacy theories focus on motivation of the players. According to the self determination theory, autonomy, competence and relatedness are main psychological needs of people (Ryan & Deci, 2017). Customization in games can support feelings of autonomy (Kim et al., 2015) while achievements such as positive feedback, coins, and badges promote feeling of competence (Peng et al., 2012). It is also stated that teams and social networks foster the feeling of relatedness (Xi & Hamari, 2019). Similarly, self-efficacy theory states that people need to feel that they can successfully perform the duty for effective learning to occur during that experience (Bandura, 1982). It is believed that GAMESIRE 2.0 model utilizes self-determination and self-efficacy theories by suggesting the use of positive and encouraging feedback after all the correct answers. As the model suggested, personalized feedback in alignment with the answer of the players and using the names of the player in the feedback might also enhance the motivating effect of the feedback.

Constructivist Learning Theory

Constructivist learning theory proposes that learning is an active process and effective learning takes place through actively constructing the knowledge instead of theoretically communicating it (Duffy & Cunningham, 1996). With this perspective, Jonassen (1999) hypothesizes that modeling, coaching and scaffolding are three main instructional activities that foster learning. He also explains that clearly stating the relevance of the goals, adaptive content and motivational aspects are also important for effective construction of knowledge. In addition, sociocultural constructivism highlightes that learners should be supervised for an incremental and step-by-step development (Vygotsky, 1978). In this regard, GAMESIRE 2.0 applies constructivist learning theory in that it aims to facilitate the design of authentic and scenario-based learning environments so that players can learn by relating their previous knowledge with realistic scenarios. In alignment with sociocultural contructivism theory, GAMESIRE 2.0 also intends to support a step-by-step knowledge development by providing the order of functions to be used in scenario development based on their intricacy level.

Experiential Learning Theory and Situated Learning Theory

Experiential learning theory states that knowledge is learned as a result of personal experiences and interactions with the environment, instead of the instruction itself (Kolb, 1984). This theory conceptualize learning as an iterative process that includes the steps of *concrete experience, reflective observation, abstract conceptualization and active experimentation* (Kolb & Kolb, 2013). Kolb and Kolb (2013) furher explain that there are nine learning styles that employ at least one of these steps and these learning styles are *Initiating, Experiencing, Imagining, Reflecting, Analyzing, Thinking, Deciding, Acting and Balancing*. Similarly, situated learning theory emphasizes that learning conceptual knowledge is closely related with the situations in which it is learned (Brown et al., 1989). Hence, both theories support the design of authentic learning environments in a way to enable problem-solving experiences (All et al., 2017). In alignment with these theories, GAMESIRE 2.0 model conceptualizes observable behaviors as the core of the scenarios in order to facilitate the design of authentic problem-solving experiences that are specific to tanker ships.

Educational Alignment

Educational alignment is the conformity between objectives, instruction, and assessment aspects of educational practices (Anderson & Krathwohl, 2001). Educational alignment is believed to be of significant importance for the success of educational practices (Marzano, 2003). Roach et al. (2008) report that strong alignment between these aspects of education and trainings helps the learners not only be successful in assessment but also transfer what they learned to real world. For ensuring educational alignment, these aspects need to be considered together focusing on the relationship in between, rather than designing them separately (Anderson, 2002). GAMESIRE 2.0 decomposes the main objective of the serious game into 5 cognitive functions and creates scenarios for each of them. This way, game objective is fully covered with the scenarios. As the game scenarios include both instruction and assessment, the game objective is in fact covered in the game with a holistic approach.

RESULTS

Preliminary Design of GAMESIRE 2.0 Module-1

This section presents the application of the GAMESIRE 2.0 model for the preliminary design of a maritime serious game in SIRE 2.0 context.

Step-1: Topic

Game topic is chosen from the SIRE 2.0 Question Library Part 1 document as Clause # 4.2.1 which is "Were the Master and navigating officers familiar with the company passage planning procedures and had all voyages been appraised, planned, executed, and monitored in accordance with company procedures, industry best practice, and both local and international rules" (OCIMF, 2023c; p.178). The target group of the training is defined as navigating officers on tanker ships.

Step-2: Objective

In the same document, the objective of the Clause # 4.2.1 is explained as "To ensure that passages are planned and executed from berth to berth in accordance with international/local rules and industry best practice guidance", which is also taken as the game objective.

Step-3: Behaviors

Observable behaviors are created for 5 cognitive functions as:

F1-Collecting Information: Collecting necessary information from the radar, Electronic Chart Display Information System (ECDIS), radio devices, and bridge team.
F2-Understanding/Sense-Making: Undertanding from the collected information that there might be a risky passing situation with other ships.
F3-Decision Making: Choosing the right ship maneuver for avoiding collision with other ship.
F4-Action: Applying the decision in the collision avoidance sitiuation correctly and timely.
F5-Teamwork: Communicating with and leading the bridge team correctly and effectively for the application of the decision.

Step-4: Scenarios

In Module-1, the player is the navigation officer of the tanker ship M/T GAMESIRE 2.0. The player is on the bridge, where a navigational watch is kept. One lookout and one helmsman are also on the bridge with the navigation officer. The helmsman's duty is timely and correct application of the rudder (steering) orders that the officer in charge (navigation officer) issues. The lookout stays at alert against dangers to navigation and reports the situation to the officer in charge. M/T GAMESIRE 2.0 is approaching for the passage of Çanakkale Strait from North to South.

Based on this general situation, the scenarios are created for the causes of error under each cognitive functions.

F1C1-Info not perceived: Another ship is dangerously approaching to M/T GAMESIRE 2.0 from her port bow. The navigational radar sounds an alarm regarding Closest Point of Approach (CPA) of 500 yards to warn the bridge against the danger. The player is expected to check beforehand if the sound of the alarm is turned down to make sure he/she can hear it.

F1C2-Info mis-perceived: The player receives a call on VHF radio concerning another ship's intention to overtake M/T GAMESIRE 2.0. However, the communication with other station was not very clear because of the language barrier. The player is expected to call other station again and clarify the situation not to misperceive the information.

F1C3-Info perceived but not considered: The lookout reports another vessel with the intention of passing from the bow of M/T GAMESIRE 2.0. The player hears the report and expected to check the boat himself/herself as every information is important at sea and must be taken into account.

F2C1-Error in detecting problems: ECDIS (Electronic Chart Display System) shows the location of the ship closer to the shore than it is in reality. Before the Çanakkale Strait entrance from the North (in the southern direction), a paper chart is shown to the player. The player is supposed to detect the problem with the ECDIS by comparing it with the paper chart.

F2C2-Error in identifying problems: If the player decides to check the vessel in the Scenario F1C3, he/she will be provided distance, course, speed, and bearing information of that vessel. He/she is then supposed to notice that the bearing of that vessel does not change (which means the risk of collision is imminent). If the player decides not to check the boat in the Scenario F1C3, he/she can not identify that the bearing does not change and receives no point.

F2C3-Error in projecting future states: If the player could not identify that the bearing of that vessel does not change, then he/she is given that information as a hint. After he/she has this information (either as a hint or noticing himself/ herself) he is expected to decide that stable bearing of the vessel tells high risk of collision.

F3C1-Incorrect goal or priority setting: Now the distance of other vessel to M/T GAMESIRE 2.0 is 1000 yards. The speed of our vessel is 8 knots (nauticel miles an hour) and the speed of other vessel is 10 knots. She is approaching to our ship from port (left) side and will be aboard in 2 minutes. There is a call on VHF radio from another ship which is 4 nautical miles behind our ship and there is not a dangerous situation with that ship. The player is not supposed to answer the VHF call not to lose time as the situation with the closer vessel is the highest priority.

F3C2-Incorrect judgement of the situation: Now the situation with the vessel on 1000 yards is risky. The player is asked about the situation with different options including;

a) The ship will clearly pass to enter the strait before our ship,
b) The ship will wait our ship and enter the strait afterward,
c) The situation is risky and needs further investigation.

The options might be explained differently and increased in number, but the player is supposed to state that the situation is risky.

F3C3-Incorrect simulation/evaluation of the options: The options are depicted as but not limited to the ones below in a multiple choice format. The player is then asked to choose which might be possible options.

a) Increase speed to pass other ship,
b) Decrease speed to wait that ship to pass,
c) Keeping our speed and waiting other vessel to take action,
d) Call that ship on VHF radio to clarify the situation,
e) Letting the captain know the situation.

Possible options are a, b, and d because c is wrong and e is a late action to take (considering there is about 1.5 minutes to decide and apply our maneuver).

F4C1-*Failed to try required action*: The player is asked which action to take in this situation among the possible options. The correct action is supposed to be calling that ship on VHF to clarify the situation. Depending on the dynamics of the situation (weather and sea state, other ships around etc.) it might be conducted together with decreasing the speed.

F4C2-*Executed the required action incorrectly:* Whether the player failed in Scenario F4C1 or not, he/she is asked how to conduct the VHF communication among similar options below:

a) Ask other ship about her intention,
b) Tell other ship to keep clear of M/T GAMESIRE 2.0.
c) Tell other ship to slow down and stay on our port (left) side.

The correct reaction of the player is supposed to be “c” as others are not the suitable for the urgency of the situation. The player needs to be clear and direct.

F4C3-*Timing error for the required action*: The player is asked when to conduct the VHF communication. Options are below:

a) Conduct as soon as possible,
b) Conduct when that ship comes to 500 yards (instead of 1000 yards)
c) Ask the captain and conduct when ordered

Correct reaction is supposed to be “a” as other options cause losing time and thus incorrect.

F5C1-*Communication error*: Regardless of his/her answers, the player knows that he/she is supposed to tell other ship on VHF to slow down and stay on our port (left) side as soon as possible. In this scenario, the player is asked which sentence to use on VHF for telling this.

a) You may want to slow down and stay on our port (left) side,
b) Slow down and stay on our port (left) side right away,
c) If ok for you, you can slow down and stay on our port (left) side.

Correct answer is "b" as the communication must be clear and effective.

F5C2: *Leadership error* and F5C3: *Collaboration and cooperation error* are covered in one scenario. That scenario is applied if the reaction in the scenario F4C3 is incorrect and shows up right after that scenario before the feedback for the wrong answer. In this regard, this scenario gives a second chance for scenario F4C3. If the answer in the scenario F4C3 is already correct, then this scenario does not show up.

In this scenario, the helmsman whose duty is applying the helm order, advises that the player should conduct VHF communication as soon as possible instead of other options. The player's reaction in that case is asked among following options.

a) Listen to helmsman's advice,
b) Tells to helmsman to consider his own business,
c) Does not say anything to helsman, not taking his advice.

Correct reaction is supposed to be "a". Because a good leader considers advice from team members and is in effective collaboration and cooperation with them.

Step-5: Feedback

In this step, hints and feedback are created. No matter they are correct or wrong, feedback should be provided after all answers. For instance, a possible feedback for the wrong answer in Scenario F5C1 (Communication error) might be "Wrong answer! Not a good example of communication. All communication onboard ship should be clear and effective. Communication that might be misunderstood or misinterpreted is to be eliminated. You should state what you mean directly and very clearly without leaving anything hanging. The terms "you may want to" and "if it is ok for you" are not clear enough." Possible feedback for the correct answer might be "Correct. A good example of communication. Communication onboard ship must be clear and effective like you did". Similarly, hints should be added for enhancing the flow of the game as in Scenario F2C3 (Error in projecting future states). This hint is provided if the player could not identify that the bearing of another vessel does not change. Such an hint could be "You should check the bearing of the vessel. It looks like it does not change". Similar feedback should be created also for other scenarios.

Step-6: Assessment

Point values of each question in the game is depicted in Table 3. It should be noted that there are 2 questions about Teamwork function in the last level of the game, each of which worths 10 points. However, the second question, which is also the the final question of the game is a bonus question which shows up only if the question in the scenario F4C3 is incorrect. The minimum score to win the game can be applied as 80.

Table 3. Point values of the questions

Cognitive Function	Value of Each Question about the Function	Total Value of Questions about the Function
Collecting Information	5	15
Understanding/ Sense-Making	5	15
Decision Making	8	24
Action	12	36
Teamwork	10	10
Total	-	100

Step-7: Control

In this step, game design is controlled and finalized.

DISCUSSION

In spite of the important potential serious games propose for the maritime domain, the literature still needs a fundamental methodology for designing serious games. In this regard, current chapter offers a serious game design model, namely GAMESIRE 2.0, which is specific to SIRE inspection trainings in tanker shipping. In broader perspective, this study intends to contribute to safety of tanker shipping by providing an enhanced training approach for eliminating the deficiencies and thus possible incidents and accidents.

GAMESIRE 2.0 model is an updated version of the SGDM model which has been utilized by Gurbuz and Celik (2022) for the preliminary design of a maritime serious game in preparation for SIRE 2.0 inspections. Based on the experiences from this study, GAMESIRE 2.0 model is developed for fulfilling the specific needs of SIRE inspection trainings in various ways. GAMESIRE 2.0 model guides the designer to create the game scenarios based on possible causes of errors for defined cognitive functions. It is believed that this approach might help elimination of possible errors (non-conformities) in SIRE inspections better than SGDM model. It is also regarded that error-based approach can provide the designer with more specific guidance (than the SGDM model) in design of game scenarios as these errors form the theme of the scenarios.

Utilizing GAMESIRE 2.0 model for designing serious games about SIRE inspection trainings offers an important advantage in comparison with using other models. As GAMESIRE 2.0 model is specific to the maritime domain and SIRE inspections in particular, it employs the educational theories which are specifically chosen to enhance the effectiveness of game-based SIRE inspection trainings. In this regard, GAMESIRE 2.0 model is believed to offer a more significant potential than other models for providing step-by-step guidance in serious game-based SIRE inspection trainings. Utilizing specifically defined educational theories might also contribute to designing serious games which are more effective in elimination of SIRE inspection non-conformities.

As the next step of our further development plan, we firstly aim to acquire the final version of the preliminary design proposed in this study. Final version of the design is then to be developed as a 3D game prototype. Conducting experimental study with navigation officers of tanker ships and continuously improving the game prototype based on their feedback is the next step in our study. Quantitative pre-test/post-test experiments with officers of tanker ships are also necessary for proving the efficiency of the developed game and thus the GAMESIRE 2.0 model. We also plan to use the GAMESIRE 2.0 model for designing more serious games in preparation for SIRE inspection trainings. Enhancing the GAMESIRE 2.0 model based on our experiences is the next step of our further development plan. Finally, we aim to develop an open online platform which includes the serious games developed in preparation for SIRE 2.0 inspections.

CONCLUSION

This chapter proposes the GAMESIRE 2.0 model for designing maritime serious games in preparation for SIRE inspections. Besides, application of the model for the preliminary design of a serious game is also conducted for providing researchers and practitioners with practical guidance for designing similar games. In this regard, it is believed that current study provides valuable insight into gamification of SIRE 2.0 inspection trainings.

It is believed that this study has both practical and theoretical contributions to the literature as well as different actors in the maritime domain. To start with, the proposed GAMESIRE 2.0 model and our methodology can be utilized for designing similar maritime serious games in preparation for SIRE 2.0 inspections. In this regard, MET institutions, shipping companies, online maritime training companies as well as maritime start-ups can significantly benefit from this study for SIRE 2.0 based serious game design. Secondly, our study can be benefited by academicians for developing similar serious game design models which are specific to maritime domain. In fact, it is regarded that the error-based approach proposed in this study has the potential to be helpful in providing practical guidance for serious game scenario design outside the scope of SIRE 2.0 inspections.

Moreover, functions of the GAMESIRE 2.0 model can be extended in maritime domain. Firstly, GAMESIRE 2.0 can be developed as an online game-based training platform for SIRE inspections and serious games can be designed and developed as modules of this platform. In addition, it is also believed that GAMESIRE 2.0 model also be used for designing serious game- based trainings in preparation for other maritime inspection regimes. Therefore, our approach offers a significant potential for enhanced safety and environmental protection in maritime domain.

In spite of the novel approach, current study also has some limitations. Most importantly, as the GAMESIRE 2.0 model is new, it needs to be further used to prove its validity and efficiency. In this regard, final design and development of the serios game as well as experimental study with officers must be conducted. Moreover, the model is employed for the preliminary design of a serious game for teaching navigational procedures. For analyzing its applicability, the model needs to be utilized for the design of similar trainings in SIRE 2.0 concept. Despite the limitations, it is believed that this study creates a fundamental basis for the gamification of maritime inspection regimes.

ACKNOWLEDGMENT

This chapter is produced by extending the results from the initial stages of Ph.D. dissertation research entitled 'A Conceptual Approach for Design and Development of Serious Game in Maritime Domain' which is being executed in a Ph.D. Programme in Maritime Transportation Engineering of Istanbul Technical University Graduate School.

REFERENCES

Abt, C. C. (1970). Serious games. Viking press.

Akyuz, E., & Celik, E. (2018). The role of human factor in maritime environment risk assessment: A practical application on Ballast Water Treatment (BWT) system in ship. *Human and Ecological Risk Assessment*, 24(3), 653–666. DOI: 10.1080/10807039.2017.1396184

All, A., Plovie, B., Nunez Castellar, E. P., & Van Looy, J. (2017). Pre-test influences on the effectiveness of digital-game based learning: A case study of a fire safety game. *Computers & Education, 114*, 24–37. https://doi.org/.compedu.2017.05.018 .DOI: 10.1016/j

Anderson, L. W. (2002). Curricular alignment: A re-examination. *Theory into Practice*, 41(4), 255–260. DOI: 10.1207/s15430421tip4104_9

Anderson, L. W., & Krathwohl, D. R. (2001). *A taxonomy for learning, teaching, and assessing: A revision of Bloom's taxonomy of educational objectives: complete edition*. Addison Wesley Longman, Inc.

Arslan, O., Aydemir, B., & Kececi, T. (2016, September). Review of Tanker Ship SIRE Inspection Findings in Turkey. *International Conference on Maritime Safety and Human Factors*.

Bai, S., Hew, K. F., & Huang, B. (2020). Does gamification improve student learning outcome? Evidence from a meta-analysis and synthesis of qualitative data in educational contexts. *Educational Research Review*, 30, 100322. DOI: 10.1016/j.edurev.2020.100322

Bandura, A. (1982). Self-efficacy mechanism in human agency. *The American Psychologist*, 37(2), 122–147. DOI: 10.1037/0003-066X.37.2.122

Benkhedda, S., & Bendella, F. (2019). FASim: A 3D serious game for the first aid emergency. *Simulation & Gaming*, 50(6), 690–710. DOI: 10.1177/1046878119865913

Bhardwaj, S., & Pazaver, A. (2014). Establishing the underpinning theories of maritime education and training for on-board competencies. *Amet Marit. J.*, 55–73.

Bordwell, D. (1989). A Case for Cognitivism. *IRIS*, 9, 11–41.

Brown, J. S., Collins, A., & Duguid, P. (1989). Situated cognition and the culture of learning. *Educational Researcher*, 18(1), 32–42. DOI: 10.3102/0013189X018001032

Bruzzone, A. G., Massei, M., Solis, A. O., Poggi, S., Bartolucci, C., & Capponi, L. D. A. (2013, July). Serious games as enablers for training and education on operations on ships and off-shore platforms. In *Proceedings of the 2013 summer computer simulation conference* (pp. 1-8).

Chan, K., & Zary, N. (2019). Knowledge, use and barriers to Serious Games in undergraduate medical education.*OSF Preprints*. DOI: 10.31219/osf.io/2f7rw

Chow, C. Y., Riantiningtyas, R. R., Kanstrup, M. B., Papavasileiou, M., Liem, G. D., & Olsen, A. (2020). Can games change children's eating behaviour? A review of gamification and serious games. *Food Quality and Preference*, 80, 103823. DOI: 10.1016/j.foodqual.2019.103823

Christensen, M. (2013). *A qualitative study of the review and verification process of the Safety Management System within companies servicing the Norwegian Continental Shelf* (Master's thesis, Høgskolen i Vestfold).

Creamare. (2022). Project Overview. Accessed: August 30, 2023 from https://creamare.eu/project/

Csikszentmihalyi, M. (1975). Beyond boredom and anxiety: Experiencing flow in work and play. Jossey-Bass. https://psycnet.apa.org/record/2000-12701-000

Csikszentmihalyi, M. (2014). Flow and the foundations of positive psychology. In Flow and the foundations of positive psychology. DOI: 10.1007/978-94-017-9088-8

Deltares. (2018). Port of the Future Serious Games. Accessed August 30, 2023 from https://www.deltares.nl/en/software-and-data/products/port-of-the-future-serious-game

Dimitriadou, A., Djafarova, N., Turetken, O., Verkuyl, M., & Ferworn, A. (2021). Challenges in Serious Game Design and Development: Educators' Experiences. *Simulation & Gaming*, 52(2), 132–152. DOI: 10.1177/1046878120944197

Djaouti, D., Alvarez, J., & Jessel, J. P. (2011). Classifying serious games: the G/P/S model. In *Handbook of research on improving learning and motivation through educational games: Multidisciplinary approaches* (pp. 118–136). IGI global. DOI: 10.4018/978-1-60960-495-0.ch006

Duffy, T. M., & Cunningham, D. J. (1996). Constructivism: Implications for the design and delivery of instruction. In Handbook of research for educational communications and technology (pp. 170–198). https://doi.org/. x.DOI: 10.1111/j.1467-8535.2009.00994_9

Evans, K. H., Daines, W., Tsui, J., Strehlow, M., Maggio, P., & Shieh, L. (2015). Septris: A novel, mobile, online, simulation game that improves sepsis recognition and management. *Academic Medicine*, 90(2), 180–184. DOI: 10.1097/ACM.0000000000000611 PMID: 25517703

Fokides, E. (2018). Digital educational games and mathematics. Results of a case study in primary school settings. *Education and Information Technologies*, 23(2), 851–867. DOI: 10.1007/s10639-017-9639-5

Fotiadis, A. K., & Sigala, M. (2015). Developing a framework for designing an Events Management Training Simulation (EMTS). *Journal of Hospitality, Leisure, Sport and Tourism Education*, 16, 59–71. DOI: 10.1016/j.jhlste.2015.03.001

Fu, K., Hainey, T., & Baxter, G. (2016, October). A systematic literature review to identify empirical evidence on the use of computer games in business education and training. In *European Conference on Games Based Learning* (p. 232). Academic Conferences International Limited.

Fusco, N. M., Jacobsen, L. J., Klem, N., Krzyzanowicz, R., & Ohtake, P. J. (2022). A serious game employed to introduce principles of interprofessional collaboration to students of multiple health professions. *Simulation & Gaming*, 53(3), 253–264. DOI: 10.1177/10468781221093816

Gray, S. I., Robertson, J., Manches, A., & Rajendran, G. (2019). BrainQuest: The use of motivational design theories to create a cognitive training game supporting hot executive function. *International Journal of Human-Computer Studies*, 127, 124–149. DOI: 10.1016/j.ijhcs.2018.08.004

Gurbuz, S. C. (2021). A conceptual approach for design and development of serious game in maritime domain [Unpublished Doctoral Dissertation Progress Report-1]. Istanbul Technical University, İstanbul, Türkiye.

Gurbuz, S. C., & Celik, M. (2022). A preliminary design of a 3D maritime gamified mentoring platform to support tanker pre-vetting inspection training: 'Maritime Gamentor'. *Ships and Offshore Structures*, 18(12), 1627–1637. DOI: 10.1080/17445302.2022.2133878

Gurbuz, S. C., & Celik, M. (2023). A brief overview on serious gaming research and entrepreneurship ecosystem in maritime field. In *Abstract Book of International Conference on Information Technology for Higher Education-ICITHE-23* (p.17). Association for Scientific and Academic Research (ASAR) Explore Publishing.

Hamari, J., & Sjöblom, M. (2017). What is eSports and why do people watch it? *Internet Research*, 27(2), 211–232. DOI: 10.1108/IntR-04-2016-0085

Haruna, H., Zainuddin, Z., Mellecker, R. R., Chu, S. K., & Hu, X. (2019). An iterative process for developing digital gamified sexual health education for adolescent students in low-tech settings. *Information and Learning Science*, 120(11), 723–742. Advance online publication. DOI: 10.1108/ILS-07-2019-0066

Hjelmervik, K., Nazir, S., & Myhrvold, A. (2018). Simulator training for maritime complex tasks: An experimental study. *WMU Journal of Maritime Affairs*, 17(1), 17–30. DOI: 10.1007/s13437-017-0133-0

ICLE (International Center for Leadership in Education). (2012). Rigor/Relevance Framework. Retrieved February 21 2024, from http://www.cssvt.org/wp/wp-content/uploads/2012/08/Rigor-Relevance-Framework.pdf

International Chamber of Shipping. (2020). *Annual Review 2020*. International Chamber of Shipping. Retrieved April 18 2021, from https://www.ics-shipping.org/wp-content/uploads/2020/11/annual-review-2020-final-compressed.pdf

Johnson, D., Horton, E., Mulcahy, R., & Foth, M. (2017). Gamification and serious games within the domain of domestic energy consumption: A systematic review. *Renewable & Sustainable Energy Reviews*, 73, 249–264. DOI: 10.1016/j.rser.2017.01.134

Jonassen, D. (1999). Designing constructivist learning environments. In Reigeluth, C. (Ed.), *Instructional-design theories and models: A new paradigm of instructional theory* (pp. 215–239). DOI: 10.4324/9781410603784-16

Khan, M. A., Merabet, A., Alkaabi, S., & Sayed, H. E. (2022). Game-based learning platform to enhance cybersecurity education. *Education and Information Technologies*, 27(4), 1–25. DOI: 10.1007/s10639-021-10807-6

Kim, K., Schmierbach, M. G., Bellur, S., Chung, M. Y., Fraustino, J. D., Dardis, F., & Ahern, L. (2015). Is it a sense of autonomy, control, or attachment? Exploring the effects of in-game customization on game enjoyment. *Computers in Human Behavior*, 48, 695–705. DOI: 10.1016/j.chb.2015.02.011

Kolb, A. Y., & Kolb, D. A. (2013). *The Kolb learning style inventory version 4.0: A comprehensive guide to the theory, psychometrics, research on validity and educational applications*. Experience Based Learning Systems, Inc.

Kolb, D. A. (1984). *Experiential learning: Experience as the source of learning and development*. Prentice Hall. DOI: 10.1016/B978-0-7506-7223-8.50017-4

Korhonen, T., Halonen, R., Ravelin, T., Kemppainen, J., & Koskela, K. (2017, September). A Multidisciplinary Approach to Serious Game Development in the Health Sector. In *MCIS* (p. 30).

Koupritzioti, D., & Xinogalos, S. (2020). PyDiophantus maze game: Play it to learn mathematics or implement it to learn game programming in Python. *Education and Information Technologies*, 25(4), 2747–2764. DOI: 10.1007/s10639-019-10087-1

Landers, R. N. (2014). Developing a Theory of Gamified Learning: Linking Serious Games and Gamification of Learning. *Simulation & Gaming*, 45(6), 752–768. DOI: 10.1177/1046878114563660

Laporte, L., & Zaman, B. (2018). A comparative analysis of programming games, looking through the lens of an instructional design model and a game attributes taxonomy. *Entertainment Computing*, 25, 48–61. DOI: 10.1016/j.entcom.2017.12.005

Lee, J. (2020). Problem-based gaming via an augmented reality mobile game and a printed game in foreign language education. *Education and Information Technologies*, 1–29.

Loon, M., Evans, J., & Kerridge, C. (2015). Learning with a strategic management simulation game: A case study. *International Journal of Management Education*, 13(3), 227–236. DOI: 10.1016/j.ijme.2015.06.002

Mallam, S. C., Nazir, S., & Renganayagalu, S. K. (2019). Rethinking maritime education, training, and operations in the digital era: Applications for emerging immersive technologies. *Journal of Marine Science and Engineering*, 7(12), 428. DOI: 10.3390/jmse7120428

Margoudi, M., Oliveira, M., & Waddell, G. (2016, October). Game-based learning of musical instruments: A review and recommendations. In *European Conference on Games Based Learning* (p. 426). Academic Conferences International Limited.

Marlisco (Marine Litter in European Seas: Social Awareness and Co-Responsibility). (2015). Sea Dream Team: A Serious Game on Marine Litter for Youngsters. Accessed: August 30, 2023 from https://www.marlisco.eu/serious-game.en.html

Marzano, R. J. (2003). *What works in schools: Translating research into action*. ASCD.

Navas de Maya, B., Arslan, O., Akyuz, E., Kurt, R. E., & Turan, O. (2022). Application of data-mining techniques to predict and rank maritime non-conformities in tanker shipping companies using accident inspection reports. *Ships and Offshore Structures*, 17(3), 687–694. DOI: 10.1080/17445302.2020.1862530

Nicholson, S. (2015). A recipe for meaningful gamification. In *Gamification in education and business* (pp. 1–20). Springer. DOI: 10.1007/978-3-319-10208-5_1

Nikitakos, N., Sirris, I., Dalaklis, D., Papachristos, D., & Tsoukalas, V. D. (2017). Game-based learning for maritime education and training: The case of Trader of the World. *WMU Journal of Maritime Affairs*, 16(2), 265–291. DOI: 10.1007/s13437-016-0119-3

Nygren, N. V., Kankainen, V., & Brunet, L. (2022). Offsetting Game—Framing Environmental Issues in the Design of a Serious Game. *Simulation & Gaming*, 53(6), 615–644. DOI: 10.1177/10468781221126786

Oil Companies International Marine Forum. (2023a). Ship Inspection Report Program (SIRE). https://www.ocimf.org/programmes/sire

Oil Companies International Marine Forum. (2023b). SIRE 2.0. https://www.ocimf.org/programmes/sire-2-0

Oil Companies International Marine Forum. (2023c). SIRE 2.0. Question Library Part-1 Chapters 1-7 Version 2.0. https://www.ocimf.org/document-libary/630-sire-2-0-question-library-part-1-chapters-1-to-7-version-1-0-january-2022/file

Oil Companies International Marine Forum. (2023d). SIRE 2.0. Question Library Part-2 Chapters 8-12 Version 2.0. https://www.ocimf.org/document-libary/631-sire-2-0-question-library-part-2-chapters-8-to-12-version-1-0-january-2022/file

Oil Companies International Marine Forum (OCIMF). (2016). *Ship Inspection Report (SIRE) Programme*. 2014 Edition Rev.1.2.

Oil Companies International Marine Forum (OCIMF). (2021, August 01). *Ship Inspection Report Program (SIRE)*. Retrieved from https://www.ocimf.org/programmes/sire

Oren, M., Pedersen, S., & Butler-Purry, K. L. (2020). Teaching Digital Circuit Design With a 3-D Video Game: The Impact of Using In-Game Tools on Students' Performance. *IEEE Transactions on Education*, 64(1), 24–31. DOI: 10.1109/TE.2020.3000955

Peng, W., Lin, J. H., Pfeiffer, K. A., & Winn, B. (2012). Need satisfaction supportive game features as motivational determinants: An experimental study of a self-determination theory guided exergame. *Media Psychology*, 15(2), 175–196. DOI: 10.1080/15213269.2012.673850

Philbin-Briscoe, O., Simon, B., Mudur, S., Poullis, C., Rizvic, S., Boskovic, D., . . . Skarlatos, D. (2017, September). A serious game for understanding ancient seafaring in the Mediterranean sea. In *2017 9th international conference on virtual worlds and games for serious applications (VS-games)* (pp. 1-5). IEEE. DOI: 10.1109/VS-GAMES.2017.8055804

Poullis, C., Kersten-Oertel, M., Benjamin, J. P., Philbin-Briscoe, O., Simon, B., Perissiou, D., Demesticha, S., Markou, E., Frentzos, E., Kyriakidis, P., Skarlatos, D., & Rizvic, S. (2019). Evaluation of "The Seafarers": A serious game on seaborne trade in the Mediterranean sea during the Classical period. *Digital Applications in Archaeology and Cultural Heritage*, 12, e00090. DOI: 10.1016/j.daach.2019.e00090

Pruyn, J. (2023). The use of digital games in academic maritime education: A theoretical framework and practical applications. *Maritime Policy & Management*, 1–14.

Roach, A. T., Niebling, B. C., & Kurz, A. (2008). Evaluating the alignment among curriculum, instruction, and assessments: Implications and applications for research and practice. *Psychology in the Schools*, 45(2), 158–176. DOI: 10.1002/pits.20282

Rodríguez, R. L. (2022). Engaging future engineers: The case study of a serious game implementation. *Education and Information Technologies*, 1–31.

Ryan, R. M., & Deci, E. L. (2000). Self-determination theory and the facilitation of intrinsic motivation, social development, and well-being. *The American Psychologist*, 55(1), 68–78. DOI: 10.1037/0003-066X.55.1.68 PMID: 11392867

Ryan, R. M., & Deci, E. L. (2017). *Self-determination theory. Basic psychological needs in motivation, development and wellness.* The Guilford Press. DOI: 10.1521/978.14625/28806

Sanfilippo, F. A. (2017). Multi-sensor fusion framework for improving situational awareness in demanding maritime training. *Reliability Engineering & System Safety*, 161, 12–24. DOI: 10.1016/j.ress.2016.12.015

Sartini, S. (2020). Kahoot in Maritime English Teaching: Its Impact on Nautical Science Cadet's Oral Reproduction and Vocabulary. *English Language Teaching Educational Journal*, 3(1), 41–51. DOI: 10.12928/eltej.v3i1.1667

Sharma, A., Kim, T. E., & Nazir, S. (2021). Implications of Automation and Digitalization for Maritime Education and Training. In *Sustainability in the Maritime Domain* (pp. 223–233). Springer. DOI: 10.1007/978-3-030-69325-1_11

Silva, F. G. (2020). Practical methodology for the design of educational serious games. *Information (Basel)*, 11(1), 1–13. DOI: 10.3390/info11010014

Steenbeek, J., Romagnoni, G., Bentley, J., Heymans, J. J., Serpetti, N., Gonçalves, M., Santos, C., Warmelink, H., Mayer, I., Keijser, X., Fairgrieve, R., & Abspoel, L. (2020). Combining ecosystem modeling with serious gaming in support of transboundary maritime spatial planning. *Ecology and Society*, 25(2), art21. DOI: 10.5751/ES-11580-250221

Tribaldos, T., & Schneider, F. (2021). Enabling players to develop theories of change for sustainable development: A serious game. *Simulation & Gaming*, 52(5), 664–678. DOI: 10.1177/10468781211022399

Türkistanli, T. T., & Kuleyin, B. (2022). Game-based learning for better decision-making: A collision prevention training for maritime transportation engineering students. *Computer Applications in Engineering Education*, 30(3), 917–933. DOI: 10.1002/cae.22494

Turner, P. E., Johnston, E., Kebritchi, M., Evans, S., & Heflich, D. A. (2018). Influence of online computer games on the academic achievement of non-traditional undergraduate students. *Cogent Education*, 5(1), 1437671. DOI: 10.1080/2331186X.2018.1437671

Veronica, R., & Calvano, G. (2020). Promoting sustainable behavior using serious games: Seadventure for ocean literacy. *IEEE Access : Practical Innovations, Open Solutions*, 8, 196931–196939. DOI: 10.1109/ACCESS.2020.3034438

Vygotsky, L. (1978). *Mind in society. The development of higher psychological processes*. Harvard University Press.

Wang, Q., & Abbas, M. (2018). Designing web-games for transportation engineering education. *Computer Applications in Engineering Education*, 26(5), 1699–1710. DOI: 10.1002/cae.22031

Westera, W. (2015). Games are motivating, aren't they? Disputing the arguments for digital game-based learning. *International Journal of Serious Games*, 2(2). Advance online publication. DOI: 10.17083/ijsg.v2i2.58

Westera, W. (2019). Why and How Serious Games can Become Far More Effective: Accommodating Productive Learning Experiences, Learner Motivation and the Monitoring of Learning Gains. *Journal of Educational Technology & Society*, 22(1), 59–69.

Whaley, A. M. (2016). *Cognitive basis for human reliability analysis*. US Nuclear Regulatory Commission, Office of Nuclear Regulatory Research.

Xi, N., & Hamari, J. (2019). Does gamification satisfy needs? A study on the relationship between gamification features and intrinsic need satisfaction. *International Journal of Information Management, 46*, 210–221. https://doi.org/. ijinfomgt.2018.12.002.DOI: 10.1016/j

Ye, L., Zhou, X., Yang, S., & Hang, Y. (2022). Serious game design and learning effect verification supporting traditional pattern learning. *Interactive Learning Environments*, 1–15.

Yıldırım, İ., & Şen, S. (2021). The effects of gamification on students' academic achievement: A meta-analysis study. *Interactive Learning Environments*, 29(8), 1301–1318. DOI: 10.1080/10494820.2019.1636089

Zainuddin, Z., Shujahat, M., Haruna, H., & Chu, S. K. W. (2020). The role of gamified e-quizzes on student learning and engagement: An interactive gamification solution for a formative assessment system. *Computers & Education*, 145, 103729. DOI: 10.1016/j.compedu.2019.103729

KEY TERMS AND DEFİNİTİONS

Constructivist Learning Theory: The theory that explains that learning is an active process and effective learning takes place through actively constructing the knowledge instead of theoretically communicating it.

Educational Alignment: The conformity between objectives, instruction, and assessment of educational applications.

Experiential Learning Theory: The theory that put forwards that knowledge is learned as a result of personal experiences and interactions with the environment, instead of the instruction itself.

Gamification: Adding game features to a non-game content.

Serious Game: Games with educational purpose and not intended to be played primarily for amusement.

SIRE: (Ship Inspection Report). The programme started by the Oil Companies International Marine Forum (OCIMF) in 1993 for conducting inspections with the purpose of minimizing the risk on tanker ships.

STCW: (International Convention on Standards of Training, Certification and Watchkeeping). The primary convention that defines the standards for training, certification and watchkeeping in the maritime domain.

Section 6
"Not All That Glitters Is Gold": A Critical Perspective

Chapter 9
The Relationship as the Protagonist in Role-Playing Games

Angelo Stera
International Institute for Gestalt Therapy and Psychopathology (IPSIG), Italy

ABSTRACT

The idea for this analysis arises from the curiosity to circumscribe the phenomenon and better understand the critical issues just described, particularly how the evolution of digital technologies in recent years has radically transformed the world of work, redefining the very concept of professionalism. Among the most disruptive innovations, artificial intelligence and collaborative platforms stand out, offering new tools and modes of interaction that are revolutionizing the way people interact, work, and collaborate.

INTRODUCTION

We owe to J. L. Moreno (1934), the conception of the expression: role-playing. The term, in a broader sense, is part of the curative intervention combining psychotherapy and theater devised by the Romanian psychiatrist. Play represents an experiential function involving the individual within a group. At the basis of the game there are always two fundamental components: relationships and communication which generate interpersonal connections. *«Interpersonal connections shape the*

DOI: 10.4018/979-8-3693-1172-1.ch009

mind by facilitating the emergence of new states within interactions with others» (Siegel, 2013).

In a world where communication is one of the most important elements of human life, where it is impossible not to communicate, it is interesting to observe how people interact with each other using this rich and powerful tool, increasingly mediated by pervasive technology. A word, a glance, a gesture, or even a whole body conveys much more than simple information. Through communication, each individual tells their own story while simultaneously "nourishing" themselves with the stories of others, in a continuous exchange of ideas, thoughts, and emotions. In a broader sense, we can affirm that communication has contributed to making human history, as people have always traveled alongside a combined vector of communication and discoveries.

In the last thirty years, we have witnessed significant changes due to a rapid transformative process in technology, particularly in the evolution of computers. Between the late 1980s and early 1990s, universities, companies, and even ordinary people began to connect via the Internet. The widespread adoption of the Internet and the integration of various tools—phone, PC, radio, television, etc.—gave rise to what we now commonly call digital devices. These increasingly advanced and multifunctional devices have become an integral part of our lives to such an extent that Canadian sociologist Marshall McLuhan described them as "an extension of the senses" that influence our sensory experience by altering our relationship with the surrounding environment (McLuhan, 1967).

The advent of social networks has renewed the interaction between web users and information technologies. All these transformations undoubtedly affect each of us, for better or worse, altering our subjectivity, intersubjectivity, corporeality, and perception of reality. New frontiers have emerged: blockchain, augmented reality, and the metaverse, artificial intelligence (AI), new places in which to talk about oneself, in which to listen to others, in which to gain experience. «These technologies are like «a rhizomatic organism that is made up of countless machines, both social techniques – the structures in which we live and that give us shelter, both in a physical and psychological sense» (Floridi & Cabitza, 2021).

New forms of learning have also developed, among which the most significant are:

- Online Learning (E-learning)
- Mobile Learning (M-learning)
- Artificial Intelligence-Based Learning (AI)
- Immersive Learning (Virtual and Augmented Reality)
- Microlearning
- Gamification
- Collaborative Online Learning

- Data-Driven Learning (Learning Analytics)
- Personalized Learning
- MOOCs (Massive Open Online Courses)
- Blended Learning

All of this has altered the ways of individual, social, and professional interaction. The use of digital tools has spread on a global scale, without distinction of gender, age, culture, educational level, or social class. The involvement is global. This inevitably prompts reflection and perhaps sociocultural reorganization. Various disciplines are called upon to study this phenomenon, including computer science, mathematics, engineering, ergonomics, cognitive and social sciences, sociology, and others. It is also a field of interest for psychology, which has recently introduced a new specialization called "cyberpsychology." This discipline studies digital natives, the hyperconnected generation, the "mobile born," who, according to recent brain imaging studies, develop certain areas of the brain in a completely unique way.

Not everything is positive; the web presents several critical issues: the domestication of the masses, the excess of information that often turns into misinformation, privacy protection, loss of contact with reality, isolation, cyberbullying, voyeurism, deepfakes, the dark web, and more.

The idea for this analysis arises from the curiosity to circumscribe the phenomenon and better understand the critical issues just described, particularly how the evolution of digital technologies in recent years has radically transformed the world of work, redefining the very concept of professionalism. Among the most disruptive innovations, artificial intelligence and collaborative platforms stand out, offering new tools and modes of interaction that are revolutionizing the way people interact, work, and collaborate. Platforms like Microsoft Teams, Slack, Asana, and Trello, to name a few, have enabled an unprecedented level of coordination and communication, integrating project management, document sharing, and real-time teamwork. These tools allow professionals to collaborate effectively, overcoming geographical and temporal barriers. This change has not only "increased operational efficiency" but has also profoundly impacted individuals' professional lives, promoting a more flexible, connected, and collaborative work culture. The adoption of these platforms is reshaping internal dynamics within organizations, posing new challenges and opportunities for today's professionals.

The primary focus of this work is the observation of the relationship between technology and the user (individual aspects) and between technology and interacting groups (social aspects). My interest is particularly centered on how Relationships, which are the protagonists in role-playing games and dynamics between human beings, are the *conditio sine qua non* for the activation of the game itself: without relationships, without exchange, the game does not exist. It is now evident that even relational games—mediated by digital tools—are increasingly influenced by the use of artificial intelligence.

This paper deals only superficially with the technical aspect of technological innovations in order to delve more deeply into the human and relational aspects. The critical points analyzed will therefore have a decidedly narrow scope. The concluding part of this paper proposes some suggestions for improving the quality of communication and relational games through the use of these tools.

BACKGROUND

Collaborative platforms have become essential for modern organizations, facilitating communication and project management in increasingly dynamic and complex work environments. Among the most significant advantages, in my opinion, is the implementation of specific devices and software that enable people with disabilities to actively participate in the world of education and work, reducing deficits and generating greater inclusivity compared to the past, *«machines that can perform cognitive tasks are even more important than machines that can perform physical ones»* (Brynjolfsson & McAffee, 2014).

Recently, the integration of artificial intelligence (AI) into these platforms has ushered in a new era of efficiency and automation, further expanding the potential of collaborative work. AI is transforming how people interact with these tools, improving task organization, information management, and decision-making processes. However, like any technological innovation, the introduction of AI presents both significant benefits and challenges that must be carefully considered.

AI has been integrated into many leading collaborative platforms, such as Microsoft Teams, Slack, and Asana, offering advanced features that go beyond traditional management and communication capabilities. These include virtual assistants, predictive analytics, workflow automation, natural language recognition tools, simultaneous translators, augmentative and alternative communication (AAC) systems, etc. These technologies are changing the context of platform usage, making them not only smarter but also more inclusive and proactive in supporting work teams.

Below is a brief list of the main advantages of AI integration:

- **Automation of Repetitive Tasks**: AI enables the automation of repetitive tasks such as task assignment, deadline tracking, and workflow management. The benefit for employees is that it allows them to focus on more strategic and creative activities.
- **Productivity Improvement**: With AI, collaborative platforms can analyze work data and provide intelligent suggestions to enhance efficiency. For ex-

ample, virtual assistants can propose the best sequence of tasks to follow or identify potential bottlenecks in the workflow.

- **Personalization of User Experience**: AI can tailor the interface and features of platforms to the specific needs of users, offering personalized suggestions and optimizing the work environment based on individual habits and preferences.
- **Advanced Analytics and Insights**: AI can collect and analyze large amounts of data generated from interactions within collaborative platforms, providing useful insights for continuous improvement. This data can help managers make more informed decisions and predict future trends.
- **Improved Communication and Language Understanding**: Thanks to natural language recognition and automatic translation, AI facilitates communication among global teams, overcoming language barriers and enhancing mutual understanding. Collaborative platforms offer an integrated environment where teams can communicate more effectively, surpassing the limitations of traditional emails. Tools like Slack and Microsoft Teams enable organized conversations by channels, promoting clear communication accessible to all team members.
- **Operational Efficiency**: Tools like Asana and Trello enable more structured project management, with the ability to assign tasks, track progress, and meet deadlines. This increases operational efficiency, reducing the risk of errors and improving the transparency of ongoing activities.
- **Flexibility and Accessibility**: Collaborative platforms are accessible from any internet-connected device, allowing employees to work from anywhere and at any time. This is particularly advantageous for companies adopting hybrid or fully remote work models.
- **Integration of Tools and Resources**: Many collaborative platforms offer integrations with other business tools such as CRM, document management software, and calendars, centralizing resources and facilitating information management.

Alongside the advantages, there are also some disadvantages:

- **Privacy and Data Security Concerns**: AI requires access to large amounts of data to function effectively, raising concerns about privacy and information security. Inadequate data management can lead to privacy breaches and legal risks. Storing sensitive data on online platforms exposes organizations to potential security risks. Data breaches or unauthorized access to confidential information can have severe legal and financial consequences.

- **Information Overload and Complexity**: The introduction of AI features can make platforms more complex to use. Users may feel overwhelmed by the amount of data analyzed and notifications generated by AI, leading to distractions and decreased productivity.
- **Dependency on Technology and Loss of Control**: Advanced automation can lead to excessive dependence on technology, reducing users' ability to manage tasks manually or intervene in unexpected situations. This could diminish human control over critical decisions.
- **Artificial Intelligence Bias**: AI can introduce bias into decision-making processes if the data it relies on is skewed or if the algorithms are not adequately designed. This can lead to unfair or discriminatory decisions, compromising the integrity of collaborative work.
- **Implementation and Maintenance Costs**: Integrating AI into collaborative platforms can involve significant costs, both in terms of implementation and maintenance. Companies must invest in technological infrastructure and staff training to fully exploit these technologies.
- **Dependency on Technology**: The intensive adoption of collaborative platforms can create a dependency on technology, making potential malfunctions, service interruptions, or access difficulties problematic. Additionally, the lack of paper or offline alternatives can be an issue in emergency situations.
- **Information Overload**: With the growing amount of communications and notifications from different platforms, employees may feel overwhelmed, risking distractions and reduced productivity. Managing the flow of information thus becomes a crucial challenge.
- **Resistance to Change and Learning Curve**: Introducing new platforms may encounter resistance from employees, especially if they are not accustomed to working with digital tools. The learning curve associated with adopting new systems can slow down initial operations and require investments in training.

Critical Perspectives

Beyond the advantages and disadvantages that unstoppable technology can bring, I believe it is useful to develop critical thinking, focusing on the effects these changes have on individuals, workgroups, organizations, and human relationships in general.

The underlying idea of this contribution is to go beyond the technical-practical vision that analyzes technology in an engineering manner and in terms of potential, leaving in the background those purely human and relational aspects that are equally important. In my opinion, there is an imbalance that needs to be rebalanced between research aimed at developing disruptive technologies and research focused on user well-being. While investments and interest in developing these technologies continue to grow, there remains a significant gap in understanding their impact on people, *«in the short term, companies will still need real employees to satisfy customers and ensure economic success»* (Brynjolfsson & McAffee, 2014).

A recent survey, conducted and published by the American Psychology Association (2023)[1], highlights the growing concern among American workers about the spread of AI. This new form of fear, specifically termed AI Anxiety, is generating the development of widespread psychological and emotional malaise. The main fear for workers is that they will be obsolete and useless and consequently easily replaced by technology. The survey recorded that 64 percent of people surveyed manifest this form of AI Anxiety. As a related effect, irritability toward colleagues or customers (23% vs. 16% of those who worry about AI); lack of motivation (33% vs. 21%); and feeling of emotional exhaustion (37% vs. 27%) are highlighted. In addition, many workers feel less satisfied and loyal to the company and do not rule out seeking new employment.

An overly stressed and struggling worker generates a negative cost for any organization. In recent years, many psycho-emotional disorders have emerged, originating from the pervasive use of continuously developing digital technology, not only in terms of speed and computing power but also in terms of pervasiveness in users' private lives.

The instant nature of global communication has catapulted humanity into a reality where everything happens in real-time, exerting increasing pressure on the psycho-emotional dimension. How does each individual user manage these rapid and continuous transformations? What are the effects on the mind and emotions? Does a boundary between professional and private life still exist? Among the many critical issues, the anxiety of instantaneity is evident: the need to monitor and immediately respond to messages, emails, and notifications generates a constant sense of urgency, leading to increased stress and anxiety. This phenomenon, known as information overload or infobesity, creates constant pressure on the ability to process information and make decisions, negatively impacting emotional well-being, *«the process of modeling and progressive adaptation required by interaction with a new medium is never without difficulty.* Bolter and Gruisin (1996) called this process remediation: *on the one hand the new medium imitates some traits of the old; on the other hand it presents itself, explicitly or implicitly, as an improvement or overcoming"* (Riva, 2004).

On a daily basis, we use the Internet to browse for information that we need concretely or more simply for entertainment. The web is a vast space in which it is easy to "get lost" falling into the trap of information overload. The flood of stimuli to which browsing subjects us often becomes difficult to govern with lucid awareness.

As early as the 1980s, American psychologist Craig Brod coined the term Technostress to describe the disorder caused by the inability to handle modern information technology in a healthy manner. Technostress can be considered as *«the stress that users experience due to application multitasking, constant connectivity, information overload, frequent system updates, continuous learning and the resulting insecurities inherent to work and technical problems related to the organizational use of ICT"»* (Tarafdar, Tu, Ragu-Nathan & Ragu-Nathan, 2007). With this book, the author explores for the first time the topic of stress resulting from the use of technologies and its psycho-physiological impact. The study was helpful in describing the sense of fatigue and tiredness to which today are added as effects: information overload, hyperconnectivity, dependence on digital devices, and fear of losing important information or being outclassed or replaced by technology. In recent years, the number of studies investigating the impact of new technologies on mental health and well-being has grown, with a focus on the young and the elderly.

One of the most concerning side effects is the decline in attentional capacity. The speed with which technology bombards us with stimuli significantly impacts our ability to concentrate. Continuous exposure to notifications, social media updates, and fragmented online content has drastically reduced the ability to maintain focus on a task for extended periods. This decline in attention not only affects productivity but also fuels a sense of frustration and dissatisfaction, as it seems we can never complete what we set out to do. All of this also has negative consequences on interpersonal relationships. Conversations are reduced to quick exchanges of messages, depriving human interactions of their richer emotional context. This can lead to a sense of isolation, even when we are constantly in contact with others, as that level of empathetic connection that characterizes face-to-face relationships is lacking.

In virtual communication, individuals are freed from bodily constraints, losing parts of important and sometimes essential information for understanding messages. Users become "disembodied," with the medium partially replacing the expressive aspects of the body, offering instead a virtual representation made up of fragmented images and narratives capable of generating inevitable and dangerous emotional illiteracy.

Giuseppe Riva, professor of Communication Psychology at the Catholic University of Milan, where he directs LICENT - Laboratory for the Study of Communicative Interaction and New Technologies, argues that a subject becomes "disembodied" when "the physicality of the body is replaced by that of the medium. More precisely, the physicality and immediacy of the real body are replaced by a virtual body" (Riva, 2004). The use of collaborative platforms further contributes to disembodying relationships between people. Working remotely in asynchronous mode is an advantage for those, for example, working from countries with different time zones, but it is a disadvantage for relationships since each person contributes to the activity in complete solitude. Of course, all platforms ensure the possibility of working synchronously on the same project, but even in this mode, communication between individuals is less rich.

Below are some advantages and disadvantages of both modes:

Advantages of Synchronous Work

- **Immediate Communication**: The ability to interact in real-time allows for clarifying doubts, making quick decisions, and solving problems immediately. This can be particularly useful for strategic meetings or brainstorming sessions.
- **Greater Team Engagement**: Synchronous work promotes a sense of belonging and cohesion within the team, as all members are simultaneously involved in discussions and activities.
- **Instant Feedback**: In a synchronous environment, participants can receive and provide immediate feedback, helping to maintain a high work pace and quickly correct any errors or misunderstandings.

Disadvantages of Synchronous Work

- **Limited Flexibility**: Synchronous work requires all team members to be available at the same time, which can be challenging to manage in teams distributed across multiple time zones or with flexible work hours.
- **Frequent Interruptions**: The need to be available in real-time can lead to frequent interruptions, reducing concentration and productivity, especially in tasks that require a high level of attention.
- **Stress and Time Pressure**: The need to respond immediately can generate stress and anxiety, especially in high-intensity work environments where a quick response to any communication is required.

Advantages of Asynchronous Work

- **Flexibility and Autonomy:** Asynchronous work allows team members to manage their time autonomously, enabling them to work during their peak productivity periods or at times that are most convenient for them.
- **Better Time Management:** Without the need to attend continuous meetings, workers can organize their time more efficiently, dedicating uninterrupted blocks of time to tasks that require deep concentration.

- **Access to Global Talent:** Asynchronous work facilitates collaboration among teams distributed globally, as there is no need to coordinate work schedules across different time zones.

Disadvantages of Asynchronous Work

- **Slower Communication:** The lack of real-time interaction can slow down communication and problem-solving, as responses may take hours or even days.
- **Social Isolation:** Working asynchronously can lead to a sense of isolation, as there is a lack of direct and immediate interaction with colleagues, which can reduce the sense of belonging to the team.
- **Risk of Miscommunication:** Written or delayed communication can lead to misunderstandings or misinterpretations, as it is not always possible to immediately clarify doubts or accurately interpret tone and context.

This brief overview of the advantages and disadvantages highlights another critical issue: one of the key differences between traditional and virtual communication is sensory contact, especially involving the body. In feedback, the presence or absence of the body generates substantial communicative differences. Thanks to McLuhan's studies (1967), we know that digital tools alter the relationship between the senses, influence mental functioning, and modify the perception of reality. Another critical aspect to consider is the loss of time for shared reflection. Constant immersion in technology leaves little room for contemplation and introspection. This can lead to a disconnection from our ability to engage in critical thinking, which requires extended time and dedicated spaces. Without moments for pause and reflection, we risk living in a constant state of cognitive and emotional superficiality.

Emerging Evidence

Reflecting on the initial idea that inspired the writing of this article—namely, that every relationship is essentially a role-playing game, and as such, becomes the comfortable and uncomfortable Protagonist of every social interaction—let's consider what happens in relationships mediated by collaborative platforms.

Whether it's an intimate, private relationship or a professional one, each individual, as a social actor/user, inevitably finds themselves playing a role where the success or failure of any project or goal is heavily influenced by the quality and intensity of the relationship. This is the critical point. How can we restore the quality and intensity in relationships mediated by digital devices, and specifically by collaborative platforms? Distance, speed, and hyperconnectivity do not help; in fact, they often "contaminate" communication quality, generating entropy.

In my opinion, a mistaken belief is the idea that in a professional context, one only needs to focus on being prepared, organized, and efficient. With these ingredients, the quality of the relationship is guaranteed. However, the human being is much more complex; emotions, sensations, and desires constantly move within us, extending far beyond rationality. This happens even in the most cold and detached individuals. Perhaps, in a somewhat forced manner, we could say that human and "intimate" relationships are the basic ingredient for activating a personal and professional game in which the rules are often unclear and need to be constantly nurtured and renegotiated.

Eric Berne (1958), the father of Transactional Analysis, published a very interesting book in 1964 titled *Games People Play*, which quickly became a classic in psychology. Through his insights and studies, Berne developed a new orientation in psychotherapy towards the end of the 1950s. This model is still used today as a tool for reading, understanding, and interpreting human relationships. The innovation was the introduction of the term "game" to express, in a simple and comprehensible way, the position and role a person, consciously or unconsciously, takes in relation to themselves, their environment, or another individual.

Transactional analysis, as both a method and theory, allows those who practice it to identify the role they tend to repeat in the game, thereby laying the foundation for a critical autonomy from these mechanisms, and perhaps for liberation.

While the studies and considerations of the past remain valid, it is interesting to critically observe how technologies have modified, are modifying, and will modify Relationships within these games. Perhaps rather than the word "modify," it would be more useful to use the word "condition." The significant conditioning is due to the disruptive impact that the introduction and use of platforms and devices for almost all activities have had on the world of work in recent years. What are the advantages and disadvantages? What effect do they have on the concept of inclusion? What effect do they produce on the quality of relationships? These are the recurring questions that should guide us in observing this phenomenon. To do so, I propose using the Negative Capability Map (Fig.1)

Figure 1. Negative capability map (Author elaboration from De Sario, 2010)

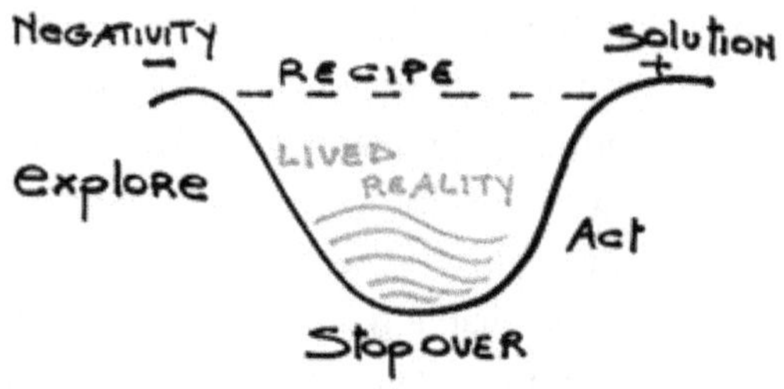

The invention of this map is credited to social psychologist Pino De Sario, who teaches the course in Mediation Communication at the University of Pisa. De Sario views negativity not only as a disturbance but also as a resource, asserting that: "Negative capability is that distinctive quality of accepting moments of indeterminacy and discomfort and recognizing their potential for understanding and action, developing skills in vigilant exploration, capable of investigating and processing emotional and operational content. The strategic importance lies in welcoming, containing, and transforming" (De Sario, 2010).

I find that this definition of "negativity" contains the necessary ingredients to objectively and subjectively observe and understand the challenges that arise from using collaborative platforms, and more broadly, any digital device. Simply put, De Sario's advice is as follows: let's expand the time for human interaction and communication, listen to each other more, give space to feelings and emotions, and respect our nature as human beings. Furthermore, starting from Marshall McLuhan's axiom "the medium is the message" and working with the ingredients proposed by Prof. De Sario—observation, acceptance in the sense of acknowledgment, containment with the idea of being present and aware in usage, and transformation with the idea of recovering and integrating those human aspects that ensure communicative quality—I believe it is possible to imagine a more conscious and ecological use of these systems, and consequently, an improvement in the quality of those relational "games" that always underlie any human relationship, both personal and professional.

CONCLUSION

In-depth analysis of the issue at hand undoubtedly requires further space for further study. In summary, it can be argued that professional and personal interactions mediated by collaborative platforms exert a significant and transformative impact on contemporary society. However, the currently available research devoted to exploring the effects of such platforms on individuals determines a potentially dangerous knowledge gap. Filling that gap requires a multidisciplinary and shared effort aimed at placing human well-being in all its facets at the center of inquiry. Only through such an approach will it be possible to ensure that technological innovations contribute to a future characterized by equity and sustainability for the entire community.

REFERENCES

Berne, E. (1958). Transactional analysis: A new and effective method of group therapy. *American Journal of Psychotherapy*, 12(4), 735–743. DOI: 10.1176/appi.psychotherapy.1958.12.4.735 PMID: 13583264

Bolter, J. D., & Grusin, R. A. (1996). Remediation. *Configurations*, 4(3), 311–358. DOI: 10.1353/con.1996.0018

Brod, C. (1984). *Technostress: the human cost of computer revolution*. Academic Press.

Brynjolfsson, E., & Mcafee, A. (2015). *La nuova rivoluzione delle macchine*. Feltrinelli.

Floridi, L., & Cabitza, F. (2021). *Intelligenza artificiale -L'uso delle nuove macchine*. Bompiani.

McLuhan, M. (1967). *Gli strumenti del comunicare*. Il Saggiatore.

Moreno, J. L. (1934). Who shall survive? A new approach to the problem of human interrelations.

Riva G. (2004), *Psicologia dei nuovi media*, Milano: il Mulino.

Siegel, D. J. (2013). *La mente relazionale*. Raffaello Cortina.

Tarafdar, M., Tu, Q., Ragu-Nathan, B. S., & Ragu-Nathan, T. S. (2007). The impact of technostress on role stress and productivity. *Journal of Management Information Systems*, 24(1), 304–305. DOI: 10.2753/MIS0742-1222240109

ENDNOTE

1 Retrieved from: https://www.apa.org/pubs/reports/work-in-america/2023-work-america-ai-monitoring

Compilation of References

Abeza, G., & O'Reilly, N. (2014). Social media platforms' use in building stakeholder relationships: The case of national sport organizations. *Journal of Applied Sport Management*, 6(3), 10.

Abt, C. C. (1970). Serious games. Viking press.

Abt, C. C. (1970). *Serious Games*. Viking Press.

Abt, C. C. (1987). *Serious games*. University Press of America.

Abuladze, L. (2023). Use of Gamification in Employee Training and Development. DOI: 10.53465/EDAMBA.2022.9788022550420.1-10

Adams, C. A., & Abhayawansa, S. (2022). Connecting the COVID-19 pandemic, environmental, social and governance (ESG) investing and calls for 'harmonisation'of sustainability reporting. *Critical Perspectives on Accounting*, 82, 102309. DOI: 10.1016/j.cpa.2021.102309

Adeabah, D., Gyeke-Dako, A., & Andoh, C. (2019). Board gender diversity, corporate governance and bank efficiency in Ghana: A two-stage data envelope analysis (DEA) approach. Corporate Governance. *Corporate Governance (Bradford)*, 19(2), 299–320. DOI: 10.1108/CG-08-2017-0171

Afolabi, H., Ram, R., & Rimmel, G. (2022). Harmonization of sustainability reporting regulation: Analysis of a contested arena. *Sustainability (Basel)*, 14(9), 5517. DOI: 10.3390/su14095517

Afyouni, I., Rehman, F. U., Qamar, A. M., Ghani, S., Hussain, S. O., Sadiq, B., Rahman, M. A., Murad, A., & Basalamah, S. (2017). A therapy-driven gamification framework for hand rehabilitation. *User Modeling and User-Adapted Interaction, 27*(2), 215–265. Advance online publication. DOI: 10.1007/s11257-017-9191-4

Aggrawal, S., & Boowuo, H. (2023). Enhancing Teamwork Through Games: A Systematic Literature Review. *Proc. Front. Educ. Conf. FIE*. DOI: 10.1109/FIE58773.2023.10343284

Ahmad, S. J., O'Regan, N., & Ghobadian, A. (2005). Leadership, decision making and internal stakeholder engagement. *International Journal of Management and Decision Making*, 6(3-4), 345–358. DOI: 10.1504/IJMDM.2005.006559

Aini, Q. (2019). Understanding How Gamification Influences Behaviour in Education. *International Journal of Advanced Trends in Computer Science and Engineering, 8*(1.5), 269–274. DOI: 10.30534/ijatcse/2019/4781.52019

Aini, Q., Azizah, N., Salam, R., Santoso, N. P. L., & Millah, S. (2022). iLearning Education Based on Gamification Blockchain. *Indonesian Journal of Electrical Engineering and Computer Science*, 26(1), 531. DOI: 10.11591/ijeecs.v26.i1.pp531-538

Aini, Q., Lutfiani, N., & Zahran, M. S. (2021). Gamification based on blockchain technology to enhance student centered learning. *CCIT Journal*, 14(1), 100–110. DOI: 10.33050/ccit.v14i1.1268

Ainscow, M. (2020). Promoting inclusion and equity in education: Lessons from international experiences. *Nordic Journal of Studies in Educational Policy*, 6(1), 7–16. DOI: 10.1080/20020317.2020.1729587

Akyuz, E., & Celik, E. (2018). The role of human factor in maritime environment risk assessment: A practical application on Ballast Water Treatment (BWT) system in ship. *Human and Ecological Risk Assessment*, 24(3), 653–666. DOI: 10.1080/10807039.2017.1396184

Alessi, S. M., & Trollip, S. R. (1984). *Computer-based instruction: Methods and development*. Prentice-Hall, Inc.

Alföldi-Rosenbaum, E. (1971). *The finger calculus in antiquity and in the Middle Ages: Studies on Roman game counters I*. Walter de Gruyter.

All, A., Plovie, B., Nunez Castellar, E. P., & Van Looy, J. (2017). Pre-test influences on the effectiveness of digital-game based learning: A case study of a fire safety game. *Computers & Education, 114*, 24–37. https://doi.org/.compedu.2017.05.018 .DOI: 10.1016/j

All, A., Castellar, E. P. N., & Van Looy, J. (2014). Measuring effectiveness in digital game-based learning: A methodological review. *International Journal of Serious Games*, 1(2). Advance online publication. DOI: 10.17083/ijsg.v1i2.18

All, A., Castellar, E. P. N., & Van Looy, J. (2015). Towards a conceptual framework for assessing the effectiveness of digital game-based learning. *Computers & Education*, 88, 29–37. DOI: 10.1016/j.compedu.2015.04.012

Almuhailib, B., & Al-Ahdal, A. A. M. H. (2021). Learner-Centered Teaching in Saudi Context: Exploring the challenges from pre-service EFL teachers' perspective. *Journal of Positive Psychology and Wellbeing*, 5(4), 1170–1181.

Alon, I., & Herath, R. K. (2014). Teaching international business via social media projects. *Journal of Teaching in International Business, 25*(1), 44-59.

Alonso-Martínez, D., Jiménez-Parra, B., González-Álvarez, N., Godos-Díez, J. L., & Cabeza-García, L. (2019). Taking advantage of students' passion for apps in sustainability and CSR teaching. *Sustainability (Basel)*, 11(3), 779. DOI: 10.3390/su11030779

AlSaad, F. M., & Durugbo, C. M. (2021). Gamification-as-innovation: A review. *International Journal on Management of Innovation & Technology*, 18(05), 2130002. DOI: 10.1142/S0219877021300020

Alsawaier, R. S. (2018). The effect of gamification on motivation and engagement. The International Journal of Information and Learning Technology, 35(1), 56-79.

Al-Smadi, M. (2014). Gameducation: using gamification techniques to engage learners in online learning. *European Summit on Immersive Education*, 85-97.

Amory, A., Naicker, K., Vincent, J., & Adams, C. (1999). The use of computer games as an educational tool: Identification of appropriate game types and game elements. *British Journal of Educational Technology*, 30(4), 311–321. DOI: 10.1111/1467-8535.00121

Amory, A., & Seagram, R. (2003). Educational game models: conceptualization and evaluation: the practice of higher education. *South African Journal of Higher Education*, 17(2), 206–217.

Ampatzidou, C., & Gugerell, K. (2018). Participatory Game Prototyping – Balancing Domain Content and Playability in a Serious Game Design for the Energy Transition. *CoDesign*, 15(4), 345–360. DOI: 10.1080/15710882.2018.1504084

Amran, A., Jalil, H. A., Muhamad, M., & Nasharuddin, N. A. (2021). Factors Contributing to Collaborative Game-Based Learning (CGBL) Effectiveness. *Asian Social Science, 17*(11). DOI: 10.5539/ass.v17n11p1

Anand, R., & Winters, M.-F. (2008). A Retrospective View of Corporate Diversity Training From 1964 to the Present. *Academy of Management Learning & Education*, 7(3), 356–372. DOI: 10.5465/amle.2008.34251673

Andersen, R., & Rustad, M. (2022). Using Minecraft as an educational tool for supporting collaboration as a 21st century skill. *Computers and Education Open*, 3, 100094. Advance online publication. DOI: 10.1016/j.caeo.2022.100094

Anderson, L. W. (2002). Curricular alignment: A re-examination. *Theory into Practice*, 41(4), 255–260. DOI: 10.1207/s15430421tip4104_9

Anderson, L. W., & Krathwohl, D. R. (2001). *A taxonomy for learning, teaching, and assessing: A revision of Bloom's taxonomy of educational objectives: complete edition*. Addison Wesley Longman, Inc.

Anderson, L. W., & Krathwohl, D. R. (Eds.). (2001). *A Taxonomy for Learning, Teaching, and Assessing: A Revision of Bloom's Taxonomy of Educational Objectives*. Addison Wesley Longman, Inc.

Andon, P., Chong, K. M., & Roebuck, P. (2010). Personality Preferences of Accounting and non-Accounting Graduates Seeking to Enter the Accounting Profession. *Critical Perspectives on Accounting*, 21(4), 253–265. DOI: 10.1016/j.cpa.2010.01.001

Andreoni, V., & Richard, A. (2023). Exploring the interconnected nature of the sustainable development goals: The 2030 SDGs Game as a pedagogical tool for interdisciplinary education. *International Journal of Sustainability in Higher Education*, 25(1), 21–42. DOI: 10.1108/IJSHE-11-2022-0378

Andreu-Cabrera, E., & González, M. C. (2010). Play and childhood in ancient Greece. *Journal of Human Sport and Exercise*, 5(3), 339–347. DOI: 10.4100/jhse.2010.53.04

Andrews, R. (2011). Social Capital and Public Service Performance: A Review of the Evidence. *Public Policy and Administration*, 27(1), 49–67. DOI: 10.1177/0952076710394399

Andrews, R., & Wankhade, P. (2014). Regional Variations in Emergency Service Performance: Does Social Capital Matter? *Regional Studies*, 49(12), 2037–2052. DOI: 10.1080/00343404.2014.891009

Angafor, G. N., Yevseyeva, I., & He, Y. (2020). Game-based learning: A review of tabletop exercises for cybersecurity incident response training. *Security and Privacy*, 3(6), e126. DOI: 10.1002/spy2.126

Annan-Diab, F. A., & Molinari, C. (2017). Interdisciplinarity: Practical approach to advancing education for sustainability and for the Sustainable Development Goals. *International Journal of Management Education*, 15(2), 73–83. DOI: 10.1016/j.ijme.2017.03.006

Ansell, C., & Gash, A. (2018). Collaborative platforms as a governance strategy. *Journal of Public Administration: Research and Theory*, 28(1), 16–32. DOI: 10.1093/jopart/mux030

Apostolakis, K. C., Kaza, K., Psaltis, A., Stefanidis, K., Thermos, S., Dimitropoulos, K., . . . Daras, P. (2016). Path of Trust: A prosocial co-op game for building up trustworthiness and teamwork. In Games and Learning Alliance: 4th International Conference, GALA 2015, Rome, Italy, December 9-11, 2015, Revised Selected Papers 4 (pp. 80-89). Springer International Publishing. DOI: 10.1007/978-3-319-40216-1_9

Argandoña, A. (1998). The stakeholder theory and the common good. *Journal of Business Ethics*, 17(9/10), 1093–1102. DOI: 10.1023/A:1006075517423

Arias Aranda, D., Bustinza Sánchez, O. F., & Djundubaev, R. (2016). Effects of gamified business simulations on entrepreneurial attitude at high school level. *Revista de Educacion, 2016*(371), 126–149. *Scopus*. Advance online publication. DOI: 10.4438/1988-592X-RE-2015-371-311

Armostrong, M. B., & Landers, R. N. (2018). Gamification of employee training and development. *International Journal of Training and Development*, 22(2), 162–169. DOI: 10.1111/ijtd.12124

Arnab, S., & Clarke, S. (2017). Towards a trans-disciplinary methodology for a game-based intervention development process. *British Journal of Educational Technology*, 48(2), 279–312. DOI: 10.1111/bjet.12377

Arnab, S., Walaszczyk, L., Lewis, M., Kernaghan-Andrews, S., Loizou, M., Masters, A., Calderwood, J., & Clarke, S. (2021). Designing mini-games as micro-learning resources for professional development in multi-cultural organisations. *Electronic Journal of e-Learning*, 19(2), 44–58. DOI: 10.34190/ejel.19.2.2141

Arslan, O., Aydemir, B., & Kececi, T. (2016, September). Review of Tanker Ship SIRE Inspection Findings in Turkey. *International Conference on Maritime Safety and Human Factors.*

Arthi, V., & Parman, J. (2021). Disease, downturns, and wellbeing: Economic history and the long-run impacts of COVID-19. *Explorations in Economic History*, 79, 101381. DOI: 10.1016/j.eeh.2020.101381 PMID: 33162564

Ashforth, B. E., & Humphrey, R. H. (1993). Emotional Labor in Service Roles: The Influence of Identity. *Academy of Management Review*, 18(1), 88–115. https://www.jstor.org/stable/258824. DOI: 10.2307/258824

Attanasio, G., Preghenella, N., De Toni, A. F., & Battistella, C. (2022). Stakeholder engagement in business models for sustainability: The stakeholder value flow model for sustainable development. *Business Strategy and the Environment*, 31(3), 860–874. DOI: 10.1002/bse.2922

Aureli, S. (2008). *La gestione delle differenze culturali nell'attività di impresa*. Giappichelli.

Ayala, I., Cuenca-Amigo, M., & Cuenca, J. (2020). Examining the state of the art of audience development in museums and heritage organisations: A Systematic Literature review. *Museum Management and Curatorship*, 35(3), 306–327. DOI: 10.1080/09647775.2019.1698312

Badal, S., & Harter, J. K. (2014). Gender diversity, business-unit engagement, and performance. *Journal of Leadership & Organizational Studies*, 21(4), 354–365. DOI: 10.1177/1548051813504460

Baecher-Lind, L., Sutton, J. M., Bhargava, R., Chen, K. T., Fleming, A., Morgan, H., Morosky, C. M., Schaffir, J., Sonn, T., Royce, C., Stephenson-Famy, A., & Sims, S. M. (2023). Strategies to Create a More Gender Identity Inclusive Learning Environment in Preclinical and Clinical Medical Education. *Academic Medicine*, 98(12), 1351–1355. DOI: 10.1097/ACM.0000000000005334 PMID: 37478137

Bagozzi, R. P., & Kimmel, S. K. (1995). A comparison of leading theories for the prediction of goal-directed behaviours. *British Journal of Social Psychology*, 34(4), 437–461. DOI: 10.1111/j.2044-8309.1995.tb01076.x

Bai, S., Hew, K. F., & Huang, B. (2020). Does gamification improve student learning outcome? Evidence from a meta-analysis and synthesis of qualitative data in educational contexts. *Educational Research Review*, 30, 100322. DOI: 10.1016/j.edurev.2020.100322

Bakker, A. B. (2011). An evidence-based model of work engagement. *Current Directions in Psychological Science*, 20(4), 265–269. DOI: 10.1177/0963721411414534

Bakker, A. B., & Demerouti, E. (2007). The job demands-resources model: State of the art. *Journal of Managerial Psychology*, 22(3), 309–328. DOI: 10.1108/02683940710733115

Baldissin, N., De Toni, A. F., & Nonino, F. (2007). Evolution of the management games: Towards the massive multiplayer online role-playing game. *Learning with Games*, 9-16.

Baldissin, N., De Toni, A. F., & Nonino, F. (2013). What is a Business Game? Historical background and evolution of business games in serious games context. *Business game-based learning in management education, 3.*

Bandura, A. (1982). Self-efficacy mechanism in human agency. *The American Psychologist*, 37(2), 122–147. DOI: 10.1037/0003-066X.37.2.122

Bandura, A. (1986). *Social foundations of thought and action.*

Baptista, G., & Oliveira, T. (2017). Why So Serious? Gamification Impact in the Acceptance of Mobile Banking Services. *Internet Research*, 27(1), 118–139. DOI: 10.1108/IntR-10-2015-0295

Bapuji, H., Ertug, G., Soundararajan, V., & Shaw, J. D. (2024). Invisible Inequalities: Barriers, Challenges, and Opportunities. *Journal of Management*, 50(3), 835–848. DOI: 10.1177/01492063231205294

Barnabè, F., Armenia, S., Nazir, S., & Pompei, A. (2023). Critical Thinking Skills Enhancement through System Dynamics-Based Games: Insights from the Project Management Board Game Project. *Systems*, 11(11), 554. DOI: 10.3390/systems11110554

Batish, A., Gordon, A., Kepler, J. D., Larcker, D. F., Tayan, B., & Yu, C. (2021). Human Capital Disclosure: What Do Companies Say About Their 'Most Important Asset'? Rock Center for Corporate Governance at Stanford University Working Paper Forthcoming.

Bauman, Z. (2013). Liquid modernity. John Wiley & Sons.

Bax, K. (2023). Do diverse and inclusive workplaces benefit investors? An Empirical Analysis on Europe and the United States. *Finance Research Letters*, 52, 103509. DOI: 10.1016/j.frl.2022.103509

Baxter, R. J., Holderness, D. K.Jr, & Wood, D. A. (2017). The effects of gamification on corporate compliance training: A partial replication and field study of true office anti-corruption training programs. *Journal of Financial Accounting Research*, 2(1), A20–A30. DOI: 10.2308/jfar-51725

Bear, S., Rahman, N., & Post, C. (2010). The impact of board diversity and gender composition on corporate social responsibility and firm reputation. *Journal of Business Ethics*, 97(2), 207–221. DOI: 10.1007/s10551-010-0505-2

Beauchamp, G., & Kennewell, S. (2010). Interactivity in the classroom and its impact on learning. *Computers & Education*, 54(3), 759–766. DOI: 10.1016/j.compedu.2009.09.033

Becker, G. S. (2009). *Human capital: A theoretical and empirical analysis, with special reference to education*. University of Chicago press.

Becker, M. (1967). *The ancient Roman world*. Holt, Rinehart and Winston.

Behl, A., Pereira, V., Sindhwani, R., Bhardwaj, S., Papa, A., & Hassan, Y. (2022). Improving Inclusivity of Digitalization for Employees in Emerging Countries Using Gamification. *IEEE Transactions on Engineering Management*, 1–15. Advance online publication. DOI: 10.1109/TEM.2022.3216553

Bell, R. (1979). *Board and table games from many civilizations*. Oxford University Press.

Beltadze, G. N. (2016). Game theory-basis of higher education and teaching organization. *International Journal of Modern Education and Computer Science*, 8(6), 41. DOI: 10.5815/ijmecs.2016.06.06

Benkhedda, S., & Bendella, F. (2019). FASim: A 3D serious game for the first aid emergency. *Simulation & Gaming*, 50(6), 690–710. DOI: 10.1177/1046878119865913

Bennani, S., Maalel, A., & Ghezala, H. B. (2021). Adaptive Gamification in E-learning: A Literature Review and Future Challenges. *Computer Applications in Engineering Education*, 30(2), 628–642. DOI: 10.1002/cae.22477

Berger, P. L., & Huntington, S. P. (Eds.). (2002). *Many globalizations: Cultural diversity in the contemporary world*. Oxford University Press. DOI: 10.1093/0195151461.001.0001

Berne, E. (1958). Transactional analysis: A new and effective method of group therapy. *American Journal of Psychotherapy*, 12(4), 735–743. DOI: 10.1176/appi.psychotherapy.1958.12.4.735 PMID: 13583264

Bernstein, R. S., Bulger, M., Salipante, P., & Weisinger, J. Y. (2020). From diversity to inclusion to equity: A theory of generative interactions. *Journal of Business Ethics*, 167(3), 395–410. DOI: 10.1007/s10551-019-04180-1

Berzosa, A., Bernaldo, M. O., & Fernández-Sanchez, G. (2017). Sustainability assessment tools for higher education: An empirical comparative analysis. *Journal of Cleaner Production*, 161, 812–820. DOI: 10.1016/j.jclepro.2017.05.194

Bešić, E., Paleczek, L., Ladenstein, J., & Gasteiger-Klicpera, B. (2023). Reaching the 'Hard to Reach': Implementing "Education for All" by Participative Action Research and Students' Voices. In Shaping Tomorrow Today–SDGs from multiple perspectives (pp. 141-160). Wiesbaden: Springer Fachmedien Wiesbaden. DOI: 10.1007/978-3-658-38319-0_7

Bettelheim, B. (1972). Play and education. *The School Review*, 81(1), 1–13. DOI: 10.1086/443059

Betz, J. A. (1995). Computer games: Increase learning in an interactive multidisciplinary environment. *Journal of Educational Technology Systems*, 24(2), 195–205. DOI: 10.2190/119M-BRMU-J8HC-XM6F

Bezanilla, M., Arranz, S., Rayn, A., Rubio, I., Menchaca, I., Guenaga, M., & Aguilar, E. (2014). A proposal for generic competence assessment in a serious game. *Journal of New Approaches in Educational Research*, 3(1), 42–51. DOI: 10.7821/naer.3.1.42-51

Bhardwaj, S., & Pazaver, A. (2014). Establishing the underpinning theories of maritime education and training for on-board competencies. *Amet Marit. J.*, 55–73.

Bhattacherjee, A. (2001). Understanding information systems continuance: An expectation–confirmation model. *Management Information Systems Quarterly*, 25(3), 351–370. DOI: 10.2307/3250921

Billen, A. (1993). Could it be the end for Super Mario? *The Observer*, *27*, 51.

Birindelli, G., Dell'Atti, S., Iannuzzi, A., & Savioli, M. (2018). Composition and activity of the board of directors: Impact on ESG performance in the banking system. *Sustainability (Basel)*, 10(12), 1–10. DOI: 10.3390/su10124699

Birnir, J. K., & Waguespack, D. M. (2011). Ethnic inclusion and economic growth. *Party Politics*, 17(2), 243–260. DOI: 10.1177/1354068810391149

Biscaccianti, A. (2003). Business ethics and profit-The impact of corporate social responsibility programs on corporate strategic planning. *Cahiers du CEREN*, 5, 14–27.

Blanchard, K. (1995). *The anthropology of sport: An introduction*. ABC-CLIO.

Blanco-Portela, N., Benayas, J., Pertierra, L. R., & Lozano, R. (2017). Towards the integration of sustainability in Higher Education Institutions: A review of drivers of and barriers to organisational change and their comparison against those found of companies. *Journal of Cleaner Production*, 166, 563–578. DOI: 10.1016/j.jclepro.2017.07.252

Blasco-Arcas, L., Buil, I., Hernández-Ortega, B., & Sese, F. J. (2013). Using clickers in class. The role of interactivity, active collaborative learning and engagement in learning performance. *Computers & Education*, 62, 102–110. DOI: 10.1016/j.compedu.2012.10.019

Blau, F. D., & Kahn, L. M. (2007). The gender pay gap. *The Economists' Voice*, 4(4). Advance online publication. DOI: 10.2202/1553-3832.1190

Bleumers, L., Mariën, I., Looy, J. V., Stewart, J., Schurmans, D., & All, A. (2013). Best practices for deploying digital games for personal empowerment and social inclusion. *Eur. Conf. Game. Base. Learn., 1*, 53–61. https://www.scopus.com/inward/record.uri?eid=2-s2.0-84893696104&partnerID=40&md5=9af6dc0cd58bff46acb2e3d169531943

Bloomberg. (2019). Accelerating D&I is essential to remain competitive and attract a new generation of investors. Retrieved from https://www.bloomberg.com/professional/blog/accelerating-di-essential-remain-competitive-attract-new-generation-investors/

Blumberg, F. C., Almonte, D. E., Anthony, J. S., & Hashimoto, N. (2012). *Serious Games: What are they? What do they do? Why should we play them? The Oxford Handbook of Media Psychology*. Oxford University Press.

Blythe, J. (2006). *Fondamenti di marketing*. Pearson Italia Spa.

Boghian, I., & Cojocariu, V. M. (2023). Using games to build social emotional learning skills. Revista Romaneasca pentru Educatie Multidimensionala, 15(1), 622-656.

Bolter, J. D., & Grusin, R. A. (1996). Remediation. *Configurations*, 4(3), 311–358. DOI: 10.1353/con.1996.0018

Boni, A., & Lozano, J. F. (2007). The generic competences: An opportunity for ethical learning in the European convergence in higher education. *Higher Education*, 54(6), 819–831. DOI: 10.1007/s10734-006-9026-4

Bordwell, D. (1989). A Case for Cognitivism. *IRIS*, 9, 11–41.

Borlido, T., & Coromina, L. (2018). Social Capital as Cause and Consequence of Rural Touristic Development: The Case of Lindoso (Portugal). *European Journal of Tourism Research*, 19, 71–85. DOI: 10.54055/ejtr.v19i.326

Boulianne, E., Keddie, L. S., & Postaire, M. (2018). (Non) coverage of sustainability within the French professional accounting education program. Sustainability Accounting. *Management and Policy Journal*, 9(3), 313–335.

Boulton, W. B. (1974). *The language of games: An aesthetic criticism*. Springer.

Bourdieu, P. (2011). The forms of capital (1986). Cultural theory: An anthology, 1(81-93), 949.

Boyle, E. A., Hainey, T., Connolly, T. M., Gray, G., Earp, J., Ott, M., Lim, T., Ninaus, M., Ribeiro, C., & Pereira, J. (2016). An update to the systematic literature review of empirical evidence of the impacts and outcomes of computer games and serious games. *Computers & Education*, 94, 178–192. DOI: 10.1016/j.compedu.2015.11.003

Brauner, P., & Ziefle, M. (2022). Beyond playful learning – Serious games for the human-centric digital transformation of production and a design process model. *Technology in Society*, 71, 102140. Advance online publication. DOI: 10.1016/j.techsoc.2022.102140

Brod, C. (1984). *Technostress: the human cost of computer revolution*. Academic Press.

Brown, J. S., Collins, A., & Duguid, P. (1989). Situated cognition and the culture of learning. *Educational Researcher*, 18(1), 32–42. DOI: 10.3102/0013189X018001032

Bruce, P., & Shelley, R. (2010). Assessing stakeholder engagement. *Communication Journal of New Zealand*, 11(2), 30–48.

Bruzzone, A. G., Massei, M., Solis, A. O., Poggi, S., Bartolucci, C., & Capponi, L. D. A. (2013, July). Serious games as enablers for training and education on operations on ships and off-shore platforms. In *Proceedings of the 2013 summer computer simulation conference* (pp. 1-8).

Brynjolfsson, E., & Mcafee, A. (2015). *La nuova rivoluzione delle macchine*. Feltrinelli.

Buckley, P., & Doyle, E. (2016). Gamification and student motivation. *Interactive Learning Environments*, 24(6), 1162–1175. DOI: 10.1080/10494820.2014.964263

Buckley, P., Noonan, S., Geary, C., MacKessy, T., & Nagle, E. (2019). An empirical study of gamification frameworks. *Journal of Organizational and End User Computing, 31*(1), 22–38. Advance online publication. DOI: 10.4018/JOEUC.2019010102

Buemi, M., Guazzo, G., & Conte, M. (2015). *Il Diversity Management per una crescita inclusiva: strategie e strumenti*. FrancoAngeli.

Burke, B. (2014). *Gartner Redefines Gamification*. Gartner Blog Network.

Calandra, D., Oppioli, M., Sadraei, R., Jafari-Sadeghi, V., & Biancone, P. P. (2024). Metaverse meets digital entrepreneurship: A practitioner-based qualitative synthesis. *International Journal of Entrepreneurial Behaviour and Research, 30*(2–3), 666–686. Advance online publication. DOI: 10.1108/IJEBR-01-2023-0041

Calvo-Morata, A., Rotaru, D. C., Alonso-Fernández, C., Freire-Morán, M., Martínez-Ortiz, I., & Fernández-Manjón, B. (2018). Validation of a cyberbullying serious game using game analytics. *IEEE Transactions on Learning Technologies*, 13(1), 186–197. DOI: 10.1109/TLT.2018.2879354

Calza-Perez, M., Perez-Ruiz, P., Enri-Peiró, S., Martínez-Climent, C., & Sánchez-García, J. (n.d.). Key factors influencing knowledge acquisition through game-based learning. *Psychology & Marketing*. DOI: 10.1002/mar.21966

Cambi, F., & Staccioli, G. (2007). *Il gioco in Occidente. Storia, teorie, pratiche*. Armando Editore.

Camerer, C., & Knez, M. (1997). Coordination in organizations: A game-theoretic perspective. Organizational decision making, 158-188

Campbell, J. L. (2007). Why would corporations behave in socially responsible ways? An institutional theory of corporate social responsibility. *Academy of Management Review*, 32(3), 946–967. DOI: 10.5465/amr.2007.25275684

Cantone, J. A., & Wiener, R. L. (2017). Religion at work: Evaluating hostile work environment religious discrimination claims. *Psychology, Public Policy, and Law*, 23(3), 351–366. DOI: 10.1037/law0000132

Capatina, A., Juarez-Varon, D., Micu, A., & Micu, A. (2024). Leveling up in corporate training: Unveiling the power of gamification to enhance knowledge retention, knowledge sharing, and job performance. *Journal of Innovation & Knowledge*, 9(3), 100530. Advance online publication. DOI: 10.1016/j.jik.2024.100530

Capellán-Pérez, I., Álvarez-Antelo, D., & Miguel, L. J. (2019). Global sustainability crossroads: A participatory simulation game to educate in the energy and sustainability challenges of the 21st century. *Sustainability (Basel)*, 11(13), 3672. Advance online publication. DOI: 10.3390/su11133672

Caponetto, I., Earp, J., & Ott, M. (2014, October). Gamification and education: A literature review. In European conference on games based learning (Vol. 1, p. 50). Academic Conferences International Limited

Cardona-Reyes, H., Trujillo-Espinoza, C., Arevalo-Mercado, C., & Muñoz-Arteaga, J. (2021). Training of Drone Pilots through Virtual Reality Environments under the Gamification Approach in a University Context. *Interaction Design and Architecture*, 49(49), 64–83. DOI: 10.55612/s-5002-049-004

Carenys, J., & Moya, S. (2016). Digital game-based learning in accounting and business education. *Accounting Education*, 25(6), 598–651. DOI: 10.1080/09639284.2016.1241951

Carlier, S., Naessens, V., Backere, F. D., & Turck, F. D. (2023). A Software Engineering Framework for Reusable Design of Personalized Serious Games for Health: Development Study *(Preprint)*. DOI: 10.2196/preprints.40054

Carter, B. (2020). Achieving diversity, inclusion and equity in the nursing workforce. *Revista Latino-Americana de Enfermagem*, 28, e3254. DOI: 10.1590/1518-8345.0000-3254 PMID: 32074212

Chakraborty, S. K., & Chatterjee, L. (2020). Rationales of Gender Diversity Management Policies and Practices in India: An Exploratory Empirical Study in the Indian IT/ITeS Industry. *Equality, Diversity and Inclusion*, 39(6), 667–688. DOI: 10.1108/EDI-04-2019-0124

Chan, K., & Zary, N. (2019). Knowledge, use and barriers to Serious Games in undergraduate medical education.*OSF Preprints*. DOI: 10.31219/osf.io/2f7rw

Chebotareva, I., Pashutina, O., & Makhova, V. (2020, May). Digital Gamification as a Leading Factor in the Educational and Learning Process of Law Students. In 6th International Conference on Social, economic, and academic leadership (ICSEAL-6-2019) (pp. 228-234). Atlantis Press. DOI: 10.2991/assehr.k.200526.034

Chee, Y. S. (2007). Embodiment, embeddedness, and experience: Game-based learning and the construction of identity. *Research and Practice in Technology Enhanced Learning*, 02(01), 3–30. DOI: 10.1142/S1793206807000282

Chen, F.-H., & Ho, S.-J. (2022). Designing a Board Game about the United Nations' Sustainable Development Goals. *Sustainability (Basel)*, 14(18), 11197. Advance online publication. DOI: 10.3390/su141811197

Cho, H. J., & Park, J. I. (2011). Cost accounting game model for education and operating method. *Advanced Materials Research*, 199, 1667–1670. DOI: 10.4028/www.scientific.net/AMR.199-200.1667

Chomsky, R. (2023), Measuring Sustainability in Business. Sustainability Review. Retrieved from: https://sustainablereview.com/measuring-sustainability-in-business/

Chow, C. Y., Riantiningtyas, R. R., Kanstrup, M. B., Papavasileiou, M., Liem, G. D., & Olsen, A. (2020). Can games change children's eating behaviour? A review of gamification and serious games. *Food Quality and Preference*, 80, 103823. DOI: 10.1016/j.foodqual.2019.103823

Christensen, M. (2013). *A qualitative study of the review and verification process of the Safety Management System within companies servicing the Norwegian Continental Shelf* (Master's thesis, Høgskolen i Vestfold).

Cicchiello, A. F., Marrazza, F., & Perdichizzi, S. (2023). Non-financial disclosure regulation and environmental, social, and governance (ESG) performance: The case of EU and US firms. *Corporate Social Responsibility and Environmental Management*, 30(3), 1121–1128. DOI: 10.1002/csr.2408

Coda, V. (1995). Dilemmas of Business Ethics. *Economia Aziendale*, 14, 7–14.

Cojocariu, V. M., & Boghian, I. (2014). Teaching the relevance of game-based learning to preschool and primary teachers. *Procedia: Social and Behavioral Sciences*, 142, 640–646.

Cole, A., & Zammit, J. (2020). *Cooperative gaming: Diversity in the games industry and how to cultivate inclusion*. CrC Press. DOI: 10.1201/9780429324826

Cole, B. M., & Salimath, M. S. (2013). Diversity identity management: An organizational perspective. *Journal of Business Ethics*, 116(1), 151–161. DOI: 10.1007/s10551-012-1466-4

Coleman, K. (2000). Entertaining Rome. *OXFORD UNIVERSITY SCHOOL OF ARCHAEOLOGY MONOGRAPH*, 54, 210–258.

Collier, P. (2001). Implications of ethnic diversity. Economic policy, 16(32), 128-166; Aigner, P. (2014). Ethnic diversity management in theory and practice. *Journal of Diversity Management (Online)*, 9(2), 111.

Corbett, J. (2001). Teaching approaches which support inclusive education: A connective pedagogy. *British Journal of Special Education*, 28(2), 55–59. DOI: 10.1111/1467-8527.00219

Cormier, D., Aerts, W., Ledoux, M. J., & Magnan, M. (2009). Attributes of social and human capital disclosure and information asymmetry between managers and investors. Canadian Journal of Administrative Sciences/Revue Canadienne des Sciences de l'Administration, 26(1), 71-88.

Corral, R. J. P. (2024). Impact of Hybrid and on-Site Work Arrangements on Employee Motivation and Job Satisfaction in the BPO Industry: A Cross-Sectional Study. *Open Journal of Social Sciences*, 12(02), 205–230. DOI: 10.4236/jss.2024.122013

Correa Ruiz, C. (2013). A commentary on 'integrated reporting: A review of developments and their implications for the accounting curriculum'. *Accounting Education*, 22(4), 360–362. DOI: 10.1080/09639284.2013.817800

Council of European Union. (2004). Joint report by the Commission and the Council on social inclusion 7101/04.

Cox, T. (1994). *Cultural diversity in organizations: Theory, research and practice*. Berrett-Koehler Publishers.

Cox, T. H., & Blake, S. (1991). Managing cultural diversity: Implications for organizational competitiveness. *The Academy of Management Perspectives*, 5(3), 45–56. DOI: 10.5465/ame.1991.4274465

Cranton, P. (2016). *Understanding and promoting transformative learning: A guide to theory and practice*. Routledge.

Creamare. (2022). Project Overview. Accessed: August 30, 2023 from https://creamare.eu/project/

Csikszentmihalyi, M. (1975). Beyond boredom and anxiety: Experiencing flow in work and play. Jossey-Bass. https://psycnet.apa.org/record/2000-12701-000

Csikszentmihalyi, M. (1990). The domain of creativity.

Csikszentmihalyi, M. (2014). Flow and the foundations of positive psychology. In Flow and the foundations of positive psychology. DOI: 10.1007/978-94-017-9088-8

Csikszentmihalyi, M. (2013). *Flow: The psychology of happiness*. Random House.

Curay Correa, P., & Ramón, L. P. (2021). Storytelling in gamification: Planning an educational guide. *Revista de Ciencias Humanísticas y Sociales*, 6(2), 110–123.

Dankbaar, M. E., Alsma, J., Jansen, E. E., van Merrienboer, J. J., van Saase, J. L., & Schuit, S. C. (2016). An experimental study on the effects of a simulation game on students' clinical cognitive skills and motivation. *Advances in Health Sciences Education : Theory and Practice*, 21(3), 505–521. DOI: 10.1007/s10459-015-9641-x PMID: 26433730

Dasen, V., & Vespa, M. (2021). Ancient play and games: In search of a definition. Play and Games in Classical Antiquity: Definition, Transmission, Reception, 5-16;

Davies, H. (2016). The Growing Pervasiveness of Games and Play. *Digital Games Research Association (DiGRA) Australia Queensland Symposium*.

Davis, F., & Venkatesh, V. (2004). Toward pre-prototyping user acceptance testing of new information systems: Implications for software project management. *IEEE Transactions on Engineering Management*, 51(1), 31–46. DOI: 10.1109/TEM.2003.822468

Davis, P. J., Frolova, Y., & Callahan, W. (2016). Workplace diversity management in Australia: What do managers think and what are organisations doing? *Equality, Diversity and Inclusion*, 35(2), 81–98. DOI: 10.1108/EDI-03-2015-0020

De Freitas, S., & Oliver, M. (2006). How can exploratory learning with games and simulations within the curriculum be most effectively evaluated? *Computers & Education*, 46(3), 249–264. DOI: 10.1016/j.compedu.2005.11.007

De Oliveira Nunes, M., & Mayer, V. F. (2014). Mobile technology, games and nature areas: The tourist perspective. *Tourism & Management Studies*, 10(1), 53–58.

de Souza Gandra Camilo, V. Y. (2024). *Articulations of inclusivity within in-game concerts: A comparative multi-case study* [MRes, University of Glasgow]. https://theses.gla.ac.uk/84035/

Del Baldo, M., & Baldarelli, M. G. (2017). Educating for sustainability: Perspectives and critical notes on accounting scholars' role in higher education. *Scientific Annals of Economics and Business*, 64(4), 411–422. DOI: 10.1515/saeb-2017-0032

Delaney, J. (2022). Minecraft and Playful Public Participation in Urban Design. *Urban Planning*, 7(2). Advance online publication. DOI: 10.17645/up.v7i2.5229

Deltares. (2018). Port of the Future Serious Games. Accessed August 30, 2023 from https://www.deltares.nl/en/software-and-data/products/port-of-the-future-serious-game

Delwiche, A. (2006). Massively multiplayer online games (MMOs) in the new media classroom. *Journal of Educational Technology & Society*, 9(3), 160–172.

Deterding, S., Dixon, D., Khaled, R., & Nacke, L. (2011). From game design elements to gamefulness: defining "gamification". In Proceedings of the 15th international academic MindTrek conference: Envisioning future media environments (pp. 9-15). DOI: 10.1145/2181037.2181040

Deterding, S., Dixon, D., Khaled, R., & Nacke, L. (2011, September). From game design elements to gamefulness: defining" gamification". In Proceedings of the 15th international academic MindTrek conference: Envisioning future media environments (pp. 9-15).

Dewey, J. (2022). *How we think*. DigiCat.

Dicheva, D., Dichev, C., Agre, G., & Angelova, G. (2015). Gamification in education: A systematic mapping study. *Journal of Educational Technology & Society*, 18(3), 75–88.

Dickinson, J. R., & Faria, A. J. (1997). A random strategy criterion for validity of simulation game participation. *Simulation & Gaming*, 28(3), 263–275. DOI: 10.1177/1046878197283003

Diller, J. V. (2014). *Cultural Diversity*. Cengage Learning.

Dimitriadou, A., Djafarova, N., Turetken, O., Verkuyl, M., & Ferworn, A. (2021). Challenges in Serious Game Design and Development: Educators' Experiences. *Simulation & Gaming*, 52(2), 132–152. DOI: 10.1177/1046878120944197

DiTomaso, N., Post, C., & Parks-Yancy, R. (2007). Workforce diversity and inequality: Power, status, and numbers. *Annual Review of Sociology*, 33(1), 473–501. DOI: 10.1146/annurev.soc.33.040406.131805

Dixit, R. K., Nirgude, M., & Yalagi, P. S. (2018). Employ gamification to make "I&CS" more interesting. *Journal of Engineering Education Transformations*, 32(2), 55–60.

Djaouti, D., Alvarez, J., & Jessel, J. P. (2011). Classifying serious games: the G/P/S model. In *Handbook of research on improving learning and motivation through educational games: Multidisciplinary approaches* (pp. 118–136). IGI global. DOI: 10.4018/978-1-60960-495-0.ch006

Douglas, B. D., & Brauer, M. (2021). Gamification to prevent climate change: A review of games and apps for sustainability. *Current Opinion in Psychology*, 42, 89–94. DOI: 10.1016/j.copsyc.2021.04.008 PMID: 34052619

Drucker, P. F. (2002). They're not employees, they're people. *Harvard Business Review*, 80(2), 70–77. PMID: 11894680

Duffy, T. M., & Cunningham, D. J. (1996). Constructivism: Implications for the design and delivery of instruction. In Handbook of research for educational communications and technology (pp. 170–198). https://doi.org/. x.DOI: 10.1111/j.1467-8535.2009.00994_9

Duncanson, C., & Woodward, R. (2015). Regendering the Military: Theorizing Women's Military Participation. *Security Dialogue*, 47(1), 3–21. DOI: 10.1177/0967010615614137

Dunne, D. J. (2014). Brechtian alienation in videogames. *Press Start*, 1(1), 79–99.

Dyer, R. (2021). Gamified Emissions Through the Wisdom of Crowds. In A. Spanellis & J. T. Harviainen (Eds.), *Transforming Society and Organizations through Gamification* (pp. 129–150). Springer International Publishing. DOI: 10.1007/978-3-030-68207-1_8

Earp, J., Ott, M., Popescu, M., Romero, M., & Usart, M. (2014). Supporting human capital development with serious games: An analysis of three experiences. *Computers in Human Behavior*, 30, 715–720. DOI: 10.1016/j.chb.2013.09.004

Ebner, M., & Holzinger, A. (2007). Successful implementation of user-centered game based learning in higher education: An example from civil engineering. *Computers & Education*, 49(3), 873–890. DOI: 10.1016/j.compedu.2005.11.026

Ebron, K. T., Luzynski, C., & Nath Komanski, C. S. (2023). Leave No One Behind: How systemic racism impacts Sustainable Development Goals. *International Journal of Public Leadership*, 19(1), 31–44. DOI: 10.1108/IJPL-02-2022-0010

ECGBL 2017 11th European Conference on Game-Based Learning. (2017). Academic Conferences and publishing limited.

Egan, M. (2021). Diversity, Inclusion, and the Opportunities for Accounting Research [D]. *Social and Environmental Accountability Journal*, 41(3), 201–207. DOI: 10.1080/0969160X.2021.1986088

Ekambaram, A., & Petersen, S. A. (2017). Enhancing Stakeholder Management Competences in Construction Projects using Serious Games. In *Proceedings of the 9th Nordic Conference on Construction Economics and Organization.*

Elbannan, M. A. (2016). IFRS adoption, legal systems and the voluntary disclosure of human capital: Cross-country evidence from the banking industry. *Accounting and Finance Research*, 5(4), 30–48. DOI: 10.5430/afr.v5n4p30

Elliott, L. (2004). *Children and Games in the Middle Ages*. Crabtree Publishing Company.

Ellis, K., Leaver, T., & Kant, M. (2023). Gaming Disability. Disability Perspective on Contemporary Videogames. Routledge.

Ely, R. J., & Thomas, D. A. (2001). Cultural diversity at work: The effects of diversity perspectives on work group processes and outcomes. *Administrative Science Quarterly*, 46(2), 229–273. DOI: 10.2307/2667087

Ely, R. J., & Thomas, D. A. (2020). Getting serious about diversity. *Harvard Business Review*, 98(6), 114–122.

European Commission. (2017). Key Skills for a Societal Change. https://op.europa.eu/en/publication-detail/-/publication/297a33c8-a1f3-11e9-9d01-01aa75ed71a1/language-en

Evans, K. H., Daines, W., Tsui, J., Strehlow, M., Maggio, P., & Shieh, L. (2015). Septris: A novel, mobile, online, simulation game that improves sepsis recognition and management. *Academic Medicine*, 90(2), 180–184. DOI: 10.1097/ACM.0000000000000611 PMID: 25517703

Ewers, H. H. (2019). Children's Games and Children's Literature between the Enlightenment and Romanticism. *Filoteknos*, (9), 86–97.

Exley, K., & Dennick, R. (2007). *Teaching in small groups in Higher Education.* Narcea.

Fabricatore, C., & Lopez, X. (2012). Sustainability learning through gaming: An exploratory study. *Electronic Journal of e-Learning*, 10(2), 209–222.

Fabricatore, C., & Lopez, X. (2012). Sustainability Learning through Gaming: An Exploratory Study. *Electronic Journal of e-Learning*, 10(2), 209–222.

Fandos Herrera, C., Jiménez Martínez, J., Orús Sanclemente, C., Peligero Domeque, M., & Pina Pérez, J. M. (2015). Learning strategies, expectations and attitude: Do I like to act as a narrator or do I prefer to be told? In *XXVII Marketing Congress AEMARK 2015* (pp. 1239-1254). ESIC Editorial.

Faria, A. J., Hutchinson, D., Wellington, W. J., & Gold, S. (2009). Developments in business gaming: A review of the past 40 years. *Simulation & Gaming*, 40(4), 464–487. DOI: 10.1177/1046878108327585

Farndale, E., Biron, M., Briscoe, D. R., & Raghuram, S. (2015). A global perspective on diversity and inclusion in work organisations. *International Journal of Human Resource Management*, 26(6), 677–687. DOI: 10.1080/09585192.2014.991511

Farouk, A. D. (2021). The role of sustainable development goals (SDGs) in social inclusion. Available at *SSRN* 3984863. DOI: 10.2139/ssrn.3984863

Feagin, J. R., & Eckberg, D. L. (1980). Discrimination: Motivation, Action, Effects, and Context. *Annual Review of Sociology*, 6(1), 1–20. DOI: 10.1146/annurev.so.06.080180.000245

Feldman, M. S., Khademian, A. M., Ingram, H., & Schneider, A. S. (2006). Ways of knowing and inclusive management practices. *Public Administration Review*, 66(s1), 89–99. DOI: 10.1111/j.1540-6210.2006.00669.x

Fielding, N. (2004). Working in hostile environments. Qualitative research practice, 248-260.

Finkel, I. (2007). Ancient board games in perspective: *Papers from the 1990 British Museum colloquium, with additional contributions*. British Museum Press.

Flavin-McDonald, C., & Barrett, M. H. (1999). The Topsfield Foundation: Fostering Democratic Community Building Through Face-to-Face Dialogue. *New Directions for Adult and Continuing Education*, 1999(81), 25–36. DOI: 10.1002/ace.8103

Fleming, K., Abad, J., Booth, L., Schueller, L., Baills, A., Scolobig, A., & Leone, M. F. (2020). The use of serious games in engaging stakeholders for disaster risk reduction, management and climate change adaption information elicitation. *International Journal of Disaster Risk Reduction*, 49, 101669.

Flood, R. L., & Romm, N. (1996). Diversity management. Critical Systems Thinking, 81-92.

Flood, R. L., & Romm, N. R. (1996). Contours of diversity management and triple loop learning. *Kybernetes*, 25(7/8), 154–163. DOI: 10.1108/03684929610149747

Florea, R., & Florea, R. (2013). Stakeholders interests analyse and harmonization-starting point of strategic approach. *Economy Transdisciplinarity Cognition*, 16(1), 130.

Florida, R., & Gates, G. (2001). *Technology and Tolerance: The Importance of Diversity to High-Technology Growth*. The Brookings Institution.

Floridi, L., & Cabitza, F. (2021). *Intelligenza artificiale -L'uso delle nuove macchine*. Bompiani.

Fokides, E. (2018). Digital educational games and mathematics. Results of a case study in primary school settings. *Education and Information Technologies*, 23(2), 851–867. DOI: 10.1007/s10639-017-9639-5

Fonseca, I., Caviedes, M., Chantré, J., & Bernate, J. (2023). Gamification and Game-Based Learning as Cooperative Learning Tools: A Systematic Review. *International Journal of Emerging Technologies in Learning*, 18(21), 4–23. DOI: 10.3991/ijet.v18i21.40035

Fornell, C., & Larcker, D. (1981). Evaluating structural equation models with unobservable variables and measurement error. *JMR, Journal of Marketing Research*, 18(1), 39–50. DOI: 10.1177/002224378101800104

Foster, M. K., Meinhard, A., & Berger, I. E. (2021). *The Role of Social Capital: Bridging*. Bonding or Both., DOI: 10.32920/ryerson.14638890

Fotiadis, A. K., & Sigala, M. (2015). Developing a framework for designing an Events Management Training Simulation (EMTS). *Journal of Hospitality, Leisure, Sport and Tourism Education*, 16, 59–71. DOI: 10.1016/j.jhlste.2015.03.001

Fottler, M. D., Blair, J. D., Whitehead, C. J., Laus, M. D., & Savage, G. T. (1989). Assessing key stakeholders: Who matters to hospitals and why? *Journal of Healthcare Management*, 34(4), 525–546.

Francoeur, C., Labelle, R., & Sinclair-Desgagné, B. (2008). Gender diversity in corporate governance and top management. *Journal of Business Ethics*, 81(1), 83–95. DOI: 10.1007/s10551-007-9482-5

Freeman, R. E. (1984). *Strategic Management: A Stakeholder Approach Pitman Publishing Inc.*

Freeman, R. E., Wicks, A. C., & Parmar, B. (2004). Stakeholder theory and "the corporate objective revisited". *Organization Science*, 15(3), 364–369. DOI: 10.1287/orsc.1040.0066

Friedman, M. (1962). *Capitalism and freedom. Friedman*. The University of Chicago.

Friedrich, J., Becker, M., Kramer, F., Wirth, M., & Schneider, M. (2020). Incentive design and gamification for knowledge management. *Journal of Business Research*, 106, 341–352. DOI: 10.1016/j.jbusres.2019.02.009

Fritzsche, D. J., Leonard, N. H., Boscia, M. W., & Anderson, P. H. (2014). Simulation Debriefing Procedures, Development Business Simulation Experience Learning Process Annuary ABSEL Conference, 31(0).

Fu, K., Hainey, T., & Baxter, G. (2016, October). A systematic literature review to identify empirical evidence on the use of computer games in business education and training. In European Conference on Games Based Learning (p. 232). Academic Conferences International Limited.

Fusco, N. M., Jacobsen, L. J., Klem, N., Krzyzanowicz, R., & Ohtake, P. J. (2022). A serious game employed to introduce principles of interprofessional collaboration to students of multiple health professions. *Simulation & Gaming*, 53(3), 253–264. DOI: 10.1177/10468781221093816

Garg, S., & Sangwan, S. (2021). Literature review on diversity and inclusion at workplace, 2010–2017. *Vision (Basel)*, 25(1), 12–22. DOI: 10.1177/0972262920959523 PMID: 33806403

Garneli, V., Giannakos, M., & Chorianopoulos, K. (2017). Serious games as a malleable learning medium: The effects of narrative, gameplay, and making on students' performance and attitudes. *British Journal of Educational Technology*, 48(3), 842–859. DOI: 10.1111/bjet.12455

Gartner Says By 2015, More Than 50 Percent of Organizations That Manage Innovation Processes Will Gamify Those Processes. (2011). Gartner Newsroom. Retrieved November 7, 2013, from https://www.gartner.com/newsroom/id/1629214

Gast, I., Schildkamp, K., & van der Veen, J. T. (2017). Team-based professional development interventions in higher education: A systematic review. *Review of Educational Research*, 87(4), 736–767. DOI: 10.3102/0034654317704306 PMID: 28989192

Gatian, A. W. (1994). Is user satisfaction a valid measure of system effectiveness? *Information & Management*, 26(3), 119–131. DOI: 10.1016/0378-7206(94)90036-1

Gatti, L., Ulrich, M., & Seele, P. (2019). Education for sustainable development through business simulation games: An exploratory study of sustainability gamification and its effects on students' learning outcomes. *Journal of Cleaner Production*, 207, 667–678. DOI: 10.1016/j.jclepro.2018.09.130

Gazzola, P., Pezzetti, R., Amelio, S., & Grechi, D. (2020). Non-Financial Information Disclosure in Italian Public Interest Companies: A Sustainability Reporting Perspective. *Sustainability (Basel)*, 12(15), 6063. DOI: 10.3390/su12156063

Gee, J. P. (2007). *Good video games and good learning: Collected essays on video games, learning, and literacy*. Peter Lang. DOI: 10.3726/978-1-4539-1162-4

Georgeac, O. A., & Rattan, A. (2023). The business case for diversity backfires: Detrimental effects of organizations' instrumental diversity rhetoric for underrepresented group members' sense of belonging. *Journal of Personality and Social Psychology*, 124(1), 69–108. DOI: 10.1037/pspi0000394 PMID: 35679195

Gilbert, J. A., Stead, B. A., & Ivancevich, J. M. (1999). Diversity management: A new organizational paradigm. *Journal of Business Ethics*, 21(1), 61–76. DOI: 10.1023/A:1005907602028

Gilson, L. L., & Goldberg, C. B. (2015). Editors' comment: So, what is a conceptual paper? *Group & Organization Management*, 40(2), 127–130.

Glavas, C., & Schuster, L. (2020). Design principles for electronic work integrated learning (eWIL). *The Internet and Higher Education*, 47, 100760. DOI: 10.1016/j.iheduc.2020.100760

Göbel, S., Wendel, V., Ritter, C., & Steinmetz, R. (2010). Personalized, adaptive digital educational games using narrative game-based learning objects. In *Entertainment for Education. Digital Techniques and Systems* (pp. 438–445). Springer. DOI: 10.1007/978-3-642-14533-9_45

Goldhill, S. (2017). Play in Ancient Greece: An interview with Simon Goldhill. *American Journal of Play*, 9(3), 287–299.

Goller, A., & Rieckmann, M. (2022). What do we know about teacher educators' perceptions of Education for Sustainable Development? A Systematic Literature Review. *Journal of Teacher Education for Sustainability*, 24(1), 19–34. DOI: 10.2478/jtes-2022-0003

Goodpaster, K. E. (1991). Business ethics and stakeholder analysis. *Business Ethics Quarterly*, 53–73.

Gould, R., Harris, S. P., Mullin, C., & Jones, R. (2020). Disability, Diversity, and Corporate Social Responsibility: Learning From Recognized Leaders in Inclusion. *Journal of Vocational Rehabilitation*, 52(1), 29–42. DOI: 10.3233/JVR-191058

Graham, R. G., & Gray, C. F. (1969). Business games handbook.

Granic, I., Lobel, A., & Engels, R. M. (2014). The benefits of playing video games. *The American Psychologist*, 69(1), 66–78. DOI: 10.1037/a0034857 PMID: 24295515

Granovetter, M. S. (1973). The strength of weak ties. *American Journal of Sociology*, 78(6), 1360–1380. DOI: 10.1086/225469

Gray, S. I., Robertson, J., Manches, A., & Rajendran, G. (2019). BrainQuest: The use of motivational design theories to create a cognitive training game supporting hot executive function. *International Journal of Human-Computer Studies*, 127, 124–149. DOI: 10.1016/j.ijhcs.2018.08.004

Gredler, M. E. (2013). Games and simulations and their relationships to learning. In *Handbook of research on educational communications and technology* (pp. 571–581). Routledge.

Greenlaw, P. S., Herron, L. W., & Rawdon, R. H. (1962). Business simulation in industrial and university education.

Greenwald, H. P., & Beery, W. L. (2001). Reducing Isolation Among Inner-City Elders: An Outcome Evaluation. *Health Promotion Practice*, 2(3), 233–241. DOI: 10.1177/152483990100200307

Greenwood, M. (2007). Stakeholder engagement: Beyond the myth of corporate responsibility. Journal of Business Ethics, 74, 315–327.

Greipl, S., Moeller, K., & Ninaus, M. (2020). Potential and limits of game-based learning. *International Journal of Technology Enhanced Learning*, 12(4), 363–389. DOI: 10.1504/IJTEL.2020.110047

Griffin, R. W., Phillips, J. M., & Gully, S. M. (2020). Organizational behavior: Managing people and organizations. CENGAGE Learning.

Griffiths, M. D., & Davies, M. N. (2005). Does video game addiction exist. Handbook of computer game studies, 359, 372.

Groenewald, E. S. (2024). *Inclusive Workplaces: The Key Strategies for Sustainable Diversity Practices*. DOI: 10.5281/ZENODO.11032466

Guest, D. E. (2002). Perspectives on the study of work-life balance. *Social Sciences Information. Information Sur les Sciences Sociales*, 41(2), 255–279. DOI: 10.1177/0539018402041002005

Guillén-Nieto, V., & Aleson-Carbonell, M. (2012). Serious games and learning effectiveness: The case of It'sa Deal! *Computers & Education*, 58(1), 435–448. DOI: 10.1016/j.compedu.2011.07.015

Gurbuz, S. C. (2021). A conceptual approach for design and development of serious game in maritime domain [Unpublished Doctoral Dissertation Progress Report-1]. Istanbul Technical University, İstanbul, Türkiye.

Gurbuz, S. C., & Celik, M. (2023). A brief overview on serious gaming research and entrepreneurship ecosystem in maritime field. In *Abstract Book of International Conference on Information Technology for Higher Education-ICITHE-23* (p.17). Association for Scientific and Academic Research (ASAR) Explore Publishing.

Gurbuz, S. C., & Celik, M. (2022). A preliminary design of a 3D maritime gamified mentoring platform to support tanker pre-vetting inspection training: 'Maritime Gamentor'. *Ships and Offshore Structures*, 18(12), 1627–1637. DOI: 10.1080/17445302.2022.2133878

Gurbuz, S. C., & Celik, M. (2022). Serious Games in Future Skills Development: A Systematic Review of the Design Approaches. *Computer Applications in Engineering Education*, 30(5), 1591–1612. DOI: 10.1002/cae.22557

Haigh, M., & Hazelton, J. (2010). Incorporating Sustainability into Accounting Curricula. *Accounting Education*, 19(1&2), 159–178.

Hamari, J., & Koivisto, J. (2013, June). Social Motivations To Use Gamification: An Empirical Study Of Gamifying Exercise. In ECIS (Vol. 105, No. 5, pp. 18-19). https://aisel.aisnet.org/ecis2013_cr/105

Hamari, J., Koivisto, J., & Sarsa, H. (2014, January). Does gamification work? a literature review of empirical studies on gamification. In 2014 47th Hawaii international conference on system sciences (pp. 3025-3034). IEEE.

Hamari, J., & Sjöblom, M. (2017). What is eSports and why do people watch it? *Internet Research*, 27(2), 211–232. DOI: 10.1108/IntR-04-2016-0085

Hambrick, D. C., & Mason, P. A. (1984). Upper echelons: The organization as a reflection of its top managers. *Academy of Management Review*, 9(2), 193–206. DOI: 10.2307/258434

Hammedi, W., Leclerq, T., & Riel, A. C. R. (2017). The Use of Gamification Mechanics to Increase Employee and User Engagement in Participative Healthcare Services. *Journal of Service Management*, 28(4), 640–661. DOI: 10.1108/JOSM-04-2016-0116

Haque, S., Panda, D., & Ghosh, A. (2024). Gamifying sustainability with self-efficacy: Motivating green behaviours in large industrial firms. *International Journal of Organizational Analysis, 32*(11), 74–93. Advance online publication. DOI: 10.1108/IJOA-08-2023-3951

Harrison, D., & Klein, K. (2007). What's the difference? Diversity constructs as separation, variety, or disparity in organizations. *Academy of Management Review*, 32(4), 1199–1228. DOI: 10.5465/amr.2007.26586096

Harrison, J. S., Bosse, D. A., & Phillips, R. A. (2010). Managing for stakeholders, stakeholder utility functions, and competitive advantage. *Strategic Management Journal*, 31(1), 58–74. DOI: 10.1002/smj.801

Harteveld, C., Javvaji, N., Machado, T., Zastavker, Y. V., Bennett, V., & Abdoun, T. (2020). Gaming4All: Reflecting on Diversity, Equity, and Inclusion for Game-Based Engineering Education. 2020 IEEE Frontiers in Education Conference (FIE), 1-9. DOI: 10.1109/FIE44824.2020.9274176

Hartt, M., Hosseini, H., & Mostafapour, M. (2020). Game on: Exploring the effectiveness of game-based learning. *Planning Practice and Research*, 35(5), 589–604. DOI: 10.1080/02697459.2020.1778859

Haruna, H., Zainuddin, Z., Mellecker, R. R., Chu, S. K., & Hu, X. (2019). An iterative process for developing digital gamified sexual health education for adolescent students in low-tech settings. *Information and Learning Science*, 120(11), 723–742. Advance online publication. DOI: 10.1108/ILS-07-2019-0066

Hebl, M., Cheng, S. K., & Ng, L. C. (2020). Modern Discrimination in Organizations. *Annual Review of Organizational Psychology and Organizational Behavior*, 7(1), 257–282. DOI: 10.1146/annurev-orgpsych-012119-044948

Helm, S. (2007). One reputation or many? Comparing stakeholders' perceptions of corporate reputation. *Corporate Communications*, 12(3), 238–254. DOI: 10.1108/13563280710776842

Heras-Saizarbitoria, I., Urbieta, L., & Boiral, O. (2022). Organizations' engagement with sustainable development goals: From cherry-picking to SDG-washing? *Corporate Social Responsibility and Environmental Management*, 29(2), 316–328. DOI: 10.1002/csr.2202

Herodotou, C., Rienties, B., Hlosta, M., Boroowa, A., Mangafa, C., & Zdrahal, Z. (2020). The scalable implementation of predictive learning analytics at a distance learning university: Insights from a longitudinal case study. *The Internet and Higher Education*, 45, 100725. DOI: 10.1016/j.iheduc.2020.100725

Herring, C. (2009). Does diversity pay?: Race, gender, and the business case for diversity. *American Sociological Review*, 74(2), 208–224. DOI: 10.1177/000312240907400203

Himmelstein, J., & Gopalakrishnan, G. (2017). Tackling implicit and explicit bias through games that teach workplace diversity. In *Proc. Eur. Conf. Games Based Learn., ECGBL* (pp. 244–252). Academic Conferences and Publishing International Limited. https://www.scopus.com/inward/record.uri?eid=2-s2.0-85036460892&partnerID=40&md5=bd35599d1451282b4607d3f0b17fa705

Hitt, M. A., Ireland, R. D., & Hoskisson, R. E. (2009). *Strategic Management: Concepts & Cases Competitiveness and Globalization* (8th ed.). South-Western Cangage Learning.

Hjalager, A.-M., Graakjær Smed, S., & Jensen, J. F. (2022). E-Tools for Tourism Innovation Management: A New Typology. In *Handb. Of e-Tourism* (pp. 1465–1489). Springer International Publishing; DOI: 10.1007/978-3-030-48652-5_79

Hjelmervik, K., Nazir, S., & Myhrvold, A. (2018). Simulator training for maritime complex tasks: An experimental study. *WMU Journal of Maritime Affairs*, 17(1), 17–30. DOI: 10.1007/s13437-017-0133-0

Hofer-Bonfim, B., Savych, Z., & Schnitzer, J. (2023). Comparing Diversity & Inclusion (D&I) disclosures across nine countries. In Diversity and Inclusion across languages (pp. 83-108). Frank & Timme, Berlin.

Høiseth, M., Alsos, O. A., Holme, S., Ek, S., & Gabrielsen, C. T. (2021). Serious Game Design to Support Children Struggling With School Refusal. *International Journal of Serious Games*, 8(2), 109–128. DOI: 10.17083/ijsg.v8i2.416

Hossain, M., Atif, M., Ahmed, A., & Mia, L. (2020). Do LGBT workplace diversity policies create value for firms? *Journal of Business Ethics*, 167(4), 775–791. DOI: 10.1007/s10551-019-04158-z

Huang, W. H., Huang, W. Y., & Tschopp, J. (2010). Sustaining iterative game playing processes in DGBL: The relationship between motivational processing and outcome processing. *Computers & Education*, 55(2), 789–797. DOI: 10.1016/j.compedu.2010.03.011

Huizinga, J. (1955). *Homo ludens: A study of the play-element in culture*. Beacon Press.

Hung, A. C. Y. (2018). Gamification as Design Thinking. *International Journal on Teaching and Learning in Higher Education*, 30(3), 549–559.

Hunicke, R., LeBlanc, M., & Zubek, R. (2004). MDA: A formal approach to game design and game research. *Proceedings of the AAAI Workshop on Challenges in Game AI*, 4(1).

Hunt, V., Layton, D., & Prince, S. (2015). Diversity matters. McKinsey & Company.

Huntington, F. (1984). The Learning Machine: Thinking Is an Adventure. *InCider*, 2(10), 33–36.

Hunt, V., Layton, D., & Prince, S. (2015). Diversity matters. McKinsey & Company.

Hurtado, S., Alvarado, A. R., & Guillermo-Wann, C. (2015). Creating inclusive environments. *Journal Committed to Social Change on Race and Ethnicity*, 1(1), 60–81.

Hwang, G.-J., Chiu, L.-Y., & Chen, C.-H. (2015). A contextual game-based learning approach to improving students' inquiry-based learning performance in social studies courses. *Computers & Education*, 81, 13–25. DOI: 10.1016/j.compedu.2014.09.006

ICLE (International Center for Leadership in Education). (2012). Rigor/Relevance Framework. Retrieved February 21 2024, from http://www.cssvt.org/wp/wp-content/uploads/2012/08/Rigor-Relevance-Framework.pdf

Ifenthaler, D., Eseryel, D., & Ge, X. (2012). Assessment for game-based learning. In *Assessment in game-based learning: Foundations, innovations, and perspectives* (pp. 1–8). Springer New York. DOI: 10.1007/978-1-4614-3546-4_1

Interdisciplinary Design of Game-based Learning Platforms: A Phenomenological Examination of the Integrative Design of Game, Learning, and Assessment | SpringerLink. (n.d.). Retrieved January 27, 2024, from https://link.springer.com/book/10.1007/978-3-030-04339-1

International Chamber of Shipping. (2020). *Annual Review 2020*. International Chamber of Shipping. Retrieved April 18 2021, from https://www.ics-shipping.org/wp-content/uploads/2020/11/annual-review-2020-final-compressed.pdf

Isabelle, D. (2020). Gamification of Entrepreneurship Education. *Decision Sciences Journal of Innovative Education*, 18(2), 203–223. DOI: 10.1111/dsji.12203

Ismail, M. F., Iksan, Z. H., & Ariffin, R. (2021). Effects of Using Gamification Techniques on Achievement in Science Subject. *International Journal of Academic Research in Business & Social Sciences*, 11(12). Advance online publication. DOI: 10.6007/IJARBSS/v11-i12/11769

Ismail, M. S., & Klischewski, R. (2020). BP-IT alignment in SMEs: a game-based learning approach to increase stakeholders' maturity. *Business Process Management: 18th International Conference, BPM 2020, Seville, Spain, September 13–18, 2020 Proceedings, 18*, 400–416.

Itam, U., & Bagali, M. M. (2019). Diversity and inclusion management: a focus on employee engagement. In Gender and Diversity: Concepts, Methodologies, Tools, and Applications (pp. 1771-1788). IGI Global. DOI: 10.4018/978-1-5225-6912-1.ch093

Janakiraman, S., Watson, S. L., & Watson, W. R. (2018). Using Game-based Learning to Facilitate Attitude Change for Environmental Sustainability. *Journal of Education for Sustainable Development*, 12(2), 176–185. DOI: 10.1177/0973408218783286

Janssens, M., & Zanoni, P. (2014). Alternative diversity management: Organizational practices fostering ethnic equality at work. *Scandinavian Journal of Management*, 30(3), 317–331. DOI: 10.1016/j.scaman.2013.12.006

Jean, S., Medema, W., Adamowski, J., Chew, C., Delaney, P., & Wals, A. (2018). Serious Games as a catalyst for boundary crossing, collaboration and knowledge co-creation in a watershed governance context. *Journal of Environmental Management*, 223, 1010–1022. DOI: 10.1016/j.jenvman.2018.05.021 PMID: 30096742

Johnson, D., Horton, E., Mulcahy, R., & Foth, M. (2017). Gamification and serious games within the domain of domestic energy consumption: A systematic review. *Renewable & Sustainable Energy Reviews*, 73, 249–264. DOI: 10.1016/j.rser.2017.01.134

Jonassen, D. (1999). Designing constructivist learning environments. In Reigeluth, C. (Ed.), *Instructional-design theories and models: A new paradigm of instructional theory* (pp. 215–239). DOI: 10.4324/9781410603784-16

Jones, B. D. (2009). Motivating students to engage in learning: The MUSIC model of academic motivation. *International Journal on Teaching and Learning in Higher Education*, 21(2), 272–285.

Jones, B. D., Epler, C. M., Mokri, P., Bryant, L. H., & Paretti, M. C. (2013). The effects of a collaborative problem-based learning experience on students' motivation in engineering capstone courses. *The Interdisciplinary Journal of Problem-Based Learning*, 7(2), 2. DOI: 10.7771/1541-5015.1344

Jost, M. (2011). Transformative learning and complex problem-solving among hospitality and tourism students. *Tourism & Management Studies*, 1025–1028.

Jungmin, K., & Youngsun, L. (2016). Serious games for the job training of persons with developmental disabilities. *Computers & Education*, 95, 328–339. DOI: 10.1016/j.compedu.2016.02.001

Kamp-Roelands, N. (2013). A commentary on 'Integrated reporting – a review of developments and their implications for the accounting curriculum'. *Accounting Education*, 22(4), 357–359. DOI: 10.1080/09639284.2013.817799

Kapilashrami, A., Otis, M., Omodara, D., Nandi, A., Vats, A., Adeniyi, O. V., Speed, E., Potter, J., Eder, B., Pareek, M., & Bhui, K. (2021). Ethnic Disparities in Health &Amp; Social Care Workers' Exposure, Protection, and Clinical Management of the COVID-19 Pandemic in the UK. *Critical Public Health*, 32(1), 68–81. DOI: 10.1080/09581596.2021.1959020

Kapp, K. M. (2012). *The gamification of learning and instruction: game-based methods and strategies for training and education*. John Wiley & Sons.

Kapralos, B., Fisher, S., Clarkson, J., & van Oostveen, R. (2015). A course on serious game design and development using an online problem-based learning approach. *Interactive Technology and Smart Education*, 12(2), 116–136. DOI: 10.1108/ITSE-10-2014-0033

Kavesh, M. A. (2024). Welcoming the foreigner: Notes on the possibility of multispecies hospitality. *American Anthropologist*, 126(1), 109–119. DOI: 10.1111/aman.13938

Keesee, G. S. (2012). Educational games. Teaching and learning resources. http://teachinglearningresources.pbworks.com/w/page/35130965/Educational%20Games.

Kent, S. (2001). *The ultimate history of video games: From Pong to Pokémon and beyond...the story behind the craze that touched our lives and changed the world*. Crown.

Khan, M. A., Merabet, A., Alkaabi, S., & Sayed, H. E. (2022). Game-based learning platform to enhance cybersecurity education. *Education and Information Technologies*, 27(4), 1–25. DOI: 10.1007/s10639-021-10807-6

Khan, N., Korac-Kakabadse, N., Skouloudis, A., & Dimopoulos, A. (2019). Diversity in the workplace: An overview of disability employment disclosures among UK firms. *Corporate Social Responsibility and Environmental Management*, 26(1), 170–185. DOI: 10.1002/csr.1669

Kiili, K. (2005). Digital game-based learning: Towards an experiential gaming model. *The Internet and Higher Education*, 8(1), 13–24. DOI: 10.1016/j.iheduc.2004.12.001

Kim, K., Schmierbach, M. G., Bellur, S., Chung, M. Y., Fraustino, J. D., Dardis, F., & Ahern, L. (2015). Is it a sense of autonomy, control, or attachment? Exploring the effects of in-game customization on game enjoyment. *Computers in Human Behavior*, 48, 695–705. DOI: 10.1016/j.chb.2015.02.011

Kim, P., Hong, J. S., Bonk, C., & Lim, G. (2011). Effects of group reflection variations in project-based learning integrated in a Web 2.0 learning space. *Interactive Learning Environments*, 19(4), 333–349. DOI: 10.1080/10494820903210782

Kim, T. W., & Werbach, K. (2016). More than just a game: Ethical issues in gamification. *Ethics and Information Technology*, 18(2), 157–173. DOI: 10.1007/s10676-016-9401-5

Kinzie, M. B. (1990). Requirements and benefits of effective interactive instruction: Learner control, self-regulation, and continuing motivation. *Educational Technology Research and Development*, 38(1), 5–21. DOI: 10.1007/BF02298244

Kinzie, M. B., & Sullivan, H. J. (1989). Continuing motivation, learner control, and CAI. *Educational Technology Research and Development*, 37(2), 5–14. DOI: 10.1007/BF02298286

Kirriemuir, J., & McFarlane, A. (2004). Literature review in games and learning: https://telearn.hal.science/hal-00190453/document

Kirton, G. (2020). Diversity and inclusion in a changing world of work. In *The future of work and employment* (pp. 49–64). Edward Elgar Publishing. DOI: 10.4337/9781786438256.00011

Kolb, A. Y., & Kolb, D. A. (2013). *The Kolb learning style inventory version 4.0: A comprehensive guide to the theory, psychometrics, research on validity and educational applications*. Experience Based Learning Systems, Inc.

Kolb, D. A. (1984). *Experiential learning: Experience as the source of learning and development*. Prentice Hall. DOI: 10.1016/B978-0-7506-7223-8.50017-4

Kolk, A. (2003). Trends in sustainability reporting by the Fortune Global 250. *Business Strategy and the Environment*, 12(5), 279–291. DOI: 10.1002/bse.370

Köllen, T. (2021). Diversity management: A critical review and agenda for the future. *Journal of Management Inquiry*, 30(3), 259–272. DOI: 10.1177/1056492619868025

Kopp, S. (2018). The Power of Play: How to Spark Adult Learning and Innovation. https://www.mckinsey.com/featured-insights/themes/how-to-unlock-the-power-of-learning

Korhonen, T., Halonen, R., Ravelin, T., Kemppainen, J., & Koskela, K. (2017, September). A Multidisciplinary Approach to Serious Game Development in the Health Sector. In *MCIS* (p. 30).

Korteling, J. E., Helsdingen, A. S., Sluimer, R. R., Van Emmerik, M. L., & Kappé, B. (2011). *Transfer of Gaming: Transfer of training in serious gaming*. TNO.

Koster, R. (2004). *Theory of Fun for Game Design*. O'Reilly Media.

Koupritzioti, D., & Xinogalos, S. (2020). PyDiophantus maze game: Play it to learn mathematics or implement it to learn game programming in Python. *Education and Information Technologies*, 25(4), 2747–2764. DOI: 10.1007/s10639-019-10087-1

Krath, J., Schürmann, L., & Von Korflesch, H. F. (2021). Revealing the theoretical basis of gamification: A systematic review and analysis of theory in research on gamification, serious games and game-based learning. *Computers in Human Behavior*, 125, 106963. DOI: 10.1016/j.chb.2021.106963

Kraus, S., Schleich, M., Tröster, A., & Roig-Tierno, N. (2019). Cultural diversity in large enterprises: A qualitative analysis from the Alpine Rhine Valley. *Journal of Promotion Management*, 25(5), 640–663. DOI: 10.1080/10496491.2019.1585570

Krosnick, J. A. (2018). Questionnaire design. The Palgrave handbook of survey research, 439-455. DOI: 10.1007/978-3-319-54395-6_53

Kuknor, S. C., & Bhattacharya, S. (2022). Inclusive leadership: New age leadership to foster organizational inclusion. *European Journal of Training and Development*, 46(9), 771–797. DOI: 10.1108/EJTD-07-2019-0132

Kuppers, P. (2016). Diversity: Disability. *Art Journal*, 75(1), 93–97. DOI: 10.1080/00043249.2016.1171549

Kurke, L. (1999). Ancient Greek board games and how to play them. *Classical Philology*, 94(3), 247–267. DOI: 10.1086/449440

Laamarti, F., Eid, M., & El Saddik, A. (2014). An overview of serious games. *International Journal of Computer Games Technology*, 2014(1), 358152.

Lai, C.-L., & Hwang, G.-J. (2016). A self-regulated flipped classroom approach to improving students' learning performance in a mathematics course. *Computers & Education*, 100, 126–140. DOI: 10.1016/j.compedu.2016.05.006

Landers, R. N. (2014). Developing a Theory of Gamified Learning: Linking Serious Games and Gamification of Learning. *Simulation & Gaming*, 45(6), 752–768. DOI: 10.1177/1046878114563660

Landers, R. N., Armstrong, M. B., & Collmus, A. B. (2017). How to use game elements to enhance learning: Applications of the theory of gamified learning. In *Serious games and edutainment applications* (pp. 457–483). Springer. DOI: 10.1007/978-3-319-51645-5_21

Landow, G. P. (2009). *Victorian types, Victorian shadows: Biblical typology in Victorian literature, art, and thought*. Routledge.

Laporte, L., & Zaman, B. (2018). A comparative analysis of programming games, looking through the lens of an instructional design model and a game attributes taxonomy. *Entertainment Computing*, 25, 48–61. DOI: 10.1016/j.entcom.2017.12.005

Larsen, T. J., Sørebø, A. M., & Sørebø, Ø. (2009). The role of task-technology fit as users' motivation to continue information system use. *Computers in Human Behavior*, 25(3), 778–784. DOI: 10.1016/j.chb.2009.02.006

Larson, K. (2020). Serious games and gamification in the corporate training environment: A literature review. *TechTrends*, 64(2), 319–328. DOI: 10.1007/s11528-019-00446-7

Lavander, T. (2011). Video Games as Change Agents—The Case of Homeless: It's No Game | The Homeless Hub, McMaster. *Journal of Communication*, 7(1), 13–36.

Lavoué, E., Monterrat, B., Desmarais, M., & George, S. (2019). Adaptive Gamification for Learning Environments, in IEEE Transactions on Learning Technologies, 12(1), 16-28. .DOI: 10.1109/TLT.2018.2823710

Lee, C. (2022). Coming Out in the University Workplace: A Case Study of LGBTQ+staff Visibility. *Higher Education*, 85(5), 1181–1199. DOI: 10.1007/s10734-022-00884-y PMID: 35730026

Lee, H. (2023). Collaborative governance platforms and outcomes: An analysis of Clean Cities coalitions. *Governance: An International Journal of Policy, Administration and Institutions*, 36(3), 805–825. DOI: 10.1111/gove.12702

Lee, H., & Reade, C. (2014). Ethnic Homophily Perceptions as an Emergent IHRM Challenge: Evidence From Firms Operating in Sri Lanka During the Ethnic Conflict. *International Journal of Human Resource Management*, 26(13), 1645–1664. DOI: 10.1080/09585192.2014.958514

Lee, J. (2020). Problem-based gaming via an augmented reality mobile game and a printed game in foreign language education. *Education and Information Technologies*, 1–29.

Lee, K., & Fanguy, M. (2022). Online exam proctoring technologies: Educational innovation or deterioration? *British Journal of Educational Technology*, 53(3), 475–490. DOI: 10.1111/bjet.13182

Lee, Y. J. (2011). A study on the effect of teaching innovation on learning effectiveness with learning satisfaction as a mediator. *World Transactions on Engineering and Technology Education*, 9(2), 92–101.

Legaki, N. Z., Xi, N., Hamari, J., Karpouzis, K., & Assimakopoulos, V. (2020). The Effect of Challenge-Based Gamification on Learning: An Experiment in the Context of Statistics Education. *International Journal of Human-Computer Studies*, 144, 102496. DOI: 10.1016/j.ijhcs.2020.102496 PMID: 32565668

Lehan, T., Hussey, H., & Babcock, A. (2020). Mission unaccomplished: Beyond "talk [ing] a good game" to promote diversity and inclusion. *Journal of Educational Research and Practice*, 10(1), 12. DOI: 10.5590/JERAP.2020.10.1.12

Lepper, M. R., & Cordova, D. I. (1992). A desire to be taught: Instructional consequences of intrinsic motivation. *Motivation and Emotion*, 16(3), 187–208. DOI: 10.1007/BF00991651

Lepper, M. R., & Malone, T. W. (2021). Intrinsic motivation and instructional effectiveness in computer-based education. In *Aptitude, learning, and instruction* (pp. 255–286). Routledge.

Lerbinger, O. (2006). *Corporate public affairs: Interacting with interest groups, media, and government*. Routledge. DOI: 10.4324/9781410617262

Leslie, L. M., Snyder, M., & Glomb, T. M. (2013). Who Gives? Multilevel Effects of Gender and Ethnicity on Workplace Charitable Giving. *The Journal of Applied Psychology*, 98(1), 49–62. DOI: 10.1037/a0029943 PMID: 22985116

Liang, X., Chen, M., & Leung, V. C. M. (2011). A game-theoretic approach for relay assignment over distributed wireless networks. *IWCMC - Int. Wirel. Commun. Mob. Comput. Conf.*, 1557–1562. DOI: 10.1109/IWCMC.2011.5982770

Libe, C., Grenouillat, A., Lagoutte, J., Jean, C., & Maranzana, N. (2020). *Creativity and Innovation for Children: Presentation and First Experiment of New (Serious).* Game., DOI: 10.35199/EPDE.2020.40

Liboriussen, B., & Martin, P. (2016). Games and gaming in China. *Games and Culture*, 11(3), 227–232. DOI: 10.1177/1555412015615296

Lier, L. M., & Breuer, C. (2020). The motivating power of gamification: Does the inclusion of game elements increase the effectiveness of worksite health promotion programs? *International Journal of Workplace Health Management, 13*(1), 1–15. Advance online publication. DOI: 10.1108/IJWHM-04-2019-0055

Ligorio, L., Venturelli, A., Rosato, P., & Campo, R. (2023). Fostering sustainable development goals through gamification. *Journal of Management & Organization*, 1–22. Advance online publication. DOI: 10.1017/jmo.2023.54

Lippincott, B., & Pergola, T. M. (2009). Use of a job cost simulation to engage gen Y students. *Journal of the International Academy for Case Studies*, 15(1), 107.

Loon, M., Evans, J., & Kerridge, C. (2015). Learning with a strategic management simulation game: A case study. *International Journal of Management Education*, 13(3), 227–236. DOI: 10.1016/j.ijme.2015.06.002

Lopes, A. P., & Soares, F. (2018). Perception and performance in a flipped Financial Mathematics classroom. *International Journal of Management Education*, 16(1), 105–113. DOI: 10.1016/j.ijme.2018.01.001

Lorbiecki, A., & Gavin, J. (2000). Critical turns in the evolution of Diversity Management. *British Journal of Management*, 11(s1), 11. DOI: 10.1111/1467-8551.11.s1.3

Loureiro, S. M. C., Bilro, R. G., & de Aires Angelino, F. J. (2020). Virtual reality and gamification in marketing higher education: a review and research agenda. *Spanish Journal of Marketing-ESIC.*

Lozano, R. (2007). Collaboration as a pathway for sustainability. *Sustainable Development (Bradford)*, 15(6), 370–381. DOI: 10.1002/sd.322

Lozano, R. (2011). Addressing stakeholders and better contributing to sustainability through game theory. *Journal of Corporate Citizenship*, 2011(43), 45–62. DOI: 10.9774/GLEAF.4700.2011.au.00004

Lyons, R. M., Fox, G., & Stephens, S. (2023). Gamification to enhance engagement and higher order learning in entrepreneurial education. *Education and Training. Education + Training*, 65(3), 416–432. Advance online publication. DOI: 10.1108/ET-05-2022-0204

Maji, S., Yadav, N., & Gupta, P. (2023). LGBTQ+ in Workplace: A systematic Review and Reconsideration. *Equality, Diversity and Inclusion*, 43(2), 313–360. DOI: 10.1108/EDI-02-2022-0049

Malaquias, R. F., Malaquias, F. F. D. O., Junior, D. M. B., & Zambra, P. (2018). The use of a serious game and academic performance of undergraduate accounting students: An empirical analysis. *Turkish Online Journal of Distance Education*, 19(2), 117–127. DOI: 10.17718/tojde.415825

Mallam, S. C., Nazir, S., & Renganayagalu, S. K. (2019). Rethinking maritime education, training, and operations in the digital era: Applications for emerging immersive technologies. *Journal of Marine Science and Engineering*, 7(12), 428. DOI: 10.3390/jmse7120428

Malone, T. (1981, May). What makes computer games fun? In *Proceedings of the Joint Conference on Easier and More Productive Use of Computer Systems (Part-II): Human Interface and the User Interface-Volume 1981* (p. 143).

Malone, T. W. (1980). *What makes things fun to learn? A study of intrinsically motivating computer games*. Stanford University.

Malone, T. W. (1981a). Toward a theory of intrinsically motivating instruction. *Cognitive Science*, 5(4), 333–369.

Mann, B. D., Eidelson, B. M., Fukuchi, S. G., Nissman, S. A., Robertson, S., & Jardines, L. (2002). The development of an interactive game-based tool for learning surgical management algorithms via computer. *American Journal of Surgery*, 183(3), 305–308. DOI: 10.1016/S0002-9610(02)00800-0 PMID: 11943132

Mara, L. C., Ginieis, M., & Brunet-Icart, I. (2021). Strategies for coping with LGBT discrimination at work: A systematic literature review. *Sexuality Research & Social Policy*, 18(2), 339–354. DOI: 10.1007/s13178-020-00462-w

Marczewski, A. (2013). Gamification: a simple introduction.

Margoudi, M., Oliveira, M., & Waddell, G. (2016, October). Game-based learning of musical instruments: A review and recommendations. In *European Conference on Games Based Learning* (p. 426). Academic Conferences International Limited.

Mariappanadar, S. (2024). Improving Quality of Work for Positive Health: Interaction of Sustainable Development Goal (SDG) 8 and SDG 3 from the Sustainable HRM Perspective. *Sustainability (Basel)*, 16(13), 5356. DOI: 10.3390/su16135356

Marlisco (Marine Litter in European Seas: Social Awareness and Co-Responsibility). (2015). Sea Dream Team: A Serious Game on Marine Litter for Youngsters. Accessed: August 30, 2023 from https://www.marlisco.eu/serious-game.en.html

Marquart-Pyatt, S. T. (2016). Environmental trust: A cross-region and cross-country study. *Society & Natural Resources*, 29(9), 1032–1048. DOI: 10.1080/08941920.2016.1164265

Martin, A. (2000). The design and evolution of a simulation/game for teaching information systems development. *Simulation & Gaming*, 31(4), 445–463. DOI: 10.1177/104687810003100401

Marzano, R. J. (2003). *What works in schools: Translating research into action*. ASCD.

Matuleviciene, M., & Stravinskiene, J. (2015). The importance of stakeholders for corporate reputation. *The Engineering Economist*, 26(1), 75–83.

Maxfield, S., Wang, L., & Magaldi de Sousa, M. (2018). The effectiveness of bank governance reforms in the wake of the financial crisis: A stakeholder approach. *Journal of Business Ethics*, 150(2), 485–503. DOI: 10.1007/s10551-016-3116-8

Mayr, K., & Teller, C. (2024). The ethical edge: Unveiling the power of virtuousness in retailing from employees' perspectives. *Journal of Retailing and Consumer Services*, 81, 104025. DOI: 10.1016/j.jretconser.2024.104025

Mazur, B. (2010). Cultural diversity in organisational theory and practice. Journal of intercultural management, 2(2), 5-15.

Mazur, B. (2014). Building diverse and inclusive organizational culture-best practices: A case study of Cisco Co. Journal of Intercultural Management, 6(4.1), 169-179;

Mazure, C. M., & Jones, D. P. (2015). Twenty Years and Still Counting: Including Women as Participants and Studying Sex and Gender in Biomedical Research. *BMC Women's Health*, 15(1), 94. Advance online publication. DOI: 10.1186/s12905-015-0251-9 PMID: 26503700

McKee, V. (1992). Out of sight—and out of mind. *Life and Times, The Times, 22*, 5–22.

McLuhan, M. (1967). *Gli strumenti del comunicare*. Il Saggiatore.

McMillan-Capehart, A., Aaron, J. R., & Cline, B. N. (2010). Investor reactions to diversity reputation signals. *Corporate Reputation Review*, 13(3), 184–197. DOI: 10.1057/crr.2010.20

Mello-Carpes, de Paiva Abreu, Staniscuaski, Souza, Campagnole-Santos, & Irigoyen. (2019). Actions developed by the Brazilian Physiological Society to promote women's participation in science. Academic Press.

Meshcheryakova, A. O., & Hemmert, F. (2023). Tales from the Future: Exploring Game Design Strategies for Creativity and Play. In *Lect. Notes Educ. Technol.* (pp. 565–574). Springer Science and Business Media Deutschland GmbH. DOI: 10.1007/978-981-99-0942-1_59

Meske, C., Brockmann, T., Wilms, K., & Stieglitz, S. (2017). Social collaboration and gamification. Gamification: Using game elements in serious contexts, 93-109;

Meya, J. N., & Eisenack, K. (2018). Effectiveness of gaming for communicating and teaching climate change. *Climatic Change*, 149(3-4), 319–333. DOI: 10.1007/s10584-018-2254-7

Mezirow, J. (1991). *Transformative dimensions of adult learning*. Jossey-Bass.

Mezirow, J. (2000). Learning to think like an adult: Core concepts of transformation theory. In Mezirow, J. (Eds.), *Learning as transformation: Critical perspectives on a theory in progress* (pp. 3–33). Jossey-Bass.

Michael, D., & Chen, S. (2006). *Serious games: Games that educate, train, and inform*. Thomson Course Technology.

Mikkelson, G. M. (2013). Growth is the problem; equality is the solution. *Sustainability (Basel)*, 5(2), 432–439. DOI: 10.3390/su5020432

Miller, S. G. (2004). *Ancient Greek athletics*. Yale University Press.

Mitchell, A., & Savill-Smith, C. (2004). The use of computer and video games for learning. A review of the literature, 88(10), 1397-1399.

Mitchell, R. K., Agle, B. R., & Wood, D. J. (1997). Toward a theory of stakeholder identification and salience: Defining the principle of who and what really counts. *Academy of Management Review*, 22(4), 853–886. DOI: 10.2307/259247

Modarelli, G. (2023). Editorial: Combining CSR, public-private policies, inclusiveness and complex challenges for integral well-being by reciprocity relations — An agenda for global governance. *Corporate and Business Strategy Review*, 4(2), 4–6. DOI: 10.22495/cbsrv4i2editorial

Modarelli, G. (2023). The "gaming society" between homologation and diversity: Trends, evolutions, perspectives and critical aspects of the fragmented self in organized and hyperlinked relations. *Journal of Organizational Culture Communications and Conflict*, 27(S3), 1–4.

Modarelli, G., Rainero, C., & Amelio, S. (2024). Games, diversity and occupation: A bidimensional CSR perspective for adaptive organisations. *Social Responsibility Journal*, 20(9), 1787–1808. DOI: 10.1108/SRJ-07-2023-0390

Modell, S. (2022). Accounting for institutional work: A critical review. *European Accounting Review*, 31(1), 33–58. DOI: 10.1080/09638180.2020.1820354

Möhlen, L. K., Handle-Pfeiffer, D., Proyer, M., Schmölz, A., & Kremsner, G. (2018, November). Playful Social Inclusion: Approaching Inclusive Thinking and Acting Through Game Based Learning. In *Proceedings of the 17th European Conference on e-Learning* (pp. 383-93)

Molnár, C., Csehné Papp, I., & Juhász, T. (2024). Organizational strategies and tools of employee well-being as perceived by employees. *Management & Marketing*, 19(2), 336–361. DOI: 10.2478/mmcks-2024-0015

Mor Barak, M. E., & Daya, P. (2013). Fostering inclusion from the inside out to create an inclusive workplace. Diversity at work: The practice of inclusion, 391-412.

Moreno, J. L. (1934). Who shall survive? A new approach to the problem of human interrelations.

Morini, L., Chen, Y.-F., Adefila, A., Mahon, D., Dawson, M., Mohamad, F., Minoi, J. L., & Schwartz, G. (2022). Playful Participatory Mapping: Co-creating Games to Foster Systems Thinking. In Costa C. (A c. Di), *Proc. European Conf. Games-based Learn.* (pp. 387–395). Dechema e.V. https://www.scopus.com/inward/record.uri?eid=2-s2.0-85141169336&partnerID=40&md5=fa24c927511ab71026d9a80bad4cd1b3

Morris, A. D. (1984). *The origins of the civil rights movement.* Simon and Schuster.

Mosleh, W., Bäckstroem, I., Manfrini, C., & Leue-Bensch, C. (2024). Organizing employee-driven innovation (EDI) through game-based formats: Understanding participation. *Creativity and Innovation Management*, caim.12625. Advance online publication. DOI: 10.1111/caim.12625

Mousa, M., Massoud, H. K., & Ayoubi, R. M. (2020). Gender, diversity management perceptions, workplace happiness and organisational citizenship behaviour. *Employee Relations*, 42(6), 1249–1269. DOI: 10.1108/ER-10-2019-0385

Munsell, E. G. S., Kudla, A., Su, H., Wong, J., Crown, D., Capraro, P., Trierweiler, R., Park, M., & Heinemann, A. W. (2022). Employers' Perceptions of Challenges and Strategies in Hiring, Retaining, and Promoting Employees With Physical Disabilities. *Rehabilitation Counseling Bulletin*, 67(3), 177–189. DOI: 10.1177/00343552221130304

Murray, H. J. R. (1997). *Hamlet on the Holodeck: The future of narrative in cyberspace*. MIT press.

Mylonas, G., Hofstaetter, J., Giannakos, M., Friedl, A., & Koulouris, P. (2023). Playful interventions for sustainability awareness in educational environments: A longitudinal, large-scale study in three countries. *International Journal of Child-Computer Interaction, 35.International Journal of Child-Computer Interaction*, 35, 100562. Advance online publication. DOI: 10.1016/j.ijcci.2022.100562

Nadeem, M., Oroszlanyova, M., & Farag, W. (2023). Effect of Digital Game-Based Learning on Student Engagement and Motivation. *Computers, 12*(9). https://doi.org/ DOI: 10.3390/computers12090177

Nafukho, F. M., Roessler, R. T., & Kacirek, K. (2010). Disability as a Diversity Factor: Implications for Human Resource Practices. *Advances in Developing Human Resources*, 12(4), 395–406. DOI: 10.1177/1523422310379209

Nah, F. F. H., Zeng, Q., Telaprolu, V. R., Ayyappa, A. P., & Eschenbrenner, B. (2014). Gamification of education: a review of literature. *HCI in Business: First International Conference, HCIB 2014, Held as Part of HCI International 2014, Heraklion, Crete, Greece, June 22-27, 2014Proceedings*, 1, 401–409.

Navas de Maya, B., Arslan, O., Akyuz, E., Kurt, R. E., & Turan, O. (2022). Application of data-mining techniques to predict and rank maritime non-conformities in tanker shipping companies using accident inspection reports. *Ships and Offshore Structures*, 17(3), 687–694. DOI: 10.1080/17445302.2020.1862530

Nederveen Pieterse, A., Van Knippenberg, D., & Van Dierendonck, D. (2013). Cultural diversity and team performance: The role of team member goal orientation. *Academy of Management Journal*, 56(3), 782–804. DOI: 10.5465/amj.2010.0992

Neumark, D. (2021). Age discrimination in hiring: Evidence from age-blind vs. non-age-blind hiring procedures. *The Journal of Human Resources*.

Neville, B. A., Bell, S. J., & Mengüç, B. (2005). Corporate reputation, stakeholders and the social performance-financial performance relationship. *European Journal of Marketing*, 39(9/10), 1184–1198. DOI: 10.1108/03090560510610798

Newman, J. (2004). *Videogames*. Routledge. DOI: 10.4324/9780203642900

Nguyen, C. T. (2017). Philosophy of games. Philosophy Compass, 12(8), e12426.
Noemí, P.M., & Máximo, S.H. (2014). Educational games for learning. *Universal Journal of Educational Research*, 2(3), 230–238.

Nicholson, S. (2015). A recipe for meaningful gamification. In *Gamification in education and business* (pp. 1–20). Springer. DOI: 10.1007/978-3-319-10208-5_1

Nikitakos, N., Sirris, I., Dalaklis, D., Papachristos, D., & Tsoukalas, V. D. (2017). Game-based learning for maritime education and training: The case of Trader of the World. *WMU Journal of Maritime Affairs*, 16(2), 265–291. DOI: 10.1007/s13437-016-0119-3

Noemí, P. M., & Máximo, S. H. (2014). Educational games for learning. *Universal Journal of Educational Research*, 2(3), 230–238. DOI: 10.13189/ujer.2014.020305

Noland, J., & Phillips, R. (2010). Stakeholder engagement, discourse ethics and strategic management. *International Journal of Management Reviews*, 12(1), 39–49. DOI: 10.1111/j.1468-2370.2009.00279.x

Núñez Barriopedro, E., Penelas Leguía, A., & Cuesta Valiño, P. (2014). The development of web 3.0 as an innovation in teaching marketing and market research. *Caracciolos, revista digital de investigación en docencia, 2*(1).

Nygren, N. V., Kankainen, V., & Brunet, L. (2022). Offsetting Game—Framing Environmental Issues in the Design of a Serious Game. *Simulation & Gaming*, 53(6), 615–644. DOI: 10.1177/10468781221126786

O'Neil, H. F., Wainess, R., & Baker, E. L. (2005). Classification of learning outcomes: Evidence from the computer games literature. *Curriculum Journal*, 16(4), 455–474. DOI: 10.1080/09585170500384529

O'Reilly, C. A.III, Williams, K. Y., & Barsade, S. (1998). Group demography and innovation: Does diversity help? In Gruenfeld, D. H. (Ed.), *Composition* (pp. 183–207). Elsevier Science/JAI Press.

Oblinger, D. G. (2004). The Next Generation of Educational Engagement. *Journal of Interactive Media in Education*, 8(1), 1–18. DOI: 10.5334/2004-8-oblinger

Oelrich, S., Siebold, N., & Ketelhut, K. (2024). Diversity at work: Firms' strategic responses to mandatory diversity disclosure. *Accounting Horizons*, 38(1), 123–138. DOI: 10.2308/HORIZONS-2022-083

Oil Companies International Marine Forum (OCIMF). (2016). *Ship Inspection Report (SIRE) Programme*. 2014 Edition Rev.1.2.

Oil Companies International Marine Forum (OCIMF). (2021, August 01). *Ship Inspection Report Program (SIRE)*. Retrieved from https://www.ocimf.org/programmes/sire

Oil Companies International Marine Forum. (2023a). Ship Inspection Report Program (SIRE). https://www.ocimf.org/programmes/sire

Oil Companies International Marine Forum. (2023b). SIRE 2.0. https://www.ocimf.org/programmes/sire-2-0

Oil Companies International Marine Forum. (2023c). SIRE 2.0. Question Library Part-1 Chapters 1-7 Version 2.0. https://www.ocimf.org/document-libary/630-sire-2-0-question-library-part-1-chapters-1-to-7-version-1-0-january-2022/file

Oil Companies International Marine Forum. (2023d). SIRE 2.0. Question Library Part-2 Chapters 8-12 Version 2.0. https://www.ocimf.org/document-libary/631-sire-2-0-question-library-part-2-chapters-8-to-12-version-1-0-january-2022/file

Oliveira, M., & Petersen, S. (2014). The choice of serious games and gamification. In *International Conference on Serious Games Development and Applications*. Springer. DOI: 10.1007/978-3-319-11623-5_18

Oliver, R. L. (1980). A cognitive model of the antecedents and consequences of satisfaction decisions. *JMR, Journal of Marketing Research*, 17(11), 460–469. DOI: 10.1177/002224378001700405

Olken, B. A. (2009). Do Television and Radio Destroy Social Capital? Evidence From Indonesian Villages. *American Economic Journal. Applied Economics*, 1(4), 1–33. DOI: 10.1257/app.1.4.1

Olmo-Muñoz, J. (2023). Exploring Gamification Approaches for Enhancing Computational Thinking in Young Learners. *Education Sciences*, 13(5), 487. DOI: 10.3390/educsci13050487

O'Mara, J., & Richter, A. (2011). Global diversity and inclusion benchmarks: Standards for organizations around the world. O'Mara and Associates.

Omar, M., Williams, R. L.Jr, & Lingelbach, D. (2009). Global brand market-entry strategy to manage corporate reputation. *Journal of Product and Brand Management*, 18(3), 177–187. DOI: 10.1108/10610420910957807

Oprescu, F., Jones, C., & Katsikitis, M. (2014). I PLAY AT WORK—Ten principles for transforming work processes through gamification. *Frontiers in Psychology*, 5. Advance online publication. DOI: 10.3389/fpsyg.2014.00014 PMID: 24523704

Oren, M., Pedersen, S., & Butler-Purry, K. L. (2020). Teaching Digital Circuit Design With a 3-D Video Game: The Impact of Using In-Game Tools on Students' Performance. *IEEE Transactions on Education*, 64(1), 24–31. DOI: 10.1109/TE.2020.3000955

Orlandini, P., & Amelio, S. (2022). *Un percorso aziendale verso la sostenibilità*. Giappichelli.

Ortega-Arranz, A., Asensio-Pérez, J. I., Martínez-Monés, A., Bote-Lorenzo, M. L., Ortega-Arranz, H., & Kalz, M. (2022). GamiTool: Supporting instructors in the gamification of MOOCs. *IEEE Access : Practical Innovations, Open Solutions*, 10, 131965–131979. DOI: 10.1109/ACCESS.2022.3228762

Orús, C., Barlés, M. J., Belanche, D., Casaló, L., Fraj, E., & Gurrea, R. (2014). Affective and objective consequences of using a YouTube channel to support teaching in marketing. National Marketing Congress AEMARK, 17-19 September, Elche (España).

Orús, C., Barlés, M. J., Belanche, D., Casaló, L., Fraj, E., & Gurrea, R. (2016). The effects of learner-generated videos for YouTube on learning outcomes and satisfaction. *Computers & Education*, 95, 254–269. DOI: 10.1016/j.compedu.2016.01.007

Owen, P. (2017). How gamification can help your business engage in sustainability. In *How Gamification Can Help Your Business Engage in Sustainability* (p. 77). Taylor and Francis. DOI: 10.4324/9781351275606

Owen, G. (2013). A rejoinder to commentaries on 'integrated reporting: A review of developments and their implications for the accounting curriculum'. *Accounting Education*, 22(4), 363–365. DOI: 10.1080/09639284.2013.817801

Özbilgin, M. (2009). Equality, diversity and inclusion at work: yesterday, today and tomorrow. Equality, diversity and inclusion at work: a research companion, 1-16.

Özsözgün Çalişkan, A. (2014). How accounting and accountants may contribute in sustainability? *Social Responsibility Journal*, 10(2), 246–267. DOI: 10.1108/SRJ-04-2012-0049

Page, M. J., McKenzie, J. E., Bossuyt, P. M., Boutron, I., Hoffmann, T. C., Mulrow, C. D., Shamseer, L., Tetzlaff, J. M., Akl, E. A., Brennan, S. E., Chou, R., Glanville, J., Grimshaw, J. M., Hróbjartsson, A., Lalu, M. M., Li, T., Loder, E. W., Mayo-Wilson, E., McDonald, S., & Moher, D. (2021). The PRISMA 2020 statement: An updated guideline for reporting systematic reviews. *BMJ (Clinical Research Ed.)*, (71), n71. Advance online publication. DOI: 10.1136/bmj.n71 PMID: 33782057

Pagés, T., Hernández, C., Abadía, A. R., Bueno, C., Ubieto-Artur, I., Márquez Cebrián, M., Sabaté Diaz, S., & Jorba Noguera, H. (2016). Innovation as a teaching competence at the university: Innovation aimed at improving learning. Aloma. *Revista de Psicologia i Ciències de l'Educació*, 34(1), 33–43.

Parizi, R. M., & Dehghantanha, A. (2018, August). On the understanding of gamification in blockchain systems. In 2018 6th international conference on Future Internet of Things and Cloud Workshops (FiCloudW) (pp. 214-219). IEEE DOI: 10.1109/W-FiCloud.2018.00041

Park, J., Montiel, I., Husted, B. W., & Balarezo, R. (2022). The Grand Challenge of Human Health: A Review and an Urgent Call for Business–Health Research. *Business & Society*, 61(5), 1353–1415. DOI: 10.1177/00076503211073519

Patricio, R., Moreira, A., Zurlo, F., & Melazzini, M. (2020). Co-creation of new solutions through gamification: A collaborative innovation practice. *Creativity and Innovation Management*, 29(1), 146–160. DOI: 10.1111/caim.12356

Patrick, H. A., & Kumar, V. R. (2012). Managing workplace diversity: Issues and challenges. *SAGE Open*, 2(2). DOI: 10.1177/2158244012444615

Pedersen, C., Togelius, J., & Yannakakis, G. N. (2010). Modeling player experience for content creation. *IEEE Transactions on Computational Intelligence and AI in Games*, 2(1), 54–67. DOI: 10.1109/TCIAIG.2010.2043950

Peloza, J., Loock, M., Cerruti, J., & Muyot, M. (2012). Sustainability: How stakeholder perceptions differ from corporate reality. *California Management Review*, 55(1), 74–97. DOI: 10.1525/cmr.2012.55.1.74

Peng, W., Lee, M., & Heeter, C. (2010). The Effects of a Serious Game on Role-Taking and Willingness to Help. *Journal of Communication*, 60(4), 723–742. DOI: 10.1111/j.1460-2466.2010.01511.x

Peng, W., Lin, J. H., Pfeiffer, K. A., & Winn, B. (2012). Need satisfaction supportive game features as motivational determinants: An experimental study of a self-determination theory guided exergame. *Media Psychology*, 15(2), 175–196. DOI: 10.1080/15213269.2012.673850

Pereira, J., Echeazarra, L., Sanz-Santamaría, S., & Gutierrez, J. (2014). Student-generated online videos to develop cross-curricular and curricular competencies in nursing studies. *Computers in Human Behavior*, 31, 580–590. DOI: 10.1016/j.chb.2013.06.011

Peterková, J., Repaská, Z., & Prachařová, L. (2022). Best Practice of Using Digital Business Simulation Games in Business Education. *Sustainability (Basel)*, 14(15), 8987. DOI: 10.3390/su14158987

Petersen, S. A., & Ekambaram, A. (2016, October). Interaction, Experience, Reflection: Enhancing Project Management Training using Serious Games. In European Conference on Games Based Learning (p. 521). Academic Conferences International Limited.

Petrov, A. (2014), Using Minecraft in Education: A Qualitative Study on Benefits and Challenges of Game-Based Education, TSpace Repository OISE, Master of Teaching Research Project, University of Toronto, https://hdl.handle.net/1807/67048

Philbin-Briscoe, O., Simon, B., Mudur, S., Poullis, C., Rizvic, S., Boskovic, D., . . . Skarlatos, D. (2017, September). A serious game for understanding ancient seafaring in the Mediterranean sea. In *2017 9th international conference on virtual worlds and games for serious applications (VS-games)* (pp. 1-5). IEEE. DOI: 10.1109/VS-GAMES.2017.8055804

Phillips, R. (1999). On stakeholder delimitation. *Business & Society*, 38(1), 32.

Phillips, R. (2003). *Stakeholder theory and organizational ethics*. Berrett-Koehler Publishers.

Piaget, J., & Cook, M. T. (1954). The development of object concept.

Piazza, F. (2006). L'argomentazione come gioco linguistico. Il punto di vista aristotelico. *Giornale di Metafisica*, 389–396.

Pineda-Martínez, M., Llanos-Ruiz, D., Puente-Torre, P., & García-Delgado, M. Á. (2023). Impact of Video Games, Gamification, and Game-Based Learning on Sustainability Education in Higher Education. *Sustainability (Basel)*, 15(17), 13032. DOI: 10.3390/su151713032

Pivec, M. (2004). *Guidelines for Game-based Learning*. Pabst Science Publishers.

Plass, J. L., Homer, B. D., & Kinzer, C. K. (2015). Foundations of game-based learning. *Educational Psychologist*, 50(4), 258–283. DOI: 10.1080/00461520.2015.1122533

Plato, . (1992). *Laws*. Cambridge University Press.

Plummer, E. M.The Olympic Games in Ancient Times. (1898). II. The Olympic Games in Ancient Times. *American Physical Education Review*, 3(1), 1–18. DOI: 10.1080/23267224.1898.10649670

Polo-Peña, A. I., Fernández-Ruano, M. L., & Frías-Jamilena, D. M. (2024). The role of gamified environmental interpretation in boosting destination perceived value. *Tourism & Management Studies*, 20(2), 55–68. DOI: 10.18089/tms.20240205

Ponomareva, Y., Uman, T., Bodolica, V., & Wennberg, K. (2022). Cultural diversity in top management teams: Review and agenda for future research. *Journal of World Business*, 57(4), 101328. DOI: 10.1016/j.jwb.2022.101328

Poonsawad, A., Srisomphan, J., & Sanrach, C. (2022). Synthesis of problem-based interactive digital storytelling learning model under gamification environment promotes students' problem-solving skills. *International Journal of Emerging Technologies in Learning*, 17(5), 103–119. DOI: 10.3991/ijet.v17i05.28181

Porter, G. G. (2013). Minecraft for children with autism. Retrieved from Autism Key: https://www.autismkey.com/minecraft-for-children-with-autism/

Post, J. E., Preston, L. E., & Sachs, S. (2002). Managing the extended enterprise: The new stakeholder view. *California Management Review*, 45(1), 6–28. DOI: 10.2307/41166151

Poullis, C., Kersten-Oertel, M., Benjamin, J. P., Philbin-Briscoe, O., Simon, B., Perissiou, D., Demesticha, S., Markou, E., Frentzos, E., Kyriakidis, P., Skarlatos, D., & Rizvic, S. (2019). Evaluation of "The Seafarers": A serious game on seaborne trade in the Mediterranean sea during the Classical period. *Digital Applications in Archaeology and Cultural Heritage*, 12, e00090. DOI: 10.1016/j.daach.2019.e00090

Prado, A. M., Arce, R., Lopez, L. E., García, J., & Pearson, A. A. (2020). Simulations Versus Case Studies: Effectively Teaching the Premises of Sustainable Development in the Classroom. *Journal of Business Ethics*, 161(2), 303–327. DOI: 10.1007/s10551-019-04217-5

Prasad, K. D. V., Mruthyanjaya Rao, M., & Vaidya, R. (2019). Gamification and resource pooling for improving operational efficiency and effective management of human resources: A case study with an ecommerce company. *International Journal of Management, 10*(6), 76–87. Advance online publication. DOI: 10.34218/IJM.10.6.2019.008

Prensky, M. (2001). Fun, play and games: What makes games engaging. Digital game-based learning, 5(1), 5-31.

Prensky, M. (2003). Digital game-based learning. Computers in entertainment (CIE), 1(1), 21-21.

Prensky, M. (2003). Digital game-based learning. *Computers in Entertainment*, 1(1), 21–21. DOI: 10.1145/950566.950596

Prosen, M. (2022). Nursing Students' Perception of Gender-Defined Roles in Nursing: A Qualitative Descriptive Study. *BMC Nursing*, 21(1), 104. Advance online publication. DOI: 10.1186/s12912-022-00876-4 PMID: 35509039

Provost, J. A. (1990). Work, play, and type: Achieving balance in your life.

Pruyn, J. (2023). The use of digital games in academic maritime education: A theoretical framework and practical applications. *Maritime Policy & Management*, 1–14.

Puncheva, P. (2008). The role of corporate reputation in the stakeholder decision-making process. *Business & Society*, 47(3), 272–290. DOI: 10.1177/0007650306297946

Putnam, R. D. (2000). Bowling alone: America's declining social capital. In *Culture and politics: A reader* (pp. 223–234). Palgrave Macmillan US.

Qian, M., & Clark, K. R. (2016). Game-based Learning and 21st century skills: A review of recent research. *Computers in Human Behavior*, 63, 50–58. DOI: 10.1016/j.chb.2016.05.023

Quinn, G. P., Sánchez, J., Sutton, S. K., Vadaparampil, S. T., Nguyêñ, G. T., Green, B. L., Kanetsky, P. A., & Schabath, M. B. (2015). Cancer and Lesbian, Gay, Bisexual, Transgender/Transsexual, and Queer/Questioning (LGBTQ) Populations. *CA: a Cancer Journal for Clinicians*, 65(5), 384–400. DOI: 10.3322/caac.21288 PMID: 26186412

Rajashekar, S., & Jain, A. (2024). A Thematic Analysis on "Employee Engagement in IT Companies from the Perspective of Holistic Well-being Initiatives". *Employee Responsibilities and Rights Journal*, 36(2), 165–187. DOI: 10.1007/s10672-023-09440-x

Ranchhod, A., Gurău, C., Loukis, E., & Trivedi, R. (2014). Evaluating the educational effectiveness of simulation games: A value generation model. Information Sciences, pp. 264, 75–90.

Rauschenberger, M., Willems, A., Ternieden, M., & Thomaschewski, J. (2019). Towards the use of gamification frameworks in learning environments. *Journal of Interactive Learning Research*, 30(2), 147–165.

Redman, A., Wiek, A., & Barth, M. (2021). Current practice of assessing students' sustainability competencies: A review of tools. *Sustainability Science*, 16(1), 117–135. DOI: 10.1007/s11625-020-00855-1

Rehbein, F., Psych, G., Kleimann, M., Mediasci, G., & Mößle, T. (2010). Prevalence and risk factors of video game dependency in adolescence: Results of a German nationwide survey. *Cyberpsychology, Behavior, and Social Networking*, 13(3), 269–277.

Richards, M. B., Becker, K. L., & Stollings-Holder, J. (2024). Escaping generational conflict: Using gamification to examine intergenerational communication & problem-solving. *Review of Managerial Science, 18*(6), 1597–1616. Advance online publication. DOI: 10.1007/s11846-023-00669-2

Rich, B. L., Lepine, J. A., & Crawford, E. R. (2010). Job engagement: Antecedents and effects on job performance. *Academy of Management Journal*, 53(3), 617–635. DOI: 10.5465/amj.2010.51468988

Riemer, V., & Schrader, C. (2015). Learning with quizzes, simulations, and adventures: Students' attitudes, perceptions and intentions to learn with different types of serious games. *Computers & Education*, 88, 160–168. DOI: 10.1016/j.compedu.2015.05.003

Rijamampianina, R., & Carmichael, T. (2005). A pragmatic and holistic approach to managing diversity. *Problems and Perspectives in Management*, (1), 109–117.

Riva G. (2004), *Psicologia dei nuovi media*, Milano: il Mulino.

Roach, A. T., Niebling, B. C., & Kurz, A. (2008). Evaluating the alignment among curriculum, instruction, and assessments: Implications and applications for research and practice. *Psychology in the Schools*, 45(2), 158–176. DOI: 10.1002/pits.20282

Roberson, Q. M. (2006). Disentangling the meanings of diversity and inclusion in organizations. *Group & Organization Management*, 31(2), 212–236. DOI: 10.1177/1059601104273064

Roberts, P. W., & Dowling, G. R. (2002). Corporate reputation and sustained superior financial performance. *Strategic Management Journal*, 23(12), 1077–1093. DOI: 10.1002/smj.274

Robison, L. J., Schmid, A. A., & Barry, P. J. (2002). The Role of Social Capital in the Industrialization of the Food System. *Agricultural and Resource Economics Review*, 31(1), 15–24. DOI: 10.1017/S1068280500003439

Rodela, R. (2013). The Social learning discourse: Trends, Themes and interdisciplinary influences in current research. *Environmental Science & Policy*, 25, 157–166. DOI: 10.1016/j.envsci.2012.09.002

Rodrigues, M. A. B., & Morais, A. I. (2021). How to challenge university students to work on integrated reporting and integrated reporting assurance. *Sustainability (Basel)*, 13(19), 10761. DOI: 10.3390/su131910761

Rodríguez-Gómez, D., & Gairín Sallán, J. (2015). Innovation, organizational learning and knowledge management in educational institutions. *Education*, 24(46), 73–90.

Rodríguez, R. L. (2022). Engaging future engineers: The case study of a serious game implementation. *Education and Information Technologies*, 1–31.

Roithmayr, D. (2003). Locked in inequality: The persistence of discrimination. *Michigan Journal of Race & Law*, 9, 31.

Romero, M. (2015). Work, games and lifelong learning in the 21st century. *Procedia: Social and Behavioral Sciences*, 174, 115–121. DOI: 10.1016/j.sbspro.2015.01.634

Rosati, F., & Faria, L. G. D. (2019). Business contribution to the Sustainable Development Agenda: Organizational factors related to early adoption of SDG reporting. *Corporate Social Responsibility and Environmental Management*, 26(3), 588–597. DOI: 10.1002/csr.1705

Royal Decree 1393/2007, of October 29, which establishes the organization of official university education. Recovered from: https://www.boe.es/buscar/pdf/2007/BOE-A-2007-18770-consolidado.pdf

Royall, S., McCarthy, V., & Miller, G. J. (2022). Creating an inclusive workplace: The effectiveness of diversity training. *J. Glob. Econ. Trade Int. Bus*, 3, 39–55.

Rudestam, K. E., & Newton, R. R. (2014). Surviving your dissertation: A comprehensive guide to content and process. Sage publications.

Ryan, J., Hawdon, J., & Branick, A. (2002). The political economy of diversity: Diversity programs in fortune 500 companies. *Sociological Research Online*, 7(1), 26–40. DOI: 10.5153/sro.702

Ryan, R. M., & Deci, E. L. (2000). Intrinsic and extrinsic motivations: Classic definitions and new directions. *Contemporary Educational Psychology*, 25(1), 54–67. DOI: 10.1006/ceps.1999.1020 PMID: 10620381

Ryan, R. M., & Deci, E. L. (2000). Self-determination theory and the facilitation of intrinsic motivation, social development, and well-being. *The American Psychologist*, 55(1), 68–78. DOI: 10.1037/0003-066X.55.1.68 PMID: 11392867

Ryan, R. M., & Deci, E. L. (2017). *Self-determination theory. Basic psychological needs in motivation, development and wellness*. The Guilford Press. DOI: 10.1521/978.14625/28806

Said, H., & Kamel, N. A. (2023). Linking e-leadership to innovative and proactive work behaviors in tourism higher education institutions: A moderated mediation model using SEM. *Tourism & Management Studies*, 19(4), 47–60. DOI: 10.18089/tms.2023.190404

Sainath, K. L., & Sai, K. T. (2023). Supply Chains Are Playing Games: A Review Literature on Gamification in Supply Chain. *Journal of Future Sustainability*, 3(1), 59–66. DOI: 10.5267/j.jfs.2022.11.005

Salcedo, P., & Alejandra, A. (2023). *Enhancing Students' Motivation in the EFL Classroom Through Life is Strange: A Digital Game-Based Learning Scenario Proposal*. https://diposit.ub.edu/dspace/handle/2445/200580

Salido, P. S., & Breviescas, B. D. (2024). Unlocking Potential: Best Practices for Promoting Independence and Life Skills in Intellectual Disability Learners of Special Education Class of Alubijid Central School. *Best Practices in Disability-Inclusive Education, 3*(1). https://publication.seameosen.edu.my/index.php/diebook/chapter/view/395

Samudhram, A., Stewart, E., Wickramanayake, J., & Sinnakkannu, J. (2014). Value relevance of human capital based disclosures: Moderating effects of labor productivity, investor sentiment, analyst coverage and audit quality. *Advances in Accounting*, 30(2), 338–353. DOI: 10.1016/j.adiac.2014.09.012

Samuels, M. A. B., De Angelis, K., Gibson, H., Han, J., Laurence, J., Matthew, K. E., & Yu, J. (2023). *Inclusion in the American military: A force for diversity*. Rowman & Littlefield.

Sanclemente, F. J., Gamero, N., Medina, F. J., & Mendoza-Denton, R. (2024). A multilevel model of job inclusion of employees with disabilities: The role of organizational socialization tactics, coworkers social support, and an inclusive team context. *Applied Psychology*, 73(3), 887–909. DOI: 10.1111/apps.12390

Sanfilippo, F. A. (2017). Multi-sensor fusion framework for improving situational awareness in demanding maritime training. *Reliability Engineering & System Safety*, 161, 12–24. DOI: 10.1016/j.ress.2016.12.015

Sang, K., Calvard, T., & Remnant, J. (2021). Disability and Academic Careers: Using the Social Relational Model to Reveal the Role of Human Resource Management Practices in Creating Disability. *Work, Employment and Society*, 36(4), 722–740. DOI: 10.1177/0950017021993737

Sang, K., & Powell, A. (2013). Equality, diversity, inclusion and work–life balance in construction. In *Human resource management in construction* (pp. 163–196). Routledge.

Sanin, J. R. (2020). "I Don't Belong Here": Understanding Hostile Spaces. In Me Too Political Science (pp. 112-121). Routledge.

Sartini, S. (2020). Kahoot in Maritime English Teaching: Its Impact on Nautical Science Cadet's Oral Reproduction and Vocabulary. *English Language Teaching Educational Journal*, 3(1), 41–51. DOI: 10.12928/eltej.v3i1.1667

SASB. (2017) Sustainability Accounting Standard Board-Conceptual framework, Retrieved from: https://sasb.org/wp-content/uploads/2020/02/SASB_Conceptual-Framework_WATERMARK.pdf

Sasson, I., Yehuda, I., & Miedijensky, S. (2022). Innovative learning spaces: Class management and universal design for learning. *Learning Environments Research*, 25(3), 725–739. DOI: 10.1007/s10984-021-09393-8

Scarborough, W. J., Lambouths, D.III, & Holbrook, A. (2019). Support of Workplace Diversity Policies: The Role of Race, Gender, and Beliefs About Inequality. *Social Science Research*, 79, 194–210. DOI: 10.1016/j.ssresearch.2019.01.002 PMID: 30857662

Scavarelli, A., Arya, A., & Teather, R. J. (2021). Virtual reality and augmented reality in social learning spaces: A literature review. *Virtual Reality (Waltham Cross)*, 25(1), 257–277. DOI: 10.1007/s10055-020-00444-8

Schindeler, E. (2021). Workplace: Hostile Environment. In *Encyclopedia of Security and Emergency Management* (pp. 947–953). Springer International Publishing. DOI: 10.1007/978-3-319-70488-3_256

Schmeer, K. (1999). Stakeholder analysis guidelines. *Policy Toolkit for Strengthening Health Sector Reform, 1*, 1-35.

Schmölz, A., Karpouzis, K., Pfeiffer, D., & Koulouris, P. (2017). Doing Social Inclusion: Aiming to Conquer Crisis through Game-Based Dialogues and Games.

Schnepfleitner, F. M., & Ferreira, M. P. (2021). Transformative Learning Theory–Is It Tıme to Add A Fourth Core Element? *Journal of Educational Studies and Multidisciplinary Approaches*, 1(1), 40–49. DOI: 10.51383/jesma.2021.9

Schöbel, S., Janson, A., Hopp, J. C., & Leimeister, J. M. (2019, July). Gamification of online training and its relation to engagement and problem-solving outcomes. In Academy of Management Proceedings (Vol. 2019, No. 1, p. 11949). Briarcliff Manor, NY 10510: Academy of Management. DOI: 10.5465/AMBPP.2019.11949abstract

Schrader, C. (2023). Serious games and game-based learning. In *Handbook of Open, Distance and Digital Education* (pp. 1255–1268). Springer Nature Singapore. DOI: 10.1007/978-981-19-2080-6_74

Schreiber, E. (2021). The Virtue of Play: Games and Stories for Children in Three Pedagogical Texts of the Enlightenment. *Eighteenth-Century Studies*, 54(3), 613–632. DOI: 10.1353/ecs.2021.0041

Sczesny, S., Moser, F., & Wood, W. (2015). Beyond sexist beliefs: How do people decide to use gender-inclusive language? *Personality and Social Psychology Bulletin*, 41(7), 943–954. DOI: 10.1177/0146167215585727 PMID: 26015331

Seaborn, K., & Fels, D. I. (2015). Gamification in theory and action: A survey. *International Journal of Human-Computer Studies*, 74, 14–31. DOI: 10.1016/j.ijhcs.2014.09.006

Sebbane, M. (2001). Board games from Canaan in the Early and Intermediate Bronze Ages and the origin of the Egyptian Senet game. *Tel Aviv : Journal of the Institute of Archaeology of Tel Aviv University*, 28(2), 213–230. DOI: 10.1179/tav.2001.2001.2.213

Selwyn, N., & Facer, K. (2007). Beyond the digital divide: Rethinking digital inclusion for the 21st century.

Senaratne, S., Gunarathne, N., Herath, R., Samudrage, D., & Cooray, T. (2022). Institutional pressures and responses to the introduction of integrated reporting into accounting curricula: The case of Sri Lankan universities. *Accounting Education*, 31(5), 536–566. DOI: 10.1080/09639284.2022.2032775

Serra, M. (2018). *Il gioco del disaccordo: persuasione, comunità, linguaggio in Wittgenstein e Platone (con un terzo incomodo)/The game of disagreement: persuasion, community, language in Wittgenstein and Plato (with a third wheel).* Rivista Italiana di Filosofia del Linguaggio.

Shan, H., Cheng, A., Peikazadi, N., & Kim, Y. (2021). Fostering diversity work as a process of lifelong learning: A partnership case study with an immigrant services organisation. *International Review of Education*, 67(6), 771–790. DOI: 10.1007/s11159-021-09929-3 PMID: 34840346

Sharma, A., Kim, T. E., & Nazir, S. (2021). Implications of Automation and Digitalization for Maritime Education and Training. In *Sustainability in the Maritime Domain* (pp. 223–233). Springer. DOI: 10.1007/978-3-030-69325-1_11

Sharma, U., & Kelly, M. (2014). Students' perceptions of education for sustainable development in the accounting and business curriculum at a business school in New Zealand. *Meditari Accountancy Research*, 22(2), 130–148. DOI: 10.1108/MEDAR-12-2012-0042

Shliakhovchuk, E. (2018). Using video games in intercultural, diversity and inclusion education. In *ICERI2018 Proceedings* (pp. 10326-10336). IATED DOI: 10.21125/iceri.2018.0946

Shore, L. M., Cleveland, J. N., & Sanchez, D. (2018). Inclusive workplaces: A review and model. *Human Resource Management Review*, 28(2), 176–189. DOI: 10.1016/j.hrmr.2017.07.003

Shore, L. M., Randel, A. E., Chung, B. G., Dean, M. A., Holcombe Ehrhart, K., & Singh, G. (2011). Inclusion and diversity in work groups: A review and model for future research. *Journal of Management*, 37(4), 1262–1289. DOI: 10.1177/0149206310385943

Showalter, D. S. (2022) The Role of Accounting in ESG Reporting: A Q&A with D. Scott Showalter. Retrieved from NC state university: https://mac.ncsu.edu/news/2023/03/02/the-role-of-accounting-in-esg-reporting-a-qa-with-d-scott-showalter/

Siala, H., Kutsch, E., & Jagger, S. (2020). Cultural influences moderating learners' adoption of serious 3D games for managerial learning. *Information Technology and People, 33*(2), 424–455. Advance online publication. DOI: 10.1108/ITP-08-2018-0385

Siano, A., Kitchen, P. J., & Confetto, M. G. (2010). Financial resources and corporate reputation: Toward common management principles for managing corporate reputation. *Corporate Communications*, 15(1), 68–82. DOI: 10.1108/13563281011016840

Sicart, M. (2011). *The ethics of computer games*. MIT Press.

Siegel, D. J. (2013). *La mente relazionale*. Raffaello Cortina.

Sierra, J., & Rodríguez-Conde, M.-J. (2021). The Microfinance Game: Experiencing the dynamics of financial inclusion in developing contexts. *International Journal of Management Education*, 19(3), 100540. DOI: 10.1016/j.ijme.2021.100540

Silva, F. C., Clark, T. N., & Cabaço, S. (2013). Culture on the Rise: How and Why Cultural Membership Promotes Democratic Politics. *International Journal of Politics Culture and Society*, 27(3), 343–366. DOI: 10.1007/s10767-013-9170-7

Silva, F. G. (2020). Practical methodology for the design of educational serious games. *Information (Basel)*, 11(1), 1–13. DOI: 10.3390/info11010014

Sinicropi, S., & Cortese, D. (2021). (Re) Thinking diversity within sustainable development: A systematic mapping study. *Corporate Social Responsibility and Environmental Management*, 28(1), 299–309. DOI: 10.1002/csr.2050

Sisodia, R., Wolfe, D., & Sheth, J. N. (2003). *Firms of endearment: How world-class companies profit from passion and purpose*. Pearson Prentice Hall.

Sitzmann, T. (2011). A meta-analytic examination of the instructional effectiveness of computer-based simulation games. *Personnel Psychology*, 64(2), 489–528. DOI: 10.1111/j.1744-6570.2011.01190.x

Skillman, A. (2023). An Analysis of Gamification and Game-Based Learning as Strategies for Anti-Oppressive Education. *Social Justice and Community Engagement Major Research Papers*. https://scholars.wlu.ca/sjce_mrp/12

Skinner, B. F. (1963). Operant behavior. *The American Psychologist*, 18(8), 503–515. DOI: 10.1037/h0045185

Slavich, G. M., & Zimbardo, P. G. (2012). Transformational teaching: Theoretical underpinnings, basic principles, and core methods. *Educational Psychology Review*, 24(4), 569–608. DOI: 10.1007/s10648-012-9199-6 PMID: 23162369

Soboleva, E. V., Suvorova, T. N., Zenkina, S. V., & Bocharov, M. I. (2021). Developing Computational Thinking of Specialists of the Future Through Designing Computer Games for Educational Purposes. *European Journal of Contemporary Education, 10*(2), 462–475. Advance online publication. DOI: 10.13187/ejced.2021.2.462

Sona, A. J., Santana, J. L., & Saitta, E. K. H. (2022). Looking Through a Prism: A Systematic Review of LGBTQ+ STEM Literature. *Journal of Chemical Education*, 100(1), 125–133. DOI: 10.1021/acs.jchemed.2c00391

Sousa, C. (2020). Empowerment and ownership in intellectual disability gaming: Review and reflections towards an able gaming perspective (2010-2020). *International Journal of Film and Media Arts, 5*(1), 14–23. Advance online publication. DOI: 10.24140/ijfma.v5.n1.02

Sousa, M. J., & Rocha, Á. (2019). Leadership styles and skills developed through game-based learning. *Journal of Business Research*, 94, 360–366. DOI: 10.1016/j.jbusres.2018.01.057

Spalding, E., & Wilson, A. H. (2006). Bowling Together. *English Education*, 38(2), 102–122. DOI: 10.58680/ee20065073

Squire, K. (2005). Game-based learning: Present and future state of the field. New York, NY: Masie Center E-Learning Consortium.

Squire, K., & Jenkins, H. (2003). Harnessing the power of games in education. *Insight (American Society of Ophthalmic Registered Nurses)*, 3(1), 5–33. PMID: 12703249

Stanitsas, M., Kirytopoulos, K., & Vareilles, E. (2019). Facilitating sustainability transition through serious games: A systematic literature review. *Journal of Cleaner Production*, 208, 924–936. DOI: 10.1016/j.jclepro.2018.10.157

Steenbeek, J., Romagnoni, G., Bentley, J., Heymans, J. J., Serpetti, N., Gonçalves, M., Santos, C., Warmelink, H., Mayer, I., Keijser, X., Fairgrieve, R., & Abspoel, L. (2020). Combining ecosystem modeling with serious gaming in support of transboundary maritime spatial planning. *Ecology and Society*, 25(2), art21. DOI: 10.5751/ES-11580-250221

Stefan, I. A., Stefan, A., Goldbach, I. R., & Hamza-Lup, F. (2019). Exploring the use of gamified systems in training and work environments. In *eLearning Softw. Educ. Conf.* (pp. 11–19). National Defence University - Carol I Printing House. DOI: 10.12753/2066-026X-19-001

Steinkuehler, C., & Squire, K. D. (2012). Games, learning, and society: Learning and meaning in Stevens, F. G., Plaut, V. C., & Sanchez-Burks, J. (2008). Unlocking the benefits of diversity: All-inclusive multiculturalism and positive organizational change. *The Journal of Applied Behavioral Science*, 44(1), 116–133.

Streicher, A., & Smeddinck, J. D. (2016). *Personalized and Adaptive Serious Games*. DOI: 10.1007/978-3-319-46152-6_14

Su, C. H. (2016). The effects of students' motivation, cognitive load and learning anxiety in gamification software engineering education: A structural equation modeling study. *Multimedia Tools and Applications*, 75(16), 10013–10036. DOI: 10.1007/s11042-015-2799-7

Sukhov, A. (2019). Ethical issues of simulation video games. *Proc. European Conf. Games-Based Learn., 2019-October*, 705–712. DOI: 10.34190/GBL.19.060

Sung, Y., Cho, K., & Um, K. (2012). A Development Architecture for Serious Games Using BCI (Brain Computer Interface) Sensors. *Sensors (Basel)*, 12(11), 15671–15688. DOI: 10.3390/s121115671 PMID: 23202227

Sun, Z., & Xie, K. (2020). How do students prepare in the pre-class setting of a flipped undergraduate math course? A latent profile analysis of learning behavior and the impact of achievement goals. *The Internet and Higher Education*, 46, 100731. DOI: 10.1016/j.iheduc.2020.100731

Susi, T., Johannesson, M., & Backlund, P. (2007). Serious games: An overview.

Susi, T., Johannesson, M., & Backlund, P. (2007). Serious games: An overview: https://www.diva-portal.org/smash/get/diva2:2416/FULLTEXT01.pdf

Sutton-Smith, B. (1997). *The ambiguity of play*. Harvard University Press.

Swaddling, J. (1999). *The ancient Olympic games*. University of Texas Press.

Szendrői, L., Dhir, K. S., & Czakó, K. (2020). Gamification in for-profit organisations: A mapping study. *Business: Theory and Practice, 21*(2), 598–612. Advance online publication. DOI: 10.3846/btp.2020.11864

Taber, K. S. (2020). Mediated learning leading development—the social development theory of Lev Vygotsky. In *Science education in theory and practice* (pp. 277–291). Springer. DOI: 10.1007/978-3-030-43620-9_19

Taliento, M., Favino, C., & Netti, A. (2019). Impact of environmental, social, and governance information on economic performance: Evidence of a corporate 'sustainability advantage' from Europe. *Sustainability (Basel)*, 11(6), 1738. DOI: 10.3390/su11061738

Tan, G. (2018). Gamification in Education: What is it and How Does it Work? https://edtechmagazine.com/higher/software/gamification

Tanner, C., Schmocker, D., Katsarov, J., & Christen, M. (2022). Educating moral sensitivity in business: An experimental study to evaluate the effectiveness of a serious moral game. *Computers & Education*, 178, 104381. Advance online publication. DOI: 10.1016/j.compedu.2021.104381

Tarafdar, M., Tu, Q., Ragu-Nathan, B. S., & Ragu-Nathan, T. S. (2007). The impact of technostress on role stress and productivity. *Journal of Management Information Systems*, 24(1), 304–305. DOI: 10.2753/MIS0742-1222240109

Taylor, E. W. (2007). An update of transformative learning theory: A critical review of the empirical research (1999–2005). *International Journal of Lifelong Education*, 26(2), 173–191. DOI: 10.1080/02601370701219475

Thielsch, M. T., & Niesenhaus, J. (2017). User experience, gamification, and performance. The Wiley Blackwell handbook of the psychology of the internet at work, 79-101.

Thirumalesh Madanaguli, A., Dhir, A., Kaur, P., Mishra, S., & Srivastava, S. (2023). A systematic literature review on corporate social responsibility (CSR) and hotels: Past achievements and future promises in the hospitality sector. *Scandinavian Journal of Hospitality and Tourism*, 23(2–3), 141–175. DOI: 10.1080/15022250.2023.2221214

Thomas, C. (2014). Disability and diversity. In *Routledge international handbook of diversity studies* (pp. 43–51). Routledge.

Thomas, P., & Macredie, R. (1994). Games and the design of human-computer interfaces. *Educational & Training Technology International*, 31(2), 134–142. DOI: 10.1080/0954730940310208

Tilak, S., Glassman, M., Kuznetcova, I., Peri, J., Wang, Q., Wen, Z., & Walling, A. (2020). Multi-User Virtual Environments (MUVEs) as alternative lifeworlds: Transformative learning in cyberspace. *Journal of Transformative Education*, 18(4), 310–337. DOI: 10.1177/1541344620932224

Timbó, S., de Melo Bezerra, J., & Hirata, C. M. (2019). Supporting Gamified Experiences for Informal Collaborative Groups. In *Lect. Notes Bus. Inf. Process.* (Vol. 363, pp. 42–57). Springer Verlag. DOI: 10.1007/978-3-030-26169-6_3

Titus, S., & Ng'ambi, D. (2023). Digital Gaming for Cross-Cultural Learning: Development of a Social Constructivist Game-Based Learning Model at a South African University. *International Journal of Game-Based Learning*, 13(1), 1–20. DOI: 10.4018/IJGBL.331995

Tobias, S., Fletcher, J. D., & Wind, A. P. (2014). Game-based learning. Handbook of research on educational communications and technology, 485-503. DOI: 10.1007/978-1-4614-3185-5_38

Toda, A. M., Valle, P. H., & Isotani, S. (2017). The dark side of gamification: An overview of negative effects of gamification in education. In *Researcher links workshop: higher education for all* (pp. 143–156). Springer International Publishing.

Tomé Klock, A. C., Palomino, P. T., Rodrigues, L. A. L., Toda, A. M., Simanke, S., Spors, V., Santana, B. S., & Hamari, J. (2024). Gamification towards and alongside equity, diversity and inclusion: Looking back to move forward. *New Media and Society.New Media & Society*. Advance online publication. DOI: 10.1177/14614448241254028

Toribio López, A., & Robles Rojas, E. (2021). *Gamification: An Educational Strategy to Improve the Commercial Training in the Sales Force*. Yearbook Faculty of Economics and Business Sciences.

Tremblay, M. S. (2019). The Importance of Play in Promoting Healthy Development in Children. https://publications.aap.org/pediatrics/article/119/1/182/70699/The-Importance-of-Play-in-Promoting-Healthy-Child

Triana, M. D. C., Gu, P., Chapa, O., Richard, O., & Colella, A. (2021). Sixty years of discrimination and diversity research in human resource management: A review with suggestions for future research directions. *Human Resource Management*, 60(1), 145–204. DOI: 10.1002/hrm.22052

Tribaldos, T., & Schneider, F. (2021). Enabling players to develop theories of change for sustainable development: A serious game. *Simulation & Gaming*, 52(5), 664–678. DOI: 10.1177/10468781211022399

Tschopp, D., & Nastanski, M. (2014). The Harmonization and Convergence of Corporate Social Responsibility Reporting Standards. *Journal of Business Ethics*, 125(1), 147–162. DOI: 10.1007/s10551-013-1906-9

Türkistanli, T. T., & Kuleyin, B. (2022). Game-based learning for better decision-making: A collision prevention training for maritime transportation engineering students. *Computer Applications in Engineering Education*, 30(3), 917–933. DOI: 10.1002/cae.22494

Turner, P. E., Johnston, E., Kebritchi, M., Evans, S., & Heflich, D. A. (2018). Influence of online computer games on the academic achievement of non-traditional undergraduate students. *Cogent Education*, 5(1), 1437671. DOI: 10.1080/2331186X.2018.1437671

UNESCO. (2015). Education 2030: Incheon Declaration and Framework for Action. https://uis.unesco.org/sites/default/files/documents/education-2030-incheon-framework-for-action-implementation-of-sdg4-2016-en_2.pdf

UNICEF. (2019). State of the World's Children 2019: Children in a Changing World. https://www.unicef.org/reports/annual-report-2019

United Nations General Assembly. (2015). *Transforming Our World: The 2030 Agenda for Sustainable Development. Draft resolution referred to the United Nations summit for the adoption of the post- 2015 development agenda by the General Assembly at its sixty-ninth session.*

United Nations. (2015). Transforming our world: the 2030 Agenda for Sustainable Development: https://documents-dds-ny.un.org/doc/UNDOC/GEN/N15/291/89/PDF/N1529189.pdf?OpenElement

United Nations. (2018). The World's Future – A Sustainable Development Goals Game that highlights the interlinkages among the SDGs and targets. Available at: https://sdgs.un.org/partnerships/worlds-future-sustainable-development-goals-game-highlights-interlinkages-among-sdgs

Van der Heijden, B. I. J. M., Burgers, M. J., Kaan, A. M., Lamberts, B. F., Migchelbrink, K., Van den Ouweland, R. C. P. M., & Meijer, T. (2020). Gamification in Dutch Businesses: An Explorative Case Study. *SAGE Open, 10*(4). *SAGE Open*, 10(4). Advance online publication. DOI: 10.1177/2158244020972371

Van Diepen, N. M., Stefanova, E., & Miranowicz, M. (2009). Mastering skills using ICT: An active learning approach. Research, Reflections and Innovations in Integrating ICT in Education, 226-233.

Van Eck, R. (2006). Digital Game-Based Learning: It's Not Just the Digital Natives Who Are Restless. *EDUCAUSE Review*, 41(2), 16–30.

Van Leeuwen, L., & Westwood, D. (2008). Adult play, psychology and design. *Digital Creativity (Exeter)*, 19(3), 153–161. DOI: 10.1080/14626260802312665

Van Toorn, C., Kirshner, S., & Gabb, J. (2022). Gamification of query-driven knowledge sharing systems. *Behaviour & Information Technology*, 41(5), 959–980. DOI: 10.1080/0144929X.2020.1849401

Varvasovszky, Z., & Brugha, R. (2000). A stakeholder analysis. *Health Policy and Planning*, 15(3), 338–345.

Vate-U-Lan, P. (2014). Redesign principles of game-based learning: expectations from stakeholders in a developing country. Paper presented at the 8th European Conference of Game-based Learning (ECGBL2014).

Vaz Torres, C., Vasques-Menezes, I., & Presotti, L. (2017). Cultural diversity and inclusion in organizations: State of the art and challenges. Organizational Psychology and Evidence-Based Management: What Science Says About Practice, 227-242.

Venter, R., & Hodgson, H. K. G. (2020). Strategies for Inclusive Medical Imaging Environments for Sexual and Gender Minority Patients and Radiographers: An Integrative Literature Review. *Journal of Medical Imaging and Radiation Sciences*, 51(4), S99–S106. DOI: 10.1016/j.jmir.2020.05.009 PMID: 32622654

Venturelli, A., Fasiello, R., & Pizzi, S. (2021). CSR education in economia aziendale curricula: An overview. *Administrative Sciences*, 11(4), 137. DOI: 10.3390/admsci11040137

Verdeyen, V., Put, J., & van Buggenhout, B. (2004). A social stakeholder model. *International Journal of Social Welfare*, 13(4), 325–331. DOI: 10.1111/j.1468-2397.2004.00328.x

Veronica, R., & Calvano, G. (2020). Promoting sustainable behavior using serious games: Seadventure for ocean literacy. *IEEE Access : Practical Innovations, Open Solutions*, 8, 196931–196939. DOI: 10.1109/ACCESS.2020.3034438

Vithana, K., Soobaroyen, T., & Ntim, C. G. (2021). Human resource disclosures in UK corporate annual reports: To what extent do these reflect organisational priorities towards labour? *Journal of Business Ethics*, 169(3), 475–497. DOI: 10.1007/s10551-019-04289-3

Vito, R., & Sethi, B. (2020). Managing change: Role of leadership and diversity management. *Journal of Organizational Change Management*, 33(7), 1471–1483. DOI: 10.1108/JOCM-04-2019-0116

Vygotsky, L. (1978). *Mind in society. The development of higher psychological processes*. Harvard University Press.

Vygotsky, L. S. (1978). *Mind in society: The development of higher psychological processes*. Harvard University Press.

Waldman, D. A., & Sparr, J. L. (2023). Rethinking diversity strategies: An application of paradox and positive organization behavior theories. *The Academy of Management Perspectives*, 37(2), 174–192. DOI: 10.5465/amp.2021.0183

Walsh, D. (2009, April). Wii can do it: Using co-design for creating an instructional game. In *Proceedings of the CHI 2009*, Boston, MA DOI: 10.1145/1520340.1520722

Wang, R. T.-C. (2022). Investigating the contribution of role-plays for social sustainability: Designing a role-play game for CSR Communication. *Developments in Business Simulation and Experiential Learning: Proceedings of the Annual ABSEL Conference, 49*. https://absel-ojs-ttu.tdl.org/absel/chapter/view/3322

Wang, C. K. J., Khoo, A., Liu, W. C., & Divaharan, S. (2008). Passion and intrinsic motivation in digital gaming. *Cyberpsychology & Behavior*, 11(1), 39–45. DOI: 10.1089/cpb.2007.0004 PMID: 18275311

Wang, J., Kim, H. R., & Tran, T. B. H. (2024). Can shared leadership stimulate team members' proactive behaviour? Exploring through the bridge of psychological empowerment. *Tourism & Management Studies*, 20(2), 69–78. DOI: 10.18089/tms.20240206

Wang, Q., & Abbas, M. (2018). Designing web-games for transportation engineering education. *Computer Applications in Engineering Education*, 26(5), 1699–1710. DOI: 10.1002/cae.22031

Wang, Y., Rajan, P., Sankar, C. S., & Raju, P. K. (2016). Let them play: The impact of mechanics and dynamics of a serious game on student perceptions of learning engagement. *IEEE Transactions on Learning Technologies*, 10(4), 514–525. DOI: 10.1109/TLT.2016.2639019

Wanick, V., & Bui, H. (2019). Gamification in Management: Analysis and research directions. *International Journal of Serious Games, 6*(2), 57–74. Advance online publication. DOI: 10.17083/ijsg.v6i2.282

Wardaszko, M. (2016). Building simulation game-based teaching program for secondary school students. *Simulation & Gaming*, 47(3), 287–303. DOI: 10.1177/1046878116635467

Weinstein, A. M. (2010). Computer and video game addiction—A comparison between game users and non-game users. *The American Journal of Drug and Alcohol Abuse*, 36(5), 268–276.

Wellington, W. J., Hutchinson, D. B., & Faria, A. J. (2017). Measuring the impact of a marketing simulation game: Experience on perceived indecisiveness. *Simulation & Gaming*, 48(1), 56–80. DOI: 10.1177/1046878116675103

Werbach, K., & Hunter, D. (2012). *For the Win: How Game Thinking Can Revolutionize Your Business*. Wharton Digital Press.

Westen, P. (1985). The concept of equal opportunity. *Ethics*, 95(4), 837–850. DOI: 10.1086/292687

Westera, W. (2015). Games are motivating, aren't they? Disputing the arguments for digital game-based learning. *International Journal of Serious Games*, 2(2). Advance online publication. DOI: 10.17083/ijsg.v2i2.58

Westera, W. (2019). Why and How Serious Games can Become Far More Effective: Accommodating Productive Learning Experiences, Learner Motivation and the Monitoring of Learning Gains. *Journal of Educational Technology & Society*, 22(1), 59–69.

Westera, W. (2022). The Devil's Advocate: Identifying Persistent Problems in Serious Game Design. *International Journal of Serious Games*, 9(3), 115–124. DOI: 10.17083/ijsg.v9i3.547

Whaley, A. M. (2016). *Cognitive basis for human reliability analysis*. US Nuclear Regulatory Commission, Office of Nuclear Regulatory Research.

What We Know and Don't Know About Corporate Social Responsibility: A Review and Research Agenda—Herman Aguinis, Ante Glavas, 2012. (n.d.). Retrieved January 27, 2024, from https://journals.sagepub.com/doi/10.1177/0149206311436079

Whitehead, D. P. (2008). Thoughts on education and innovation. *Childhood Education, 85*(2), 105-B.

Williams, D. A., & Wade-Golden, K. C. (2023). *The chief diversity officer: Strategy structure, and change management.* Taylor & Francis.

Williams, K. Y., & O'Reilly, C. A. (1998). Demography and diversity in organizations: A review of 40 years of research. *Research in Organizational Behavior*, 20(20), 77–140.

Winters, M. F. (2013). From diversity to inclusion: An inclusion equation. Diversity at work: The practice of inclusion, 205-228.

Wirba, A. V. (2023). Corporate Social Responsibility (CSR): The Role of Government in promoting CSR. *Journal of the Knowledge Economy*, 15(2), 7428–7454. Advance online publication. DOI: 10.1007/s13132-023-01185-0

Wolfe, J., Bowen, D. D., & Roberts, C. R. (1989). Team-building effects on company performance: A business game-based study. *Simulation & Games*, 20(4), 388–408. DOI: 10.1177/104687818902000401

Wolf, M. J. P. (2001). *The medium of the video game.* University of Texas Press.

Woolfson, L. M. (2024). Is inclusive education for children with special educational needs and disabilities an impossible dream? *The British Journal of Educational Psychology*, bjep.12701. DOI: 10.1111/bjep.12701 PMID: 38890011

Wouters, P., Van der Spek, E. D., & Van Oostendorp, H. (2009). Current practices in serious game research: A review from a learning outcomes perspective. Games-based learning advancements for multi-sensory human computer interfaces: techniques and effective practices, 232-250.

Wouters, E., Meulemans, H., & Rensburg, H. C. J. (2009). Slow to Share: Social Capital and Its Role in Public HIV Disclosure Among Public Sector ART Patients in the Free State Province of South Africa. *AIDS Care*, 21(4), 411–421. DOI: 10.1080/09540120802242077 PMID: 19266407

Wouters, P., van Nimwegen, C., van Oostendorp, H., & van der Spek, E. D. (2013). A meta-analysis of the cognitive and motivational effects of serious games. *Journal of Educational Psychology*, 105(2), 249–265. DOI: 10.1037/a0031311

Yamada, D. C. (1999). The phenomenon of workplace bullying and the need for status-blind hostile work environment protection. *Geological Journal*, 88, 475.

Yang, Y., Asaad, Y., & Dwivedi, Y. (2017). Examining the impact of gamification on intention of engagement and brand attitude in the marketing context. *Computers in Human Behavior*, 73, 459–469. DOI: 10.1016/j.chb.2017.03.066

Yawkey, T. D., & Pellegrini, A. D. (Eds.). (2018). *Child's play: Developmental and applied* (Vol. 20). Routledge. DOI: 10.4324/9781315099071

Yee, N. (2006). The psychology of MMORPGs: Emotional investment, motivations, relationship formation, and problematic usage. *Avatars at work and play: Collaboration and interaction in shared virtual environments, 34*, 187–207.

Ye, L., Zhou, X., Yang, S., & Hang, Y. (2022). Serious game design and learning effect verification supporting traditional pattern learning. *Interactive Learning Environments*, 1–15.

Yıldırım, İ., & Şen, S. (2021). The effects of gamification on students' academic achievement: A meta-analysis study. *Interactive Learning Environments*, 29(8), 1301–1318. DOI: 10.1080/10494820.2019.1636089

York, J., & DeHaan, J. W. (2018). A constructivist approach to game-based language learning: Student perceptions in a beginner-level EFL context. *International Journal of Game-Based Learning*, 8(1), 19–40. DOI: 10.4018/IJGBL.2018010102

Zafar, U., Khattak, M., Zafar, H., & Rehman, H. (2022). Let's Play Games: A Comparison of Case-Based Learning Approach With Gamification Technique. *Cureus*. Advance online publication. DOI: 10.7759/cureus.27612 PMID: 36059319

Zaid, M. A., & Issa, A. (2023). A roadmap for triggering the convergence of global ESG disclosure standards: lessons from the IFRS foundation and stakeholder engagement. Corporate Governance: The International Journal of Business in Society.

Zainuddin, Z., Chu, S. K. W., Shujahat, M., & Perera, C. J. (2020). The impact of gamification on learning and instruction: A systematic review of empirical evidence. *Educational Research Review*, 30, 100326. DOI: 10.1016/j.edurev.2020.100326

Zainuddin, Z., Shujahat, M., Haruna, H., & Chu, S. K. W. (2020). The role of gamified e-quizzes on student learning and engagement: An interactive gamification solution for a formative assessment system. *Computers & Education*, 145, 103729. DOI: 10.1016/j.compedu.2019.103729

Zanardi, M. (1985). Metafora e gioco nel "Cannocchiale aristotelico" di Emanuele Tesauro. Studi secenteschi, 26, 25.

Zhonggen, Y. (2019). A meta-analysis of use of serious games in education over a decade. *International Journal of Computer Games Technology*, 2019, 2019. DOI: 10.1155/2019/4797032

Zichermann, G., & Cunningham, C. (2011). *Gamification by design: Implementing game mechanics in web and mobile apps*. O'Reilly Media, Inc.

Zimmerman, E., & Chaplin, H. (2013, September 9). Manifesto: The 21st century will be defined by games. Retrieved from: https://kotaku.com/manifesto-the-21st-century-will-be-defined-by-games-1275355204

Zulmi, M. M., Prabandari, S. P., & Sudiro, A. (2021). Inclusive Human Resource Management (HRM) Practices for Employees With Disabilities as an Effort to Manage Diversity. *Estudios de Economía Aplicada*, 39(12). Advance online publication. DOI: 10.25115/eea.v39i12.6002

Zyda, M. J. (2005). From visual simulation to virtual reality to games. *Computer*, 38(9), 25–32. DOI: 10.1109/MC.2005.297

About the Contributors

Giuseppe Modarelli is Ph.D. and collaborator at the Department of Management – University of Turin. His research interests include the public sector, innovation and digital transformation for public sector organizations, comparative studies (public-private), organization and complex systems studies, motivation and group dynamics, accounting and organizational history, influences and repercussions on the introduction of new tools in the workplace, business ethics and CSR, D&I. He considers qualitative and narrative, but also mixed methods, emphasizing critical and conceptual approaches. He received awards for originality in research and scholarships, publishing a good percentage of articles in top ranking journals at national and international level. During the last years he was speaker at several national and international conferences.

* * *

Juan Miguel Alcántara-Pilar holds a PhD in Economics and Business Management from the University of Granada and is an Associate Professor of Marketing at the Faculty of Education, Economy, and Technology of Ceuta. His areas of expertise include Cross-Cultural Marketing and the Language Effect on Consumer Behavior. Alcántara-Pilar has published a book titled "Cross-Cultural Communication and Marketing," which is the outcome of extensive research in the field that has resulted in numerous publications in esteemed international journals such as the International Journal of Hospitality Management, Tourism Management, Journal of Destination Marketing & Management, Journal of Business Research, Cross Cultural Management: An International Journal, and Computers in Human Behavior.

Selena Aureli is Associate Professor at Bologna University. Before she has been Assistant Professor of Business Administration and Accounting Studies at Urbino University. She teaches Financial Reporting, Managerial Accounting and Business Planning & Control. She has published several contributions to books, essays and articles in academic reviews, both Italian and international. Her major research interests are in the field of non-financial reporting, sustainability, performance measurement, small and medium sized businesses and cultural heritage.

Barbara Barabaschi is associate professor in Università Cattolica del Sacro Cuore, Piacenza (Italy). Her main research interests concern welfare systems and labor policies with particular reference to age and gender disadvantaged groups, social sustainability, local development policies and the role of public administration. She holds a degree in Economics and Commerce and a PhD in "Sociology and Methodology of Social Research" from the Università Cattolica del Sacro Cuore in Milan. She furthered her studies at the Organization for Economic Cooperation and Development (OECD) - Local Economic and Employment Development Program (Paris) and Université Jean Moulin Lyon 3 (Lyon). She is also a member of the Research Centre for Responsibility, Ethics and Sustainability in Management—RES.m HUB.

Monica Bartolini is Associate Professor at the Forlì Campus of the University of Bologna. She is lecturer in financial and managerial accounting and also teaches in several master programs of Bologna Business School. Her main research interests include international financial reporting standards, sustainability reporting, Diversity & Inclusion reporting, performance management systems.

Andrea Caccialanza is research fellow at the Department of Management (DiSA), University of Bologna (Italy). He obtained a PhD in 2024 as candidate with Fellowship in Agrisystem - Economics, Management and Efficiency of the Agri-Food Market at the Università Cattolica del Sacro Cuore of Piacenza (Italy). He has been visiting PhD candidate at Roskilde University, Department of Social Sciences and Business, Denmark, from January to March 2023. His research covers topics such as sustainability reporting and sustainable supply chain management, UN 2030 SDGs, and sustainability impact in mega-projects. He is a member of the Center for Social and Environmental Accounting Research (CSEAR), the European Business Ethics Network (EBEN), the Italian Association for Management and Marketing studies (SIMA-SIM), and the Italian Associations SIDREA and AIDEA . He is also a collaborator of the Research Centre for Responsibility, Ethics and Sustainability in Management – RES.m HUB.

Metin Celik is a Professor of Maritime Faculty at ITU and co-founder of Blueanalytica Maritime established in 2021. He received his BSc in Marine Engineering (2003), his MSc (2006) and PhD (2009) in Maritime Transportation Engineering of ITU. He conducted risk-based decision-making studies as an international visiting scholar of LJMU, UK. He has published 3 book chapters, 65+ SCI/SSCI indexed journal papers (h-index 26; 2200+ citations in Wos/WoK) and 65+ international conference papers. He conducted granted 16 different maritime research and technology projects in Coordinator (2), Researcher (11), Advisor (2), Consultant (1) positions. He has supervised/co-supervised to 5 PhD dissertations and 10 MSc theses on human/system reliability, advance maintenance, data analytics, emergency preparedness on-board ships. Professor Celik has been featured among the World's Top 2% Scientists List, according to a Stanford University ranking study, published in 2020-2021-2022-2023. His core research themes include marine safety engineering, maritime digitalization, ship operations modelling, and future maritime solutions.

Suleyman Cihan Gurbuz received his BSc (2010) in Industrial Engineering from Turkish Naval Academy and received his MSc (2016) on Meteorology and Physical Oceanography from Naval Post Graduate School (NPS)/California- USA. He is currently having Ph.D. education on Maritime Transportation Engineering at İstanbul Technical University/İstanbul-Turkey. His main research topics include maritime education and training, serious games, technology-enabled education and training.

Giorgia Moschini, currently pursuing her PhD in Business Administration at the Polytechnic University of Marche, focuses her research on various areas including Management Accounting, Integrated Reporting, CSRD and Game-based learning. Her primary research emphasis lies in the field of Diversity & Inclusion (D&I), the topic in her doctoral work. Specifically, she explores effective methods of measuring D&I and devising a framework for D&I metrics. In addition to her academic pursuits, Giorgia serves as an experienced tutor at Bologna University within the Department of Management. She's also lecturer and tutor in several Executive MBA programs at Bologna Business School, covering subjects such as Performance Management Systems, Cost Management and Financial Accounting. Her dedication to sustainability and education is evident through her collaboration with the European Universities (Bologna University and Avans University) involved in the Erasmus + Programme INTEGRES 2020-2023. Beyond academia, Giorgia has gained experience as a strategic consultant specializing in management control.

Mª Eugenia Rodriguez-López is an Adjunct Professor in the Department of Market Research, at the Faculty of Education, Economy and Technology of Ceuta, University of Granada (Spain). Her areas of interest to research are Advertising, Tourism, Cross-Cultural Marketing, and topics related on Hospitality, in terms of Satisfaction and Customer Experience. She published a papers several journals and she has taken part in international conferences.

Álvaro J. Rojas-Lamorena has a Ph.D. in Business Administration from University of Granada (Spain). He is Assistant Professor in the Department of International and Spanish Economy, at the Faculty of Education, Economy and Technology of Ceuta, University of Granada (Spain). His areas of interest to research are Sustainability, Brand Management, Tourism and Television Marketing. He has published various peer-reviewed papers in journals such as Journal of Business Research, Technological Forecasting and Social Change or Journal of Marketing Communication. He has taken part in international conferences.

Deepak Ranjan Sahoo is an expert in the field of Accounting and Finance, offering a robust combination of academic and corporate experience. With eight years in academia and two years in the corporate sector, he provides a comprehensive perspective that enhances his professional contributions. Dr. Sahoo is currently an Assistant Professor of Finance at MIT Arts Design and Technology University, where he is committed to advancing knowledge and fostering innovation among his students. He holds an M.Com in Corporate Accounting and Financial Management, M.Phil in Business Administration, and PhD in Business Administration. His academic credentials underpin his extensive expertise in key areas of finance, including Financial Modelling and Business Valuation, Fintech, Environmental, Social, and Governance (ESG), Sustainable Development, Behavioral Finance, Derivatives, Risk Management, Fundamental and Technical Analysis, and Capital Market Operations. His dual experience in academia and the corporate world enables him to bridge theory and practice effectively, providing his students with invaluable insights and practical knowledge.

Vaishali Deepak Sahoo is an expert in the field of Accounting and Finance, offering a robust combination of academic experience. With eight years in academia, she provides a comprehensive perspective that enhances her professional contributions. Dr. Vaishali is currently an Assistant Professor of Finance at Vishwakarma University, where she is committed to advancing knowledge and fostering innovation among her students. She holds an M.Com in Corporate Accounting and Financial Management, an M.Phil. in Business Administration, and a PhD in Accountancy and Auditing. Her academic credentials underpin her extensive expertise in key areas of finance, including, Financial Management, Environmental, Social, and Governance (ESG), Sustainable Development, Behavioural Finance, Taxation, Risk Management and Capital Market Operations. Her profound understanding of these subjects enriches her teaching and informs her research and professional activities. Her experience in academia enables her to bridge theory and practice effectively, providing her students with invaluable insights and practical knowledge.

Valentina Toscano is a Ph.D. student in the Business for Society program at the University of Milano-Bicocca. She holds a master's degree in Business and law from the University of Pavia and is an alumna of IUSS Pavia - School of Advanced Studies. She received scholarships as a graduate student distinguished for her commitment and academic achievements. She was an Adjunct Professor for the course on Internationalization strategies, she serves as a tutor for several courses at the University of Milano-Bicocca, and she is a Subject Expert at the University of Pavia for the courses Financial Analysis and Business Plan, and Governance, Management, and Accounting in Public Administrations. Her current research interests concern the fields of sustainability reporting, cultural heritage, accountability, and accounting history. During the last few years, she has been a speaker at several national and international conferences.

Index